Philosophy, Humanity and Ecology

Volume I

Philosophy of Nature and Environmental Ethics

H. Odera Oruka
Editor

African Centre for Technology Studies
Nairobi, Kenya

The African Academy of Sciences
Nairobi, Kenya

1994

© International Federation of Philosophical Societies, Philosophical Association of Kenya, 1994

Published by

ACTS Press, African Centre for Technology Studies (ACTS)
P.O. Box 45917
Nairobi, Kenya

and

The African Academy of Sciences
P.O. Box 14798
Nairobi, Kenya

Printed by English Press Ltd., P.O. Box 30127, Nairobi

Cataloguing in Publication Data

Philosophy, Humanity and Ecology, Vol. I, Philosophy of Nature and Environmental Ethics/H. Odera Oruka, Editor.—Nairobi, Kenya: ACTS Press, African Centre for Technology Studies and The African Academy of Sciences, 1994.

Bibliography: p.
Includes index.

ISBN 9966-41-086-4

Contents

Preface   vii
Introduction
   H. Odera Oruka   ix
Back to the Question of Goals
   Ionna Kucuradi   xvi

Part I Environment and the Philosophy of Nature

1. Philosophy, Humanity and the Environment
   Evandro Agazzi — 3
2. Modern Science, Environmental Ethics and the Anthropocentric Predicament
   Richard T. DeGeorge — 15
3. Philosophy, Humankind and the Environment
   Kwasi Wiredu — 30
4. Science, Technology and the Natural Environment
   Thomas R. Odhiambo — 49
5. Threats to Human Survival and the Responsibility of Scholars
   Mihailo Markovic — 59
6. The Role of Philosophy of Nature Today: Nature, Custom and Reality
   J.D.G. Evans — 67
7. The Image of Humanity as the Image of Nature
   Yersu Kim — 76
8. Naturalism and Primitive Truth
   Ernest Sosa — 86
9. On Eco-ethica: New Ethics for the New Age
   Tomonobu Imamichi — 94
10. Philosophical Aspects of the Inter-play between Nature and the Artificial Environment of Man
    Wolfgang Kluxen — 98
11. The Unity of Everything Alive
    Anna-Teresa Tymieniecka — 107
12. Ecophilosophy and the Parental Earth Ethics
    H. Odera Oruka and Calestous Juma — 115

Part II Philosophy, Politics and Language

13. Development and Environmentalism
    Robin Attfield — 133
14. Are Ideologies Dead?
    Francisco Miro Quesada C. — 150
15. Political Monism and Pluralism in Contemporary Africa
    Didier Njirayamanda Kaphagawani — 158

16. From Sun-Worship to Time-Worship: Toward a Solar Theory
    of History
    Ali A. Mazrui 165
17. Ideology and Dogma
    Mourad Wahba 177
18. The Antithetical Sequel in the African Personality
    J.M. Nyasani 181
19. What Can the Europeans Learn from African Philosophy?
    Gerd-Rudiger Hoffman 190
20. African Philosophy: Two Views
    Kate J. Wininger 198
21. Sign-Language-Cognition
    Jerzy Pelc 208
22. Re-viewing Verwoerd's Vision: Critical Reflections on the Praxis
    of Apartheid and the Thought of its Architect
    W.J. Verwoerd 212

Part III Discussions on Environmental Ethics

23. Ecology and Ethics: Exploiting Nature
    Jay Drydyk 225
24. Technology, Ethics and the 'End' of Nature
    Frederick Ferré 233
25. Ecology and Ethics: A Relationship
    A.T. Dalfovo 244
26. Deep Ecology's Approach to the Environmental Crisis
    Michael E. Zimmerman 249
27. Ethical Principles for Ecodevelopment
    Alejandro Herrera Ibáñez 256
28. The Business of Ethics: Development and the Environment
    Daniel W. Skubik 261
29. Whether the Western World Will Weather the Weather: A Neo-
    Marxist Discussion about Averting 'Ecolocaust'
    Paul Allen III 270
30. Mathematical-Scientific-Technical Comprehension of Nature versus
    Organic Image of Nature
    Karen Gloy 279
31. F.E. Abbot and the Environmental Crisis
    Creighton Peden 285
32. The Principal Attitudes of Humanity towards Nature
    Juhani Pietarinen 290
33. Humans, Animals and Environment: Indian Perspectives
    S.S. Rama Pappu 295
34. The Earth as Family: A Traditional Hawaiian View with Current
    Applications
    D.M. Dusty Gruver 301

35.	Within the Scope of Environmental Ethics Jan Wawrzyniak	306
36.	Human Nature and the Environment Vincent Luizzi	313
37.	Environmental Philosophy within the Relationships of Humanity, Environment, Culture and Economy U. Ozer	318
38.	The Environment and the Epistemological Lesson of Complementarity Henry J. Folse	321
39.	Social Ecology and the Future of the Earth J.P. Clark	329
40.	Of Suffering and Sentience: The Case of Animals Purushottama Bilimoria	336

References 345
Notes on Contributors 353
Index 359

PREFACE

We are happy to inform our contributors and readers that we have managed to bring out the first volume of the Proceedings of the Nairobi World Conference of Philosophy (July 21-25, 1991) which was on the general theme of 'Philosophy, Humanity and the Environment'. Funds permitting, we expect at least two other volumes to follow.

This volume consists mostly of the papers presented at the plenaries, symposia and colloquia. It also includes the papers that were presented in the section on Environmental Ethics. There are, nevertheless, a few papers which do not fall within those two domains, but they are either directly or indirectly of special significance to the topics of African philosophy, culture or politics. Some of the papers have been revised, while a number of them are published from the original versions delivered.

During the course of preparing this publication, we wrote to the contributors requesting biographies about themselves. We did not receive a response from everybody. Among those who did not respond, there are a few whose records were known to us from other contacts. The editors took the liberty to prepare short briefs about these contributors, using the contacts mentioned. If no briefs were received and no knowledge was available, the contributor was omitted from the 'Notes on the Contributors'. We sincerely apologize to those authors whose briefs might have been mailed but failed to reach us and to those who may not have received the request we sent.

The publication of this volume would never have been realized without the support of various institutions and personalities. We are extremely grateful to the Rockefeller Foundation, Nairobi office and its representative, Dr. David Court for their donation for the publication. We are also humbly thankful to the African Academy of Sciences (AAS) for their grant for the same purpose. We are thankful to the African Centre for Technology Studies (ACTS) for administering The Rockefeller Foundation funds and for co-publishing this volume with the AAS.

On behalf of Kenya Philosophical Association and the Kenya National Academy of Sciences, I wish to thank the International Federation of Philosophical Societies (FISP) and its then President, Professor E. Agazzi and Secretary General, Professor Ioanna Kuçuradi for sponsoring the Nairobi Conference and working tirelessly to have it realized.

Professor H. Odera Oruka
Editor and Chair, National Organizing Committee
Nairobi World Conference of Philosophy

ACKNOWLEDGEMENTS

We wish to acknowledge the services of various organizations and persons whose contributions given in kind or grant were crucial to the overall success of the Conference and the publication of this volume. These include UNESCO (Paris), UNESCO Regional Office (Nairobi), Kenya Government through its National Commission to UNESCO, CODESRIA (Senegal), Kenya National Academy of Sciences, University of Nairobi, the Philosophical Association of Kenya, African Council for Social Science Research (New York), Kenya National Council for Science and Technology, the International Council for Philosophy and Humanistic Studies and the Inter African Council for Philosophy (IACP). We also acknowledge the services from the international and local organizing committees of the Conference.

We also appreciate the services and participation of the President and Secretary General of IACP, J.O. Sodipo and P.J. Hountondji, the Chair of the closing session, Byruihaanga Akiiki, the chief rapporteur, Joseph Makhoha, Silvester Ouma (public relations officer), Jackline A. Mboya (conference services officer), Lady Diana Omondi and Maurice Onyango Oruka (conference registrations) and G.E.M. Ogutu who gave a most inspiring vote of thanks at the close of the Conference.

INTRODUCTION

H. Odera Oruka

The Nairobi World Conference of Philosophy (July 21-25, 1991) attracted up to 550 participants and observers from all over the world. The total number of countries represented was 55. One-fifth of the participants were from Africa. The conference had four plenary sessions, two symposia and two colloquia. There were 28 sections and 10 special panels organized by various societies. It should be noted that the Nairobi Conference was an extra-ordinary *World Congress of Philosophy* and organized in the exact tradition of the World Congresses of Philosophy.

The scope of international representation of speakers at the plenaries were drawn from Europe, North America, Asia, and Africa. At the level of plenary sessions, Europe was represented by Prof. Evandro Agazzi (University of Fribourg), Prof. W. Kluxen (University of Bonn) and Prof. Jerzy Pelc (Warsaw University); North America by Prof. Richard T. De George (University of Kansas); Asia by Prof. K.S.Murty (India) and Prof. I. Imamichi (Japan); and Africa by Prof. Ali Mazrui (Kenya), Kwasi Wiredu (Ghana) and Prof. Thomas R. Odhiambo (Kenya).

Themes

All four plenary sessions were based on the common assumption that the status of the world environment poses a threat to human and non-human beings leading to a philosophical concern as to what should be done to alleviate the situation even if not to avert ecological disaster.

As it turned out, every speaker portrayed an element of nostalgia for the primeval universe when human and non-human beings lived in harmony and a time when humans showed a sensitivity towards the environment that bordered on respect, admiration and awe. The extreme of such nostalgia emerged in Prof. Kluxen's suggestion that humanity and nature should enter a dialogue. However, the dilemma that emerged in each of the speaker's presentation was the question of the feasibility of such a dialogue in the face of science and technology. The spirit of all four sessions turned out to be an attempt at resolving this dilemma.

The four plenary sessions were as follows:
    Plenary Session 1: Philosophy and the human environment today
    Plenary Session 2: Science, technology and natural environment
    Plenary Session 3: Peace and national boundaries
    Plenary Session 4: Philosophical aspects of the interplay between the

Session 1
Philosophy and the human environment today

Prof. Wiredu and Prof. Agazzi were the key speakers on this theme. Arguing their cases from different cultural perspectives, the two concurred on the need for humankind to change its attitudes towards nature and the environment. Prof. Wiredu challenged the Western industrialized countries to emulate African communalism as a moral basis for interaction between humanity, the environment and nature. He argued that African communalism made it imperative for society to regard the earth and all that it carries with respect, In the communal system of ownership, he argued, the land belonged not to an individual but to the entire community. Such collective ownership meant that land and all its resources had to be harnessed for the dead, the living, and those yet to be born. This, he concluded, should be the philosophy of science and technology about the environment. Wiredu's appeal to his fellow philosophers was to strive to include in the realm of human rights, a new concern namely: *The right to a livable environment.*

Prof. Agazzi on the other hand is heavily influenced by European tradition regarding the philosophy of the definition of humanity *vis a vis* nature and the environment. From the Socratic to the Judeo-Christian perceptions and renaissance of the reality of humanity and the environment, he argued for the dignified status of humanity *vis a vis* non-human beings. Such a dignified status does not render humanity separate from the environment but part of it. This has to be the case because humanity's knowledge of nature and its secrets is limited. Hence, humanity's attitude towards nature should not be that of dominating and possessing nature, but rather that of being in 'exchange' with it, an exchange, which obviously does not exclude the use of nature, the adaptation of nature to the needs of humanity, but at the same time does not reduce humanity's relation to nature to evil, and recognizes in nature the possession of an intrinsic value which as such deserves respect. Such was Prof. Agazzi's challenge to the participants: the need for a broad perspective on the environment emanating from a suitable philosophical reflection on nature and humanity.

Discussion

A major issue of concern that emerged from the discussion during this session was the question of priorities when it comes to striking harmony between the needs of humans and non-humans. Related to this was the question of ethics and intrinsic values when it comes to human patterns of consumerism. Much of the time, it is the humans consuming other beings for survival. It was agreed that a balance can be reached or approximated when individual interests are restricted to the interests of others.

The issue of African communalism as a basis for morality in human attitudes to nature was also raised, with some wondering whether the system can be extended to global dimensions. It was agreed that communalism is meaningful when localized. Beyond a certain focus it stops being communalism. Hence, African communalism can only serve as a model for others but not for all peoples in their relation to nature and the environment.

There was the issue of humanity as a superior product of cultural evolution. To what extent can such evolution be ethical in relation to nature considering humanity's selfish inclinations? It was agreed that there is a consciousness emerging culturally in respect to a mutually beneficial development between humanity and the environment. Yet, this consensus can hardly be sustained considering the theory of deterministic chaos. What is the basis for prediction of such harmony between humanity and nature? It was suggested that one way out of this predicament is to set goals for society. Although there is no certainty such goals will be achieved, they would form a basis for responsibility.

Emerging from the above was the issue of accommodation of the condition of nature and life. How would we accommodate the two against the syndrome of dependency and the less industrialized economies? It was agreed this is a complicated issue. The question was: How do you modernize without losing cultural identity? It was suggested that philosophers should establish a scale of values out of which a balance can hopefully be struck.

Session 2
Science, technology and natural environment

Prof. Richard De George, Prof. Mihailo Markovic, and Prof. Thomas R. Odhiambo were the key speakers. Prof. De George confined himself to the topic 'Modern Science and Global Environmental Ethics'. In his presentation, Prof. De George unmasked the dilemma between the Western view of science and technology on the one hand, and the need for values and ethics in present-day modernization approaches. In the Western sense, all non-beings are objects at the disposal of human beings in their scientific advances. Even a dead human-being becomes an object of scientific inquiry. How then can one talk of science and ethics? De George experiments with three escape routes out of this dilemma:

- Basic decisions on the environment should be made by the people affected, not scientists or technologists (*the misplaced expertise* thesis).
- Given the presuppositions of science and technology, only an anthropocentric ethics is compatible with them and so only such an ethic is truly viable in the West (the anthropocentric thesis)–this could cause adverse effects on human beings by actions that have an adverse impact on nature.
- Given the different views of nature worldwide, joint efforts in solving international and global ecological problems are most likely to be fruitful if focused on the level of action rather than on theory (the coherence compromise thesis).

Prof. Markovic focused on the threats to human survival and the responsibility of scholars. His concern was the deteriorating status of the environment as a result of natural and human-made efforts and the role of a scholar. Can science–computers and all–provide a rational solution? Yes. Computers liberate the scholar from routine tasks. He should hence utilize his freedom to investigate solutions. In doing so, the scholar would use his knowledge for the good of the people. He should eschew contamination of such knowledge by ideological biases. He can do this through:

- *Self-reflection:* consciousness about his consciousness and a sense of honour.
- *Objectivity*: the concern here is with the environment of a scholar, the question is whether the natural scientist is any better off than the social scientist. As it turns out, both have a responsibility for the consequences of their research. Whether sceptic, apologist or neutralist, every scholar has a moral responsibility to work for the good of humanity and nature.

Africa received one of her most instructive lectures in the presentation of Prof. Odhiambo entitled 'Science, Technology and the Natural Environment'. He developed a new paradigm for a sustainable development agenda, namely:

- Food security, assured through the sustainable use of physical resources and environment.
- Basic economic security, which guarantees the fullest employment of each individual's talents and skills, through both the formal sector and the household mobilization system.
- National institutional security from the establishment and sustainable operation of national systems responsible for the mobilization of geographical and geoeconomic support for its priority programme for long-term national development, including a dynamic sense of national peace, security, and cohesion.
- The development of a national, vibrant *knowledge industry*, consisting of university institutions, a scientific research and technological development (R and D)

system, the agro-business and industrial domain, the publishing industry and entrepreneurial institutions, all designed to underpin the inputs into and extend the outputs from the first three components of sustainable development, given above. Africa has a conscience (*inner voice*) that says that the continent has the capacity to leapfrog history and catch up with the rest of the continents. This can be done through scientific dialogue on the continent, provided we:

- Relax trans-boundary travel and trans-national recruitment of African scientists and scholars.
- Create and nurture a vigorous and scholarly press for intellectual discourse that will foster intra-continental dialogue.
- Rehabilitate and redesign the entire university system in Africa to suit the needs of the time.
- Re-establish a national sense of purpose in Africa's R and D community as an engine in science-led national development.

Discussion

As in the previous session, the question as to whether nature has intrinsic values and how they can be prioritized arose. The question of humanity's dependence on non-human resources still stands in the way of resolving the dilemma. It was concluded that humanity should own up to its responsibilities, since there is no moral standing between humanity and nature. This is made all the more unachievable as humanity cannot effectively dialogue with nature.

Session 3
Peace and national boundaries

Prof. Murty and Prof. Mazrui were the key speakers. In his paper entitled 'Critique of Nationalism' Murty explained the problem of the concept of nationalism from the perspective of Indian philosophers and sages. He argued that nationalism as a product of the ideas of Western philosophy does not promote peace but creates antagonism. In its place should be the ideal of spiritual freedom as a basis for liberty and equality. This would create brotherhood in the world transcending national boundaries. This would then lead to world peace through a 'free world union in diversity'.

Prof. Mazrui in an innovative and amusing paper entitled 'From Sun-worship to Time-worship–Towards a Solar Theory of History', concluded that Africa lags behind other continents in technology due to the limbo between 'sun-worship' and 'time-worship'. Mazrui reckons that Africans are caught in between the challenges of the industrialized world in which the value of time dictates motion and transaction on the one hand, and the traditional timeless world in which the sun was the source of all knowledge, fortune and life. His appeal to his fellow Africans was to emulate the Japanese who have successfully managed to combine their traditions of worshipping the sun while catching up with the Western treatment of time as money. If Africans were more conscious of time and its value, they would be better planners and more efficient managers of resources, concluded Prof. Mazrui.

Discussion

The solar theory of history proved quite controversial especially in its justification for boundaries of race, religion and gender. Most of the curiosity was explained by the limited time of the conference which could not allow for full ramification of the theory. What emerged as useful for Africa was the value of time. A little time-consciousness might improve Africa's management of resources.

Session 4
Natural and artificial environments of humanity

Prof. Imamichi, Prof. Kluxen and Prof. Pelc were the key speakers. Prof. Imamichi of Tokyo University, suggested a new type of relationship between the philosophical definition of *subject* and *object*. While in Aristotelian logic aims directed and determined the means, in the modern technological age means control the aims, Imamichi concluded. In this sense he points to the fact that modern humans seems to have become a slave as opposed to a master of technology. This new ethic is contrary to the traditional ethics where *God* was the directing principle of action. Now, it would seem that action is what makes good, rendering the entire relationship inconsistent. He advocated eco-ethics and what he termed 'social technology' if ecological disaster is to be averted.

Prof. Kluxen insisted that technology is an extension of humanity's natural environment and should not be considered as being against nature. He suggested that there should be a dialogue between humanity and nature. Such a dialogue is possible as in the case of nature responding to humanity's quest for survival through cultivation. Technology should be at the service of humanity and nature because through it, nature is empowered and enhanced. Technology can 'emancipate' nature by waking up its forces.

Prof. Pelc spoke on sign-language and cognition. Although this was a symposium paper, it dovetailed smoothly into the plenary session. It provoked discussion in view of Prof. Kluxen's call for a dialogue between humanity and nature. The question arose as to whether animals have a language and whether they are capable of thought. It was agreed that animals cannot learn, understand, nor use language. Animals use a code, not a language. However, animals are capable of holding a dialogue with humanity through signs and non-verbal communication. Emotional transmission facilitates this special communication. In a moral sense, animals cannot be subjects.

The plenary sessions had a clear message for the world, especially the industrialized north, i.e. science and technology are the main culprits in the destruction of the natural environment. However, the two are necessary evils in humanity's endeavours to improve the quality of his life. What is called for is *ethics,* the conference concluded. *Ethics* to ensure that science and technology do not exclude humanity from nature nor nature from society, but rather blend humanity's existence with that of non-human beings.

Conference resolutions

Closing comments were issued by Prof. H. Odera Oruka, as the host of the conference; Prof. Nigel Dower; Prof. Zeynep Davran; Prof. E. Agazzi; Prof. Ionna Kuçuradi; Prof. K. Wiredu; Prof. J. O. Sodipo; Dr. G. E. M. Ogutu (vote of thanks); Prof. M. Wahba; Prof. A. B. T Akiiki; and Mr. Joseph Makokha (Chief Rapporteur).

It was resolved that:
1. Conference proceedings be published.
2. That as far as possible all the publishing be done in Nairobi.
3. Conference publications be circulated to all important information centres in Africa and outside as a monument to the first-ever World Conference of Philosophy in Africa.
4. An International Centre for Environmental Philosophy be established in some convenient part of the world. The Centre will be an institution of advanced research and shall hold seminars in all matters pertaining to environment and philosophy. It would, however, be open to researchers in other disciplines in so far as they relate to the problems of environment and philosophy (Kenya was suggested as an attractive candidate for such a centre).

Papers from the plenary sessions, symposia and colloquia are in Part I and Part II of the volume. In Part III we have published a selection of papers that were presented at the section on Environmental Ethics. A number of the papers were not formally intended for that section, but they are of much value. We expect to print the remaining publishable papers in the subsequent volume(s).

H. Odera Oruka
Professor of Philosophy

BACK TO THE QUESTION OF GOALS

Ioanna Kuçuradi
Secretary General of FISP

The central theme of our Conference is 'environment', i.e. our environment in the last decade of the 20th century. Environmental or ecological problems constitute a set of problems that we call today global, or world problems. They constitute a category of facts[1] or deadlocks to which, after the Second World War, mankind was led, without noticing it – in spite of the warning of a few scientists – until some of them became obvious and urgent.

Pollution of the air and of waters, the accumulation of wastes, an increase of the concentrations of carbondioxide and chlorofluorocarbons in the atmosphere, of nitrogen and sulphur compounds in the troposphere, and the climatic changes they cause, deforestation, desertification, erosion, soil salination, the disappearance of non-renewable resources and the scarcity of energy[2] are usually enumerated among these problems. There are other problems which have not yet called public attention.

We have become aware of these dangers since they started jeopardizing human life on the planet, and in the case of some of them, after they started threatening the welfare of the industrialized countries. All these environmental problems, though they are not of the same nature, are usually considered to have somehow to do with humanity's relationship with nature. It is also a widespread opinion that many environmental problems arose from 'indiscriminate technological use of scientific knowledge',[3] or, that they are the outcome of so-called technological development.

However, such claims lose sight of certain factors which have caused the entanglement of various independent events and facts that lie at the origin of the situation in which we find ourselves. We sense only some symptoms and are not sufficiently aware of the factors that caused them. These factors, which we lose sight of, are our global decisions, and the actions we perform to carry them out.

Now, if we take a look at what has happened in this respect, since the end of the Second World War, it appears that at the origin of the deadlocks faced especially, but not only, in industrialized countries at this moment, are due not really to 'technological development' or 'indiscriminate technological use of scientific knowledge' but to the global decisions we took and the actions we performed in this respect; i.e. they are due not to an indiscriminate but to a voluntary technological use of scientific knowledge in view of given objectives which have been our direct responsibility. To put it plainly, behind these problems we find 'development' – which is still our *idee fixe* – after the Second World War, as the principal objective of national policies in almost all the countries of the world.

Developmental policies, followed in most of the industrialized countries, not only opened the way to 'indiscriminate technological use of scientific knowledge', but also promoted it, without thinking of its effects on human beings and on nature. These easily predictable effects, were probable at that time but are now a reality. The policies which were determined in the industrialized countries by 'the-bigger-the-better-principle', and coupled with political calculations, promoted unlimited industrial production, including the production of all kinds of weapons for the cold war between the 'blocks', as well as for selling them to those who were not able to produce them (the so-called, until recently, 'Third World'). Is this an 'indiscriminate' technological use of scientific knowledge or a voluntary and conscious one?

The effects of these policies followed in industrialized countries have consequences, including environmental ones, for the so-called 'countries on the way to industrialization.' However for these countries besides the environmental problems they now face, they also have policies aiming at the increase of *per capita* income, industrialization and development of their technologies. A complicating factor is the unlimited increase of population in these countries. Between 1950 and 1975 the world population increased from 2,500 billion to 4,000 billion, and it is now estimated to be at about 5,000 billion.[4]

This increase in population in the 'countries on the way to industrialization', coupled with poverty, prevailing in most of them, together with their developmental policies, causes rapid urbanization with all its special effects that we see today in many cities in Asia, Africa and Latin America, i.e. migration from rural areas to the cities which give rise to wretched shanty towns and slums and migration from these countries to oil-producing countries and industrialized countries and the accompanying ghettos we see there. All these are well known facts. Still it escapes our attention that some of them are at the origin of the environmental problems we face, and some others are their outcome. If we wish to master these problems, we must not confuse them and must treat them differently, in our endeavour to find solutions.

In this fourth decade of development (1990-2000) we find ourselves in an environment which itself is threatening human existence on the planet – an environment which we did not intend to create, but which we have, nevertheless, created directly or indirectly, in a comparatively short period of time, because we did not sufficiently scrutinize epistemologically and axiologically the specificities of the goals and/or objectives we decided to put to our national and international policies. Did we do that with respect to our anticipated solutions? I am afraid not, at least not yet. This conference, which is basically a philosophy conference, is, in my opinion, an opportunity to do so.

Just at this moment, we find ourselves in an environment which alarms us and it is in a world remarkably different from the one in which the global decisions which have created this environment were taken. This different world is a chance for us only if we do not miss it. One wise person once told me that chance is like a train without a timetable, which stops only for one second at the stations on the line; to catch it, one has to be at the station when it passes. Are we at the station? Are our decision-makers at the station? We should not miss this chance.

This is why I wish to say here a few words on our anticipated solutions – not, of course words concerning ecological problems, most of which presuppose professional knowledge in different fields of the natural sciences – but concerning the framework in which the solutions of ecological as well as of other global problems are sought.

These solutions we see anticipated in the documents of the U.N. and Unesco, seem to move, in spite of their intentions, within the same framework, where from these problems themselves originated; i.e. they are based, essentially, on the same ideas and conceptions lying behind the decisions taken in different historical conditions– decisions which are among the factors that have produced the problems we complain about. We have to break this framework.

Why and how?

Let me give you in a nutshell the reasons behind my claim: after the obvious global problems that developmental policies have created, people have ascribed the 'failure' of these policies to lead towards the ends wished for (i.e. they ascribed the broadening gap between the rich and the poor, in and among countries, and the environmental problems they caused etc.), to the fact that development, was understood only as economic development i.e. development which does not take into consideration the human or cultural dimension of progress.

This explanation led to the consideration that the 'human dimension' should be taken into account within the policies aiming at economic development. Thus nowadays we see 'development' qualified by various epithets such as 'indigenous development', 'self-reliant development', 'cultural development', and lately, 'sustainable development'. These attempts reflect different needs, as well as the wish to shape a new idea of development – once the old one proved to be insufficient. Still, 'development' – whatever its content might be – is usually not questioned but taken for granted as an idea put as the main objective of national and international policies.

The debates going on just now, concern the ways to integrate into development the 'human dimension', which many think is missing in it. Sporadic attempts to scrutinize the idea of development as the main objective, have not, for the moment, attracted sufficient attention.[5] What ongoing debates concerning development reflect is a questioning of what was understood by 'development', since people think, that it is this understanding that has led us to deadlocks; but nobody questions the almost religious belief in development, as the main objective. Those involved in this debate, try to shape a new conception of this idea, which, they think, would answer our needs – our different needs. Thus, we see that what is questioned, in fact, in these debates, is not the idea of development, but the objectives set to national and international policies, and the activities carried out under and in the name of 'development'– activities which have also produced the environmental problems which alarm us.

Can the *idea of development*, even with a 'human dimension', be a global objective? Even the inevitably different ways of understanding it in the so – called developed and developing countries during the past decades, could be a sign that it is not an appropriate choice. Global goals must be ideas of different epistemological and ethical specificity, on which I shall not dwell here.[6] An example of such ideas is what we call human rights.

The protection of human rights now appears to be the only candidate to become a global goal, which once set consciously as the principal goal of our national and international policies, would imply the setting of different objectives, and different action in different countries and regions of our world–different objectives, which still have to be pursued in common.

Dear Colleagues, allow me to conclude, by saying that if we are decided, as we avow in our international documents, to create a world 'free from fear and want' in the 21st century–if we feel ourselves 'responsible for future generations' – we have, together with all our other endeavours, to promote and broaden philosophical education–an education which aims at making young people conscious of their human identity, and trains them to evaluate each case in itself, in the light of human rights and in the knowledge of ethical value in general.

Back to the Question of Goals

Notes
1. For the specificity of these kinds of world problems, see my 'Speech' in *Philosophy Facing World Problems*, Ankara, 1988, pp.7-13.
2. See Unesco's Draft Medium-Term Plan (1984-1989), par. 66-86.
3. *Ibid.*
4. *Ibid.*
5. Among which we see an attempt of Unesco's Division of Philosophy, which organized, among others, relevant meetings such as one on 'The Goals of Development' (Budapest, October 1986, published in 1988) – a title that seems to reflect an attempt to question 'development', not as a goal or objective, but in connection with the question of goals; the Seminar organized by the Philosophical Society of Turkey on 'Philosophy Facing World Problems' (Ankara, July 1986, published in 1988); and the Symposium organized by FISP and the Philosophical Society of Turkey on 'The Idea of Development, Between its Past and its Future' (Ankara, September 1990).
6. For these specificities, see my *Etik* (Ankara, 1977a, 1986b) pp. 70-74, and 'A Different Approach to Ethics', in *Traditional Cultures, Philosophy and the Future,* Jakarta, in print.

PART I

ENVIRONMENT AND THE PHILOSOPHY OF NATURE

Evandro Agazzi

1 PHILOSOPHY, HUMANITY AND THE ENVIRONMENT

Evandro Agazzi
President of FISP, 1988-1993
University of Fribourg, Switzerland

The problem of the environment has become one of the most discussed for at least the last ten years, and has even become fashionable. This is not however a proof of its significance: what is fashionable can become 'old fashioned', if some more intrinsic reasons of importance are not made explicit through deeper scrutiny. The fact that everybody speaks of environment and that environment has already created a 'big business' may indeed render the appreciation of the real reasons of its significance more difficult to uncover. This is why a philosophical reflection on this problem, appears to be particularly necessary: in many fields of our life, we are continuously faced with the problem of distinguishing what is 'urgent' from what is important. Wisdom should consist in giving priority to what is important more than to what is urgent. However, this is a very difficult enterprise (essentially because urgency has itself a certain importance).

It is hardly deniable that the problem of the environment has presented itself with the characteristics of urgency, or, to be more explicit, with the connotations of fear. Unfortunately, fear is not the best ground for rational evaluations, and one of the reasons why the discussions on environmental problems failed to produce a clear appreciation of the issues involved is because they have often consisted of an emphasis on opposite fears. The degradation of the environment has often been presented under the light of an imminent danger of extinction of humankind due to an uncontrolled development of technology, and stopping this development has been claimed to be the only appropriate measure to remove this danger. On the other hand, the opponents of this position have stressed that, stopping technological development, would mean obliging humankind to go back to a situation of poverty, to give up any hope of solving present economic and social problems, to condemn the advanced societies to a rapid and tragic decline, as well as to prevent the less

Philosophy, Humanity and the Environment

advanced societies from reaching a satisfactory 'development'. It has also been claimed that technology is intrinsically able to put under control its own products and avoid the terrific consequences portrayed by its enemies.

Both these lines of reasoning are based on fear, which is certainly quite far from any philosophical attitude, but if we try to see the implicit 'rationale' of both positions, we easily see that it lies within their common pretension of being the only correct way of ensuring the protection of humankind. The first position claims that this protection coincides with the protection of Nature, while the second claims that protection of humankind coincides with his becoming more and more the master of Nature through technology. Common to both is therefore something which we could call an anthropocentric perspective, but they also share an implicit identification of the notion of environment with that of Nature. A reasonable task for a philosophical investigation of this issue can therefore be the following: accepting at a first stage the adoption of an anthropocentric perspective and seeing to what extent it is tenable to identify environment with Nature; then putting under scrutiny at a second stage the anthropocentric view itself.

What is environment? The first step in answering this question is to recognize that the concept of environment is not absolute, but relative: environment always is the environment of something, which also depends on the 'point of view' from which we consider this something. For a cell in a living organism, the proper environment is the tissue to which this cell belongs; only in a broader sense can it be the whole organism, and only in a much broader (almost meaningless) sense, can it be the entire system of living beings. To extend its environment to the cosmic dimension of the universe would be a completely meaningless speculative move. Let us now consider a book. From the point of view of its spatial location, its environment may be the library where it is located; from the point of view of its content, its environment may be the general field to which it belongs (science, poetry, history, philosophy, etc.), but also (if the point of view is more restricted) the specific sector of a given discipline (molecular biology, ancient Greek history, political philosophy, etc.) From the point of view of its economic value, its environment may be the book market. The exemplification could easily be continued, but we do not expect that this proliferation could be indefinite: we would never consider it sensible to say, e.g., that the environment of a book is the realm of animals, or the galactic system.

Let us turn now to our 'anthropocentric' perspective. We can assume it in a quite correct and neutral sense, i.e. precisely in the sense of assuming humankind as this 'something' for whom we try to determine the most sensible environment, (without implicitly or explicitly endowing humankind with a privileged value, in comparison with other realities belonging to his environment, or even lying outside it). Hence, the very vague and almost meaningless question, what is environment? becomes the precise and sensible question, which is the environment of humankind?

An answer to this question is implicitly provided for by the evolutionary way of thinking which has become very influential in the contemporary world; humankind is the result of biological evolution, which by natural selection has produced living beings of increasing complexity, and humankind is simply the most evaluated product of this long process. By embedding biological evolution in cosmic evolution (as is done by modern cosmology), humankind is seen as the accidental occurrence determined by a coincidence of very special physical conditions, which has made possible the apparition and evolution of life in an infinitesimal portion of the universe. If we remain within this genetic approach, we could say that the environment of humankind is primarily the system of 'living Nature' on Earth and secondly the whole nature of the Earth, and in a very remote sense, the entire universe.

However, it has subsequently been stressed that this picture may account for the first apparition of humankind on Earth, but not for further history which has been characterized by a tremendous change and development, while humankind's biological constitution has not undergone any appreciable change. In order to account for this development, the idea of cultural evolution has been introduced, with the explicit claim that the same mechanisms of 'natural selection' have been able to steer the progress of humankind from its almost 'animal-like' primitive conditions to the sophisticated forms of its present civilization. It is not our intention here to discuss the soundness of this conception of cultural evolution, but rather to stress that the new factor which distinguishes it from biological evolution is that humankind, contrary to what is typical of the other living beings, has been able to progress not by adapting to the natural environment, but by adapting this environment to peoples' needs. This has been possible because humankind has been able to construct a world of artifacts, which at first represented a kind of adaptation of Nature to human requirements, but soon became the edification of an artificial world, beside that of virgin Nature. With the advancement of civilization, this artificial world has become so broad, overwhelming and pervasive, that it has almost replaced Nature as the proper environment of humankind.

Therefore, when we speak of humankind and environment, we cannot avoid considering this 'relativized' environment, as being primarily the artificial environment constructed by humankind. Nature is no longer the real environment of humankind. Of course this does not deprive of any sense the question of the relations between this human environment and the 'broader' environment by Nature, but rather, obliges us to pose this question correctly, i.e. not as if Nature were the authentic environment of humankind, which is foolishly forgotten and attacked by modern human beings. If we now consider that this artificial environment has been constructed to a large extent through technology, it is clear that one cannot demonize technology, without at the same time ignoring the 'specific' nature of humankind as it has emerged from evolution, i.e. as the nature of a living being which continues its evolution by adapting Nature to itself, rather than the other way around.

It is already possible at this stage, to examine the claim that in order to 'protect humankind', we should stop technology and go back to Nature. This is not only practically untenable, it is philosophically unsound: this person whom we would pretend to 'protect' would actually be a non-person, i.e. an imaginary living being deprived of its specific characteristic of adapting Nature to itself. In this way, the very idea of cultural 'evolution' would be annihilated, since those features which have been said to constitute the reason for the 'evolutionary' affirmation of humankind, over the rest of the animal kingdom (features which we could summarize under the general concept of intelligence) would come to negative features, that in the long run (and we might be now just at the end of this run) would imply the disappearance of this species from the face of Earth. The real problem is a different one: we must see how we can make the human environment compatible with the natural environment, or to put it differently, make cultural evolution compatible with natural evolution.

The problem is not simple, because the coordination or harmonization of different systems usually requires the adoption of a 'point of view', which is in a way 'supra-systemic' with respect to them: the adoption of a point of view 'of the whole', which cannot be secured from within a single system. But this is the very traditional aim of philosophy, which makes the effort of investigating from the point of view of the whole through a reflection of a global nature the sense of the isolated parts of reality. In particular, a traditional task which philosophy has attributed to itself has been that of interpreting the position of humanity in the universe. Today we are confronted with this very problem, since the problem of environment is itself a particular articulation of this general question.

If we take a quick view of the history of Western philosophy, we can see that at the beginning it concentrated on the understanding of Nature without singling out a special place for humankind (this was the attitude of the pre-Socratic philosophers) while, after more than a century later, the Sophists became especially concerned with the world of humankind (political and social life) and neglected the study of Nature. With Socrates, the question about the specific nature of humankind became the most important philosophical problem, and he identified that nature with the spiritual features of intelligence and moral consciousness inaugurating the division between humankind and Nature, which was subsequently deepened by Plato who explicitly introduced a metaphysical 'supernatural' dimension of reality, to which also the human soul belongs, while the material world was reduced to a radically inferior level. The idea that humankind must become master of Nature and use it for his purposes already existed there mainly in the form of the moral imperative to free oneself from the slavery of instincts and naturalistic appetites (which also obscure the correct intellectual insight), but also as a social and political prominence, attributed to those who are less involved in material occupations and preoccupations, It was only Aristotle who rejoined humankind and Nature by considering a human being as a 'rational animal', and performing the study of his rational features with the same methods used for the study of the other 'animated' beings: he did not deny the excellence of humankind, but at the same time, he did not present this as a sign of his being apart from Nature. But the Platonic tradition become prevalent since it could find an easy encounter with the Judeo-Christian conception according to which humankind are privileged beings, having been separately created by God and endowed with an immortal spiritual soul, which makes them an image of God having been entitled by God to put Nature at God's service. The Islamic conception essentially incorporated these basic views.

At the same time these 'creationist' conceptions were able to provide a framework in which the relation of humankind with Nature could preserve a balance. Nature, after all, was also created by God and as such expressed God's perfection and deserved intrinsic respect; humankind was allowed to avail himself of Nature, but remained an integral part of the ethical code of these religions until now. It was this 'theocentric' perspective that could provide the 'supra-systemic' outlook in which humankind and Nature were harmonized. But with the Renaissance this outlook began to decline and an 'anthropocentric' view clearly emerged: the 'dignity of humanity' was strongly vindicated (not in contrast with, but in a way independently of religious considerations). The new natural science inaugurated a study of Nature free of any theological conditioning and offered to humanity the most efficient means for putting Nature to work. Soon thereafter applied science put at humanity's disposal an incredibly rich world of artifacts and machines in such a way that the technological system started becoming the direct environment of humankind, replacing the traditional natural environment.

This had far-reaching consequences. The machine was not simply an artifact at the service of humanity, but a model for interpreting humankind, Nature and society: different 'mechanisms' were introduced for explaining the functioning of organisms, humanity's psychic features and social institutions, while the method of the natural sciences, which had permitted the increase in knowledge of Nature and the construction of material machines for solving a great deal of concrete problems, was extended to the study of humankind and to the design of several mechanisms for the regulation of individual and social life. The technological environment in which we now live is therefore constituted not simply by the legion of material artifacts which surround us, but by a no less complex net of immaterial artifacts in which our human life is embedded. This, in particular, explains why it would be naive to imagine that we could simply stop technology in the sense of stopping the attainment of material artifacts, which have a direct impact on the natural environment. Such an operation would leave the much more complex 'technological system' intact, in all its non-material components, but this system, on the other hand, would continue to demand the production of new and increasingly sophisticated material artifacts for its survival.

At first glance the historical process sketched above could be interpreted as a progressive erosion of the pole of Nature which has become almost entirely absorbed in the pole of humanity, more or less in the form of a 'humanization of Nature', which has now reached such an excessive dimension that it seriously threatens to lead to the extinction of humankind. But the same process may be read (and perhaps more significantly) as a naturalization of humankind. In fact, we have seen that the constitution of the 'technological system' is essentially the consequence of having applied to the interpretation of humanity the same methodology (and even the same basic concepts) used in the natural sciences. This is particularly clear in the case of the theory of evolution and is no less true in the case of hundreds of 'human' sciences, in which 'scientific' methods have been invented for interpreting human realities at the individual, social, economic and political levels. These methods have led to the proposal of using related technologies for solving almost all 'human problems'. Now what is typical of the approach of the natural sciences is that they limit their comprehension to what is empirically ascertainable and verifiable by testing, that is to what can be quantified and measured in the consideration of cause-effect relations, and to the establishment of factual regularities, while they exclude from their consideration unobservable features such as moral, aesthetic or religious values, the consideration of goals or motivations, or of duties and obligations. Therefore it is clear that an interpretation of human realities which ignores all these dimensions can only lead to a 'naturalized' image of humankind and to the construction of a technological 'environment' of humankind which is not 'natural', because it is artificial, and is also not really 'human'. It is constructed, after all, according to the conceptual and technical models of the natural sciences. It is no wonder that in the construction of this environment, little attention is paid to Nature since no real attention is paid even to humanity: in fact the criticisms of the non-human character of the technological environment have been developed much earlier than the present criticisms concerning the disregard for the natural environment. One could even say that it is this wrong way of conceiving and realizing the human environment which has led to a wrong attitude towards the natural environment.

We have already seen that the determination of an environment depends on the selection of the 'point of view' from which we consider the entity, and this is why one and the same entity usually belongs to several environments at the same time. For this reason we may define the 'global environment' of an entity, the set of all the environments to which this entity directly belongs, according to the different points of view. It is worth noting that these different environments, are usually of quite different natures (think of the above example of a book, where we considered a material environment such as a library, and an abstract environment such as the special field of knowledge of a certain discipline). In the most interesting cases this global environment of an entity can be conceived of in systems-theoretic terms and as the organized system of all those sub-systems which correspond to the different conditions of existence of that entity. We have said 'conditions of existence' and not 'conditions for existence' since we want to include in our consideration not only those features without which a certain reality could not become or remain existent, but more generally those features which characterize its way of existing.

Now in turning to humankind, it is clear that those specific features that have made this 'cultural animal' determine the way of existence in all its dimensions. This means not only that humankind needs appropriate environments for satisfying intellectual, artistic, moral, religious, and effective dimensions, but also for satisfying biological needs in a 'cultural' way, i.e. by passing through technological achievements and systems (cultivation of the earth for nutrition, the production of clothes for bodily protection etc). The consequence is that the global environment of humankind must be such that it includes and brings to a correct functioning a series of sub-systems suitable for securing the satisfaction of all dimensions. Using current terminology, we could say that the overall goal of this global environment should be that of granting to humankind the best possible quality of life. Here one sees why conditions 'for' existence, and conditions 'of' existence must be distinguished.

The technological system of which we have spoken above, can satisfy in the most efficient way most biological needs of humankind, since these are describable using the knowledge accumulated by the natural sciences and are able to be satisfied through the technological tools provided by the application of this knowledge. However, if a parallel satisfaction of the other non-biological dimensions of humankind is not secured, the consequence will be a frustration that seriously diminishes the 'quality of life'. This occurs these days in many of our affluent societies, and the most tragic aspect of this situation is that too many people cultivate the illusion that we can find a technological solution to the problem of satisfying the non-biological needs of humankind, so that they do not even search for a correct solution to this problem. On the contrary, the acceleration of the growth of technological development increases the atrophization of the other human non-biological energies and renders less and less 'human' the global environment of humankind.

Nature has remained practically absent from this whole discourse since it does not seem to belong to the global environment of humankind, which has been defined as the system of all those sub-systems to which humankind directly belongs. However, this is only a superficial impression: humankind remains embedded in Nature in spite of the fact that many (although not all) aspects of the interchange with Nature have become only indirect and mediated through technology. Humanity still needs the oxygen from the atmosphere, no less than water from the rivers, while plants and animals necessary for nutrition are still far from being more or less artificially produced or reproduced on a purely technological basis. The technological system has ignored Nature; this is because Nature cannot be produced, and the technological system is only concerned with what can be produced.

Therefore the sudden alarm which has been raised against the potential destruction of Nature through technology is perfectly similar to the alarm raised against the atrophization of non-biological human dimensions through a unilateral development of technology of which we have spoken above. The difference is that, in the case of Nature, what appears to be in danger are not so much the conditions of life, as the very conditions for life for humankind. It is this difference, in particular, that explains why the appeal in favour of respecting Nature presents itself as 'urgent': conditions for life (or conditions characterizing the 'quality of life').

However, this approach is still too narrow. It reduces the relation of humanity to Nature to the level of pure biological survival. Therefore it is unable to truly refute the claim of the supporters of the technological system when they say that technology will be able to control the exploitation of Nature, so that humankind will be protected against the risk of extinction, and at the same time it will offer to humankind that better 'quality of life', which would never be enjoy by going back to a 'state of Nature'. Now the real point is that this relation to Nature also belongs to the satisfaction of those non-biological dimensions of humankind which inevitably affect the quality of life. Contact with Nature has been for thousands of years an occasion for contemplation, a source of inspiration, a stimulation to reflect on the meaning of life, and occasions which have nourished humanity's art, poetry, religious feelings, philosophy and science. The fact that the technological system more and more separates humankind from Nature is only further evidence that this system has tended to ignore those non-biological dimensions of humankind which it cannot satisfy, or wrongly tries to reduce them to a material level where they could receive a technological solution. Therefore, the vindication of a correct relation of humankind with Nature for non-biological reasons is part of the vindication of a better quality of life.

The different reflections we have developed so far may now be summarized by recognizing that humankind possesses, with respect to other living beings, certain non-biological features, which we would certainly call supra-biological in a correct non-reductionist perspective. Most of us would also be ready to frankly call them 'spiritual', but we shall refrain from using this term in order to avoid quarrels which would be of no interest here. These features contradistinguish humankind with respect to the rest of Nature, but do not segregate people from Nature, which remains in any case the root, the background and the framework for the proper environment. This human environment is constructed to a great extent by humankind through a process of adapting Nature to humankind. But this is clearly possible only if Nature still remains as a root and background for this adaptive transformation. Moreover, Nature constitutes the framework, or the frame of reference, of humankind in several senses. First of all, he cannot stop being a biological entity which necessarily belongs to the general environment of the biosphere: secondly, Nature remains, in humankind's deepest feeling the 'broader context' in which the human environment itself is located; and thirdly, Nature seems to constitute a harmonious 'whole' in which everything has a function and a role, and this contributes to the satisfaction of humankind's search for a global meaning of existence. If we become aware of all this, the 'anthropocentric' outlook mentioned at the beginning receives its necessary corrections.

Of course, Nature can be perceived according to these attitudes only if humanity approaches it with all the richness of these dimensions, i.e. including the supra-biological ones: a sense of contemplation, astonishment before beauty, respect for beings, intellectual curiosity and at the same time a humble admission of the limitation of this knowledge of its secrets. All this implies two things. The first is that the basic attitude cannot be that of dominating and possessing Nature, but rather that of being in 'exchange' with it, and secondly this is an exchange which obviously does not exclude the use of Nature, the adaptation of Nature to the needs of humankind, but at the same time recognizes in Nature the possession of an intrinsic value, which as such deserves respect.

It follows that such a perspective cannot emerge from a simple scientific reading of Nature, since the categories of science exclude the intervention of value judgments of the sort that we have exemplified. The necessary broadness of perspective might come from a suitable philosophical reflection on Nature and humanity, i.e. from a reflection which does not prejudicially delimit its conceptual and methodological tools to those prescribed by the sciences. Unfortunately, most current philosophical conceptions of humankind and Nature try to take full account of the contributions of the sciences but are unable to complement the scientific optic with other principles. The consequence is a picture of humankind and Nature as being the result of purely random material occurrences, with no intention behind it and with no intrinsic value. In these conditions it is hard to imagine how one could seriously propose the idea of a respect for Nature, or for humanity. What remains is simply the spontaneous tendency of any existing biological species for self-preservation, a tendency which instrumentalizes everything, and, at most, must accept being protected against the risk of committing 'mistakes' which would lead to its own extinction.

Owing to this fact, it is in a way a fortunate circumstance that the debate over environment has exploded at a moment of human history when an opening and exchange among very different cultures is gradually taking place. Many of these cultures have preserved in their fundamental approaches to reality an attitude of respect, contemplation, friendly cohabitation, even of sacrality with regard to Nature, and this should complement the extremely narrow attitude implicit in the strict scientific approach characteristic of the West and, in general, of those cultures and societies which have been most deeply marked by technology. The fact that the problem of humanity and environment is going to be discussed here in a philosophical context in which many representatives of differing cultures are going to propose their reflections is a good omen for us. If the true environment of humankind is a global environment in which Nature, artifacts, institutions, culture, art, religion, and values must find their place and role, in order to allow humankind to fully expand all dimensions it is clear that finding a suitable solution to the problem of the relation of humankind and the environment would no longer mean appeasing fears, but would propose to humankind a valuable project for future development.

2 MODERN SCIENCE, ENVIRONMENTAL ETHICS AND THE ANTHROPOCENTRIC PREDICAMENT

Richard T. De George
*University of Kansas, Lawrence
U.S.A.*

In its common Western sense modern science is the study of nature and its laws; technology is the application of science and the laws of nature to specific human practical projects. Both presuppose a certain view of nature — a view not shared by all peoples. However, whatever their virtues, other views of nature — e.g., the Buddhist or the animist – have not led to the development of science and technology in the same way or to the same extent that the modern view of nature has.

The concept of nature dominant in the development of modern science and technology yields three dichotomies, despite a methodological thrust towards materialistic monism. First, nature is material reality, opposed to and different from mind or spirit. Nature/spirit is the first dichotomy. There are other views of nature such as animism, which deny this division. For the animist, spirit inhabits nature. But for Western scientists nature is devoid of spirit, and, if spirit exists, it is beyond science's ken. Exorcising spirit from nature involved giving up teleological in favour of mechanistic explanations of natural phenomena. The dilemma then became how to account for spirit or mind, — a dilemma which is blatant in psychology and the social sciences but which is most often avoided in natural science simply by ignoring it.

The second, related dichotomy, is nature-as-object/self-as-subject. For modern science nature is an *object* for thinking subjects. This division, which seems obvious to most of us, is denied, for instance, by traditional Chinese philosophy, including Confucianism, according to which human beings are one with nature.[1] The Confucian ideal of humans living in harmony with nature is not part of the Western scientific view of nature. The Western concept of nature as object helped make possible the development of modern science. For if nature is an object, then it is there for humans to interrogate, subdue, dominate, and manipulate. It is by the interrogation and manipulation of nature that we learn the laws of nature that constitute scientific knowledge.

It was only once the heavenly bodies were considered not as deities or special entities, but as physical bodies similar to the earth, that they became candidates for applications of the laws of physics. In a like manner, it was only after the human body was considered an object that could be dissected that important advances were made in human anatomy. More advances could be made in the medical realm if human beings were considered simply objects that might be studied at will, and subjected to tests that are now precluded. The Nazi experiments with hypothermia were performed without concern for what happened to those on whom the experiments were performed. Those experiments are condemned from an ethical point of view. Yet from a scientific point of view there is little doubt that we could learn more if human beings did not have to be treated as subjects but simply as objects.

The third dichotomy is between facts and value, which modern science considers radically different. Of course natural science itself is a human enterprise and many scientists admit it is value-laden in many ways. Nonetheless the claim that its object, nature, is value free is the salient point.

The separation of body from mind or spirit and the separation of fact from value, at least as the object of study, go together. There is nothing special to respect in matter, as opposed to spirit, and given the dichotomies, values go with spirit and not with matter. Hence one result of the absence of value in matter is the absence of value in nature, where nature is defined as separate from spirit.

When Mount St. Helen's erupted in May of 1979, it killed at least sixty people, damaged 220,000 acres of timberland, befouled the Touttle, Cowlitz and Columbia Rivers, and emitted enormous amounts of sulfur which spread in measurable amounts across the United States. In anthropomorphic terms we can say that the volcano, and so nature, did not care about the devastation that it wrought. In the scientific view of nature, there is no better or worse in the state of the mountain before and after the eruption. Clearly the laws of nature operated and operate in both environments. Whether there are trees, animals, and clear rivers, or whether there are dead carcasses, and rivers stopped up with debris makes no difference to the mountain or to nature, because the mountain and nature are objects. As such it makes no sense to say that they care, or that the existence of certain species makes any difference to nature. These things cannot make a difference to it. They may make a difference to us. But that says something about us, not about nature. Human beings are the only part of nature that can in a literal sense care about nature, and it is only human beings who can take care of it as a shepherd or caretaker.

Since no physical state is more natural than any other from the point of view of the physicist, nature not only does not care but also can give no guidance in what it means to be a caretaker or shepherd, and no environment is any more or less natural than any other. Through technology we produce results, some of which may be deleterious to us and to our environment. Yet in the scientific view we cannot say that we are destroying nature. For whatever we do there will always be nature, even if what we leave behind is a desolate wasteland surrounded by toxic clouds carrying radiation that wipes out all life. The laws of physics will still operate, as they operate in all the universe. The barren surface of some of the other planets is no more or less natural than the variegated surface of the earth. The earth is the exception, certainly in our solar system, possibly in our galaxy, maybe in the entire universe. If values enter they do not enter from nature as studied by physicists, but they enter only through human beings. If there are values that exist independent of human beings, they are not the object of study of natural science.

Given this uneasy set of dualisms, modern Western philosophy has tended to give up natural law and to treat human beings as the measure of all things. Ethics, or the study of how human beings should act, comes not from the scientific study of nature but from human beings — for Kant, from human reason, for Hume, from human emotions and desire, for Nietzsche, from human will. Such ethical theories, of course, cannot lay claim to being scientific — which in the contemporary period becomes not only a descriptive but an honorific term. Some Western philosophers have sought alternatives to the problems of dualism through adopting monisms of one sort or another. In a Spinozistic type of neutral monism, Nature is not an object for a subject, and mind and matter are but two different attributes of the same substance. This leads to a kind of pantheism in which Nature or God is everything, in which all are one, and in which human beings can be in harmony with nature. But as with Chinese philosophy, the harmony of human beings with the rest of nature arguably precludes human beings from manipulating nature for their own purposes, or from seeing themselves as dominators of nature who may do whatever they wish to it. Inherent respect for nature has tended historically to delay or impede the development of Western-type science both in traditional Chinese society and in many countries of Africa.

The many difficulties that we presently face because of the often unrestricted use of technology have prompted some in the developed countries to call for a different view or philosophy of nature, in the hope that by changing our view we will change our actions. To a large extent the call is futile. For the view of nature that undergirds contemporary science is not a false one, as opposed to that espoused by Confucianism, by animists, or by others. Concepts or views of nature are not true or false. At best they can be classified as more or less fruitful for certain purposes. The modern view has yielded such tremendous strides in knowledge of the laws of nature, and technology has so changed the globe and the way people live, that it is unlikely Western science or scientists or the general population in industrially developed countries will change their view of nature and adopt a Confucian or animistic one, even though these yield more harmony with nature, propose that nature be respected rather than dominated, and might inhibit the wide-scale application of available technology. Attempts at proposing and defending an alternate philosophy of nature adequate to undergird contemporary science and yet incorporating in nature values that demand respect have not yet been successful. Whether or not they are possible is a question I shall not pursue further at this time. But the failure of attempts thus far incline me to think that the answer to questions of environmental ethics do not lie in that direction.

The questions, then, are how ethical considerations can be brought to bear on ecological issues, given the modern scientific view of nature, and how those considerations can be reconciled with considerations stemming from different conceptions of nature. In considering these questions I shall state and briefly defend three theses, which I shall call the misplaced expertise thesis, the anthropocentric thesis, and the coherence-compromise thesis.

The misplaced expertise thesis
This thesis claims that basic decisions on the environment should be made by the people affected, not by scientists or technologists. If one takes the scientific view of nature at its word, then science does not and cannot tell us how to act.

It cannot direct our choices. Similarly, technology can tell us what we *can* do, and what some of the remedies are for some of the problems we face. But there is no technological fix for all our problems. Thus, it is a mistake to look to either science or scientists, technology or technologists, for guidance as to what we *should* do. The expertise of scientists and technologists simply does not entitle them to any special say in decisions of what should be done. To think otherwise is a case of misplaced expertise. Yet there is a marked tendency in many societies to defer to the scientists and technologists and to rely upon them to make decisions concerning public policy involving the environment. Pollution provides an excellent example.

Pollution is not a scientific term. What we call pollution from a scientific point of view is as natural as is anything else. Nature does not prefer a certain amount of oxygen in the atmosphere or a certain amount of sulfur. Mercury in water and fish is no more natural or unnatural than its opposite. Any mix of the two is natural, even though only certain mixes will allow the growth and development of fish, animals and human beings. There is no such thing as pollution in nature: there are simply different states. The sulfur-laden atmosphere of an erupting volcano is as natural as the clean air surrounding it before it erupts. Pollution is a value term and indicates the presence of elements, usually produced and controlled by human beings, that are in some way and for some reason undesirable from a given human perspective. It is a relative term and depends on the criteria and thresholds that one uses, no one of which is correct or true.

Better and worse, good and bad, are not terms that we find in science or technology. If nature provides no guide and does not care, neither do science and technology. To some extent, technologists are part of the problem and they tend to look only towards technological solutions, whereas part of the solution might be the reduction of the use of available technology. Science or technology cannot tell us what tradeoffs we should make. They cannot tell us how much industrialization we should have or how much of the health of the people of a country or of the globe we should be willing to sacrifice for any particular end — defense, increase in comfort and mobility, or anything else. The use or abuse of nature, and the trade-offs that people wish to make, are issues that require not technical expertise but decisions based on values. Since no one has special expertise with respect to values, any decisions taken should be made by all of those directly affected.

Decisions about pollution are a three-step process. Science and technology can provide scientific and technical knowledge about which chemicals at which levels in water and air will produce certain rates of cancer, and they can describe the effects of denuding the forests. This is the first, or knowledge, step in the process. Upon this the people affected should decide what risk they are willing to take to achieve the ends that they have chosen. This is the second, or value and decision, step. The third, or implementing, step is ascertaining whether the standards set by the people affected are adhered to by all – which is again a question of measurement and technology.

The first and third steps are operative in many countries. What is lacking in almost all is a way of developing and determining informed consensus on the risks people are willing to knowingly take to achieve ends they have collectively decided to pursue. There is no one ethically correct standard. We are all morally precluded from harming others. But with respect to pollution we are often concerned with allowable tradeoffs, any number of which are morally acceptable. If we want cheaper cars, then we must accept certain levels of pollution; cleaner cars and hence cleaner air are expensive. Who should decide how clean our air and water should be? Since the decisions should be made by all those affected, this means the population in general should make them. There is no reason to think that people in Mexico and people in the United States must decide the issue in the same way, providing neither country pollutes the other. Yet the people in any country are given little information about the trade-offs they as a society are actually making. Most countries leave it up to governments or to industries to determine what degree of pollution is dangerous and whether to come up with regulations that will prevent that level from being reached, or what to do if the levels are reached or exceeded. Few people ever vote on alternatives, rarely are they told what the alternatives are, what risks they are being subjected to or what they are trading off against what. Few countries have any comprehensive environmental package. Most action is taken piecemeal, is claimed to be technical, and is left up to technicians and their technologies.

For those interested in an environment ethic, the first task is to establish the mechanisms to enable those affected to decide. The second is to help structure the ethical discussion of the values at stake so that it produces fruitful results.

Richard T. De George

This approach assumes that people are the ones to choose, and that ethics is the exclusive preserve of human beings. I think this inevitable, because even if animals are affected, there is no way we can let them choose. The best we can do is consider them and perhaps give them some moral standing in our calculations. Ultimately, it is we who will choose. This states an anthropocentric position, which I believe is inevitable and which leads me to my second thesis.

The anthropocentric thesis
This thesis asserts that given the presuppositions of science and technology, only an anthropocentric ethics is compatible with them and so only such an ethic is truly viable in the West. Since nature is seen by science as an object and without intrinsic value, traditional modern ethical theory has focused on persons and has paid little attention to nature. The only road open for adopting an ethics of the environment compatible with the presuppositions of contemporary science and mainstream ethical theory is to argue for the adverse effect on human beings of actions that impact on nature. Polluting streams is not wrong because of what it does to rivers or fish, but because of what it does to human beings. Endangering or eliminating species of animal or vegetable life is not wrong because of what it does to those species but because of what it does or might do to human beings, given the interconnections of the ecosystem that supports life.

Those who argue that nature cares in some sense; that life is valuable in whatever form it is found; that a balanced ecosystem is more natural than a disrupted, dysfunctional one; that nature deserves respect; that there is an 'ought' as well as an 'is' embedded in nature, cannot take the point of view of modern science and look upon nature simply as an object to be used and manipulated. Any attempt to find values in nature or to find a basis for respecting nature in its own right, important as it is, fails to find acceptance in the developed nations of the West because it violates the cannons that make science and technology possible. The response, 'So much the worse for science,' puts one outside the mainstream.

Historically we know that the members included in the moral community have grown over the ages. In ancient Greece it covered only male freemen. Slowly it was extended to include women and then all human beings. Should we further extend the moral community to animals, to mountains, to ecosystems, to nature as a whole? Some like Tom Regan advocate animal rights, some like Aldo Leopold propose a land ethic, some like Christopher Stone argue that even trees should have standing. Those who argue in these ways in the West belong to something of a counter-culture,[2] since they implicitly attack the view of nature upon which modern science is built, and hence modern science itself. The traditional Western ethic refuses to extend the moral community to animals, trees, or nature.[3]

The claim that modern Western ethics is anthropocentric is thus correct, and given the Western view of nature and science, this is the only kind of ethics compatible with them in the West. Hence any concern for nature must be translated into adverse effects on human beings or their interests. Thus the destruction of forests is not unethical because of what it does to forests but because it carries with it certain results — consequent flooding, changes in temperature and climate, famine if the land is not able to sustain crops, and so on. This does not preclude consideration of the forest in its totality — the animals, birds, insects, plants, shrubs, trees, streams, that is, the total ecosystem that it supports and of which it is a part. But ultimately the question is how any change impinges on human beings. Fortunately, this is enough to preclude wanton destruction, such as burning forests without considering the results, and to foster consideration of how a forest is to be cut — how much, how fast, in what way — and whether reforestation and replanting are possible and implemented.

Few people would deny that if one were to weigh the worth or importance or value of a human life against that of a rabbit that might supply the food needed to keep the human being alive, the life of the human being should take precedence. Whether one human life is so precious as to justify the destruction of many thousands of animals will for many people be less clear. The traditional ethicist will have ultimately to argue this issue in terms of its effects on human beings.

Yet it does not follow on the traditional ethical view that we are free to treat animals, forests, ecosystems, or nature any way we want.[4] How should we treat them? Ultimately it is we who have to decide, and it will be our interests that carry weight in the decision. The fact that animals can suffer and that they in some ways have interests are facts or claims that we can consider and that we can factor into our moral evaluations.[5] But animals do not form a community of peers with us, and any talk of rights on their behalf cannot carry with them obligations towards us on their part. In this way, some have argued, they have a status similar to infants and the mentally incompetent, whom we nonetheless regard as having human rights and no correlative obligations.

The analogy is in part well taken. but all it shows is that we can treat animals as if they have rights, just as we treat infants as if they have rights. It does not follow that we should treat animals as if they had rights just because we have decided or agreed to treat infants as if they have rights. Moreover, the extension of rights to infants and the mentally incompetent is based on a metaphysics that pushes us in that direction and that justifies our extending rights to them. If that metaphysics is based on the notion of a human soul, then the argument is that as human beings they have a human soul, even though its expression is limited by an undeveloped or malformed body. If moral worth is based on the possession of reason, then it is argued that the baby has it in potency, as a member of the human race, and the mentally defective either once had it or also has it potentially. The same kind of argument cannot plausibly be made for animals. Nor if we were to adopt ethical talk about animal rights is it at all clear — even to its proponents — how we are to weigh the claims of animal rights against conflicting claims of human rights.

However this issue is resolved, it must clearly be resolved by human beings, and those who claim that animals have rights will have to argue for them as their representatives, just as those who argue for the rights of infants must be human beings capable of making out the case for them.

Those, such as Leopold, who argue for a land ethic and who claim that the land, and implicitly all of nature, deserve respect and have intrinsic value, are stating their beliefs and values. With respect to a land ethic it is necessarily and only other human beings who can assert the intrinsic value of the land or nature. All that nature can do is follow its laws. But as in the case of Mt. St. Helen's, a lush green thriving mountainside is no more or less natural than one swept clean by erupting lava and the scorched earth that results from the fires it sets.

This is what I call the *anthropocentric predicament.* Extending morality, which is a human institution, to the land, to animals, to species, is something that we humans can do. But it is something that only we can do. And in extending our ethics in this way, all we are extending is a human ethics. This new broad ethic is as much a human ethic as is a narrower one which includes concern primarily for human beings. The claim that our ethics is too narrow if we consider only human beings as its center fails to realize that ethics must place human beings at its center, at least in the sense that ethics is a human institution.[6] If we wish to grant animals rights and henceforth do not raise them for slaughter, if we all become vegetarians and stop fishing and hunting, if we cease clearing land in which animals live in the wild, these are all decisions that we take for our reasons. We can take them. But in doing so we should not be confused about what we are doing. If this is the result of adopting an ethic that requires these actions, it is we who are adopting this ethic. It is no less a human ethic simply because it precludes certain actions with respect to beings other than human beings. The crucial question, of course is why we should — if we should — adopt such an ethic. Is it because, for instance, animals have rights, but we have simply ignored them or failed to see them? Or is it because we extend rights to them? The difficulty of explaining what it means for animals to have rights comes from the fact that rights are claims or entitlements that have developed within the framework of ethical and legal language and institutions, and do not exist in any way comparable to physical objects. To claim that animals have rights seems to be at best a claim that makes sense only given those human institutions and language. It makes no sense, for instance, to say that cats should respect the rights of mice, or that lions should respect the rights of wildebeests.

From this perspective, whatever view anyone takes is a human view. Even if someone attempts to think or feel like a mountain or a river, it is a human being doing so, and the values attributed to nature and its parts, even if found there and respected as such by some, are attributed by human beings, weighed by human beings, and defended by human beings. Having made this point, my aim is not to resolve the issue of whether nature has value in itself, or whether we should for some reason respect nature as valuable in itself or view animals as having rights. Rather, granting that people disagree on these questions, and given that we are in the anthropocentric predicament, can we adequately handle questions of environmental ethics, and if so, how?

The answer, I suggest, is yes we can handle them, and to do so we do not need to have everyone agree on a new environmental ethic. The defense of that claim becomes clearer if we move to the global level, rather than staying within our own borders. This anthropocentric thesis and the misplaced expertise thesis provide the basis for my third thesis, which concerns an approach to solving the many ecological problems that are global in scope.

The coherence-compromise thesis

This thesis says that given the different views of nature and of ethics worldwide, joint effort in solving international and global ecological problems is most likely to be fruitful if focused on the level of action rather than theory. I take the global issues as paradigmatic because on the global level we have both different views of nature as well as different views of ethics. But what works on the global level will work as well on the national level.

Although it is unlikely that any non-anthropocentric view will prevail in the West, views that claim that nature has value in itself are a vital counterweight to the dominant scientific view. They have helped raise consciousness in the West about ecological issues, and they present an important ideal that should not be lost, even though it is, according to my second thesis, a human ideal. These views are important because they give expression to certain deep human feelings and values, even if the defenses or justifications for them have not been totally convincing.

If we preclude imposing one view on all, and if it is unlikely that any single view will be adopted by all in the short run, the approach I propose is to see whether on practical issues, such as pollution and deforestation, all sides might agree on practical programs and practices. Such agreement may well involve some compromise. To many moral theorists compromise is anathema and opposed to principle. It need not be. In environmental issues, just as in issues of justice, we should not expect any easy reconciliation of opposing views. But we can hope for and work for agreement on the practical rather than the theoretical level.

There are three aspects of the anthropocentric view that make it amenable to compromise, that leave it open to the development of an environmental ethic, and that allow for a tempering of its sometimes arrogant and potentially destructive tendencies.

First, since it claims that values come from human beings, it is possible to argue for the limiting of applications of technology on the basis of known deleterious effects on nature that in turn produce harm to human beings. If nature does not deserve respect in its own right, if rivers may be polluted and fish killed without consideration of rivers or fish, human beings, according to this view, do deserve respect, and polluting rivers and killing fish harms people who depend on them. We know enough about the effects of many of our actions to know that they must be restrained. Thus there is ground for arguing within the anthropocentric view for what those who respect nature at least in part want. In fact, a case can be made that those interested in preserving the environment and in environmental issues can defend most of their practical objectives in these terms.

The second aspect that allows an opening to counter the disrespect towards nature that science allows comes from the respect due to the views and interests of all human beings. According to the anthropocentric view, whatever view anyone takes is a human view. The interest in nature of those who respect it thus carries weight within mainstream ethical theories, even if nature itself is seen as having no intrinsic value. Their respect for and interest in mountains, wilderness, species, or animals deserves consideration, just as do the views and interests of those who think differently.

Thus the snail darter may not have any right to continued existence as a species. It is difficult to see how that right can be forcefully argued. Yet the fact that a significant number of people are interested in the continuation of the species of snail darters is not something that can simply be ignored, no matter what approach one takes to ethical issues. It is the interest and rights of those people rather than the rights of the snail darter that carry weight in the anthropocentric ethic. But since the former does carry weight, those interested in developing an environmental ethic can join forces with those wedded to an anthropocentric ethic to achieve results that they both may desire.

The third opening that allows for some affinity with those who respect nature in a strong sense comes from the limits of science and the inherent acknowledgement of vast ignorance. There is an enormous amount that science does not know. This provides the basis for an argument from ignorance. For instance, we do not know the role of every species in the ecological system. Those who argue for the preservation of species – take the snail darter again – often argue as if all species for some reason deserve preservation in their own right, even though nature itself, independent of human beings, destroys species.

Richard T. De George

The argument from ignorance allows for a course of action that preserves species. Species as parts of nature may deserve no special respect. But since we do not know what role in the ecosystem many species play, or what changes will take place if we eliminate any one of them, the argument from ignorance, joined with prudence and concern for human beings, gives us good reason to preserve as many species as possible. The diversity in nature has produced an ecosystem on which humans depend, and we tamper with it in ignorance at our peril. Such an approach to the preservation of species is not the same as respect for nature in its own right. But it does provide a basis for joint action with those who claim that nature deserves respect in its own right. Thus both those who take an enlightened view of human well-being and those who respect nature for its own sake can join forces in opposing the wanton destruction of forests, the denuding of land, the poisoning of rivers and fish, and the degradation of the environment in which we live.

Where there is lack of agreement, negotiation and compromise are necessary, and the key to just progress in the international as well as the national arena is reciprocity. Reciprocity means that each of those subject to the institution, practice, or system agrees to the acceptability of the institution, practice, or system. Such agreement implies that the practice coheres with the system of theory and practice of that society. An institution is acceptable if it is agreed to by all the representative persons of the various groups with a stake in the matter whatever conception of nature or of justice they hold. The coherence of the accepted practice with each of the different social systems in turn provides precedent and decisions with which later agreements should cohere. This is the condition on which compromise is compatible with moral principle, and the way in which it is integrity-preserving.

Any moral negotiation or compromise necessary to arrive at agreement on specific environmental practices must preserve the moral integrity of the disputants and so must cohere with their moral views. Negotiation does not mean accommodation to immoral practices, as one sees immoral practices. It means widening one's perspective of reflective equilibrium so as to include the claims of others made from a conflicting perspective. On issues of internal national policy concerning the environment, no international accommodation may be necessary, and an accepted *modus vivendi* among nations may be mutually tolerated. Thus each country might determine its own pollution levels, providing that its pollution affects that country only. On some issues, no accommodation may be possible. On other issues, such as Brazil's giving up its claimed right to cut its forests, or establishing institutions for some global determination of allowable pollution levels, accommodation does not involve acceding to injustice. Compromise, negotiation, and coherence all go together here, in the sense that the resolution must cohere with the principles, beliefs, view of nature, and so on of all the participants, though how it coheres will be different in each case. This is a methodological approach that acknowledges the very real differences that exist both nationally and internationally in conceptions, views, or theories of nature, in ethical theory, and on some ethical judgments, while overcoming the impasse to which insistence on the exclusive correctness of one's own position or on complete relativism lead us.

Global issues require a global perspective. But no single approach to nature, values, or the proper treatment of our natural environment, be it Western scientific or a monistic view of the unity of humans and nature, is either fully satisfactory or likely to be acceptable to all in the foreseeable future. The search for or hope for an all-encompassing coherent whole on the global level is at best an ideal and one that we cannot realistically achieve by replacing accepted views of nature with other views or by replacing the richness and diversity of views with a homogeneous view of what nature and human beings are or should be. But the existing pluralism need not be an obstacle to be overcome. It represents diversity that is worth preserving. The West has lived with its fundamental dualisms; Chinese, animistic, and other monistic views of nature do not fit easily with modern science. Acceptance of the latter will involve them in a practical dualism they may be willing to live with as well. Negotiation on practical issues and reciprocity between nations will not resolve the dualisms but will help prevent abuses of nature, whether considered from the viewpoint of the effects on human beings or their effect on nature.

The implications of this approach are in part conservative and in part revisionist. It is conservative to the extent that it justifies prevailing views of nature and ethics and defends such actual practices as the development of international treaties and agreements on the environment despite differences in ethical views and views of nature. It is revisionist to the extent that it undercuts the presuppositions of some theoretical debates, since it claims that it is wrong to insist on any view being the only correct one. It is conciliatory to the extent that it claims that many positions have valuable insights and are potentially or actually fruitful. It advocates compromise not on principle but on practices. Finally, it suggests a method of resolving practical problems, no matter what view one holds of nature, and so of science and technology.

My proposed solution will not satisfy those who believe that nature deserves respect in its own right. But that complaint is really beside the point. For my purpose is not to reach consensus on the truth of the matter but to reach consensus on what we — whatever collective is at stake, whether it be a community, a nation or the world — should do. Environmental issues are pressing and demand action now. My suggestion is that it is easier to agree on what action is necessary and appropriate, given our common concern for human beings and their future, than it is to agree on the basis for that action. Environmentalists can and perhaps should continue to try to convince the majority that nature has intrinsic value and that rights talk makes sense beyond the domain of rights for human beings. But a sane environmental policy does not depend on convincing people of the truth of these. My claim is that such assertions are caught within the anthropocentric predicament just as much as are the claims of standard ethical theory. The important point is not to achieve agreement on philosophical principle (which is of major concern to philosophers), but to come to agreement on action. It is action, not philosophical or theoretical agreement, that will make a difference to us and to those who come after us.

Notes
1. See, among other sources, Kuide, 1989.
2. Regan, 1983; Stone, 1974.
3. Callicott, 1989, is sensitive to this charge, and sees that a new environmental ethic requires also a new metaphysics, and implicitly a new philosophy of science.
4. This position is stated clearly by Frankena, 1979.
5. Frankena, 1979, points out that although only human beings can be moral agents, entities other than human beings can be moral patients according to a great many modern ethical theories.
6. Singer, 1975, makes a strong case for considering animals within a utilitarian framework.
7. To put something other than human beings (for example, land) at the center of ethics is to give up ethics as we have traditionally known it. To do so would not be a true Copernican revolution because it does not simplify the moral phenomena to be explained. Astronomy is a human social endeavour, whose object is the study of heavenly bodies. Ethics is a human social endeavour, but its object is the study of how people should act. In this sense people are necessarily at its center. Even if they are to act in harmony with nature, people are still at the center.

3 PHILOSOPHY, HUMANKIND AND THE ENVIRONMENT

Kwasi Wiredu
University of South Florida, Tampa
U.S.A.

The environmental dangers of our time have become so gross as not to escape any moderately observant citizen of the modern world, philosopher or layman. Two questions that should be of a special interest to a gathering like this are, one: Is Philosophy implicated in the causation? And, two: Can it help in the solution? It cannot be assumed that these questions have the same answers, in terms of character or nuance, in every part of the world. In this discussion I propose to explore the relevant issues from an international point of view but with a special concern for Africa, a concern born not out of nationalistic special pleading but out of anguish at the contemporary plight of the continent.

What, in a few words, are the dangers in question? They are, internationally speaking, dangers of pollution, overpopulation and depletion - depletion of the natural wealth of the world. Let me, for a moment, focus on the Western world[1] and, in particular, on the U.S.A., its hyperbolic paradigm, for that is where voracious consumption and the habits of hegemony, the joint head and spring of the environmental crisis, are most in evidence. Of the problems just named, pollution is the most palpable. Industrial and defense activities have brought pollutants upon land and in water and air with consequences of death and disease and an incalculable potential of more of the same in the future. In the mounting warnings of doom from ecologists and environmental protectionists there is most likely a certain element of voluntary or involuntary exaggeration; but when all allowances are made there remains a sobering picture of an environment, already somewhat degraded through the inappropriate disposal of toxic wastes and the releasing of unsafe gasses into the air from both routine processes and accidents,[2] facing the prospects of aquatic contamination from acid rain and disastrous climatic warning through ozone reduction (the Ozone Agreement not withstanding).

The role of overpopulation in the environmental crisis or even its very existence has been subject to dispute. But it is undebatable that if world population growth remains at its exponential rate, the pollution of the environment will be aggravated, the depletion of non-renewable resources accelerated and the spread of poverty in many parts of the world exacerbated, barring, in all these scenarios, any windfall availability of cheap, clean and inexhaustible substitutes or some unforeseen world-wide increase in human wisdom. As things are now, a priori considerations alone are sufficient to induce a sense of impending shortages in the finite resources of the world. And, as a matter of fact some empirical researchers have put it at as early as within the next hundred years.[3]

What kind of environmental philosophy, it has been asked, is responsible for so incautious a use of the environment? In this connection the spotlight has been mainly on the West, for the environmental philosophies indigenous to Africa and the Orient are self-evidently harmless. It is well-known that Hinduism, Buddhism, Shintoism, Confucianism, Taoism — all in their different ways teach respect for nature. In all these systems of thoughts human beings are basically seen as fellow participants with animals, plants and non-living things in a system of organically interrelated existence pervaded in their essences by one and the same principle of ultimate reality. And, whether this is well-known or not, it is a fact that traditional African conceptions of the external world enjoin environmental circumspection, for the environment is believed, in various parts, to be changed with forces or inhabited by extra-human beings superior to humans in power and sometimes in morals. I will return to this in due course.

But, meanwhile, what does the spotlight on the West reveal? Not unexpectedly, no single monolithic of nature and of human relations with it emerges. We may begin by noting that spiristic beliefs akin to the African ones to which allusion has been made were commonplace in European antiquity, not to talk of closer epochs in rural Europe. It is sometimes suggested that this 'pagan animism' was extinguished by Christianity.[4] But, apart from anything else, Christianity itself has not been averse to belief in generically the same entities. Jesus Christ was, so we are told, once moved to exorcise entities of the same ontological status from a person and channel them into swine. For Christianity, then, the thing about such spirits is not necessarily that they are non-existent but rather that they are, when existent, evil. This, of course, does not in itself entail any particular ecological outlook.

What has been taken as the locus classics of the specifically Christian attitude to the environment is the passage in Genesis (1-3) in which at least the chosen people seem to be encouraged to dominate nature. Within the Western tradition or ensemble of traditions and environmental ideology of dominion also emerges from stoic sources according to which nature was made for the sole convenience of human beings. The historical conjunction of these two strands of thought did not presage a widespread habit of environmental solicitude in the West. Nor were the occasional remarks of an influential thinker like Aristotle or Bacon or Descartes or Kant supporting the supposed cosmic subordination of nature to human needs and purposes such as to precipitate a revolution in thought habits. Not, of course, that there have not been models of a more empathetic attitude to nature in the tradition. Genesis 2: 15, which says 'And the Lord took the man (Adam) and put him into the garden of Eden *to dress it and keep it* (my italics), has not infrequently been seen as appointing humans as stewards of nature.[5] More unproblematically, there is the example of the mystical nature-love of Saint Francis of Assisi, nominated by Lynn White as 'a patron saint for ecologists'.[6] Those less enthused with mystics might perhaps resonate somewhat more to the counter-nomination, by Rene Dumos, of Saint Benedict for the same honor on grounds of his more functional respect for nature.[7] Besides, the feel for nature expressed by the Son of Man himself, as reported by Luke (12:27), has not gone without ecologically minded attention:[8] 'Consider the lilies how they grow; they toil not, they spin not; yet I say unto you, that Solomon in all his glory was not arrayed like one of these'.[9]

To the foregoing stoic and Christian attitudes to nature (or more strictly to non-human nature) may be added what might be called simply the secular attitude. This is the attitude which regards nature, or, more particularly, of practical and aesthetic values for human beings. Nature offers possibilities of use and enjoyment of which human beings can avail themselves if they know how, subject only to the ethical imperative to avoid doing harm, in that process, to the interests of other people, now living or sure to live in the future.

If Passmore is right, this tenet of 'conventional' morality, which has always been taught as distinct, presumably from being always practical in the Western tradition, is sufficient — 'without any supplementation whatsoever' to 'justify our ecological concern, our demand for action against the polluter, the depleter of natural resources, the destroyer of species, and wildernesses'.[10] This position is disputed by philosophical advocates of a specifically environmental ethic. I will, for the time being skirt over this issue and pursue a consideration connected with the fact that Passmore's reference in this context is to conventional morality rather than to technical moral philosophy.

We meet here the remarkable fact that, historically, Western attitudes to the environment have been shaped not by technical philosophy but by folk conceptions, even if some of these are philosophical, broadly speaking. Genesis is not even technical theology. That much is obvious. What may not be obvious is that the statements made by the historical philosophers about the proper way of regarding nature reflect more the ideological bent of their socialization than the trend of their technical lucubrations. But it would be apparent, on reflection, that the historical Western philosophers did not regard human relations with the environment as a subject posing philosophical problems requiring any very earnest meditations. Thus, the industry and elaborate care which Kant, for example, expends on his search for the explanation of the possibility of *a priori* knowledge are notably absent from his treatment of the question of human lordship over nature. That humans, as rational beings, are lords over nature is pretty obvious to him while, on the other hand, he thinks that nothing short of an intellectual revolution is needed for solving the problem of *a priori* knowledge.

It was not until quite recently, when the effects of the ravages wrought upon the environment through industrial and war-related activities manifestly became not only life-threatening but also life-destroying on a large scale, that philosophers, following the much earlier cries of ecologists, perceived the environmental situation as philosophically problematic and began to devote intensive professional attention to it. If, then, Philosophy as a discipline has any guilt in the genesis of the environmental crisis, it is one of omission, not commission. And if 'ought' implies 'can', then the assessment of blame must be predicated on how far-sighted we are entitled to suppose that human beings can be. History gives no unambiguous clues.

But what of the charter of dominion, alluded to previously, which, according to the Genesis, God, having created men and women after his own image, gave to them? Saith the Lord: 'Be fruitful, and multiply, and replenish the earth, and subdue it: and have dominion over the fish of the sea, and over the fowl of the air, and over every living thing that moveth upon the earth' (Genesis 1: 28). Surely, herein lies the root of all (or much) environmental evil? I am not a Christian, but I do not think so. Whoever issued that exhortation cannot plausibly be supposed to have intended to recommend a policy of either careless or wanton destruction. Nor is it necessary to suppose that the recipients of the advice interpreted it in that way. To hold dominion is not necessarily to destroy or despoil and to multiply at a time when population may have been relatively sparse might well have been a sensible idea. As for subduing the earth, it is not such an inappropriate metaphor if you consider, for example, the manifold inclemencies of the elements, which, even now in spite of all the marvels of modern technology, human beings struggle inconclusively to *overcome*. Note, by the way, how natural this last metaphor (of overcoming) sounds in this connection. Think how devastating a hurricane can still be in the United States of America, for example.

The real cause of the environmental problem is to be found, I believe, in the fact that technology tends to grow ahead of knowledge, which, in turn, tends to grow ahead of wisdom and moral virtue. Technology, of course, presupposes knowledge – knowledge both of fact and technique. But when once this productive resource has delivered the product, questions may arise regarding the consequences, for humans and for the environment, of its use, and, in some cases, its disposal of which the inventors and the manufactures may be, and often are, in the dark. Yet such consequences may have the gravest import for both the living and the non-living. The case of pesticides is a notorious illustration of this. Here ignorance is the primary cause of trouble, though secondary factors like carelessness, greed and wickedness may ramify the consequences. The basic reason why ignorance is such an intractable problem in such matters is because the relations subsisting among the various components of the total ecological system of which human and non-human beings and existences are sub-systems are so complex and subtle and so delicately balanced that any intervention at any one point is apt to touch off a whole chain of unforeseen reverberations. It is in this sense that knowledge tends to lag behind technology to the peril of man, woman, beast and earth.

Suppose that this problem of knowledge is significantly alleviated through conscientious research and patient computation. I say alleviated, not solved, for only omniscience can accomplish that. Assume, then, that there is a fair knowledge of the consequences of a technological innovation. There is still no guarantee that it will be used to the good of humankind generally or for the proper maintenance of the environment. What if the technology in question is one easily adapted to use in the premeditated destruction of life and habitat? Because of the frequent shortages of wisdom on one side or another or on all sides in human confrontations such uses of knowledge are not at all rare. This is a reflection that presses on our attention the lack of equation between knowledge and wisdom. The point was known to Heraclitus and is common place in African folklore. Heraclitus said that the learning of many things does not suffice to make one wise. With high technology and fair knowledge but not enough wisdom is it any wonder that our species endangers itself and its surroundings and vice versa?

This relation between technology and knowledge, on the one hand, and danger, on the other, as mediated by insufficient wisdom, calls for at least a slight elaboration. Whatever else technological advances may mean, they mean increased power to affect the environment in terms both of rate and scope. But to err is human, and this characteristic of the species appears to be stable in frequency. Hence, the application of technology is liable to bring in its trail dangers proportionate to its own magnitude. This tendency is no respecter of cultures, and one might almost call it a law of human interactions with nature. It is only in the light of this apparent law that one can understand the despoliation of the environment that took place in, for instance, medieval China. If knowledge and technique are available, human beings will use them and the Chinese, who until the seventeenth century were superior to Europe in science and technology, used their capabilities with vim, little inhibited by their culture of reverence for nature. They built large cities – large, even by today's standards – and manufactured a variety of products, laying waste large expanses of forest and causing considerable land erosion, among other things.

If technology is such a mixed blessing, why not give it up? In truth we can sooner give up breathing than do that. To know or not to know? That is not an option. To want to know is human, and so also is to want to make use of what is known. So, one way or another, we have to live with technology and use and cultivate it and try to thrive on it without destroying our environment. But how best may we do this? Obviously, knowledge and wisdom are needed, and so also is morality. Of these, perhaps, knowledge is the easiest to get and wisdom the hardest. But morality is the most essential, for without morality no human community is sustainable, with or without a protected environment. But, it might be asked, what is the morality that will both sustain human community and protect the environment? This brings me to a question broached earlier on but left unexplored, namely, will 'conventional' morality, unsupplemented with a specifically environmental tenet, suffice?

It is important in this connection to separate two questions. The first is whether conventional morality can provide, unaided, an adequate basis for an approach to nature aimed at reversing the environmental crisis, and the second is whether that morality is philosophically complete. Let the term 'conventional morality' stand for the moral precept that we ought not so to act as to harm the interests of others, born or unborn. Very roughly, the position of Passmore to which reference was made early in this discussion - not, by any means, his only message - is that the answer to the first question is affirmative. This position will not have been shown to be false if it should turn out that sound overall moral thinking requires that we recognize that non-human as well as human beings have, in themselves, a moral worth which we ought to respect in our dealings with our environment. This would be a negative answer to the second question. It would be a standpoint that logically transcends the concerns specifically generated by the environmental crisis. Even if we had no environmental crisis on our hand, it would still be binding upon us to respect the independent moral standing of non-human beings, if they indeed have such a status. Still, as a strategy of mass persuasion in matters environmental, it might be effective enough to show that considerations founded on human interests are enough to justify and hopefully motivate circumspection and forbearance. And when the resources of philosophy are brought to bear on this project, that is a non-trivial contribution.

Nevertheless, philosophically, the question whether the non-human world is a locus of independent moral worth cannot be shelved. Not that too much can be expected from an affirmative resolution of this issue and the universal acceptance of that point of view. Historically, neither conventional morality, as is generally manifest, nor even an ethic of reverence for nature, as is clear from the case of Medieval China has proved to be a panacea for environmental degradation. This is due, of course, to the gap between moral avowals and actual virtue created by complications of the human psyche such as self-deception, shortsightedness and the fragility of the will. Even so, we are at an epoch in human affairs where the threat of environmental disaster is so apocalyptic that it may well be capable of reinforcing the will in the implementation of good environmental intentions. Many such intentions can be expected to flow from the belief in the intrinsic moral significance of the non-human realms of nature. But are such conceptions valid? That they are is being argued by an increasing number of very astute philosophers, and some of the very best work in current Western philosophy is being done in this area of investigation. Arguments for conceptions of this sort are being expounded in works such as, to cite only two examples. Paul Taylor's *Respect for Nature,*[11] and more lately, Lawrence Johnson's *A Morally Deep World,*[12] with such clarity, rationality and systematic coherence as to challenge the most serious attention. Historical pride of place belongs, of course, to Passmore and Attfield for, so to speak, opening up this field to professional philosophy.[13]

Of course, neither Taylor nor Johnson pretends to advance knock-down arguments for their positions. Such arguments are, in any case, rare in Philosophy. Not even in Logic, if you stray from mechanical procedures, do you get such a dispensation. But beyond this there are deep conceptual problems in the notions of moral worth at work in these theories that make them rather more than averagely controversial. While this may turn out to be due more to their originality than anything else, it might seem, from the outside, to detract from their effectiveness as incentives to environmental activism. In fact, however, controversy is the mainstay of the enterprise of Philosophy, and the current debate on the environmental enlargement of ethical concerns will at least raise public consciousness about the deeper phases of the attitudinal changes required for stemming the tide of ecological disruption.

The reference to the need for changes in attitudes brings us to the second reason why the apparent contentiousness of environmental ethics is not such a drawback. The point is that a frontal approach to narrowly environmental matters is not the only way in which Philosophy can contribute to the solution of the problems under discussion. As pointed out earlier, the root cause of these problems is our combined poverty in knowledge, wisdom and virtue in the use of advancing technology and the management of our numbers on this earth.

Wisdom has a subtle connection with knowledge and virtue. It also has a no less subtle connection with Philosophy. We know already that wisdom is not identical with knowledge. Yet, it is equally clear that one cannot be wise on an empty head. The reason is that wisdom is the capacity, the skill, for certain kind of employment of knowledge. It is the quality of mind that is manifested in the use of knowledge about persons and their worlds for the satisfactory ordering of social relations and individual lives. Evidently, wisdom has a moral dimension, for without moral insight such an ordering of human affairs must be a chimerical aspiration. But wisdom is not just virtue. There can be simple-minded virtue, while wisdom, on the contrary, is nothing if not a complex form of mentality. Its complexity consists in the ability to grasp heterogeneous facts and squeeze out of them a unified significance for life.

It is exactly here, in the transcending of brute facts with an eye on the living of life, that the affinity of Philosophy with wisdom is disclosed. The preoccupations of wisdom come in degrees of abstractness. Close to the theater of day-to-day existence there is the need to base conduct on an understanding of the meaning and purpose of things. Wise pondering in this context yields principles of practical judgement and purposeful action. Further probing of these transports us into the realms of speculative abstractions, but with the same controlling quest for meaning. Here enters the philosopher.

The wise person in practical life may not be a philosopher nor, unfortunately, is the philosopher necessarily a possessor of practical wisdom. But both, relative to their appropriate levels of concern, are apt to ask the same question: 'What does it all mean?' Since at the philosophical level of abstraction 'all' means 'quite all', this question is more strictly characteristic of philosophy than any of the form of principled reflection. (These considerations are obviously germane to the etymological reference to wisdom in the English word 'philosophy'. In fact, in the Akan language of Ghana, my mother tongue, the word that most closely corresponds to 'philosopher' is 'Onyansafo', which means 'a wise person', though the designation is reserved for wise men of an abstract cast of mind).[14]

Now, my suggestion is that the inculcation of the quest for meaning into the thought habits of the generality of humankind may be Philosophy's greatest contribution to the solution of the problems of the environment and other problems too. The asking of that question may be, if not the beginning of wisdom, at least a reminder of its desirability. At all events, it should be an incitements to reflection on fundamentals. From this exercise benefits are likely to accrue to the environment in the following way. Consider, to begin with, how routine it can be for great numbers of people, especially in the so-called developed world, to live an unexamined life of acquisition and consumption, untouched by the remotest qualms about the environmental consequences of their life-style in terms of pollution and the depletion of world resources. Of course, a certain amount of acquisition and consumption is an elementary requirement of life. But money and possessions, although sought in the first instance as a means to personal satisfaction and self-realization, can become ends in themselves.

This pathology becomes even more frightening when manifested at the level of the state, for here the unrestrained quest for national wealth is compounded by an equally unrestrained quest for power and glory and for ascendancy over other peoples and nations. War, colonialism and neo-colonialism are familiar outcomes. A more constant concomitant is arms production, which takes up a respectable part of the resources of nations. Meanwhile, the resultant deterioration of the environment is a daily verification of the Akan proverb that when two elephants fight it is the earth that bears the brunt.

But imagine for a moment that people were to step aside awhile from the life of acquisition and aggrandizement to ask what it all means. The chances are that the vanity not indeed of the whole thing but of much of it will become apparent. One could then expect a reduction in consumption and its untoward consequences for the environment. Moreover, this would become possible through voluntary restraint.[15] This in itself, would, of course, be a modest gain, given the enormity of the environmental problem. But a widespread attitude of self-restraint in consumption would betoken a general outlook of sanity which would be likely to spill over into other relevant departments of conduct. For example, a more liberal allocation of funds (through a little curbing of the profit motive) on the part of corporations for research into the likely effects of intended products or into safer methods of waste disposal would be a natural sequel. And even state agencies might break loose from the inertia of bureaucracy in pursuit of a more imaginative safeguarding of the environment, which would be a special blessing in socialist countries where maintenance of the environment has not been more glorious in their capitalist counterparts.[16]

Let me follow up briefly on the matter of voluntary restraint just mentioned. We have been recommending, in the interests of environmental sobriety, what might be called a philosophical attitude to life. But here we need to take notice of problems requiring philosophical ratiocination. Suppose, for example, that voluntary restraint does not materialize. Could we foresee any sort of legitimate enforcement of limits to consumption through legislation? And on what theory of the relations of the state to the individual might this be predicated? The same questions arises with respect to population control,[17] *mutatis mutandis*. These latter are, in fact, more crucial, for population increase has an obvious impact on the magnitude of consumption. Another important question relates to the control of industrial pollution. The question is not whether governments have the right to institute anti-pollution regulations. That is an uncontroversial fact of daily experience in many parts of the world. The question is rather how far a government may go in this direction without becoming authoritarian, or worse, totalitarian, and on what criteria.

Since problems of pollution frequently cut across national boundaries, it is clear that some manner of cooperation between states is required for their solution. The Ozone Agreement, referred to earlier on, was a good example of this kind of cooperation. An idea that naturally suggests itself here is that of a world government. It seems plausible, on the face of it, that an authority of this sort is the ideal one for crafting and enforcing convenants of a global scope.[18] But, on a little reflection the very idea of what some might call a global Leviathan bristles with problems not the least of which are conceptual. Without stopping to enumerate these, it is obvious that the topic is not one to encourage philosophical complacency. Let me mention, finally but not as the last of such issues in existence, the question whether there is a human right to a liveable environment. Until recently when problems of the environment seized the attention of philosophers, the customary inventory of human rights consisted of such items as life, liberty, property, happiness, equality, education and the like. It is now being questioned whether the right to a liveable environment is not presupposed by all these.[19]

The above is a budget of problems, highlighted by the environmental crisis, which philosophy is uniquely qualified to tackle. I say 'highlighted' advisedly. These problems were not created by that crisis they have always been with humankind. The crisis has simply made them more pronounced and more terrifying. Note, as a corollary, that technology too has always been with humankind; every people at every epoch of their history have had some techniques for facilitating the arts of living. When therefore some people decry technology for bringing the environmental crisis upon us, they cannot, in good sense, mean technology as such. They can only mean modern, sophisticated technology. And even that only in part, for they can hardly pretend to be disenchanted with absolutely all the fruits of high technology. In any case, technology of itself does nothing; it is human beings who create and use it for their own purposes. Therefore, when things go wrong they must blame themselves, not the artifacts. Otherwise, they are behaving like a certain gentleman who could not drive his car into his garage without a brush every so often with the garage wall away from the driver's side. He berated the wall soundly for being so uncooperative. It is not known what comments the wall had on the man's genius for driving.

In the West such 'pathetic' fallacies about technology may be more or less harmless, for the technology is already there and in place, and such talk will not conjure it out of existence. But in Africa it might conceivably have unfortunate effects, for it could retard the acquisition of necessary technology. By 'necessary technology' I mean 'appropriate' technology, which does not always mean state-of-the-art contraptions. But the careful discriminations of the appropriate from the fanciful will not come easily to minds enamoured of obscurantist deprecations of modern technology. Similar animadversions apply to careless disparagements of science. Scientism is the belief in the omniscience of science. One need not be victim to such simple-mindedness to suggest that there is an urgent need for science and technology in Africa. The need is, in fact, a rather intensive one for we need both to acquire and apply these resources for the transformation of our societies in a comparatively short time. In this process there are a number of things that we ought to do. We have, ourselves, to assume the role and responsibility of adapting scientific knowledge and technology to the special circumstances of our continent. But we must also work to discover new knowledge and invent new things for ourselves and the rest of humanity (with any requisite adaptations in the latter case). In the first two cases we need to disentangle Western cultural particularities from the universals of knowledge, technique and practice with which they are immanently intermixed in the existing disciplines.

This last is probably the most difficult of all the foregoing desiderata to accomplish. I will here limit myself to one illustration of an environmental relevance. The Western practice of technology-seems to me to be marked by a remarkable nonchalance about the management of waste, carcinogenic or not. My own encounter with this aspect of Western culture came early in my introduction to Western society. In 1958 on my way to Oxford for graduate studies I stopped in London briefly. That was my first visit to any Western city, and I was highly impressed. I thought the streets were nice and there were many nice things all around. But in my hotel room I happened to look down through the back window and was sharply struck by the comparative filth of the place where the garbage containers were kept. It turned out that this study in contrast was not an isolated phenomenon in Western cities.

The impression has grown on me that one at least of the underlying causes of the appalling problem of pollution which has attended advanced industrialization and the large-scale production of high technology weapons and defense systems, a problem with consequences for even the non-participating regions of the world, is the same disparity that I observed between, on the one hand, the care and concentrated assiduity in the production of things and, on the other hand, the uninspired manner of waste management. The tragedy, now, is that in Africa when we have imported some technological system involving waste management we have brought it incomplete with all such cultural infelicities, except that in this case the assiduity in production has not been all that concentrated owing to certain distractions of third world existence, such as political instability and various forms of stagnation.

This leads to a more general reflection of an even more somber significance. Either through the long chain of the effects of ecological processes or through insidious human scheming abroad or through carelessness at home, some of the deleterious consequences of the environmental problems of the Western world get exported or imported into Africa, thus compounding her own ecological situation which is serious enough in itself. On account of the low level of industrialization, pollution from industrial wastes is, on the whole, not a serious problem in Africa. But, leaving natural dispersal of effects on one side, it is significant to note that there are agencies in the West that are highly motivated in trying to make Africa the dumping ground of toxic wastes from their industries. Sometimes expeditions to this purpose are forestalled by the protests of some African pressure groups. Other times they slip through by stealth. But more serious, because more open and more uninhibited, is the continuing export to Africa of pesticides whose use has been prohibited in their own country of manufacture.

By comparison with the environmental situation in the West Africa's indigenous problems of the environment derive more directly from natural than artificial processes, though it cannot be said that Africans have been altogether passive in the generation of these problems. One of the most serious long-term problems is the expansion of the Sahara desert. This tremendous expanse of desert, the size of the U.S.A. discounting only California and Alabama, has been for some time, according to some estimates, growing towards the south at the rate of about 40 kilometers per year.[20] Indeed, according to one United Nations study, 'In 1983 alone the desert advanced at least 150 kilometers to the south.[21] Mathematically, the unchecked playing out of this rate of change over time is too alarming to contemplate.

The disastrous effects of other environmental factors is a matter not of anticipatory contemplation but of lamentable fact. In recent years persistent drought has brought death to infirmity to unspeakable numbers of Africans, particularly those of tender age. Adverse weather conditions threaten to be perpetual. In the last two decades rain has consistently fallen below average in Africa, sometimes by as much as 40 per cent.[22] At the best of times, the African land is in many parts rather fragile. Although deeper down into the earth Africa is full of riches, her top soil tends not to be very deep and is easily denuded of nutrients. When subjected to long periods of hot sunshine, the rains, when and if they do come, simply wash away the top soil, leaving behind only useless sediment. Added to these apparently natural adversities of the African environment is the sting of the tsetse fly which transmits sleeping sickness to humans and various diseases to cattle. This fly, as is well-known, is peculiar to Africa. Not to be left out of account, of course, is the anopheles mosquito which afflicts African populations with debilitating malaria.

No one knows for sure to what degree, if any, human activities have had a part in the development of any of these phenomena. In terms of evolutionary time, the origin of the Sahara desert is believed to be rather recent. One commentator-remarks that Reasonable evidence exists to suggest that five to seven thousand years ago, much of the central Sahara was a rather humid area:[23] and some researchers believe that the desertification was due to agricultural forest-burning and shifting cultivation.[24] Whatever the truth in such speculation may be as far as the Sahara is concerned, there is no doubt that farming activities have contributed to the impoverishment of the soil as and the destruction of the forests. In this regard, the single most unmistakable pressure has been that of population growth. The annual population increase of 3 per cent, the highest in the world, has been putting extreme stress on the resources of the land. To me the workings of this abstract formula of multiplication acquires perfect concreteness when I reflect that when I was in elementary school in Ghana in the middle forties the population of Ghana, known in those days as the Gold Coast, was a mere two and a half million. By the 1984 census it had officially reached 14 millions, a figure that many thought was very conservative. Feeding this escalating mass of humankind has meant, in many parts of the continent, more forest clearing and more cattle grazing, leading to considerable soil degradation and a quite drastic deforestation with possible climatic consequences and other ecological side effects.

In order not to make this too long, let me conclude this sketch of Africa's environmental situation by noting the effects of two patterns of human intervention in the environment in Africa. The first is urbanization in its various forms, have created concentrations of population in physical and moral environments not totally dissimilar to the cities of the Western cities, if not in scale then certainly in character. The second pattern of intervention is one that must bring a lot of sadness to the heart. Border conflicts, one of the intractable legacies of colonialism, and civil wars of various kinds in post-independence Africa have caused death and environmental devastation, through bombings and other severities of war, in quite a few parts of Africa.

On a review of the foregoing description of Africa's environmental problems it would be apparent that the similarities with Western environmental problems are not as important as the dissimilarities. A little part of the situation is due to industrialization, and a little, though a most regrettable part, to war, but the greatest part is due either to natural agencies and processes or to-elemental human interactions within the species or with nature. In regard to these latter problems the greatest need is for knowledge, both scientific and intuitive, and technology sensitized to both the physical and cultural circumstances of Africa.

In other words, the technical as distinguishable from the ethical aspect of the environmental problem is much larger and much more urgent in Africa than in the West, so much more urgent that even if talk, in the West, of seeking to control nature may have the appearance of an aggressive disregard for whatever intrinsic worth nature may have, it does not have the same suggestiveness in Africa. On this continent we need to control desertification, and soil erosion and the activities of the tsetse fly and the anopheles mosquito. These are life and death matters. Whatever type of ethic we may subscribe to, whether it be humanocentric or biocentric or ecocentric, we have to recognize that a certain critical level of utilization of nature is presupposed by the demands of sheer human survival and, beyond that, of any reasonable form of human flourishing. In large parts of Africa it is now an open question whether even the more basic of these demands can be met. In such circumstances any philosophical problems of how to limit consumption, even if not unintelligible, must yield existential urgency to the problems of how to find something to consume, which also has its own philosophical dimensions.

Actually, the language of controlling nature does not quite make sense in my own language, the Akan language of Ghana, and I doubt whether it does in any other African language. This is because we do not set any domain of objects and processes aside from human beings and give it a designation comparable to the Western concept of nature, whose coherence cannot be taken for granted. This should be distinguished, though, from the nonsensical suggestion, sometimes heard, that Africans do not distinguish between themselves and the external world. Such claim reduces Africans to a virtually amoebic level of consciousness. Self-consciousness logically implies an awareness of something outside of oneself, and without self-consciousness there is no humanity.

The point is that the external world that the traditional African, as far as I know, recognizes includes other human beings and living and non-living beings as well as extra-human beings of various grades of power and intelligence, ranging from the super-human to the sub-human. All these are regarded as regular parts of the world order. There is, therefore, no question of trying to control or dominate this whole scheme of things and beings. One may seek to overcome specific problems deriving from specific components of this one system of reality, and one may also utilize other resources of the system in support of human life. This latter activity is, however subject to the constrains of two major considerations.

First, any object, living or non-living, may be within the immediate province of a super-human force or power, and one has to avoid reckless and, in some cases, unsupplicated appropriation and use of it. Second, in any case, the land, the most fundamental means of livelihood, belongs not to individuals but to whole clans, and individuals only have rights of use that they are obligated to exercise considerately so as not to render nugatory the similar rights of future members of the clan. The clan itself is thought of as consisting of members living in the world of ordinary sensible experience, those living in the post-mortem world of the ancestors and those yet to be born. Both the post-mortem and the pre-natal sectors of clan membership have a psychological reality which exercises very considerable influence on thought, feeling and behavior. The influence of the ancestors is as vivid in the African imagination as that of the living elders of the clan and actually more authoritative morally, since the ancestors are, as a rule, supposed to judge the conduct of the living and reward or punish them from a position of moral unimpeachability to which no mortal can lay claim.

Of all the duties owed to the ancestors none is more imperious than that of husbanding the resources of the land so as to leave it in good shape for posterity. In this moral scheme the rights of the unborn play such a cardinal role that any traditional African would be nonplussed by the debate in Western philosophy as to the existence of such rights. In the upshot there is a two-sided concept of stewardship in the management of the environment involving obligations to both ancestors and descendants which motivates environmental carefulness, all things being equal.

But all things are not always equal, and, as we saw earlier on, a world view, which, from a logical point of view, should be favorable to the environment, does not necessarily guarantee the protection of the environment. If no very extensive damage was done to the African environment through human intervention in traditional times, it was probably due, more than anything else, to the absence of the population explosions of modern times and the literal explosion of the warfare associated with these times. In any case, the African traditional world view has been, for a considerable time, under pressure from Christianity and Islam, which have sought to supplant it through prescription rather than persuasion and large numbers of Africans now profess an allegiance to Christian and Islamic world views, though without an explicit, reasoned disavowal of indigenous conceptions, which are incompatible in many points with the new faiths. Amidst the imponderable of this conceptual and psychological interplay of world views it is probably going to be fruitless, at all events, in the short term, to seek a cosmological anchorage for a popular approach to the problems of the environment in contemporary Africa. Perhaps, a more promising basis for an environmental outlook in regard, at least, to those problems of the environment whose solution requires the sacrifice of some of the interests of individuals in favor of the common good is the communalists ethic of traditional Africa, which though in some danger from the pressures of incipient industrialism, still retains appreciable vitality. The necessity for some such adjustment of interests is not the discovery of communalism; it is a presupposition of all morality. What communalism adds is the increased readiness of the individual to empathize with demands of communal welfare over an expanding field of interests.

But, in the final analysis, more can be expected, in Africa as in other places, from the adoption of the philosophical attitude to the problems of life, environmental ones included, than specific modes of ethical practice or particular philosophical insights into existence and human life. The beginning of that attitude, as we have previously indicated, is the asking of the question, 'What does it all mean?' Since, despite the fact that science, technology and industrialization have a lot to do with the environmental problems of the West and we in Africa still urgently need to cultivate these ways of knowing the world and changing it, the following special case of our very general question is of the last consequence to us. We are to ask, 'Industrialization for what?' It is the dedicated pursuit of this quest for meaning and purpose in all its ramifications that will prevent us from mindlessly imitating the industrialism of the West, pollution and all. And it is the same effort of the mind that will prevent the West from destroying its own environment and all others with her technology.

Notes
1. From the present point of view the Soviet Union and the Eastern European countries are, of course, parts of the Western world.
2. In the U.S.A. alone, 'an EPA study recorded almost 7000 accidents between 1980 and 1985,

killing 138 people, injuring more than 4700 and causing the evacuation of more than 200,000 people. Accident rates may be going even higher - more than 12,000 releases to air, water and ground were reported to the National Report Center in 1986.' Richard E. Ayres in Goldfarb, ed. 1989, p.114. Although things like the near accident at the Three Mile Island nuclear plant in the U.S.A. in 1986 are what alert the popular mind to the dangers of modern technology, the cumulative effect of these unpublicized accidents on human welfare is exceedingly negative.

3. This suggestsion, made, for example, in Meadows *et al.*, 1974 has drawn a lot of criticism, but when it is taken with all the appropriate qualifications, it should serve at least as an aid to temperance in consumption. See also in Shrader-Frechette, 1981.
4. See, for example, White, 1971, p.37.
5. The next two verses are, however, not very inspiring in this particular connection. They are: 2: 16 'And the Lord God commanded the man, saying: Of every tree in the garden thou mayest freely eat. 2: 17. But of the tree of the knowledge of good and evil thou shalt not eat of it in the day that thou eatest thereof thou shalt surely die.'
6. White, in Harney and Disch, 1971, p.42.
7. Rene Dumos, 'A Theology of the Earth' in Harney and Disch, *ibid.*
8. Carmody and Carmody, 1988, p.55.
9. Again, the next verse might, though it need not be, interpreted by some as manifesting a partiality for humans over nature: 'If, then God so clothe the grass which is today in the field and tomorrow is cast into the oven how much more will he clothe you. O ye of little faith.?'
10. Passmore, 1974, pp. 186-7.
11. Taylor, 1986.
12. Johnson, 1991.
13. Passmore, 1974; Attfield, 1983.
14. Gyekye is dead right on this: The philosopher in Akan Traditional society is not just any person who has practical wisdom: a person has to have abstract wisdom to be recognized as such. Gyekye, 1987, p. 64. See also Wiredu, 1980, pp. 140 - 143.
15. See also Shrader-Frechette, ed. 1981, chapter 7: 'The duty to limit consumption', especially, K.S. Shrader-Frechette, 'Voluntary Simplicity and the Duty to Limit Consumption.'
16. See, for example, Michael Kupilik, 'The Environment and Socialism', in Barrett, ed., 1982.
17. For opposing views on this see, eg. Garrett Hardin, 'The Tragedy of the Commons' and Daniel Callahan, 'Ethics and Population Limitation' both in Sharader-Frechette, 1981. See also Hardin's "Parenthood: Right or Priviledge" in Campbell adnd Wade, 1972.
18. Norman Cousins, writing in 1970, was in no doubt of the necessity for a world government: 'Humanity needs a world order. The fully sovereign nation is incapable of dealing with the poisoning of the environment. Worse than that, the national governments are an important part of the problem. They create anarchy on the very level where responsible interrelationships are most needed. The management of the planet, therefore, whether we are talking of the need to prevent war or the need to prevent ultimate damage to the conditions of life, requires a world government.' *Saturday Review,* Vol 53, no.10 (March 7, 1970), reprinted in Campbell and Wade, 1972, p.306.
19. For example, William T. Blackstone, 'Ethics and Ecology' in Blackstone, ed., 1974.
20. Fred W. Reed, 'Human Ecology, Desertification Nationalism, and Population Growth in the Sahara' in Barrett, 1982, p.229.
21. Brown and Wolf, 1985, p.25.
22. Brown and Wolf, 1985, p.20.
23. Fred W. Reed in Barrett, 1985, p.231.
24. Reed in Barrett, 1985, pp.232; also Brown and Wolf,1985, pp.19 ff.

4 SCIENCE, TECHNOLOGY AND THE NATURAL ENVIRONMENT

Thomas R. Odhiambo
International Centre of Insect Physiology and Ecology (ICIPE)
Nairobi, Kenya

When one of the key foci of the civilization of Mesopotamia, Uruk city state, grew most of its food within 20 km of the city wall, they could not conceive that latter-day social and institutional innovations could completely transform the distribution patterns of the then new technological innovation of irrigated farming. Two millennia later, Rome obtained most of its 200,000 tons of grain annually from its overseas colonies for its one million city dwellers by shipping it from Africa, Sardinia and Sicily.[1]

What this transformation exemplifies is the manner in which human beings respond to the challenges of significant changes in the environment, including climate. Thus, the rapidly growing population of Uruk city state and the metropolitan city, of Rome, two millennia apart, put into operation three sets of technological advances which responded dramatically to their specific global needs; hardware innovations (such as an irrigation system and new varieties of high-yielding wheat); software innovations (such as irrigation schedules and forecasts of wind performance in respect of shipping schedules); and behavioural, social and institutional innovations (such as the development of colonies and spheres of influence). Two millennia of post-Roman geopolitical reality have not modified this human response to the challenges of the environment: we still make strenuous efforts to climate-proof society, trying to make humans less subject to natural phenomena.

It is this continuing attempt to isolate human society from the natural environment, including the deleterious effects of human modification of this natural environment, that has become the global agenda in respect to the interface between technology, environment, and society. Consequently, the scientific community has a responsibility to human society, not only in utilizing its special genius for scientific discovery and technological innovation to the fullest, but also in explaining to the public the potential impact of scientific advances on advances on the environment and society. This emerging civic duty has been neglected and atrophied, in a sense because of the way that scientists are trained, as Donald Langenberg so succinctly puts it:

> In a sense, the behavioral adaptations that have made us (the scientists and engineers) so successful in untangling the rich tapestry of nature and reaping the benefits of the knowledge thereby gained have also rendered us ill-adapted to the process of transforming societal perceptions and values into societal reality.In science, fact yields perceptions, not the other way round.[2]

It is this societal reality that the scientific community must help in shaping.

Many scientific notions have recently become a matter of geopolitical and geoeconomic agenda: a sample includes the notions of agricultural sustainability, global warming, technology transfer, and industrial competitive edge. These notions have now become public slogans, while the scientists behave as if they have opted out of this public debate just when they are most needed to illumine the public understanding on these issues. In order to gauge the depth of this neglect of the civic duty by the scientific community, Langenberg has characterized such slogans as a societal perception that has been transformed into a societal reality by the political process. We should then recognize four aspects of this reality:

- first, the slogan does indeed label a complex and controversial public issue;
- second, the issue does possess an underlying body of scientific knowledge that should become a crucial feature of public debate on the issue;
- third, the public debate on the issue is more often than not shaped and controlled by opinion-makers who are not scientists and who do not have the relevant knowledge base; and
- fourth, if scientists who have the relevant knowledge on the issue are ever brought into the public debate, they are usually cast in 'the roles of costume consultant, prompter, stage-hand, or spear-carrier, rather than director or lead soprano'.[3]

There is no question then that the self-imposed isolation of the scientific community from the mainstream of public debate on science-related environmental and technological issues is a profound neglect of a civic duty they must exercise for the benefit of developing a balanced societal reality.

I have elsewhere stated this perception of civic responsibility of the scientist and academic in a different way, since by-and-large in Africa it is the universities that contain the largest number of scientists and engineers.

The 21st century African university must transform itself into a relevant knowledge institution attuned to the readjusted times and willed future of Africa. Thus, while it should be a universalized instrument for the incremental growth of human knowledge and the understanding of nature, it must contemporaneously address the application of this knowledge and understanding to human welfare. Thus, the African university should become both a global manifestation of the internationality of knowledge, and at the same time a national instrument for human and economic growth.[4]

The single most important societal reality facing Africa today is how to achieve sustainable development before continent-wide developmental crisis becomes endemic — and before the continent is consigned in its entirety to the 'Fourth World'.

Sustainable development in Africa — A new paradigm
For Africa, sustainable development implies four critical themes in its development agenda:

- first, food security, assured through the sustainable use of its physical resources and environment;
- second, basic economic security, which guarantees the fullest employment of each individual's talents and skills, through both the formal sector and the household mobilization system;
- third, national institutional security, resulting from the establishment and sustainable operation of national systems responsible for the mobilization of geopolitical support for its priority programmes for long-term national development, including a dynamic sense of national peace, security, and cohesion;
- fourth, the development of a national vibrant knowledge industry, consisting of the national universities, the scientific research and technological development (R&D) system, the agro-business and industrial domains, the publishing industry, and entrepreneurial institutions, all designed to underpin the inputs into and extend the outputs from the other three components of sustainable development.

The greatest task facing Africa's determination to achieve food security is how to transform its erstwhile self-sufficient traditional farming systems, which guaranteed a generous and diverse sustenance to her small population within an ecological agricultural technology that closely simulated the natural and diverse tropical environment, into an intensive agricultural system, more deliberately man-made, to meet the needs of a greatly expanding human population. The FAO/UNESCO *Soil Map of the World* highlights the fact that only 18.6 per cent of the soils of Africa do not exhibit inherent fertility limitation. The rest are problem soils or encompass the roughly two-thirds of the continent's landmass which is arid or semi-arid drylands. Some places are degraded, soil-eroded, or deforested wastelands; and the form of agriculture practised is overwhelmingly rain-fed. Consequently, 'the green revolution' technologies which provided the foundation on which Asia began to re-build its food security some three decades ago, are neither appropriate to the African condition nor sufficiently adequate.

Africa must go beyond the green revolution's technological approach. The long-term intensive agriculture needed by Africa demands a long-term commitment to the search for scientific knowledge, including the rationalization of traditional knowledge, that would lead to the re-designing of Africa's tropical agriculture to provide first to the needs of its peoples, and only second to the requirements of extra-African trade. Such modernized tropical African agricultural technologies must maintain soil fertility and improve soil structure for plant growth and water management; they must be parsimonious with the limited moisture found in the environment. They must also strive for an integrated farming system which interfaces productively with annual crops, tree crops, fuelwood, social forests, domesticated livestock (including insects such as honeybees and pollinating wasps), and fisheries; and they ought to strive for high-yielding crop varieties while maintaining their basic productive stability in the face of the potential environmental constraints of drought, pests, and diseases.[5]

This is a tremendously difficult goal to achieve; but nobody will want to take up this entire R&D agenda, unless the Africans themselves are committed to it, and place it as part of their vision to attain in the next three to four decades. Part of this agenda could well be what the Nobel laureate, Norman Borlaug, dreamt about 'the ideal cereal for Africa':

> One can dream of the day ... when advances in science will have produced cereal varieties which are resistant to all major diseases and pests, tolerant to abiotic stresses such as drought, higher in protein and with balanced amino acid composition, and which can fix

their own nitrogen from the air, greatly reducing the need for applying chemical fertilizers. Although I believe that many such breakthroughs eventually will come, it is highly unlikely that they will be achieved this century or even in the next 30-40 years.[6]

There are reasons to believe that we should be rather optimistic about developing Borlaug's ideal cereal for Africa. Take the example of advances towards growing cereals without the intervention of chemical insecticides at all. For instance, the International Centre of Insect Physiology and Ecology (ICIPE), during its collaborative R&D with resource-poor farming households in Kendu Bay and Oyugis in western Kenya over the last five years, has shown that using insect resistant varieties which have also other desirable agronomic characteristics, such as high-yield and an acceptable taste, and employing the intercropping of cereals with other crops to suppress the general level of pest populations (as previous ICIPE mission-oriented research had abundantly shown possible under certain species mixtures and cropping patterns) the farming households can consistently garner 40 per cent more food grains. And that result was achieved without the application of any pesticides. Indeed, the use of chemical insecticides is now receiving serious attention simply as a fire-brigade, band-aid tactic during an emergency, and therefore inadequate as a long-term measure for the management of insect pest populations. The chemical insecticide industry is a steady-income industry, worth $6.2 billion a year in the United States alone,[7] having a strong lobby throughout the world, and is unlikely to be diverted to other industrial pursuits — except for excellent commercial reasons.

Those reasons have to do with the world-wide concern about the long-term environmental impact of chemical insecticides, and the prevalent misuse and abuse of their application. Consequently, the age-old use of predators and parasites, and the new-found use of insect's own parasitic diseases to control insect pests biologically, has come into wider, more deliberate employment. Take the example of the toxin produced by the soil-living bacterium, *Bacillus thuringiensis* (B.t.) which kills the insect larva when the latter swallows the B.t. spores produced by the bacterium in the course of its normal life-cycle. This toxin and its impact on insects has been known since the early 1950's, as a highly selective natural bioinsecticide, each variant only active against a narrow range of insects, and having a short existence in the field because it is easily biodegradable. Thus, it possesses desirable environmental characteristics, but was not commercialized for a long time because of its narrow market niche. The industrial and business situation for B.t. has dramatically changed in the last five years. The B.t. can now be easily mass-produced by industrial fermentation techniques which compete favorably with the cost of production of chemical insecticides.

Molecular techniques are being utilized to expand the range of B.t.s through a deeper knowledge of the two distinct functional domains of the toxin molecule: particular interest is focused on the binding domain that determines which insect species succumb to the toxin, as the amino-acid sequence of this domain varies significantly from one species- specific B.t. strain to another, different in its functional impact. The coupling of several different binding domains to the rest of the toxin molecule which contains the larvicidal activity extends the range of insect species that succumb to this newly engineered B.t. toxin. A different, and third approach was the recently designed technique of introducing the genes for the B.t. toxin itself directly into the plant genome. Such an implantation has already succeeded in the case of cotton, potato, and tomato; and field experiments are now going on for maize.

These innovative approaches to insect pest management, going well beyond the conventional chemical insecticide age, are taking root in the present industrial world only slowly and hesitantly. For example, in the United States, only 8 per cent of the cropland is currently using these new approaches to non-insecticidal interventions.[8] This slow adoption is unfortunate in the face of the well-documented impairment of the environment through insecticidal accumulation, and the high level of human poisoning and fatalities resulting from their use. Thus, it is estimated that about 4 per cent of world-wide human deaths are due to pesticidal poisoning, 72 per cent of these occurring in the developing world.[9]

With this view of the problem of sustainable tropical agriculture I want to emphasize the new imperative for Africa's agricultural production, to create long-term security in food and nutrition. A specifically relevant, Africa-oriented knowledge industry is also necessary to direct and support Africa's modern science-led agriculture, agro-business and industry.

Africa's knowledge industry

Let us go to the beginning of the Industrial Revolution in England, which came at a time when the English population was rising rapidly, just as it was in France and Germany from about 1750 A.D. The German response to this crisis was to legislate against early marriage by the poor, and to cope with the problem of excessive numbers by instituting a massive programme of emigration. The

French solution was to control fertility within the marriage at later parities. The English solution was quite different, and in many ways a radically revolutionary idea. The idea ignored the strictly demographic balance, and instead chose the path of adjusting resources to the population. The revolutionary component of the idea was to let technology intervene to make the upcoming Industrial Revolution supply the answer towards bringing about a demographic adjustment. What was significant for our purpose was that technological change continuously changed the frontiers of what was humanly possible in the age-old quest to master the material world. The technology-aided change built up its own momentum. For instance, 'the quantum leap afforded by the substitution of inanimate, inorganic energy for natural energy (i.e. muscle energy) was equivalent to creating an industrial reserve army of slaves.'[10]

The revolutionary idea of technology-supported social and economic development is one of generic importance. But its application must arise from perceived national needs, and correspond closely to national institutions, including the socio-cultural traditions of the people. Rosenberg and Birdzell have given us two pertinent examples of the way in which Japan and the United States responded in different ways to the Industrial Revolution model.[11] The United States did borrow the notion of Industrial Revolution from England, but it made the American technologies very much resource-intensive and very much less labour-intensive. Japan, in borrowing the English notion, responded in a very different way from both the United States and England. Japan, in its first modernization beginning in the late 1860's, emphasized intensive use of labour, and optimised the use of Japan's scarcest resource — land. In the textile industry, Japan went for labour intensive, capital-poor machinery, thus expending more labour skills on its maintenance and repair in order to prolong its life. The English model 'wreaked a veritable holocaust on an overstretched peasantry desperately clinging to proto-industry as a supplement to their sub-divided holdings,' because the then modern manufacturing industry put the peasantry out of their artisan village pursuits, as Levine graphically narrates:

...(The) first phase of the Industrial Revolution (in England) destroyed its income-supplements derived from proto-industry. Simple, repetitive tasks by which women and children had contributed significantly to the domestic economy of the peasant household inexorably declined in the face of competition from, first, specialized producers and, next, machinofacture.[12]

The essential point of this short comparative review of contrasting approaches to technology-supported national development is to demonstrate that there is no one sure-fire strategy, and that each successful model has followed its own singular national ethos. It is a lesson that Africa must intimately and deliberately learn, as the modernization of Africa has clearly been derailed by listening too closely to other voices rather than trusting to our own inner voice.

The inner voice of Africa tells is that it can leapfrog certain stages in the technology-dominated modernization effort; for example, it can well get onto the frontiers of molecular sciences and biotechnology within half a generation, if the continent mobilizes fully its talents both scientific and technological, now. The inner voice of Africa tells us that we can create a dialogue among the African scientific community, synergistically interphasing with the geopolitical and geoeconomic domains, if we can create four interlocking knowledge systems within Africa on our initiative as we are now.

- First, we need to create a geopolitical environment that allows trans-boundary travel and trans-national recruitment of bona fide African scientists and scholars who are professionally committed to their tasks. In difficult cases, it may require the intervention of a scientific 'Red Cross' to negotiate protocols with national authorities, and thereby undertake the operation of 'safe havens' for displaced scholars and scientists and those needing short-term rescue, or the assignments of expatriate African specialists who need to return to Africa for short or long periods to contribute their knowledge or skills to the rebuilding of the continent.
- Second, we need to create and nurture a vigorous and enriched scholarly and scientific press, to serve as a forum for intellectual discourse and to foster intra-continental dialogue. There is no danger of Africa becoming isolationist: it is too porous for that event to occur. The crisis we are experiencing is that of not having an intimate understanding of our African neighbourhood. The Academy Science Publishers, a joint enterprise between the African Academy of Sciences, based in Nairobi, is an emerging scholarly publishing house for science worth watching in future.
- Third, we need to rehabilitate and redesign the entire university system in Africa, which is a patch-work of foreign traditions of uncertain relevance for the modern competitive world.

- Fourth, we need to re-establish a national sense of purpose in our R&D community — not as a social service, not as a sink for our best scientific and technological brains, but as an engine for science-led national development.

Africa needs self-confidence and a clear perception of its destiny to embrace this four-part interlocking knowledge universe to race up to the forefront of modern humanity. Africa was never created to be a Third World. Indeed, until the last half a millennium, we were very much in the lead. The Greek civilization, so much the foundation of the present dominance of north-western Europe, was partly the result of the symbiosis of the tribal infiltrators into the Aegean arena from the north by Indo-European speakers, which took place during the 4th and 3rd millennia B.C.; the Semites of the Levant, particularly the Phoenicians; and the Africans from Egypt and Nubia. The linguistic, mythological and archaeological evidence attests to this reality, which was only contested from the early 19th century A.D. by European purists, who did not want their civilization to have anything to do with other, earlier civilizations. Martin Bernal, in his pioneering book, *Black Athena*, strongly states this fact:

> For 18th- and 19th- century romantics and racists it was simply intolerable for Greece, which was seen not merely as the epitome of Europe but also as its pure childhood, to have been the result of the mixture of native Europeans and colonizing Africans and Semites.[13]

The impact of Bernal's finding is not so much that it corrects a distorted version of human civilization, but that it should give Africa the self-confidence to invent its positive development future, knowing that they have done it before, and that they have the determination and vision to be there once again. The words of Einstein are germane and to the point in this regard.

> Here knowledge of truth alone does not suffice; on the contrary this knowledge must be renewed by ceaseless effort, if it is not to be lost. It resembles a statue of marble which stands in the desert and is continuously threatened with burial by the shifting sand. The hands of service must ever be at work, in order that the marble continues lastingly to shine in the sun.[14]

Notes
1. Ausubel, 1991.
2. Langenberg, 1991, p. 361.
3. Langenberg, 1991, p. 362.

4. Odhiambo, 1991, p.9.
5. Norse, 1991.
6. Borlaug, 1989, p. 18.
7. Moffat, 1991.
8. Agency for International Development, 1990a. *Reports to the United States Congress*, I. Integrated Pest Management: A.I.D. Policy and Implementation, 7 pp. Washington, D.C.: U.S. Congress.
9. Agency for International Development, 1990b.
10. Levine, in press.
11. Rosenberg and Birdzell, 1990.
12. Levine, 1991.
13. Bernal, 1987, p.13.
14. French, 1979.

5 THREATS TO HUMAN SURVIVAL AND THE RESPONSIBILITY OF SCHOLARS

Mihailo Markovic
Serbian Academy of Sciences and Arts
Belgrade, Yugoslavia

The nature of various threats to human survival is now well known. The most serious among them in the long run is the ecological one. There is hardly any doubt that our natural environment is heading towards irreversible destruction. Badly polluted water, air and earth, deforestation, erosion of the soil, increasing radioactivity, acid rain, the disintegration of the ozone belt, the green house effect, chemical contamination of most foodstuffs, depletion of some energy and other resources are the generally recognized symptoms of an approaching environmental catastrophe. The situation is especially critical in the poor countries of the Third World which have pursued an environmentally hostile paradigm of material growth borrowed from developed countries and which, finding themselves under an enormous burden of debt to the Western World, are lacking necessary funds for any systematic policy of environmental conservation.[1] Whatever improvements have been achieved in most parts of the world, humanity finds itself in the same boat when it comes to the ecological threat. In order to enable them to pursue a policy of ecological stabilization perhaps for survival, therefore, a higher degree of maturity and solidarity of all humans is clearly necessary.

Ecological degradation is not the only threat to human survival. Production of huge piles of nuclear weapons is another, even more dramatic and unfair. In some parts of the world, the rise of nationalism and fundamentalism has enormous destructive potential. The main reason to focus on the ecological threat is not only because of its global nature, but also because the world is not yet ready to seriously cope with it and to pay the high price for the way out. Consequently, we do not yet have an accepted solution.

Can we reasonably expect that present day rapid development will create rational solutions? What will be the science of tomorrow if we extrapolate its prevalent present trends? The speed and accuracy of solving scientific problems will continue to grow.

Present-day microprocessors reveal capacities that go well beyond simple computing. It makes sense here to speak about man-made artificial intelligence. Scientists already use electronic equipment which is supplied with sensors that capture and store huge amounts of new information. The speed of processing this data surpasses the human brain. They tune instead of rigidly following the rules of one programme. These machines are now supplied with multiple programmes and are able to switch from one to the other with great speed and ease which gives them considerable flexibility (typical in human intelligence). The range of these programmes is still inferior to that of the human brain, but their efficiency is quite superior, both in the sense of speed and of an error-free operation. The obvious consequence for the future development of science is liberation of scientists from purely technical work, which follows some clearly definable (no matter how complex) objective rules. Future scholars will be relieved of the task of memorizing as great an amount of information as possible. Only data directly related to ideas will be stored in scientists' minds; the rest will be fed into computer memories, occupying increasingly smaller space. An entire set of books will need only one micro-chip. In this way intellectual energies will be liberated for creative tasks, producing new ideas, building new theories and conceptual paradigms, integrating knowledge, interpreting the meaning of scientific discoveries, evaluating both existing theories and the nature of reality itself.

However, there is an essential limitation in the very concept of modern science which blocks its critical function with respect to social reality, and which is responsible for enormous misuses of both scientific methodology and acquired scientific knowledge in recent times. The increasing use of science for military purposes has produced, for the first time in history, the possibility of a collective suicide of humankind. The use of science and technology for solving unlimited riddles has really contributed to environmental degradation. The onslaught on individual privacy and autonomy by the mass media and state intelligence agencies is also one of the consequences of scientific and technological progress.

All these misuses and abuses are possible because of a fatal limitation of modern, positive science. It is enormously powerful in acquiring pure knowledge of facts and structures; at the same time it is quite powerless against abuse since it lacks any implicit strategy about the use of knowledge for *the good of people*, and it is devoid of any built-in defenses against its abuse for *evil purposes*. Positive knowledge is eventually the instrument of power as was best expressed in the well known dictum of the father of modern positivism, Auguste Compte *savoir pour prevoir, prevoir pour...* (To know in order to predict, to predict in order to gain power). That scientific truth should predominantly serve power in the fundamental prejudice of the entire modern culture.

To be sure there is also a progressive emancipatory aspect in the modern scientific method as elaborated by Bacon, Galileo, Newton and Descartes. It effectively separates pursuit of factual truth from religious faith and from any sort of conservatism and mysticism. Even to this day it successfully resists the invasion of an *explicit* ideological spirit in sciences. However, it is helpless against implicit contamination of ideology. Once it is neutral and value-free, knowledge turns into a means of those social groups that enjoy the monopoly of economic, political and cultural power.

This is, of course, a modern phenomenon. In ancient culture *theoria* embraced both knowledge of reality and knowledge of virtue. Knowing that (objects were so and so) was not nearly so linked with *knowing how* (to master and produce these objects) as in modern civilization, but it was closely connected with *knowing what* (a virtuous person should do in a given situation). Truth was not merely adequacy to existing empirical reality, but also adequacy to an *ideal* possible reality.

Modernity confused religion and morality and eliminated both from science. Morality was interpreted as a sphere of subjectivity, relativity, of pure emotionality and was flatly dismissed. As a consequence, the history of philosophy from Hume to Moore, Ayer and Stevenson is a serious attempt to justify this dismissal as a consequence. Science was deprived of any internal intellectual resource that would allow it to resist its subordination to naked power. That is why so much contemporary scientific research is instrumental to military purposes, to destructive material growth, to ideological rationalization.

Electronic machines, even future 'ultra-intelligent' ones cannot reverse this trend; rather, they make it more effective. Their main differences from human beings is not that they cannot 'think' and even 'operate creatively' but that they cannot have feelings, any sense of responsibility, any conscience. There are no conceivable programmes that regulate such subjective processes and the reason is that these are not governed by objective rules but by unpredictable interactions between collective customs transferred by culture and unique personal moral experiences in a given situation. Even if emotional reactions and moral activities of humans are programmed, there is no way of finding out what these programmes are, and even if we were able to learn about these programmes, to state them explicitly and feed them into a computer, we would discover (through some kind of tuning test) that there is yet an essential difference between humans and machines. The former can unpredictably deviate from the programme. The machine can do it only if a higher level programme prescribes that under specified conditions exceptions should be made from a lower level programme. Humans are able to deviate from some acquired and internalised moral rules because of a *new immediate moral experience*, because of moral repulsion felt about the possible consequences of a programmed course of action. Feelings of disgust, of shame, of revolt, of outrage can lead humans to reverse an established trend of behaviour. Such a reversal is clearly possible in future scientific development, but it is beyond the potential of the computer. It presupposes, firstly, a new conception of science that develops its own objective ethical standards and, secondly, a new sense of moral responsibility of scholars in using their intellectual products.

As to a new conception of science that incorporates some basic and universal human values, certain values have always been present in any scientific inquiry. In a trivial sense this is true even in the case of the basic elements of the scientific method. Demands of clarity, precision, fertility, explanatory power, accuracy, applicability are in fact cognitive values. Priority assigned to some of them over the others depends on the philosophical orientation of the particular author. In a non-trivial sense, various social values are implicit in existing scholarship since individual scientists fail to get rid of various social interests, no matter how much they declare their own neutrality and impartiality. There are a number of literary and philosophical works written during the last century and a half, which tend to indicate the connection between material and spiritual values of intellectuals. The novel by the German writer Jeremias Gotthelt (1884), the study of American historian Gordon Craig about nineteenth century liberal, social bourgeois (1888), works of the anthropologist Friedrich Hansfer (1963) and of the philosopher Rudolf-Wolfgang Muttes (1977) all have the same title: *Money and Spirit*. They deal with the symbiosis between wealth and spiritual culture. The most recent contribution to this subject is by the French sociologist Pierre Bourdien. In *Homo Academicus* (1988), Bourdien has shown that the academic world, far from being purely spiritual and free from profane interests, follows similar rules and laws as an economic market — with cultural capital, production of intellectual commodities, market competition and adaptation to the judgements of market analysts, power relations and hierarchies.

If Bourdien is correct, one of the consequences is the demystification of the alleged neutrality of scientific research. It is true that the scientific method is constituted of the rules that tend to eliminate emotional impulses, cultural prejudices, ideological biases and which secure the maximum possible objectivity of the results. However, even if we disregard deliberate or unconscious violations of these rules (which can be detected and which disqualify a scholar and his research), the rules of the scientific method do not regulate all phases of research. They are very precise and articulated in the area of experimentation, statistical analysis, or logical inference. On the other hand, the selection of problems to be investigated, the choice of conceptual frames of reference which determine the area of relevant evidence, the laying down of hypotheses and building theories and systems are not governed by methodological principles. In these phases of research all kinds of worldly interests and unholy motives are smuggled in. The world of scientific research is being financed by military powers, by political establishments, by churches and by big businessmen. Of course, scholars are not simply being told what to do — although this happens too. The *Manhattan Project, Stars Wars* and similar military high-tech projects are good examples. What occurs in history and in the social sciences is rationalization, i.e. more or less unconsciously the direction of research trends towards results that would confirm and legitimize the interests of the existing powers.

It seems that the same argumentation that destroys the neutrality thesis of science also frustrates any hope that scholarship can be critical in a genuinely ethical sense. Namely, if the ordinary world of scientific endeavours is so contaminated by extra-scientific interests, how can a critique of existing social practices ever be really independent, honest and trustworthy? There is, indeed, a lot of criticism in the humanities of the view that one historical tradition, national interest or ideological position is innately superior to another.

Therefore, it is not sufficient to merely encourage scholars to be morally responsible and critical toward ethically unacceptable social practices. It is not enough to say: 'Don't pretend anymore that you are in the business of producing pure neutral knowledge. Try to bring to consciousness what you are really doing. For all brands of values and interests that unconsciously lead you, try to substitute some guiding principles and norms that can be universalised, that you honestly accept as ethical principles and norms.'

In addition to this subjective approach, it is essential to establish some objective conditions that have to be met in order to produce a truly ethically grounded social critique and a truly autonomous choice among future alternatives.

First, self-reflection of the scholar about his position in the social world and about the role he actually plays in the institution to which he belongs is needed. There is a potential for critical self-reflection in every individual. The human being has the unique capacity to be conscious of consciousness, to think about one's own thinking, evaluate one's own values and doubt one's own doubts. Another specific mental capacity of human beings is the power of negative thinking. There is an inner polarization in our minds: on the one hand is the tendency to see things and ourselves in the way that fits our preconceptions, and personal interests; on the other hand is a drive to doubt others and ourselves, and to re-examine our beliefs about the world and ourselves. The will to believe tends to temporarily produce peace within ourselves. Our sense of honour, our moral conscience, our philosophical scepticism make us restless, possibly rebellious, against our way of life and our role in society.

Second, the very possibility of ethically grounded research presumes an objective, rather independent social position of its author. Such an independent position is difficult to achieve. It might, but need not, go together with considerable material wealth. No need for employment means, of course, no pressure to conform. On the other hand, excessive wealth tends to produce a specific sense of group identity and to restrict the spiritual horizon of the owner. The most favourable case is when one is competent enough not to depend on any particular job, and has achieved a proper balance between one's material needs and income. Epictetus was, of course, right in saying that absolute freedom and independence can be achieved when one disregards 'all that is not one's own' career, whether it be a comfortable life or one's family. The problem with such an extreme view is that life devoid of most human content is too high a price for any degree of freedom. Today we know that the freedom of any person is limited by the freedom of another person, and we no longer crave freedom of mind in that absolute sense in which even a slave in chains could have been totally free from his master. The important point in Epictetus, however, is that unless we limit our material aspirations and social ambitions, we can rarely achieve enough independence to be critical of social pressures and make truly autonomous choices against them.

The third condition is the appropriation of humanist culture that affirms universal human concerns. The history of philosophy shows a high degree of consensus among recognized great thinkers concerning basic human values such as freedom, justice, truth, self-realization and care for others. This consensus does not prove anything in itself but indicates the universal character of certain norms of human life. This should not surprise us. In spite of enormous diversity among individuals of like conditions, customs and traditions, there are some invariants of the world in which we live and certain invariant features of human nature. Other conditions being equal, certain things are indeed preferable to others. For example freedom to slavery, creativity to destructiveness, reasonable care for others to sheer egoism and peace to war. After centuries of parochialism and ethnocentricism, humanity has recently reached a consensus that certain political and socio-economic conditions are necessary for survival and development of each human individual. These are labelled *human rights*: they constitute universally recognized standards in social relations all over the world.

To bring an end to these considerations about a new, critically oriented, ethically grounded conception of science and about moral responsibility of scholars in response to existing ecological and other threats to human survival, it is necessary to make an obvious distinction between natural and social scholars. A physicist or an astronomer cannot be critical of the subject-matter of research in the sense in which a social scholar can. But the researcher is also responsible for any systematic use of the results of research that would violate the rights of life, health, well being and free development of human individuals. Surely, one's responsibilities go as far as one's knowledge of possible consequences of one's actions. A scholar or researcher is not responsible for consequences impossible to foresee. And yet there is a responsibility for the consequences which can be foreseen. Accidental abuses of knowledge can be disregarded. The point is that individual scholars and entire scientific communities cannot escape responsibility for knowingly, deliberately engaging in research that leads to destructive social practices.

Surely, responsibility is not yet guilt. There are specific situations in which lesser evils must be chosen. The well known example is the moral dilemma of Einstein and Fermi before the Manhattan Project started. The greater evil was the nuclear bomb in the hands of Hitler. However in such cases a moral problem arises which must be approached seriously and solved. Out of a sense of responsibility Einstein and other physicists together with Bertrand Russell started the movement against the use of nuclear weapons.

Social scholars who try to describe, analyze, explain and interpret social reality have a moral duty to tell the truth about violations of all human rights, both political and socio-economic, which today regulate the life of the world community. Apologists who legitimize unfree and unjust societies as well as 'neutral' scholars who pretend not to see violations of human rights are nothing but disguised and cynical accomplices. Sceptics who challenge the objective character of any ethical principles have today a difficult task of casting doubt upon generally accepted ideas of human rights as reliable, objective grounds for the critical evaluation of social realities. An ethically grounded science can play a more important role in the future than ever before under one condition: that it accepts its moral responsibility for the predictable consequences of its inquiry.

Notes

1. The Kenya Freedom from Hunger Council presented a paper at a meeting of African environmentalists held in the first half of July, 1991 in which Western countries were blamed for the environmental degradation of the Third World and the demand to cancel the foreign debt owed to these countries was expressed (*Daily Nation,* Nairobi, 14 July 1991, p.6).

6 THE ROLE OF THE PHILOSOPHY OF NATURE TODAY: NATURE, CUSTOM AND REALITY

J.D.G. Evans
University of Belfast, Ireland

The philosophy of nature currently encompasses work in three rather unconnected area. First, many philosophers are interested in how and whether knowledge of natural processes can contribute to the resolution of traditional philosophical problems. This kind of interest is represented by the strategies of naturalistic epistemology and theory of meaning. The leading thought here is that ideas which are effective in natural science, can also be applied to the explanation of processes which have traditionally interested philosophers, such as learning or communicating.

Secondly, many philosophers are concerned about the moral and political issues which arise from the increasing ability of humankind to manipulate and exploit the natural environment. These issues normally form part of moral philosophy — indeed, of that burgeoning part which is known as applied ethics. Thirdly, there are philosophical questions that arise from the study of natural as opposed to artificial substances. Philosophers are interested in comparisons and contrasts; the area of philosophical enquiry which particularly addresses this interest is the philosophy of biology.

Is there a unifying theme in these three areas of philosophical enquiry? There had better be, if philosophy of nature is indeed to be regarded as a legitimate notion. But few philosophers today would in fact see much significant conceptual connection between the range of concerns which I have just outlined. In that case they should hark back to Aristotle, who introduced all three of these themes to the philosophical community, and who provided a better rationale of their connectedness than has been achieved by anyone since.

Nature and contrivance

Aristotle frequently speaks of nature as craftsman; and he reinforces the parallel between nature and contrivance by saying that nature gives evidence of even more skill than does the conscious artist. But he also says something that has caused many readers to doubt the seriousness of his comparison. This is that when we are in the business of masking something, our thought starts from what is going to be, whereas when we are studying the natural world, we start from what is already the case. Thus does Aristotle draw a sharp distinction between the processes which lead to understanding and those which lead to action. Many modern philosophers draw such a distinction; and as an almost inevitable consequence, they lack a unitary approach to the three areas of the philosophy of nature. But I shall argue that Aristotle is not to be grouped with these thinkers; on the contrary, we can learn much from him about how to integrate philosophical concerns which otherwise would seem to lack adequate motivation.

Nature, like money, is a cultural artefact. But it is an artefact with an independent power, and we ignore this power at our peril. Nature is something which we have fashioned — and continue to fashion — according to our most basic ideas. However, when these ideas are inadequate or confused, we are liable to be given the most violent external jolt. There is, then, the appearance of an antinomy. Is nature something which essentially we create — something which ultimately is malleable to our wills? Or is this true, at best, of the *concept* of nature, in which case the real thing can go on its human-independent way?

When we formulate the issue in this way, we bring together the twin poles of a contrast which Aristotle found in the intellectual background to his philosophy of nature — the poles of nature and convention. On the one hand, there is a contrast between the universal and invariant facts of nature and the different cultural forms which can be imposed on this basis in various human environments. On the other hand, it seems to be essential to at least some features of the natural world that they should be considered in terms of their reception within a human culture, for example, such things as wealth, health, knowledge and meaning.

Philosophers from Hobbes through Hume and Kant to Ayer and Bernard Williams have been inclined to posit a fundamental contrast between theoretical and practical philosophy: our relation to nature as an object of study requires a posture of inertness while as technologists we pursue a policy of active intervention in nature. Differences in the objects of study match the differences in the epistemic and volitional projects of those who study them. So the things which we try to affect must be distinct in character from what we left unchanged.

But Aristotle recognized that the division between nature and custom is to a considerable extent a false one. I shall try to build on this insight, to show how an adequate approach to our three initial philosophical areas depends on a correct analysis of the relation between custom and nature. We should aspire to a consistent philosophy of nature.

Naturalistic epistemology

First I shall consider naturalistic epistemology. This is the project of analyzing cognitive processes in terms of the principles which govern natural change. There is strong *prima facie* support for this strategy. The creatures which engage in cognitive processes, are themselves part of nature; and it is obvious that natural processes play a central role in the ways in which they obtain information — for example, the use of sensation, memory and association — and also the ways in which they transmit information through language and other signs. Moreover it is plausible to suppose that the skills which we have acquired in these psychological areas, have themselves been developed through natural processes; and here the favourite mechanism is, of course, Darwinian selection for survival.

What is it for a person's mental representation of P to constitute — *knowledge* rather than belief, or deluded fantasy — that P? What is it for a sentence S to *mean* S — rather than something closely related, such as S^*, which it would take a further semantic move to correlate with S itself? These problems are deeply sceptical in character, and essentially philosophical. And they suggest a solution along the following lines: the representation succeeds because a natural process connects the cause of the representation in the external world with the mental event which is the representation.

So according to this proposal the analysis of these representational processes is to be treated as depending on the same causal laws as operate in other aspects of the natural world. Therefore, philosophy of nature encompasses these psychological and epistemological phenomena. Our cognitive relations to the external world should be regarded as natural — just as natural as are the relations involved in breathing and respiration, or eating and nutrition.

It is straightforward to interpret breathing and eating as natural processes; they involve causal relations between items in the external world and the biological subjects which experience and undergo modifications through these processes. Differences among the external objects are systematically reflected in differences among the ways in which the biological subjects are modified. Now this sounds similar to what happens in the epistemological case. Differences in input from external reality are correlated with variation in the psychological state which is a response to such input. But a disanalogy appears when we consider the phenomenon of *error* or *mistake*. Error is a misrepresentation, but it is also a representation. It mistakenly reports a certain state of affairs A; but it actually succeeds in conveying a related state of affairs A*. By contrast, when digestion or breathing fails, as in poisoning or suffocation, we do not say that the person breathes or digests something; only that that thing is the wrong thing. In such cases there is nothing analogous to the misrepresentation.

We discovered an original motivation for naturalistic epistemology in the desire to combat scepticism. According to this line of thought, systematic error in our mental processes is excluded if we can causally tie psychological states to external reality. But it now appears that this approach is in danger of excluding the possibility of any error at all, not just the massive error which is the sceptic's concern. The answer will lie in an adjustment to the concept of nature — or better to the account of our relation to nature. The external cause of our mental states should be related not only to the correct representation but also to *misrepresentations*. The relation has to accommodate the variations imported by human subjectivity. So nature in this context is not as purely external as might first have been supposed.

In summary, there is good ground for the idea that a naturalistic analysis should be sought even for such entrenched philosophical problems as the relation between the knower and the world. The analogy between nutrition and cognition supports this strategy to a certain extent; but it also indicates how the naturalistic approach can fail to handle the phenomenon of error, unless it operates with a suitably refined concept of nature.

Philosophy and the natural environment

I turn now to what may seem a rather different topic, namely, the part which philosophical analysis can and should play where practical decisions concerning management of the natural environment are concerned. In recent decades philosophers have become interested in these problems for much the same reasons as have stimulated their work in other areas of applied ethics. The issues are so general that they transcend the narrow provinces of specialized experts; and the problems are so sufficiently open-ended that it takes a philosopher's skill at creative argument to explore the conflicting theses that can be advanced.

The questions belong with ethics: they concern whether and how people should act in various kinds of circumstances. Here we are engaged with decisions about whether we should seek to change and affect nature, rather than whether what affects us is itself natural, as in the earlier discussion. However, there is a notable difference between the answers given to these environmental problems and the answers which arise with other kinds of problems in applied ethics. The difference is that in the environmental case, unlike the others, there is a widespread tendency to conclude that once moral considerations are allowed to come into play, they provide an argument against activity which interferes with the natural course of events.

Thus there can easily arise in these discussions an opposition between two attitudes, which we may call the *technological* and the *naturalist*. The technological approach is interventionist; it sustains activity which will almost certainly alter the course of events which would otherwise occur if nature were left to itself. By contrast, the naturalist approach urges us to act only to the extent that it may be necessary to keep the course of nature moving — to intervene, as we might say, only when technological intervention compels us to do so. According to the latter conception, intervention in the natural process is something which should occur as a second-best course, as a regrettable supplement to the bad effects of the technological approach.

I shall mention some of the distinctive results of the two approaches, and the implications which this duality holds for the moral philosophy of nature. In the management of energy resources we may either seek to modify the natural processes of geology and climate, or we may try to exploit the processes without altering them. The former endeavour is realized in, for example, mining and nuclear processing, since their effect is to produce a state of affairs — a set of objects — which could never occur simply through natural processes. By contrast, the use of winds and waves to generate energy leaves the objects and events in the world unaltered.

Another example comes from the biological and botanic sphere. Natural processes have supplied many species of animals and plants. Recently, technology has made it possible to effect a significant change in this number, in two ways. First, we can eliminate species by so reducing the numbers of their members that they are unable to supply a next generation; this phenomenon is, of course, not new, but it is increasingly found through the effects of technology. Secondly, there is the radically new possibility of creating species through laboratory technology. Genetic engineering enables us to add, or replace, the existing species with others which we may judge to be more useful for various purposes. The aspiration for such manipulation is also not new; but only now does it begin to be possible to give these ambitions immediate effect.

Here then are two ways in which the contrast between a technological and a naturalistic approach can be developed in connection with environmental ethics. Now although the two approaches seem to be opposed as active and interventionist, on the one hand, and quietistic and abstentionist on the other hand, in fact it is a misconception to contrast the two styles in this way. This should become clear if we reflect on the examples. In neither case does the so-called interventionist strategy really require us to alter the natural course of events. That would be impossible, given that we have to respect the constraints of nature however overwhelming our technological ambitions may be. Programmes for developing nuclear energy or new strains of some biological organism can only have a chance of success if their exponents run with the grain of nature in their inevitable modest proposals for technical change. The chemical elements — and the much more complicated biochemical syntheses which are charted in scientific genetics — set constraints on anything that biotechnology can devise. In a word, the product has to be natural.

The abstentionist strategy suffers from a similar conceptual incoherence. It claims to advocate a policy of non-intervention in natural processes. But the wind and wave energy programmes, as well as the strategy of conserving existing biological species, are in fact thoroughly interactive with nature. We are misled if we think that in these strategies we leave nature as it was before. On the contrary, even devices and practices as apparently simple as a water-wheel or the use of herbal remedies constitute an interference with a natural order which would otherwise follow a different course. If we did not use — and perhaps also cultivate — the herbs as we do, they would have different effects on their environment and might be supplanted by other species.

There is, then, something ineradicably technological about all our practices concerning the use, abuse or failure to use the natural environment. It turns out that the thought that environmental ethics is distinctively quietistic, by comparison with other areas of applied ethics, is unsound. But what nurtures the erroneous thought is the correct insight that the best way to handle the natural environment is with a sensitivity which is informed by understanding. We are right to find fault with the interventionist approach, not because it enjoins us to try to manipulate nature, but because we sense that ill-informed and premature manipulation will not secure the best results.

Nature, custom and reality

The third area of current interest in philosophy of nature which I mentioned at the beginning, is in the philosophy of biology. Unfortunately I have no time on the present occasion to consider this topic, save to note the following. There is a significant tendency in contemporary philosophy of science to recapture an old Aristotelian insight about the primacy of biological substances among natural things and of biological methods among the modes of natural science. If those who think in this way are right, this is another significant strand in the development of philosophy of nature as a central element in the philosophical programme.

But I want now to move from survey to reasoned synthesis and conclusion. We have examined some areas of current philosophy in which the concept of nature plays an important role. Do all these ingredients in fact sustain a single coherent concept? Perhaps not. On the face of it there are tensions both within each of the parts of the concept and also between the different parts.

We found difficulties with naturalism both in epistemology and in ecological politics. In both cases the suggested diagnosis was that philosophers interpret nature as too independent of, and external to, human concerns. The problems occur alike whether the direction of causal relation is predominantly from the natural world to human sphere, as in epistemology, or the reverse, as in environmental ethics. So we must now try to clarify the relation between human social forms and the natural world.

The Role of the Philosophy of Nature Today

The ancient Greeks recognized something that is also stressed in contemporary debate: social forms are variable from culture to culture, and as such they appear to stand in contrast to the universal stability of natural phenomena. Given this contrast (about the details of which there is, of course, much room for debate), philosophers have mainly reacted in one of two ways. Either we can take the view that the variability of cultural values means that the real truth resides in the realm of nature. Or we can embrace human culture and argue that a culture-relative concept of value is the correct one.

Aristotle gave a third view — one which gives the lie to this polarization of positions. It is of the nature of value to be realized in the context of a culture, since human life cannot be lived apart from such a context. Therefore the naturally correct form of behaviour is one that reflects the local norms. But this requirement that we respect the here and now, does not entail a relativism according to which values are irreducibly distinct as between cultures. In particular it does not exclude the possibility that there should arise a single form of human culture; and indeed that possibility is definitely envisaged in the theory that ties value to something as universal as human nature. If such a possibility of a universal culture were to be realized, then there would only be one naturally correct form of behaviour for all humankind. In that possible situation the old contrast between nature and custom would be empty.

The basis of the suggested resolution is a reassessment of the relation between nature and the human sphere. I argue that it is a mistake to see nature and custom as constituting a sharply antithetical pair. Instead each is complementary to the other. Custom — the sphere of human contrivance — requires an external and independent natural order with which it can enter into causal relations. We have commented on several ways in which this relation operates — in particular, the causal input of the natural world in epistemology, and the effect on the natural world of environmental decision-making.

Let us return to the dialectic which we saw arise in the initial remarks on the relation between the human sphere and nature. Which pole in the relation is reality? If you emphasize the causality of nature — in epistemology or in ecological ethics — you get one answer. But if instead the focus of concentration is applied to ethical responsibility for the environment, there is likely to be more emphasis on the reality of human custom. I hope that the tendency of my interventions in this dialectic has been to nudge the balance in avour of the role of custom and convention.

The reality of nature is not compromised by these observations. Human customs and cultures certainly depend on the natural environments in which they arise and by which they are sustained. Nature does not remain unaffected by this causal contact — either technologically or epistemologically. There would, of course, be nature without human custom; but what that nature would be like, is beyond our comprehension — and not simply for reasons of the limitation of our knowledge. The absence of human custom would actually affect the natural world in ways which it is in principle impossible to foresee.

7 THE IMAGE OF HUMANITY AS THE IMAGE OF NATURE

Yersu Kim
Seoul National University, South Korea

Philosophy as the mirror of nature and the Kantian challenge
A conception of philosophy as the *prote philosophia* has long been dominant in the western philosophical tradition. Philosophy, according to this conception, is the discipline that defines the preconditions for all of man's systematic efforts to understand the world and his place in it, and is presumed to be in a position to provide one single, uniquely true picture of the world. It was given the role of being the 'mirror of nature',[1] enabling it to assume the privileged position of ruling over culture as a whole, including the sciences. Philosophy of nature was seen, in a grand manner typical of this tradition, as an attempt to answer the questions concerning nature, understood as the totality of the material reality and the most general species of all existing things.[2]

Today, this conception is under challenge. Encouraged by recent developments in psychology, comparative linguistics, and the philosophy of language and of science, there is a widespread acceptance of the notion that all knowledge, values and truth, which form the basis of man's intellectual as well as practical activities, are relative to cultural background or system. What we perceive, what we think true and what we deem reasonable are no longer explicated in relation to objective reality, to which philosophy alone was presumed to have access.

We can trace this recent challenge to the Kantian thesis that all perception and knowledge are products of the constructive activities of the knowing subject. Objective nature, the *Ding an sich,* is in principle unknowable by man. The world as it is known, phenomenal nature, is a construction by the knowing subject which is man. The Kantian insight has been bolstered by a more recent assertion that there cannot be a single, uniquely valid way in which such a construction may proceed. The relativistic consequences of the Kantian thesis has been diluted by the notion of the universal transcendental structure of mind that constrains all forms of knowledge acts. Now, a series of argumentations in the philosophy of language as well as of science has shown that it is impossible to accord any one conceptual scheme the privileged position of representing the world as it is, since the relationship between the world and the language which describes it is fundamentally indeterminate. There exist according to this view, many equally true but mutually incompatible conceptual schemes that interpret the world. Each of these conceptual schemes has its own standard of truth and justification, and there is no third neutral standard in terms of which each conceptual scheme can be appraised. What is accepted as real in one conceptual scheme may not be real in another. That is, the world itself becomes relative to a given conceptual scheme. Standards and norms embedded in each of the conceptual schemes are irreducible, and there is no objective rational basis for the choice of one conceptual scheme over another.

The image of nature that a given language, which expresses a given conceptual scheme, gives of it is no longer seen as being determined by nature itself. It is determined rather by the rules and presuppositions governing the use of that language, a given conceptual scheme. Some philosophers, such as Wittgenstein in his later years, simply accepted the existence of such a linguistic framework as given. Others, such as Canarp, believed that the acceptance of a linguistic framework was predicated on certain pragmatic considerations. They were however unanimous in rejecting the view that a linguistic framework was to be accepted on the basis of its link to the scheme-independent reality of some kind.

The task of philosophy thus becomes discovery, identification and formulation of that set of rules and presuppositions which together constitute a given linguistic framework. A general picture of reality is represented in these rules and presuppositions. The sciences work within the linguistic and conceptual framework constituted by these rules and presuppositions. Questions of truth and falsity about the world are decided relative to the general picture of reality as represented in these rules and suppositions.

The image of nature as the image of humanity
It is not difficult to see a connection between this relativization of the reality to the rules and presuppositions of a linguistic framework, on the one hand, and the long tradition of anthromorphization of nature, or the tradition of

formulating the conceptualization of nature in accordance with the image of man on the other hand. In the anthropomorphic cosmologies of the ancient societies, nature was seen as the activity of the spirits which were motivated by impulses and emotions similar to those of men. The spirits were then replaced by the gods and goddesses who personified, so to speak, the abstractions of thinking and language. Mythologies were of course attempts to explain nature in a systematic way, and the cosmologies as represented in these myths were representations and projections of the understanding man had of himself. The geocentric universe of Ptolemy was the systematization of these anthropocentric representations which provided for the European Middle Ages the basis of a rational and well organized world.

With the advent of the Heliocentric cosmology in the wake of the Copernican revolution, nature could no longer be seen in anthropocentric terms. The conception of nature was, nevertheless, still wedded to man in that nature became *anthropometric*, that is, man became in some sense the measure of nature. Ever since Kant, (who in principle denied any knowledge of *Ding an sich* and emphasized constructive activity of the human subject in the formation of nature as we know it) nature could no longer be defined as *an sich*, but as the image of nature, or nature as conceived by man. Heisenberg is very much in line with many scientists, including Galileo and Descartes, who attempted to represent nature in mathematical formulae, when he spoke of elementary particles in the following manner: 'The image of an objective reality of the elementary particles has therefore evaporated ... into the perspicuous clarity of mathematics, which no longer represents the image of an elementary particle, but our knowledge of this behaviour'.[3] Thus when we speak of nature we are not really dealing with an image of nature but with an image of human relationship toward nature. Indeed, one can move toward even more radical anthropocentric stance and simply identify the historical development of the conceptualization of nature with nature *per se*. Moscovici, for example, sees nature as a factor of production which has to be dominated and governed by man.[4] Man not only rules and dominates, but also 'creates' nature in so far as he produces new products and objects. Man thus becomes the Platonic *demiurgos*, a maker of nature.

One hardly needs to point out that this and other similar philosophies of nature and technology are anthromorphization of nature carried to *ad absurdum*. What is important for our context is the close interwovenness of man with the concept of nature. Natural science seems always to presuppose man not only as a spectator, but also as a 'co-actor in the drama of life'.[5] If in earlier times man saw himself as being confronted by nature, the world we live in today seems so totally changed by man that we encounter structures erected by man himself everywhere. Man is no longer a spectator, a mirror in front of nature, but an integral part of nature. The conception of man — our understanding of man's capabilities and desires and of his position within nature — becomes the very theoretical foundation on the basis of which we understand nature. The image of man thus becomes the image of nature.

The *homo economicus*

One image of man which has fundamentally influenced the way we conceptualize nature is the economic image, the *homo economicus*. Thematized by Weber and his followers, it is presented by Parsons as a system of values in explanation for the modern technological society of the capitalistic variety. This conception of man may be summarized under the following rubrics:
• Man as a rational being
• Man as a materialistic being
• Man as an autonomous entity
• Man as the conqueror of nature.[6]

The values inherent in this conception of man together constitute a highly consistent and dynamic whole. It functioned as the dynamo behind a development that brought about a fundamental transformation of nature as it had been hitherto known to mankind and enabled the most pervasive material and social improvements in the human condition man has ever seen. Futuristic passion in wishing to replace what is with that which is possible and the Faustian will to shape the world according to the wishes of man were never so strong as in this conception of man. To be sure, these values were not enough to define the particular form of this new society, but they certainly provided the basic framework within which modern industrial civilization could be built.

Considered in terms of the historical evolution of the industrial civilization, the economic image of man was originally anticipatory — a goal, the realization of which provided the focus for man's activities; a purpose, which gave meaning and direction to the life of man. With the exponential changes in

The Image of Humanity as the Image of Nature

the human condition in the wake of industrialization, there was a gradual convergence of societal conditions and the ideal image of man. We may point to certain periods in recent history in which the values constituting the economic image were realized, even if in a schematic way, in the societal conditions, for example in American society during the Pax Americana of the 50s and perhaps in European society during the 80s.

Since the economic image embraces the ideal of unlimited growth and progress, it provides the dynamics for further exponential growth in all areas of human existence, even after the convergence of the ideal and societal condition has been more or less achieved. Clear discrepancies begin then to appear between the system of values that once formed the backbone of the industrial civilization and its societal realities. The image of man, which provided the anticipatory goals and purposes in the formative stages of industrial civilization, lags behind the societal change and loses its relevance. When the discrepancy between the leading system of values and the realities it is supposed to guide reaches a certain stage, confusion sets in as to the direction for further societal change. The system of values in the image of man is no longer capable of providing the prescription for solving the problems that arise in the economic life and political institutions of a given society.

We are all now quite familiar with the issues raised by the Club of Rome report and antigrowth publications of the 70s.[7] We learned that between 1950 and 1970 the gross world product nearly tripled, greatly increasing the pressure man places on the ecological system. We learned of the danger of encroaching on the environment beyond its ability to support the demands made on it — a situation for which developed countries were primarily responsible.

The United States alone accounts for 35 per cent of all the energy used in the world, and it has consumed more minerals during the last 35 years than all mankind has used from the emergence of the species up to 1940. We are reminded in a jolting way of the bleak demographic outlook for the next two or three generations. We also have learned of the growing gap between the rich and poor parts of the world and the ensuing spectre of wars of redistribution. Finally we have become aware that alienation and depersonalization of man are the direct result of the anthropomorphization of nature which thus became something for man to conquer; so too man became an object for abstraction and quantification, thereby becoming an object for conquest. Domination and oppression of man by man are but aspects of this phenomenon of alienation.

That the system of intellectual ideas and cultural values which together form the image of man at the core of the Western industrial civilization is losing its once matter-of-fact relevance and validity is seen clearly in this gloomy picture, which, despite some modifications, remains true today. The goal of liberation from poverty was clear. But beyond the goal of development over and above the creation of material affluence there is no clear conception.

The realization that, given the destructive as well as constructive consequences of economic growth, the bigger, more and faster may not necessarily be the better has given rise to various forms of social experiments. Despite differences, they all seek an alternative mode of human existence to the present industrial-technological one by harking back to the ideas and values of more primitive traditional societies. Instead of an aggressive competitive ethics, they seek a form of human relationship based on co-operation, friendship, love and other related values. Instead of an exploitative attitude toward nature, they seek a mode of existence which is in harmony with it. However, these experiments remain only peripheral and isolated efforts in alternative modes of living, related to the social and economic realities only in an inadequate and inappropriate way. And no new synthesis of cultural ideas and moral values seems to be yet in sight that could replace the old.

Following the demise of Western colonialism, many of the emerging societies of the Third World adopted the model of industrial civilization as it is embodied in the Western conception of economy, politics and culture. By this time, however, the inner dynamics and validity of this civilization were already in disarray. Its material and institutional side were, to be sure, still basking in the splendour of high noon. The intellectual and aesthetic ideas and values of this culture, however, were undergoing, unnoticed except by a very few, a process of disintegration and transformation. One such exception was Friedrich Nietzsche, writing towards the end of the last century, in his preface to *The Will to Power*.

> What I relate is the history of the next two centuries. I describe what is coming, what can no longer come differently: the advent of nihilism. This history can be related even now; for necessity itself is at work here. This future speaks even now in a hundred signs.... For

sometime now our whole European culture has been moving toward a catastrophe, with a tortured tension that is growing from decade to decade: relentlessly, violently, headlong, like a river that wants to reach the end, that no longer reflects, that is afraid to reflect.[8]

An optimal synthesis as a regulative idea

What the foregoing amounts to is the realization that the expansionist's dynamics of the industrial civilization is coming to an end, due not merely to an accidental configuration of historical facts, but also due to the tensions and contradictions inherent in the intellectual, moral and aesthetic ideas that had been at the core of this dynamic and creative culture. Radical transformations are needed in these ideas if civilization is once again to serve the purpose for which it is intended — to ensure the survival of man and a life worthy of him. Is such a transformation possible? If so, what form would it take? And what would be the role of philosophy in such a process of transformation?

It would be intellectual hubris of the highest order to claim for any single philosophy or any single culture to be in possession of a body of knowledge and clairvoyance which could shape the course of such a transformation. We are in the dark as to the shape our lives will take 100 years from now, just as 1000 years ago the particular form of existence we are living today would have been unimaginable. But even in this state of partial knowledge and partial ignorance, cultures of each epoch and region attempt to forge a synthesis of ideas and values, which would constitute, and be internally consistent with a cohesive whole by means of which people could relate themselves to the world. These ideas, values and practices would together constitute some notion of an ordered universe, and could specify for man a set of purposes in relation to himself, his fellow men and nature. They would enable man to deal with the environment in relation to that set of purposes.

Such a set of ideas, values and practices may be called by whatever name one chooses: the idea of man, the idea of nature, or simply culture. Such as intellectual synthesis would be a kind of living organism with an internal dynamism of its own, looking beyond the boundaries set for itself. As the world and our knowledge of it change, this synthesis must change too, so as to make itself adequate to changing and changed circumstances.

Cultures of each epoch and region strive to forge an optimal cultural synthesis. Each claims for itself superiority over all others. The basis of each claim would be that it transcends the limitations of its competitors and avoids their weaknesses while at the same time incorporating their strengths. Such a synthesis would reflect a reflective equilibrium in the process of interaction and interchange of ideas and knowledge and values on the one hand, and the recalcitrant and changing environment on the other. Philosophy, with its natural bent toward argumentation and justification, would interpret and criticise these ideas and values. But above all, philosophy, to be worthy of the name, must contribute towards forging an effective and persuasive synthesis of all the ideas, knowledge and values by bringing them into a reflective equilibrium. The language of such an equilibrium must be fallibalistic, but its ambition would always be universal.

I would like to propose that we regard the possibility of an optimal intellectual synthesis as a *regulative idea* in the Kantian sense. It guides the efforts of men of different epochs and regions to form a system of ideas, knowledge and values adequate to the requirements of men and the constraints of the environment. The task would be somewhat akin to that of an archaeologist who, on the basis of meagre material at hand, attempts an overall picture of an ancient, little known civilization. As the picture offered must undergo changes, so too our knowledge of the world and our conception of how best to flourish in it undergo a continual process of disruption, correction and expansion.

Philosophical tasks ahead

Whatever form and direction this transformation may eventually take, there are a number of problems which need solutions. The increasing homogeneity of problems likely to face our respective societies is due not only to the species-specific primitive facts in man's natural history and the basic constraints the recalcitrant world places on men of all cultures and periods, but also is due to the increasing technologization and industrialization of our world.

There is, first and foremost, the problem of fundamental readjustment of man's relationship with nature. In place of the conception of man as being separate from nature, obligated to conquer it, a less exploitative outlook must be encouraged, to see man as one species among others embedded in the intricate web of natural processes that sustains and constrains all forms of life.

The Image of Humanity as the Image of Nature

Such an outlook would entail the knowledge that there are limits to all natural resources and that human intervention in natural processes is bound to have far-reaching consequences, many of which are cumulative and irreversible. Here, the Confucian culture, with its organic view of nature and man's place in it, would have something to contribute to the philosophical dialogue necessary for cultural transformation.

An attitude thus humbled toward nature and fellow men would bring in its wake a holistic sense of perspective, which balances and coordinates satisfaction among many different dimensions. It would be an outlook that places the inner satisfactions in the emotive sphere on the same, or even higher level, than the outer satisfaction of material kind. Rituals, art, music and poetry would gain commensurate places in the lives of men. Here again, one place where one may probe deeper would be the Confucian tradition that played down the material and the technical and placed supreme importance on the holistic perspective in which reason and emotion, quality and quantity, future and past, have their own appropriate places.

There is then the problem of social justice, both at the international as well as national levels. So long as the expansionistic dynamics of industrial civilization could be maintained, differences in material affluence between individuals and societies served a useful function in that they were reminders of a need for greater efforts. But once deprived of prospects for improvement in an economy whose total aggregate wealth does not keep pace with the growing population, they become a source of disruption in the fabric of society and of conflict between nations. A conception of justice, then, that goes beyond mere paternalism or utilitarianism is needed.

The problem of intra- as well as international justice can be resolved satisfactorily only if an appropriate revision of aggressive individualistic ethics that formed the backbone of industrial civilization can be tempered or even replaced by a greater concern for the common good. There have been many brave but essentially unsuccessful experiments in the west in communalistic ethics that emphasize the whole above the part, mutual cooperation rather than aggressive competition, emotional bonds rather than functional ones. Here again, a lesson can be drawn from the traditional *familism* which has been one of the essential components of Confucianism. Familism is an attitude that ascribes fundamental importance to human relations based on blood relationship. It is an attitude that places basic levels of human existence in a framework that transcends the narrow confines of individuals and binds individuals with an emotional bond. If familism could be sublimated into a normative standard for a more inclusive, human, cooperative relationship, it would contribute to the process of cultural transformation.

Notes
1. Rorty, 1979.
2. Anzenbacher, 1981.
3. Heisenberg, 1971.
4. Mocovici, 1982.
5. Heisenberg, 1971, p.115.
6. Parsons, 1963.
7. Meadows, 1972.
8. Nietzsche, 1967, p.3.

8 NATURALISM AND PRIMITIVE TRUTH

Ernest Sosa
Brown University
Providence, U. S. A.

What is the place of epistemology in a naturalist philosophy? What sort of epistemology is open to a naturalist world view? At the center of epistemology is the concept of knowledge, and more particularly, propositional knowledge. Propositional knowledge is to be distinguished from knowledge of individual things, in the broadest sense, as when one knows someone or knows a certain symphony or a certain city; and propositional knowledge is also to be distinguished from knowledge of how to do something, as in knowledge of how to play tennis or how to bake bread. Propositional knowledge is knowledge of facts, knowledge that such and such, whether the fact be ordinary or highly theoretical. Knowledge that space is relative or that arithmetic is incomplete thus counts as propositional knowledge. But so does knowledge that mangoes are edible or that Mt. Kilimanjaro is in Tanzania.

In order to know a fact you must at least accept it as such. To know that such and such you must at least believe that such and such. Of course not *every* belief amounts to knowledge. The belief may be false in which case it is surely not knowledge. And not even every *true* belief is knowledge. A gambler may believe superstitiously that the dice will come up seven or eleven, and on a certain occasion he may turn out to be right in his belief, even though the dice are fair and he has just guessed right, without really knowing. So we have arrived at three conditions that must be fulfilled if a subject S is to know that such and such: (1) S must *believe* that such and such; (2) it must be *true* that such is such; and (3) S's belief in such and such must be in some sense *appropriate* or *justified* (and cannot be just a lucky guess).

How is a naturalist world view to accommodate the possibility of human knowledge? How can a naturalist make room for our three conditions necessary for knowledge: namely, *belief, truth,* and *justification?* Most of contemporary philosophy of language, of mind, and of knowledge consists of attempts by naturalism to answer this question and other similar questions.

Here we shall leave aside the complex set of issues and arguments involved in accounting for psychological attitudes within a naturalist framework. Therefore, in particular we put aside the question of how to be a naturalist about belief, about that particular psychological attitude. Our focus shall be rather the concept of justification and, especially, that of truth.

Consider first the concept of justification, of epistemic justification or aptness. This concept is meant to help us distinguish the cheater who loads the dice and knows the outcome ahead of time from the honest player who turns out right by pure luck. Suppose we can account for such justification in terms of the concept of truth. In that case we will have reduced our overall problem to a significant extent. Accordingly, there are ways of naturalizing epistemiology that put truth at the center and explain justification in its terms. In what follows I would like to explore the prospects for truth-centered naturalized epistemology. What philosophical account of truth is available to the naturalist?

A well-known approach explicates a true belief as one that would be accepted rationally and justifiably by ideal inquirers in an ideal epistemic situation. This sort of approach goes back to Charles Sanders Peirce, and is an important alternative that deserves and has received much serious attention. Here I just want to note that if we wish to explain what is rational and justified in terms of what is true, we cannot concurrently explain truth in terms of rationality and justification. Accordingly, such epistemic accounts of truth stay on the shelf as we move on.

A second sort of account is correspondence with reality. This view of truth as correspondence has been subjected to direct criticism by some, while others have drawn from it alleged consequences that would be very unpalatable to many. Donald Davidson, for example, has argued repeatedly that there can be no correspondence of a sentence with reality, since there can be no facts to correlate with true sentences. But it is not obvious that correspondence must be with facts. Besides, Davidson's argument against the existence of facts can be met. Hilary Putnam has argued, again repeatedly, that there is no external, independent reality to which our sentences could correspond. But his main arguments involve a question-begging step from the lemma that the truth of sentences is perspective-relative to the conclusion that reality itself is perspective. Finally, Stephen Stich for his part has published a book, *The*

Fragmentation of Reason, whose main thesis is: *given* a correspondence view of truth, it follows that truth does not have the value assigned to it by our scientific and philosophical traditions, and that we should replace traditional epistemology with a more pragmatic epistemology, one that adopts more mundane and practical goals.

I believe that these arguments by Davidson, Putnam, and Stich can all be met. Nevertheless, correspondence truth does still seem problematic. Its main problem at present is not an excess of unacceptable consequences, however, so much as a deficiency of acceptable content. There are clear enough and well-explicated conceptions of correspondence: for example, the notion of one-to-one correspondence that applies to sets, or the notion of isomorphism that applies to certain well-defined structures. But the notion of a sentence's correspondence with reality is not yet clear enough or well enough explicated.

By this stage we can sense the attractions of a streamlined deflationism about the concept of truth. For deflationism, truth is not a property that needs a substantial theory such as a correspondence theory, or a coherence theory, or a pragmatist theory that the true is what works, or a relativist theory that the true is what is validated by one's culture, or any other such theory.

Deflationism comes in two main varieties: (a) noncognitivism, and (b) primitivism. Both neopragmatism and the redundancy theory are forms of noncognitivism about truth, since both *deny* to the vocabulary of truth the function of expressing any special property or set of properties, such as correspondence with reality. Instead, truth locutions are like 'Hurray' in having some other function in our speech, some pragmatic, non-cognitive function – perhaps commending, perhaps emphasizing, and so on.

For the non-cognitivist there is really no such thing as truth, nor any such thing as justification, nor anything like knowledge, any more than there is in the world any such thing as 'hurrayness'. The term 'Hurray' is a functional term which serves for venting emotion, for expressing approbation, for commending, and the like. The non-cognitivist believes that epistemic terms such as 'true', 'justified', and 'known', and their cognates, are just like 'Hurray' in that respect. In his most recent writings, Richard Rorty has opted for such noncognitivism. Consider, however, the following sentences:
(a) Some of our beliefs might be false, but many must be true.
(b) If what they said is not true, they must have lied.

(c) There are infinitely many truths expressible in English that no-one will ever express.

How can one understand the user in such sentences of the terms 'true', 'false', and their cognates, if the only function of such vocabulary is to commend, as in the case of 'Hurray'; or to emphasize, as when we use an exclamation mark; or the like? There seems no way. Noncognitivism is an offer we can and should refuse.

There is one last view of truth to consider, one that has been advocated very rarely. For reasons that will be apparent and for the sake of a convenient label let us call it 'primitivism' . Primitivism was advocated briefly by Moore and Russell in the early years of this century, and it was described later by Moore in the following passage:

> It is a theory which I myself formerly held, and which certainly has the advantage that it is very simple. It is simply this. It adopts the supposition that in the case of every belief, true or false, there is a proposition which is what is believed, and which certainly is. But the difference between a true and false belief, it says, consists simply in this, that where the belief is true the proposition, which is believed, besides the fact that it is or 'has being' also has another simple unanalyzable property which is possessed by some propositions and not by others. The propositions which don't possess it, and which therefore we call false, *are* or 'have being' – just as much as those which *do;* only they just have *not* got this additional property of being 'true'. [1]

What this view denies is that truth has a Moorean 'analysis' or definition. It does not deny that we may know *a priori* lots of propositions constituted in part by our primitive concept of truth. When Moore viewed truth as a simple, unanalyzable quality, he viewed it just the way he viewed *good* in *Principia Ethica*. So he surely would have said of truth what he did say of *good:*

> If I am asked 'What is good?' my answer is that good is good, and that is the end of the matter. Or if I am asked 'How is good to be defined?" My answer is that it cannot be defined, and that is all I have to say about it. My point is that 'good' is a simple notion, just as 'yellow' is a simple notion; that, just as you cannot, by any manner of means, explain to anyone who does not already know it, what yellow is, so you cannot explain what good is. Definition...which describe the real nature of the object or notion denoted by a word...are only possible when the object or notion in question is something complex...But yellow and good, we say, are not complex: they are notions of that simple kind, out of which definitions are composed and with which the power of further defining ceases.[2]

According to this, what you cannot define *good* or *yellow* or truth or give

an illuminating, compact, at least surveyable, Moorean analysis of it. It is in *this* sense that you cannot philosophically 'explain' any such 'simple' concept. And this leaves it open that you should have *a priori* knowledge of infinitely many propositions constituted essentially by such concepts. Among such propositions we may perhaps find the following:
    No surface that is yellow all over is blue all over.
    Pleasure is intrinsically good.
    That-snow-is-white is true if snow is white.

In what sense is primitivism a deflationary view? Clearly it is not so radically deflationary as noncognitivism. Primitivism does not deny that there is a substantive concept of truth which corresponds to a real property or aspect of reality. Primitivism does not even deny that there may be a philosophical theory of truth to be discovered. Such a theory may even take the form of a relatively simple necessary biconditional such as:
    (Tl) X is true iff X corresponds to reality.
    T2) X is true iff X coheres within a comprehensive set of beliefs.
    (T3) X is true iff X would be accepted at the end of rational inquiry.

All of these — Tl, T2, and T3 — are subject to fatal objections. But how can we be sure that no such necessary biconditional will *ever* be found? Before Galileo and Newton it would have been easy to despair of our ever finding any simple and general laws of motion. Similarly, before Euclid and his predecessors it would have been easy to despair of our ever finding any general geometry. And something similar can be said about Frege and modern logic. Universal negative *dicta* are antecedently implausible and require strong supporting arguments. I mean *dicta* such as: No theory of truth will ever be found. Accordingly, primitivism is well advised to remain noncommittal on whether such a theory of truth is in the cards. And it is *just in* this very attenuated sense that primitivism is deflationary, just in the sense that it *withholds* commitment on the prospects for a philosophical theory of truth like T1, T2, or T3.

However, if it is only in so attenuated a sense that primitivism deflates truth, does that not bring us back to our main problem: How is a naturalist to accommodate epistemology and in particular the concept of truth? It is easy to see how noncognitivism can serve naturalism. For noncognitivism there is nothing in reality corresponding to the vocabulary of truth any more than there is anything in reality corresponding to devices of commendation or emphasis such as the word 'Hurray' or the exclamation mark. But we have seen the flaws of noncognitivism. Primitivism does not have those flaws. But primitivism does grant to truth its status as a substantive concept corresponding to a *bona fide* property or aspect of reality. And so the question remains: How can a naturalist make room for such a property or aspect of reality? Where would it find a place amidst the particles, waves, and fields of force?

Primitivism grants that truth cannot be reduced to the concepts of physics or the other sciences, in the sense of being defined semantically in those terms – indeed it insists that truth is, in the relevant sense, *a primitive* concept, a concept that is indispensable though it *has* no such definition in terms of physics. Accordingly primitivism is *not* a *radical* naturalism. Radical naturalism divides our vocabulary and concepts into classes. There are the *first* class terms and concepts of science, especially physics; all other terms or concepts are *second* class or lower. The lower classes are not to be taken seriously for theoretical purposes and are thus to be *eliminated* from serious discourse. This is the view of W.V. Quine. But it suffers from a threat of pragmatic incoherence, since the discourse of the eliminativist will then itself lack seriousness. Moreover, there is little chance that we shall ever be in a position to give up all discourse except science – or that we shall even want to do so.

If philosophy and common sense cannot be definitionally reduced to physics, and if there is no prospect whatever that we shall even abandon serious affirmations of philosophy or daily life — such as 'the roses are in bloom' or 'the table is set' — then what sense is there in any class system that makes physics first class and everything else lower class? Quine speaks of the prediction of stimulations or experiences or observations as a distinguishing criterion. But such verificationism is notoriously implausible when applied far enough, and defeasible by counter examples.

Roses in bloom, table settings, the beautiful, the good, the true — none of these can be defined in terms of physics or the other sciences. Can we retain such concepts without violating naturalism? We can do so if we are willing to accept levels of reality, some more fundamental than others. 'More fundamental' — in what sense? I shall explain the sense in terms of properties (and relations), but the account can easily be extended to cover individuals, states of affairs, facts, and events.

A class of properties (and relations) C_1 is more fundamental than a class C_2 if whenever a property in C_2 is exemplified that must be in virtue of certain properties in C_1 being exemplified.

Thus the property of being a nation is less fundamental than that of being a human, the property of being a human is perhaps less fundamental than that of being a cell, which in turn is less fundamental than that of being a water molecule. And so on.

In addition, the property of being a *beautiful* vase is less fundamental than that of being a vase with a certain shape, colour or design. The property of being a *good* apple is less fundamental than that of being an apple that is sweet or juicy. And the property of being a *true* proposition is less fundamental than properties such as being snow and being white, since the truth of the proposition that snow is white derives from the whiteness of snow.

Given such a concept of a layered reality ordered by a relation of relative fundamentality, we are in a position to formulate a modest naturalism as follows:

(MN)   Some natural class of properties (and relations) is more fundamental than any non-natural class.

In conclusion, we can perhaps appreciate the attractions of the following combination of views:
- Truth is a primitive concept, and has no illuminating definition or Moorean analysis.
- There is no philosophically substantive theory of truth, one that provides *a priori* necessary and sufficient conditions for truth in terms of ideal inquirers, pragmatic working, comprehensive coherence, or causal correspondence. Or, at least, there is no such theory available at present.
- *Modest naturalism is true: reality is fundamentally natural.* And truth always supervenes more fundamental properties and relations. Once it is settled what individuals exist and how they are naturally propertied and interrelated, it will

be a supervenient consequence of that which propositions are true and which are not; in the sense that this will follow with necessity and in virtue of what was settled antecedently.
- It remains to be seen what special shortcomings may flaw such a primitive but supervenient concept of truth. What shortcomings may it have that it does not share with the many other supervenient and nonfundamental concepts used in science, or philosophy, or everyday life?
- Finally, if such a concept of truth is acceptable within a naturalist framework, then the recent development of truth-dependent epistemologies may be seen as an attempt to naturalize epistemology. Truth-dependent theories would explain justification in terms of truth. And, as we have seen, this would also help explain knowledge itself in terms acceptable to naturalism.

Notes
1. From p. 261 of the published version of Moore's 1910-11 lectures, *Some Main Problems of Philosophy* 1953. For discussion of the Moore/Russell view, see Cartwright,1987, pp. 71-95.
2. Moore, 1903, pp. 6-8.

9 ON ECO-ETHICA: NEW ETHICS FOR THE NEW AGE

Tomonobu Imamichi
Tokyo, Japan

Because the general theme of this World Congress concerns the human attitude toward the environment, it is appropriate to discuss eco-ethica as a new ethics appropriate to current ecological conditions. There are various arguments for the so-called new ethics, for example environmental ethics, bio-ethics or medical ethics. They are all important, but each of them is an applied ethics in a certain domain. If it is necessary to create new ethics, we should not be content with the form of applied ethics of traditional morality, but we must establish a new ethic such as eco-ethica which fundamentally and philosophically reflects the complexity of our techno-cultural world.

It is first important to differentialte between 'ethica in nature as traditional' moral science and 'eco-ethica' as a new morality given the present technological conjuncture. Eco-ethica includes in it techno-ethica, medico-ethica, bio-ethica, environmental ethics and various *ethica officiorum*. It means that eco-ethica is a principal ethics and a fundamental philosophical system. *Eco* derives from *oikos* in Greek, which means a house in its narrow sense and a living dimension in its wider sense. In the case of *eco-ethica, eco* as *oikos* is used in its widest sense, namely, the human living circle which is more than global, that is to say, inter-sideral (*inter* and *sidus*), cosmic.

The range of human contact fortified by modern technology can give various thoughts of impact on the cosmic condition. Experimental nuclear explosions damage and destroy life on a global scale. Freon gas depletes the ozone layer on the cosmic scale. Such damage is not only synchronic but also diachronic, that is to say, the damage continues for future generations. Moral consciousness therefore should not be limited to one's personal life, but it must be enlarged to include the destiny of humanity and its stages in nature. Eco-ethica, in the context of moral consciousness, can address three problems. The first problem concerns logical contrarity between ethics in nature and eco-ethica in its techno-ethical domain. Their ontological reversal may be seen with respect to structure in a practical syllogism. The second problem concerns the ontological difference between ethics in nature and eco-ethica in respect to the ethical object. The third problem concerns artistic creation in the eco-ethical perspective.

Let us first consider then the logical incompatibility between traditional ethics and eco-ethica. The typical representations of the traditional ethics is found in the Confucian ethics in *Lun Yu* and Aristotelian ethics in *Ethica Nicomacheia*. Because of the limited space, I will concentrate on Aristotelian ethics which is better known outside of East Asian cultural circles.

Aristotle shows us the practical syllogism very clearly: Major premise: I wish to read a book at night. (A light is wanted or needed.) Minor premise: I enumerate the means for the light (to burn some branches, to make a torch, to wait for the moon. And I choose the one means which is the easiest and the best). Conclusion: I make a torch.

Formally we schematize these propositions in the following way:
The major: I wish A.
The minor: How p, q, r and s will realize A.
The conclusion: I do r, because r is the easiest and the best.
In this logical form the major premise is self-evident as a human wish. And the minor premise is structured to decide the means through functional enumeration of possible ways of realizing the desired goal, and through moral and practical evaluation of the means as an ethical form of the human act.

This type of act is naturally found in our lives. But in the course of years technology as means has been created. But technology as a means is becoming more and more effective so much so that in place of the classical primacy of the goal, the primacy of the means has appeared as modern social phenomena. The powerful means of technology is now self-evident. We all today have the power of electricity for instance. So our practical syllogism is changed as follows: In the major premise we have the gigantic power of electricity or atomic energy. The major premise is the confirmation of the power as technology. Now, what can we realize by this gigantic power as datum? The minor premise is now the dimension of goals which can be realized through technological power. This is the dramatic reversion of the logical structure concerning the premises of practical syllogism.

The ontological change concerning the subject of actions and the object of actions should not be overlooked. At first the change of the subject is arithmetical, that is, the subject of action is more egological than noslogical. The change is from the single individual to the collective committee. We need the morality of collectivity, the ethics of the committee which is not the individual subject but the collective subject. Where is responsibility in this structure?

Concerning the object of the act in this techno-ethical syllogism, we no longer have a transcendental aim to unify us with God or to purify the soul of the sin, because our aims must be deduced from the possibilities of the material range of mechanical power like electricity or nuclear energy. So, the necessity for the secularization of morality arises. Therefore we must make efforts to evoke a non-secular aim, a transcendent sublime aim, which is not contained in mechanical power. In order to emphasize spiritual power for moral motivation, we need some key concepts which can evoke transcendent aims beyond the range of material secularity. This introduces us to the second problem under consideration.

The second problem concerns the ontological difference between ethics in nature and eco-ethica in respect of the ethical object. Traditional ethics, be it in the West or in the East, has taken as its main subject human relations. Therefore ethics in general has been *ethica ad homines*. To change savage nature into comfortable civilization has always been considered good for the sake of humanity. Therefore to destroy some natural conditions was always good on the basis of *ethica ad homines*. But in our century, not to mention the future, the range of technological power is so strong, that to change nature does not always mean to eliminate an unprofitable condition against a present evil, but also to change the whole natural system, that is to say, to destroy the cosmic harmony, wherein we live and our descendants will live. Therefore eco-ethica must include not only *ethica ad homines* but also *ethica ad naturam*. To protect nature for human survival must be one of the new key concepts which evokes transcendent aims, because to protect nature requires our temperance which is not found in mechanical power, but in spiritual power.

Our ethical consciousness must be enlarged not only to embrace nature, but also culture. In our environment there are, for example, many masterpieces of art, through which we can enjoy aesthetic happiness, spiritual ecstasy and can forget the burden of life, so that we may recreate ourselves for our future. This joy through the cultural product as masterpiece must be passed on to the future generations as completely as possible. That is our diachronical moral duty for the coming generations. The morality for the culture and the diachronical duty to the future are also very impressive key concepts, which evoke our moral motivation as transcendent aim. Unify *Ethica ad naturam* and *ethica ad culturam* in one term, *ethica ad res*.

The third problem concerns artistic creation or aesthetic expression in the eco-ethical perspective. The Greek word *arete* means, as is well known, 'virtue'. We must here think of the possibility of a new virtue in a new ethics, in our aretology.

In the previous meditation on *ethica ad res*, the necessity of the diachronicality of virtue is clear. The love for one's neighbour is the love for the visible specified persons in the synchronical relationship. But now the concept of this love must be enlarged to include the invisible, unknown, unspecified, unborn persons in the diachronical relation. That is really an unarteological revolution from the *ethica facie ad faciem* to *ethica in dimensione invisibile*. Religion which was once rejected by some ethical positions in philosophy must be taken up again in the domain of ethics, because the invisible person and the diachronicality beyond synchronicality require some religious anticipation. If we could seize the creative hold for aesthetics in the third problem, we could expect to seize it also in the second and the first problems. So, concerning a masterpiece of art we must take care of its maintenance and its value not only synchronically but also diachronically. Private possession is permitted but the idea of co-possession for humanity must be considered. The moral obligation for public exposition in a certain length of time every year must be guaranteed from the moral conviction of the owner.

Concerning nature, we must ensure ecological protection of almost all creatures because all species radiate the secret of the universe from their own structure. They are the clue for science and art. From the first problem concerning technological syllogism of action we can search noslogical ethics in contrast with egological ethics. Although ethical consciousness is deeply personal, egological access to human conduct is simply not enough for the noslogical constructive of technological conjuncture of present human dimension. We must avoid both egoism and nosism in order to realize the glory of humanity, where *ego in nobis* and *nos cum me* are compatible in moral decision.

10 PHILOSOPHICAL ASPECTS OF THE INTER-PLAY BETWEEN NATURE AND THE ARTIFICIAL ENVIRONMENT OF MAN

Wolfgang Kluxen
University of Bonn, Germany

The subject which I am invited to write on may be treated in different ways. I understand it as anthropological in the sense in which we speak of 'Philosophical Anthropology', or 'Philosophy of Humanity'. The distinction between natural and artificial is made from the standpoint of humanity. 'Natural' in the old sense, first introduced by early Greek thinkers and elaborated by Aristotle, is what 'exists by itself', without human intervention. In Aristotle, then, it is opposed to the artificial: the product not just of human action but of human intelligence (action guided by intelligence); it is the work of human beings owing its existence to human forming. Aristotle sees there an important ontological difference; he excludes works of art from theoretical consideration, and admits them only as objects of 'technology' i.e. knowledge of the way to produce them.

There are two points in Aristotle's doctrine of art which may be of interest for our topic. Aristotle says that 'production by art' proceeds in the way which Nature would take, if Nature would make the product. His constant example for this is the art of medicine; its product is health, and in producing this state, art imitates nature, supplies what nature fails to do, helps nature. Now 'health' is in itself a natural aim, but art follows nature also, when the product is non-natural, e.g. a house; it will hold when it is built just as nature would have built it (if nature would build a house). Artificial production, as it is related to naturally existing things, relies on natural forces. A work of art exists as such by human forming; its subsistence (the 'substantial' meaning of existence) remains natural. In medieval Aristotelianism, the consequence is explicitly drawn (which I have difficulty finding in Aristotle himself) that all artificial forms are accidental; all substances are natural, or 'nature' remains the only substance in the artificial.

Aristotle's second point is that not every human action upon nature transforming it, producing changes in the shape of the natural is in the strict sense artificial, or a 'work of art', i.e. a product of human intelligence in the perfection of *techne*. Such pre-technical activity may go very far: a significant early document is the first chorus of Sophocles' *Antigone*. There humankind is called *deinos* — a difficult word which I refrain from translating — because *Homo sapiens* tears up the earth, takes away the fruit, acts with violence upon nature, and is self proclaimed the master of the animals and even of the sea. Humanity is clever (one of the possible translations of *deinos*): making life by inventing ways and means to take from Nature what is not granted freely; trying to dominate, and to extend that domination. But the inventions which make this (in our view: moderate) domination possible, are, in Aristotle's sense, not yet works of art or *techne*. They belong to what Aristotle calls *empeiria* experience of experiential knowledge. Farmers and shoemakers have no *techne* but only *empeiria*. The artificial in a strict sense belongs to a higher level of productive intelligence, in modern terms, we would have to call scientific. This is a clear distinction of epistemological character. But in our context, it is interesting that it reflects two modes or stages of dealing with natural things in acting, because of immediate experience, and on the grounds of scientific technology.

We may use the words *technical* and *artificial* in a broader sense today. Then we may say that right from the beginning humankind used — and had to use — technical means to secure survival: stone-tools and fire. At a very early stage, humanity takes care of animals. As soon as people become sedentary, they begin to transform the natural environment by farming, by building shelters, houses and stables; they begin to exploit nature to make the surroundings their own.

However, we would hesitate to call these surroundings artificial, or even to speak of violence as Sophocles did. Fruits cannot be grown by violence, and when the farmer breaks up the earth, the aim is to set free natural forces, to make nature bring forth more and better fruits. Cultivating the earth is not only domination; it may be considered as a service rendered to the earth to realize its potentials; and this holds good also for breeding plants and animals. In the empirical or experiential stage humankind seeks to find out what natural things are good for; and it is no problem to see the good in what is good for humanity, and to make nature better by culture. But when people work for

Inter-play Between Nature and the Artificial Environment

their own profit, the profit depends on careful handling of what nature is in itself, on the adapting action. Then nature will reward the action. The result of the work will be the fruit of the earth. Nature responds to humanity's action, and in the successful case, will nurse humankind in a motherly way.

In a sense, this is not only a metaphor. If we consider humanity as a product of evolution, people are really the offspring of nature, and there must have been friendly conditions for the origin of the species. Should we say that human existence began naturally in concord with nature, i.e. in paradise? Now it is significant that the Biblical myth presents Paradise as a garden, i.e. as an artificial arrangement ordered by God, and thus a product of culture. Paradise is not natural, and the history of humankind begins with its loss. Humanity is entirely dependent on nature, but not in complete concord with it; there exists a break, discord, estrangement, non-identity. Nature may be friendly when it is transformed by culture, but humankind cannot be entrusted to nature nor master the contingencies which require defence and yielding: sunshine and rain, wind and weather, plagues and diseases. Thus Nature may also be hostile, and humanity must seek protection. Sometimes violence is required for survival. Therefore humanty's relationship to nature becomes ambiguous.

On the one hand, human life depends on obtaining what I called the response of nature, which it gives spontaneously. In farming and breeding or whenever we try to awaken nature's powers, or help nature, we rely on nature's spontaneity. On the other hand, people make their own life, and create an environment by cultivating the soil, and take express distance from nature when building house, villages, towns. Here nature is really dominated, treated as material for human works, and material is won by exploitation. If we call this violence — as Sophocles did — then violence is as essential an element of human culture as adaptation, the tendencies for mastery and for partnership are both given, and there exists always a certain tension between them.

Against this view, one might insist that there is a possibility of nature itself serving as material, taking on forms impressed by human action, that humanity is also a 'natural agent' of this process, and that even highly complex technology has to rely on natural forces which it sets free. In this view, the distinction of the two tendencies — for mastery, or partnership — has no objective meaning. Now this is certainly true, but it does not lead us very far: this view refers us to the theoretical level where it is clear — in accordance with Aristotle — that the artificial is substantially natural. The problem is not there, and a substantialistic, or naturalistic approach will miss the point. The ambiguity of humanity's relationship to nature is a question of meaning, and therefore cannot be reduced to an objective unity. The deeper reason for this irreducibility is that it reflects an essential structure of human existence: the problem is anthropological.

People are, first, natural beings; however, they not only are, but also have a nature. They are not just living out of a centre of activity; they can, at any time, take distance from themselves. The position, or — as a German philosopher (H. Plessner) termed it — the positionality — is eccentric. This is why humankind lives (as a nature), and also makes life (as having a nature). This structure is obvious in self-consciousness: it is a case of having presupposing a distance from the self which one is. We see also that the identity of the self which we are conscious of is not simply given; it is the result of a process in which a structural division is superseded. In so far as this division exists in the mind, it is not necessarily real, but consists in a difference of meaning. Nevertheless it is just this difference of meaning which explains the problematic character of the self by which it is capable of self-transcendence, and also exposed to self-alienation. This is not only a mental structure, though it includes that reflexivity which we ascribe to the mind. For the self is not the mind (the mind is that of a self), and the structure is that of human existence. This is of consequence for understanding humanity's relation to the environment. If we find there a certain ambiguity, this may reflect the way in which humantiy is and has a separate nature.

Considered as the nature which humanity is, *Homo sapiens* is a species among others, a product of evolution, part of the natural environment, and a living body whose relationship to the surroundings is immediate impulses and urging needs which have to be satisfied for survival of the individual or the species. For the means of survival, humanity depends entirely on nature and the surroundings, that is the earth which gives humanity space and fruit. Humankind is an earthly being, and this is the basis of human existence.

But human existence is not just a natural process. Even actions by which we satisfy urgent natural needs are not absolutely determined by nature. It is certainly urgent to eat and drink, but we prepare our food, and we introduce table manners. Nothing is more natural than sexuality, but sexual behaviour is in all humankind under strict rules which are not just natural. Humanity is certainly by nature a social animal, but the forms of social like are determined by customs and conventions, and this is true also for the general means of social communication, namely language. Humanity exists under conditions of culture, and this is natural, though this does not make culture natural. There remains a difference, and it becomes obvious in the fact that cultures exist in plural, that customs can be very different, and that in certain cases they pay no regard to, or are even in contrast to conditions of nature: alienation becomes possible. We can shape the nature which we have, and we can do that with more or less success, or even fail.

Culture means also that we transform our natural environment. *Homo sapiens* is not only a body — and as such immediately present on the earth — there is a body, and it can be used as an instrument (this is natural). It is also natural to make the surroundings one's own, so that one cannot only find the means for survival, but also a homestead for the social life which has been shaped. Humanity takes possession of the soil being lived on, and having acquired the meaning of property. People begin to mobilize the earth and its resources to create a permanent environment which is humanity's own work. One becomes a builder not just of shelters, but of solid houses constructed to last for generations, and finally of cities housing the social life of a people. As a citizen humankind lives in surroundings which are products of human skill, purposefully designed for human use, and in some cases expressing a meaning which even transcends earthly significance, as temples and cathedrals do. Urban civilization creates an essentially artificial environment.

It is clear that the decisive step towards this kind of civilization is the development of social organization. Only collective work ensures that the entire environment of human life is transformed by art. On the other hand, it is natural for a society to adapt its surroundings to its social needs, and the whole development of human culture up to the building of cities may be considered as an unfolding of that basic structure which is characterized by the category of having. In this sense, Aristotle speaks of humankind as a political animal: as the policy, the city, is the form of society in which human life becomes really good, it must be considered as the actualization of what really is meant by nature, and this includes also the work of architecture, and everything artificial belonging to the city.

If humankind is, or becomes, by nature a builder of cities or, to give a more specific example, of gothic cathedrals, it does not follow that these are natural. The remain artificial, but the artificial is, in such a case of prescientific technology, apparently of earthly character. The stone is recognizable as coming from a nature source, the construction is immediately understandable as due to the skilled use of experience in dealing with solid material; the form is determined by principles which remind us of organic structures. Such works of art are not necessarily estranged from nature; they may reveal nature's potentialities, manifest our earthly life basis, and thus change the surface of the earth not in the sense of domination, but showing it as the fundamental condition of our life.

Artificial surroundings — at least in a pre-scientific stage of technology — are still earthly, and they will show it. In this case, their meaning refers us to that nature which simply is. The nature which we are, with immediacy, remains the point of reference in all the supergrowing development of the artificial, and the latter is not alienated if the meaning of this reference is maintained. It is true that the primordial division cannot be superseded; the tension between the is and the has defines the condition of human nature. The interrelation of the artificial and the natural in our environment reflects essentially this tension which exists inside human nature, determining the structure of human existence.

This means also that complete concordance with nature is not an ideal for human existence. Reconciliation can only be sought on the level of meaning, namely in the affirmation of humanity's earthly existence. This can be expressed in concrete acts in which this affirmation becomes an element of artificial human culture: the great example is the culture of gardening, especially where it is understood in the sense of symbolic representation. This example makes also clear limits of reconciliation: it plays on the aesthetic level.

What has been said till now, refers to a technic which is experiential and earthly. Under the conditions of modern scientific technology, the tension between the natural and the artificial becomes extreme; it comes near to a break, especially in the ecological crisis of our time. Our alienation from nature becomes a real menace to our existence. This is a great and urgent subject, but I do not want to speak on the real menace: I want to make some remarks on the change of meaning which underlies the new reality. In our modern understanding of science. The distinction between theoretical knowledge, considering nature as it is (in itself), and technical knowledge, giving rules for production, has largely vanished. Since Bacon and Descartes, the mastery of nature has been proclaimed as the aim of science. Knowing means now knowing how to produce: we question nature in experimenting to find out the rules by which it produces its process — the laws of nature —, and as far as we know them, we shall be able to reproduce nature's process by technical application. On the basis of this knowledge, we can form and transform what is naturally given, so that the natural becomes mere material for our activity. For a scientific mind, the question of what nature is in itself will be meaningless; there are just facts, and matter to be dealt with, and certainly no partnership. For a scientific mind, even human existence, in so far it is natural may be considered as something to be produced, so that humankind become their own maker: the category of having takes over, and there remains no is as a point of reference.

It is obvious that scientific technology leads to an alienation, even to self-alienation of humanity, if it becomes the dominating — or even exclusively dominating — factor in the human relationship with nature. But this is more a question of our understanding of its meaning than a consequence of its real achievement. The artificial conditions of our life created by the expansion of modern technics have enriched our existence: we live easier, healthier, and longer than our ancestors, and even our chances of freedom are better. The ecological crisis does not prove that scientific technology leads us astray, and that all technics leads us to the abyss. It shows only that mastery cannot be our exclusive ideal in dealing with nature: or also, that we have not succeeded in mastering our own mind, its narrowness and one-sidedness.

Nevertheless — and this is my second remark — the narrowness of the scientific approach, its focusing on specific problems, enabled science to penetrate deeply into the analysis of natural matter. Below the level of the elements, we hit on what is no more earthly stuff, but cosmic matter. Our technology not only transforms what is given in our surroundings, it creates new ones from cosmic raw material. Modern technics becomes planetary: It has surrounded the globe with an unearthly sphere of communication — even visible in the satellites — and the eccentricity of humanity finds an analogous expression in the human ability to take an extraterrestrial standpoint. Nuclear technics may even try to reproduce on earth the process of the sun. This is also a kind of imitation of nature (though in this case nature is not friendly).

According to the old principles that what something is essentially must be judged by its utmost possibilities, modern technics is essentially marked by its unearthly, cosmic character. This character may be felt in earthly works of art which use modern technics for aesthetic achievement: buildings which deny the solidity of their earthly foundation by their form, or sculptures which float above the soil, or industrial design inspired by the fantasy of science fiction. And in the latter, we find the idea that man may even leave the earth, that generations may live in huge space ships and survive a catastrophic end of our planet. Does this indicate an alienation from the earth? Or shall we take it as a symbolic expression of the human ability to transcend the conditions of existence.

This leads me to my third remark. Even in leaving the earthlings' planet, *Homo sapiens* does not leave the earth as a birthplace; humankind takes it along, just as taking the human body, or the nature which humanity is, and just as the astronauts detected the blue planet as the only homely place in a quite unhomely cosmos. The moon was conquered by man: but the meaning of this conquest was completed by the return to the earth. This makes positively clear what, in the negative way, is taught by the ecological crisis: under the conditions of planetary technics, the planet itself, the globe as a whole, is our environment. We must try to organize humankind as that social unity which can take care of it on a global scale; and the main task will not be to shape it but to preserve it.

Which nature is to be preserved? That nature which we belong to ourselves, and in which we survive by artificial means, including scientific technology, but which remains — and should remain — the homely earth. This sounds romantic if we consider our industrialized societies and their way of disposing of the soil. But on the other hand, industrialized societies created industries to procure for their members opportunities for experience of this earth; mass tourism is such an industry, to some extent sports also falls under this heading. There are also protected areas for wild life, and the art of gardening is increasingly practised. Humanity wants to be not only a master of nature, but also as its partner: people want to be who they are. In this context there is a strong need for humanity to have a dialogue with nature on the basis of mutual understanding.

Why is it important that humanity win this counterbalance over against the technical world, when this world is the work of human freedom? The reason is that nature — human nature — is the basis of freedom, and people cannot subject it to a process of making. As a product of human making, how could nature be the ground of human freedom? How could humanity claim dignity, which demands, and is not the result of, recognition? Thus the question of the interplay between the artificial and natural environment leads back to the context in which freedom and human dignity are at stake.

1 THE UNITY OF EVERYTHING ALIVE

Anna-Teresa Tymieniecka
World Institute for Advanced Phenomenological Research and Learning
Belmont, Massachusetts, U.S.A.

Introduction: Reason and manifestation

We may approach the question of research from three different points of view. First, we may follow the Greeks and make a distinction between certain dubitable cognition, between *episteme* and *doxa*; or, second, we may adopt the critique of reason initiated by Kant and focus on the powers and operations of the human mind assumed to be the source of reason. In this study a third approach is proposed, one which is a counterpart of my previous critique of reason. In contrast to the manner in which the two approaches mentioned first divide rationality into two types (*episteme* and *doxa*; on the one hand, and 'pure reason' and the 'rationality of Nature', on the other hand), I have in my critique of reason taken the human creative act — and not the cognitive act — as the Archimedean point from which reason and rationality may be differentiated into several types and innumerable strands which sustain the cosmos, life, and the orbit of specifically human life circumscribed by the radius of the human creative genius. Having already investigated the origin of Logos, we will now raise our sights to *the vision of the entire spread of Logos in its manifestation*.

I have already elsewhere ascertained the priority in the actual work of a scholar, scientist, philosopher of *vision* over 'proving' by argumentative methods. The proving of tiny fragments of cognition is meaningless unless they be placed within an all-embracing vision.

Here I want to bring out another crucial point further supporting this view, namely, the point that meaningfulness-rationality takes place, occurs, is 'opportune', congenitally implies *manifestation*. Forces, energies, virtualities, potentialities, proficiencies, and the like, become 'meaningful' as such and come as such to be 'activated', defining themselves in their nature only when assuming rational 'forms' in their manifestation. The formless, the mute, the soundless, the invisible, the transparent, the weightless are in themselves meaningless; their concepts acquire meaningfulness only in contrast to their opposites, with reference to their generic quality. The hidden acquires meaningfulness only with reference to the obvious. It is only in the gigantic manifestation occurring, according to our myth of the sudden explosion of the cosmos into being, that its generic forces acquired/revealed themselves in their forms. The hidden and the obvious, in their opposition, lay the basis for the enigmas of life and of the human being; the canceled has meaning only with respect to the manifest. The play between the two which is one of the threads in the dramatic play of human reason, lies at the very heart of the Logos of Life.

In philosophy we are so captivated by conjecture about the hidden and the obvious that we get absorbed in it, digging like a mole our way into ever deeper corridors. We embroil ourselves in labyrinths, in the obscure, and we forget about getting back to the light and the great vision of the manifest. It is time we turn to the great vision of all that is manifested. After we have seen how the human creative act spreads its constructive rays – like the sun at its zenith – gathering the relevant synergies from the virtualities of the Human Condition, on the one hand, and from the realm of bios, on the other, as well as constructive relevances from the laws and rules of the cosmos, then this vision of the universal play of forces takes precedence over the two classical approaches to rationality/reason mentioned at the beginning.

It takes precedence over the narrow focus on human cognition which dwells upon certitudes and fallacies which restrict the horizon to the world of one living species and has but limited grasp of comparable things among ants and eagles; this horizon bounded by the faculties of the human mind introduces inflexible and illegitimate borderlines between man and the bios, nature and cosmos. Our approach, however, supersedes the classical approaches in that by it we gain access to the hitherto ignored or little considered unity-of-everything-there-is-alive. Carried by the rays of the human creative act, we reach beyond the limits of the human cognitive grasp and enter directly into the channels of our human participation in the existence/subsistence progress of life of the universe. No doubt, cognition makes preparatory forays into the inner workings of the universal forces. It fails, however, to reveal our Human Condition as *a major station in life's advance*. The overall play of bios and cosmic forces and laws in our innermost workings appears in the manifestation of the Human Condition which is incomparably fuller and of the essence than whatever our cognitive grasp with its abstract forms and approximating conjectures may yield.

Within the full panorama extending before and within us opened to view by our approach, we see clearly the fallacy of the classical philosophical approaches. We realize a sharp division, nay, sharp distinction, between the rationalities of the cosmos, life, nature, and those of human creative genius cannot be made; further, we see that cognitive rationalities are just a specific modality of human creative genius, and that in turn the human being in all his functioning *is himself a manifestation of the forces, powers, constructive rules, and proficiencies of bios, life, and the cosmos.*

Vindicating a metaphysics of manifestation over classical epistemology
Cognition on trial

Before we enter into the exfoliation of the vision of Life, we will probe further into the manifestation of the Logos of Life in its underpinnings as we sustain the contrast between cognition and the creative experience of man.

To begin with, let us state that while in cognition we are caught in the intelligible rationalities constituting the specifically human universe of life, society, and culture. Through the human creative act, which gathers all the life proficiencies, we discover, in contrast, innumerable threads of rationalities sustaining the entire life system which lies within the schema of cosmic forces and the carrying on of life's progress; these rationalities, manifest themselves through the genesis, growth and advance of life. Cognition, having its fulcrum in the human mind, meets with the manifestation of life, especially with life's individualizing genesis; cognition and the individualization of bios constitute, thus, just two different poles through which the Logos of Life processes its rational life routes. The creative act of the human being is the meeting point of the two. Through the investigations of the workings of life as it appears in the creative act of the human being we may discover the shortcomings of cognition. We may also see its hitherto shadowed features in a novel, revelatory light.

The very question of the conformity of our cognition of things, beings, events and processes, of all from our surrounding world to their assumed 'objectivity', that is, to their status independent of the cognitive processes —

the crucial question around which all the epistemological questions turn — appears in this perspective to be itself inadequately formulated. Already Edmund Husserl nurturing some hints at the inventive nature of the mind, rejected radically any identification of cognition so understood with the 'constitution' in which, according to him, the objectivities were formed and devised; the referential dependence of the cognitive processes (understood as constructive) upon any assumed 'referent' lying outside of the cognitive process is thereby disclaimed. Objectivity as such is shown by Husserl to be precisely the effect of constitution. The assumption of a direct correlation of the cognitive process with an 'object' or 'thing' lying beyond the 'object of cognition' that would represent it and mark the end of the fulfilment of this process seems to be an effect of an undue and hasty narrowing of the focus that cognition commands, and of a forgetting — or ignoring of — the fact that cognitive consciousness is, first of all, just an overgrowth of the multiple functions of human consciousness, even if it be the major one.

Cognition among the life-functions
When we envisage cognitive consciousness within the entire field of individualizing life opened to us by the creative act, and, consequently, within the evolutive progress of types, we follow consciousness from its emergence as it takes on progressively various degrees of complexity. On the rebound, we discover the dependencies and existential interconnections of the cognitive processes with the rationalities of the life process. From the simplest phases of life, from reactivity to sensitivity, to psyche, consciousness surges as a functional complex prompted by the inner workings of self-individualizing life as an organ necessary for processing life itself — an organ stemming from nature, belonging to nature, remaining in its service. Consciousness has reached its highest level in full-fledged human experience and self-awareness. In this perspective we see that the clear, distinctive intentional intelligence proper to human consciousness is the crowning point of the evolutive progress of individualizing life, but also that *at all phases of life's complexity there is essentially present a network of intelligence at work.* Following the creative tentacles of the self-individualizing progress of life, it seems that the simplest forms of life show already a shadow of intelligent activity, that is, of *intelligence understood as a sensing reactivity to inner or outer stimuli, as a*

modality of reason which sets itself apart from the rationalities governing cosmic and pre-life functional spheres.

Here we have reached the culminating point of our inquiry. The human intelligence proper to intentional constitution is inventive and creative in establishing spheres of life with rules, laws, and structures of a flexibility unprecedented in the evolving course of life. But despite the operative input of the main engine of the Human Condition, that is, *Imaginatio Creatrix* and the creative act which seems to soar above all the regulations and constraints of bios, loosening or breaking its ties, and in spite of the fact that the distinctly human intellectual qualities set the human being free from the confining provinces of instinct, again, allowing him to exercise freedom through his power of invention and leave restrictions behind as his imagination takes wing, yet — and here lies the insight to which this discussion leads — cognition/constitution does not introduce rationality per se into the orbit of life; it constitutes merely a new phase of intelligence within the spread of life.

The integrating vision

This type of intelligibility so extraordinarily different from the rationalities of the cosmos, bios, nature as well as from the processes or the simpler life functions cannot, in the last account, be set apart from them. What cognition puts asunder, what epistemology, believing in narrowing the focus and splitting the hair in ten to ensure artificial certitude, separates, the creative vision, by drawing upon the very source of all in the differentiated powers of Logos, encompasses in a discrete unity. We have to recognize, with Pascal, the grandeur of the human being. And yet as autonomous as human creative powers are in the full gamut of their 'vocal', 'graphic', 'motile', 'emotive', 'sentient' metamorphoses and in the infinitely varying voices of their expression (in marked contrast to the mute and stereotypic rationalities of the cosmos), and as revelatory of the universe in and around us are the thrust of conscious intelligence (while the rationales of the forces and powers of bios are bound by narrow tasks and repetitive cycles), it cannot be overlooked that the wondrous faculties of the human being even as they inventively and creatively transform and expand Life's orbit, and even as they have the power to open an entirely novel sphere with respect to the simple realm of bios, are the manifestation of life, nature, and the cosmos themselves, being the most striking affirmation of their powers and driving forces.

What we want to argue here is that in the novel perspective which here gives a radical anthropologic-metaphysical treatment to the nature and role of the creative function of the human being, cognition is put on trial and a radical change of perspective occurs. Instead of choosing cognition as the entry to philosophical investigation, we have opted for the creative act of man, opening then a diametrically opposed door. Through this door we have entered into the workings of life itself. Cognition proves to be just one of the moments — a crowning one, to be sure — of the functioning of life.

By this discussion we have been moving toward the discovery of *the manifestation of the Logos of Life in its accomplishments* — that is, toward a metaphysical modality of inquiry into reason and rationality — and contrasting it with one of the factors of that manifestation, the cognitive-epistemological modality. This vision, which places all of the perspectives on life within their assumed common ground, does not imply, nor does our argument warrant, any hasty adoption of naturalistic, vitalistic, or pantheistic views. In the final analysis which lies far ahead still, life itself might turn out to be beyond these categories, necessitating and calling for a special formulation.

The hidden vortex of the manifestation

Virtuality/actualization; the outward and the inward. Can we in any way describe the significance of 'manifestation' other than in contrast to its opposite the 'hidden'? In the circularity of their meaningfulness, crossing from hidden to manifest is first of all bringing out of hiding, but this implies that what is thus coming out of obscurity into the light has already been present in its fullness. When we talk about the manifestation of the Logos through life, we mean indeed, the works of Life seen in full light. But our very revelation of life is grounded in the notion of the progressive genesis of life, that is, in the conjecture of a passage from the realm of pre-life to a breaking forth in the crystallization of life.

Furthermore, the crystallization of life is partly synonymous with what Husserl called 'presencing' (*Vergegenwartgung*). Crystallization means the formation and implies simultaneous or successive steps — actually both — resulting in motion, and bringing about temporality. Here seems to lie the very knot of factors by which manifestation may be grasped — or approximated —

in its nature. 'Presencing' means the first, the clear, diaphanous appearance, apparition of intentional objects within the vast horizon, internal as well as external, of the human intentional universe; this 'apparition' is understood as an end result of the entire intentional process. Nevertheless, in our perspective we have to envisage presencing as also occurring apart from the constitutive/cognitive processes, apart from subjectivity. 'Presencing', which in the subjective sphere means from 'presentification' to ... 'appearing to us', means the progress of life's crystallization in the sphere of life's genesis; there is a passage from a virtual state, from the atemporal 'hidden', to the appearance that brings about temporality as it takes shape within a temporal phase and expands the dimension of space. The manifestation of Life consists precisely in this passage from the virtual to actualizing, self-presencing temporalization.

However, drawing upon what I discussed earlier in my cosmology (*Why Is There Something Rather Than Nothing* [Assen: Royal Van Gorcum, 1967]), in the passage from the virtual to a crystallization in the cosmos and in the realm of bios, progress is inner-outer oriented. And yet, the 'inner' workings of the cosmic forces remain cancelled; hidden, they explode into light only when attaining formative effect on a space/time axis.

Herein lies a distinction between the manifestation of life and that of the cosmic rationalities. The inner-outer orientation of the life processes leads in self-individualization-in-existence to a double dimensionality which opens and unfolds: the 'outer', the spatio/temporal, the world of movement, formation, duration and succession, of the spatio-temporality of all cosmic rationalities and the 'inner' manifestation proper which occurs concurrently within the living individual and makes up the other side of the coin, namely, the psychic forms of establishing human intelligence in the specifically human universe of existence. Let us emphasize that it is the inner/outer direction of all life or prelife processes which offers the axis for manifestation, as much as it is the spatio/temporal expansion that accounts for its forms, shapes, 'appearance', and presentification.

To conclude and set the stage for manifestation itself, let us summarize. As we follow the unfolding individualization of life, we find the Logos of Life expanding in innumerable modalities setting off from the universal schema from which life surges and then, projecting progressively, articulations for life's unfolding from its smallest and simplest forms through more complex forms to its highest complexity, that attained in the human creative phase.

When, proceeding in the contrary direction, we gaze out from the peak of the expansion of the Logos, that is, from the human creative phase, from us in whom the Logos of Life is differentiated into infinite strands through rationalities which are autonomous with respect to bios, we discover human consciousness to be the center of its work, as it processes all rationalities in all directions so that human cognitive intelligence crowns the work of creation.

Raising our sites to the metaphysical plane, we are able at last to put the epistemological plane in its proper position and to place the question of reason in its proper perspective, for manifestation covers the entire spread of the Logos as it extends now in one direction from its central point, which is the origin of life, and ramifies in its unfolding and again in the other direction, toward the cosmic logos, going from the origin of life backwards to pre-life conditions indicative of the constitutive network of the realm of life and reaching the cosmic laws upon which life's forms and play of energies are suspended. All life is suspended upon the cosmic parameters. *Cosmic* Logos/Logos of *life*/the logos of specifically *human* intelligence all of these three perspectives upon reason and rationality radiate in life's manifestation.

12 ECOPHILOSOPHY AND PARENTAL EARTH ETHICS (On the Complex Web of Being)

H. Odera Oruka
University of Nairobi, Kenya

Calestous Juma
African Centre for Technology Studies, Kenya

The Judaeo-Christian view of nature which has permeated Western philosophical thought has nurtured a form of possessive individualism which is disrupting the complex web of being in which humans are a part. The Judaeo-Christian ethic has placed humans apart from nature, a factor that has contributed to global environmental degradation. There is a need for a shift towards a new epistemological outlook in which humankind is viewed as part of a complex and systematic totality of nature. This chapter argues for an ecophilosophical approach which recognizes the totality of (spatial, temporal, spiritual and other) interlinkages in nature. We illustrate the importance of taking an ecophilosophical approach with an exposition of 'parental earth ethics'.[1]

Ecology and philosophy

> The Environment Crisis facing humanity is due in part to the philosophy of possessive individualism, a philosophy which is spreading in today's World as pluralistic democracy and free market economy become the dominant political and economic norms for humanity.[2]

It is appropriate to begin this chapter with this quotation from one of the distinguished scholars of philosophy in the Western world. It is now generally known that major concerns of the debate on environmental ethics in the West have been: (i) whether ethics should be restricted to human beings or whether non-human sentient-beings should also be subjects and agents in the domain of ethics, and (ii) whether any other matters in nature such as hills, rocks, rivers, also have moral value. If so, then ethics becomes ecocentric rather than anthropocentric.[3]

By destroying paganism, Christianity made it possible to exploit nature in a mood of indifference to the feelings of the natural objects. It is often said that for animism the Church substituted the cult of saints. True; but the cult of saints is functionally different from animism. The saint is not *in* natural objects; he may have special shrines, but his citizenship is in heaven....The spirits *in* natural objects, which formerly had protected nature from man, evaporated. Man's effective monopoly on spirit in this world was confirmed, and the old inhibitions on the exploitation of nature crumbled.[4]

Peden introduces one special view of the 19th-century American philosopher, Francis Ellingwood, (1836-1903) who argued for a philosophical shift from the anthropocentric conception of nature with its philosophy of possessive individualism to universalism based on the theory of the organic constitution of all life. A position is essentially individualistic, Peden writes, following Abbot, if it 'seeks the ideal end of individual life' in the primary ethical welfare of the individual. While on the other hand, a position is 'essentially universalistic' if it identifies the ideal end with the ethical welfare of humanity, with individuals being a part of humanity.[5]

Ethics traditionally (at least in the West) has concentrated on the ideal of the individual while ignoring the insights provided by the biological, physical and social sciences. We wish to consider and harmonize the views of Abbot with the similar views of scholars who using other cultures, have contributed to the subject of humanity and nature. And on the basis of this consideration, we shall strive to argue that the views of these scholars form sufficient grounds for the assertion of the parental earth ethics. But just before we come to that, a brief sketch of the history or nature of ecophilosophy, which is defined here as the totality of the philosophy of nature, is pertinent.

Our approach differs from the traditional worldview in which nature is seen as existing solely for satisfying the material needs of humanity. This view is clearly articulated in the Bible which has over the centuries served as a source of divine rules for a large section of the Western world.

In Genesis (1: 27-28), for example, we are taught: 'So God created man in his own image, in the image of God he created him; male and female he created them. And God blessed them, and God said to them, "Be fruitful and multiply, and replenish the earth, and subdue it: and have dominion over the fish of the sea, and over the fowls of the air, and every living thing that moves upon the earth".'

Western political thought has been equally influenced by the ideas of the classical philosophers such as Aristotle who generated hierarchial justification for the dominance of humanity over nature. In *Politics,* for example, he asserts that:

> Plants exist [for the sake of animals, while] animals exists for the sake of man, the game for use as food, the wild, if not all, at least the greater part of them, for food and for the provision of clothing and various instruments. Now if nature makes nothing incomplete, and nothing in vain, the inference must be that she has made all animals for the sake of man.[6]

Cicero, echoing similar views in *De Natura Deorum* through his character, Bulbus the Stoic reinforces this view by arguing that '[W]hat other use have sheep save that their fleeces are dressed and woven into clothing for men?...Oxen?...their necks were born for the yoke and their broad powerful shoulders for drawing the plough.' This view was articulated in the teachings and Biblical interpretations of Thomas Aquinas and acquired the status of divine wisdom. [7]

We shall depart from the anthropocentric, utilitarian and hierarchical view of the relationship between human and nature and adopt a holistic outlook in which everything is related to everything else. This inter-relatedness requires a corresponding philosophical approach that looks at nature in its totality and derives from it ethics that reflect this outlook. We shall refer to this exposition as *ecophilosophy.*

The development of ecophilosophy

The term *ecology* derives from the Greek word *oikos* which is supposed to mean a house. The earlier precursor to ecology was *œconomy,* which literally means household management. But when applied to nature, *œconomy* takes the form of the divine governance of the natural world. It is claimed that it was Sir Kenelm Digby who was the first to use the term *Œconomy* (1658).[8]

Gilbert White: Antecedents of ecophilosophy

The term *ecology* came into use in the 19th century as a better substitute for the old expression. Worster writes that '[t]he term ecology did not appear until 1866, and it took almost another 100 years before it entered the vernacular.'[9]

One of the earliest persons (in the West) to carry out the systematic study of flora and fauna was the Englishman, Gilbert White, who in 1789 published *The Natural History of Selborne*. This was a collection of letters on wildlife, seasons, and antiquities of White's Parish at Selborne.

According to White, '[n]ature is a great economist,' for she 'converts the recreation of one animal to the support of another!'[10] He adds that the 'most insignificant insects and reptiles are of much more consequence, and have much more influence in the economy of nature, than the incurious are aware of;....Earthworms though in appearance a small and despicable link in the chain of nature, yet, if lost would make a lamentable chasm.'[11]

The implication of White's observation is that we must be careful in the way we handle nature for it seems as if almost everything in it has value not just for itself but for the reality of the survival of the rest. This kind of religious-cum-stoical attitude to nature is a contrast to the views of other Western scholars such as Francis Bacon (1561-1626) who had earlier taught that 'the world is made for man' and that man is not made for the world. Bacon and even no less an institution than the Christian Church stood for exactly the opposite views to those expressed by White. They were for what Worster refers to as 'imperial ideology' of nature — where nature is a domain in which man must rule and exploit unchecked.[12] The position of Bacon and that of Christianity illustrate the Western anthropocentric view of nature.

Carl von Linné: Reverential awe of nature

Despite the onslaught of the dominating Western philosophy of irreverent exploitation of nature by man, thinkers like White were not without support from some persons of genius. The Swedish pioneer-botanist, Carl von Linné (latinized as Linnaeus) lent most of his great mind to the discovery and systematization of nature. Linnaeus wrote much, but one of his most admired essays was *The Œconomy Of Nature* (1749). From this we are taught that: 'we understand the all wise disposition of creator in relation to natural things, by which they are fitted to produce general ends, and the reciprocal uses'. In this arrangement, living beings 'are so connected, so chained together that they all aim at the same end, and to this end a vast number of intermediate ends are subservient.'[13] So for Linné, all of animate nature is bound together in a common interest 'by the chains of substance that link the living to the dead, the predator to its prey, the beetle to the dung on which it feeds.'[14]

Although Linné is known in some versions of his work to have postulated that all the arrangement of nature is designed by God for the ultimate benefit of humans, this was a mere gesture to please or reconcile his views with the forces of the anthropocentric view of nature. Living in the post-Baconian scientific world and in a dominating Christian era, Linné could not help avoid such a 'tongue-in-cheek' compromise with his community. We can thus ignore this aspect of his views and adopt the deeper aspect, i.e., his views about the inter-connectedness of the ecology of nature.

Charles Darwin: A special link in ecophilosophy

We regard ecophilosophy as the totality of the philosophy of nature. In this sense ecophilosophy is broader than such subjects as environmental studies and environmental ethics. Environmental studies have so far, restricted themselves to the study of the earth and the atmosphere. Environmental ethics has not gone much beyond the attempt to consider the possibility of extending ethics from human beings to the non-human creatures on earth.

Ecophilosophy must include the totality of both human-made as well as non-human-made philosophy about nature and the totality of the universe. Some of the non-human philosophies are studied and adopted by human beings, but such philosophies still remain non-human made. Humans have derived metaphors from the non-human world to enrich their own understanding of the world they live in or create. For example, they have derived metaphors on organizations that ensure collective living under one sovereignty from the ants. They have also derived the sense of the philosophy and technology of flying from the birds.

In ecophilosophy there is a significant link and affinity between the philosophies of White, Linné and Darwin, the father of the theory of evolution.[15] This link can be expressed as that of the earth with all its benefits as the common good for all the creatures. So that even the gains each one of the species can have as its absolute and exclusive possessions are in reality historically limited.

The observation goes well with Darwin's postulation that 'no one species can hold a particular place in the economy of nature for ever. At every moment each place is up for grabs and sooner or later a replacement will be found and the old occupant shoved out of the circle to perish alone.'[16] Now, and for beings which claim to be rational and visionary such as humans, it would appear sensible to co-operate with those who might one day replace them by the law of nature rather than turn and see their privileges as absolute and eternal possessions. Darwin's philosophies of 'conflict in nature' and the 'survival of the fittest' do not in any way, if we take a deeper conception of nature, contradict the position of White and Linné.

The practice of the survival of the fittest passes only within the level of subservient, species-limited end, but for the ultimate end the survival of the fittest is but a mere passing means to the ultimate arrangement or development of nature. Thus, Linné's observations that living beings are so connected that they all aim at the same end, link consistently with Darwin's argument that '[n]ature is web of complex relations...and no individual organism or species can live independently of that web. A parallel assumption was that even the most insignificant creatures are important to the welfare of their conjoining species.'[17] He acknowledged that even if they are not essential members of society now, some time in the past they have been and are therefore part of the historical chain of being.

Darwin's theory, like that of Linné, was indeed based on ecology and not on some form of genetics. It is notable that Darwin's thinking was to a large extent inspired by social theorists such as Herbert Spencer. The interplay between social theory and ecological thought is complex and warrants a separate assessment.[18]

The White-Linné-Darwin ecological perspective contrasts sharply with the Judaeo-Christian perspective of nature.[19] The latter we wish to refer to as the *imperial ecophilosophy* as a contrast to the former which we wish to term as the *common-earth ecophilosophy*.

Ecophilosophy in other cultures

Abbot was the first American philosopher to support Charles Darwin.[20] Abbot developed a philosophy that rejected idealism given Darwin's revolution and emphasized experience and reason as the basis for all knowledge. Considering the situation facing humanity in his day, Abbot became convinced that a shift from individualism to universalism was required as the basic principle of ethical theory.[21]

Abbot's position was a grand shift in Western philosophy from the individually centred position emanating from the philosophies of Western classics such as Aristotle, Kant and Hegel: The root of the ethical individualism of Kant and Hegel is found in the Aristotelian theory of universals in metaphysics.[22] For Kant the individual is a universally self-legislating mind declaring the categorical imperative as the source of all moral law. For Hegel, following Kant, the individual is a self-legislating will in a universal perspective and there is really no ethical authority over the subjective conscience of the individual.[23]

What Abbot brought to Western philosophy is the view of the organic constitution of all life as a shift from individualistic theories. This is the notion that every organism functions partly for the others — this means that, it is both a means and an end to itself and to others.[24] The truth of organic constitution implies that the proper principle in human life and in nature in general is the principle of reciprocity. Abbot writes in his work, *Scientific theism*: 'Reciprocity between the individual and the society is well formulated in the old saying... "each for all and all for each."'[25] Thus, Peden adds, reciprocal justice is the social ideal; it seeks to cultivate in each organism individual differences while subordinating these differences to the universal social ideal of reciprocal justice.

The Indian dharma

Pappu contrasts the basic issues in Western environmental ethics with the basic issues in Indian philosophy.[26] Ethics in Indian philosophy is not human-centred, but *dharma*-centered. All life is sacred, and the ethical relationship between humans and animals is one which demands equality. All natural objects such as trees, hills, rivers and stones are sacred and deserve respect. In Indian philosophy humans are in nature not against nature.

Morality is conceived as an aspect of *Rta*, and *Rta* is the eternal law of the universe which when applied to nature becomes the natural law and when applied to living beings becomes the moral law. *Rta* as a concept joins together with *dharma*, which means that which holds together. Pappu's claim is supported by Singh, who writes: 'Gandhi presented a manifesto of a counter culture of plain living and high thinking and ecological balance between nature and man.'[27]

Hawaiian cosmology

Gruver writes that the traditional concept of family in the Hawaiian Islands embraces a system of social relationships that was essentially pan-Polynesian.[28] In Hawaii, family means *ohana* which comprises a matrix genealogical kinship that extends to include all elements of creation. Both human beings and the rest of nature occupy a position of parity that originated from environmental union of the *earth* and the *sky*.

These two are named *Papa* (mother earth) and *Wakea* (the sky father). There are interesting details given in this oral narration of Hawaiian cosmology on how all the islands of Hawaii were given birth to and how the totality of nature is intertwined.

Dogon cosmology

Anyanwu argues that the Dogon conceptions of humans, nature, society and the universe offer a unitary and an organic view of reality in which humans, nature and society are continuous with the universal creative process.[29] This cosmology emphasizes unity in diversity. It regards myths, religions, morality, politics and economics as important forces which integrate the individual with the community.

Wiredu refers to the traditional African practice of communally based life.[30] In this practice, land — the most fundamental means of livelihood — belongs not to the individuals but to the clan. The clan itself is thought of as consisting of members currently living, those in the world of the ancestors and those not yet born. All these categories of people have a psychological reality that greatly influences the thoughts, feelings, behaviour, decisions and relationships in the community. The earth or the immediate environment on which our lives are based is thus a common good for all.

The foregoing texts lend us some solid scientific and philosophical ground on which to postulate pan-organism as the basic truth underlying all nature. This basic truth has two major philosophical implications. First, it means that all aspects of nature are interconnected, so that the ecological activities are a network. So a break or imbalance in one aspect has serious consequences in other aspects of the domain. Secondly, it exposes the empirical-*cum*-ethical plausibility of the principle of the earth as a common good to all mankind and to all creatures.

This principle is seriously objected to by those who favour exclusive individual or national survival as the fundamental truth or reality in all human and natural relations. Let us refer to this as the principle of 'exclusive individual or national survival'. One philosophical derivative of this principle is the 'life boat ethics'. This is an ethics which stands in the way of formulating a new ethic that is built on ecophilosophy i.e. the parental earth ethics.

Parental earth ethics

Ecophilosophy can provide a practical basis upon which to formulate a new ethics that would take into account the complexity and totality of nature. This would be a parental earth ethics. Parental earth ethics is not simply a product of intellectual enquiry. It is the basis upon which different cultures around the world base their environmental perceptions. The ethics can be presented in the form of principles and rules.

Imagine a family with six children. Two of the six are relatively rich and four generally poor. Among the rich, one is extremely rich while among the poor, three are very poor. The reasons for the differences in status have to do partly with the family history, partly with personal luck and partly with individual talents. Though the children have different and diverse possessions, they have certain things in common such as parents (whether alive or deceased). They are also common in that each of them has status and achievements based on the teaching which the family as a whole provided. Some made better use of that education while others may have squandered it.

The children find that their lives and relationships are guided by the unwritten ethical laws which can best be summarized under two main principles: (i) parental-debt (or bound) principle (PP), and (ii) individual luck principle (IP).

Parental debt principle

This principle consists of four related rules dealing with family security and dignity, parental debt, and individual and family survival.

The family security rule states that the fate and security (physical or welfare) of each member of a family is ultimately bound up with the existential reality of the family as a whole. Any one of the six members may, for example, be arrogant and have enough to claim self-sufficiency and independence from the rest. However, eventually the person of the person's own progeny may experience a turn of events which could make them desperately in need of protection from the family.

History abounds with such examples. Both the Roman and the Ottoman empires disintegrated and their children and dependents sought their security and fate elsewhere. Western Europe was liberated from economic ruin after the Second World War by a power from outside her borders. And today the former Soviet Union is desperately looking for rescue even from such a small power as Italy.

The kinship shame rule is that the life conditions of any member of the family affect all the others materially and emotionally, so no member can be proud of his or her situation however 'happy', if any member of the family tree lives in squalor. There is a partial non-earthian application of this rule in our current world: European powers are more inclined to help fellow Europeans out of their squalor than they are prepared to do the same for some Third World country. Today, for example, Russia and Eastern Europe are a greater concern of the West than the rest of the world including China.

The parental debt rule assumes and explains the organic relationship and debt between the family members: Whichever member of the family is affluent or destitute owes his fortune or misfortune to the parental and historical factors inherent in the development of the family. Hence, within the family no one alone is fully responsible for his affluence nor for his misfortune.

The individual and family survival rule states that no member of the family, given the above rules, has any moral obligation to refrain from interfering with the possessions of any brother or sister who ignores the obligation to abide by the rules of the family ethics. This rule allows the disadvantaged to demand assistance from the affluent, but it also allows the creative and hardworking members of the family to repossess underdeveloped possessions of the idle relatives and develop them for the welfare of humanity and for use by posterity.

The individual luck principle
This is made up of three constituent rules dealing with personal achievement,

personal supererogation, and public law. *The personal achievement rule* states that what a member possesses is due mainly to the person's special talents. This is a kind of family individualism which disregards historical experience and the organic constitution of the family. *The personal supererogation rule* provides that every member has a right to do whatever he or she wishes with his or her possessions. Finally, the *family public law rule* states that any member of the family who contravenes the right of another member as given by the second principle will be subject to the family public law, and would be punished or reprimanded and ordered to restore justice.

The parental debt principle takes precedence over the individual luck principle, in case of a conflict between the two. And this is as it should be. Why, for example, would we not see it as senseless that an individual member of a family would want to do anything she wishes with her possessions, while a number of her kith and kin may be in desperate need of help.

The basic ethical rationale for why the parental debt principle takes precedence is as follows: the individual luck principle (IP) is supported fundamentally by the 'right of first occupation', personal luck and achievement, i.e., the veil of fate. But the first principle (PP) springs from the fact of organic unity between the children, the common pool of their wealth (whatever their differences in possessions) and the need for their common security.

The ethics of common sense shows that when in any given family or community, matters of common wealth, and common security conflict with matters of the personal possession, luck or achievement, the former must prevail over the latter.

There is no country in which, for example, an individual institution would be safe-guarded if it endangers the security or the economy of the nation. And it is also clear that no country would accept the wish or a will from one of its citizens which stipulates that upon death all his achievements, however dear to the country, should be exterminated or kept out of use by anybody. The reason for such a will would be that those achievements are personal and hence, the personal supererogation rule is to prevail. The objection to the will can only be supported by invoking the issues of common origin, common security and common wealth.

We hope it is clear that the earth or the world is a kind of a family unit in which the members have kith and kin relationship with one another. So far, our discussion is driven towards the claim that the earth is a common wealth to all humanity.

We are prepared to concede that the world has no sovereign. But this does not affect the claim that planet earth—not the world—is a common good or heritage for all humankind. The question of the right by the first occupation or personal achievement does not overrule this truth. If it did, then it would make no sense to accept the territorial rights of the Europeans who migrated to the Americas after Christopher Columbus 'discovered' that continent over five hundred years ago.

The territorial rights and sovereignty in the Americas would, in that case, rightly and legitimately belong to the indigenous Indians. However, the reality today is such that indigenous Indians have no more a legitimate claim to that part of the earth than the migrants who invaded it five hundred years ago.

Again, if the right of first occupation or generally the veil of fate is to prevail over the principle of the earth as a common good for all humankind, then all that was procured through the colonization of such places like Africa and India should have been returned to these former colonies a long time ago. But nowadays it seems it does not make sense to demand that such resources be returned.

On colonialism, what we lament is the fact that those who developed themselves by it have turned their backs on those they colonized and now claim that they (the former subjects) have no share in or claim to any of their current possessions. But given the organic constitution of life and the principles of parental earth ethics, the former colonies have a legitimate claim to such possessions.

Conclusion

We wish to conclude by attempting to answer several objections which we foresee as coming from some of our readers. One such objection would be that the earth is not a common good in the sense of sharing whatever we have gained from it with everybody; the earth is a common good only in the sense that it is an open field for the survival of the fittest.

We have already cautioned against a crude interpretation of Darwin's theory of the origin of species. A more detailed interpretation reveals that nature is a web of complex relations and that no particular species can exist independent of that web. 'Survival of the fittest' may sound correct when we limit ourselves to subservient (personal, or national) ends. Such limitations have beguiled some nations to believe that their given historical domination of others would last forever.[31]

The Third Reich of Hitler was to last 1,000 years. But it lasted for only 12 years. The Roman empire of course lasted a long time, but it did not last forever. Today the descendants of (say) the British empire would surely feel some relief and pride in any historical revelation of any good which the empire did to the colonies. For it is precisely from the goods not the evils done by colonization that makes former subjects tolerant and at times even friendly to the descendants of their former oppressors.

So when we take not the subservient ends of nations, but the ultimate or organic ends of all nature, no particular species or nation could be the fittest or weakest in accordance with the historical organic shifts of nature. Perhaps what all nations which are rich and powerful need to do is to invest in the pool of service to the rest of the world, so that when their historical turn or shift to oblivion comes, others may remember them with compassion. This would be a parental earth insurance policy.

The other objection we foresee is that parental earth ethics is a quasi-religious exaggeration of the kinship relationships between all people of the earth: that it is a doctrine for preachers in churches but not relevant to the real world of the political and economic chess board.

The kinship issue is not being dragged into this matter just as a moralization of the virtue of declaring all human beings, and all species in nature as 'brothers and sisters'. It is given here as an assertion derived from the ecological truth about nature and the ultimate common fate of all creatures living on planet earth. Without the element of kinship or organic unity of nature none of the arguments of the current environmental protectionists would be valid for all peoples and nations. But given the organic unity of nature the arguments make sense, for it is clear that the pollution and the degradation of sections of the earth are likely to have consequences in the rest of the globe. This is the concern that led to the convening of the Earth Summit in Brazil in 1992. That meeting was a symbolic family gathering.

The last objection we wish to consider is one which claims that we are placing creatures such as even earthworms in the same moral level as human beings. Equality of all human beings may be understandable, but how about equality (say) between a head of state and an earthworm? The earthworm does not demand or require equality with a head of state. But nature demands that we do not extinguish earthworms as a species. Earthworms are a part of the biodiversity without which even a head of state would be non-existent.

There are basically two main reasons in the need for the sustenance of biodiversity: One is that all sentient-beings have an intrinsic value, and the other is that human life on earth is doomed to perish if we destroy biodiversity. Although the first reason is still too remote for most people to grasp, the second reason is and should be today common knowledge among reasonable adult human beings. We propose *parental earth ethics* as a basic ethics that would offer a motivation for both a global environmental concern and a global redistribution of the wealth of nations.

Notes

1. This expression was first employed in H. Odera Oruka's paper in *Quest*, Vol. VI, No. 1, June, 1993, as a reaction to G. Gardin's Life-boat ethics'.
2. Peden, this volume.
3. Rolston, 1988. For a classic review of the responsibility of humankind towards the environment, see Passmore, 1990.
4. White, 1967 p. 1203.
5. Peden.
6. Aristotle, *Politics*.
7. For a detailed examination of the ethical implication of this view, see Johnson, 1991.
8. Worster, 1985, p. 37.
9. *Ibid.*, p. xiv.
10. *Ibid.*, p. 7.
11. *Ibid.*, pp. 7-8.
12. Bacon, 1603. *Temporis Partus Masculus*.
13. Worster, 1985, pp. 37-38.
14. *Ibid.*
15. For a study of Darwinian Philosophy, see Ruse, 1986.
16. Worster, 1985, pp. 157-158.
17. *Ibid.*, p. 156.
18. Young, 1985; Heyer, 1982.
19. For a detailed analysis of the implications of the Judaeo-Christian ethic, see White, 1967.
20. Peden. this volume.
21. *Ibid.*
22. *Ibid.*
23. *Ibid.*
24. *Ibid.*
25. *Ibid.*
26. Pappu, this volume.

27. Singh, 1991.
28. Gruver, this volume.
29. Anyanwu, 1991.
30. Wiredu, this volume.
31. We see *parental earth ethics* as offering counter-examples to the sentiments of persons like Garret Hardin with their arguments under the *life-boat ethics* which find it senseless and suicidal for the rich nations to aid poor nations. See Hardin, 1974.

PART II

PHILOSOPHY, POLITICS AND LANGUAGE

13 DEVELOPMENT AND ENVIRONMENTALISM

Robin Attfield
University of Wales
Cardiff, U.K.

The days are receding when advocates of Third World development maintained that concern for the environment was a luxury which only developed countries could afford. A similar view sometimes surfaces from British conservative politicians when they claim that conservation and preservation can only be afforded out of the proceeds of development, as if at least the early stages of development could take place in their absence. There is, however, an increasing realization that the kind of 'development' which pollutes and sometimes undermines life-support systems is inimical to development worthy of the name. In this more enlightened approach, human interests tend to be paramount, but there is concern for the protection of the natural world, if only for prudential reasons.

Environmentalists, meanwhile, frequently regard development and its advocacy as the enemy which is to be opposed at all costs, or at least as often as possible. While this is not the posture of groupings such as the Green Parties of Britain and West Germany, it is often encountered in British environmentalist circles and is even more prevalent among environmentalist in North America and Australia. How deep this attitude goes depends in part on the underlying value theory and ethics professed or taken for granted, and partly on the locally accepted understanding of the causes of ecological problems and of the social and political conditions necessary to solve them. Accordingly, the ranks of environmentalists include some who recognize poverty as one of the causes of environmental deterioration and welcome sustainable development in the Third World. Yet the advocates of development still come in for criticism for caring about nature largely in the human interest.

In this chapter I shall try to explain why even the 'deeper' strain of environmentalists should support sustainable development (as opposed to undifferentiated growth), and are required to do so by their own principles, insofar as they are defensible. I shall also try to explain why developmentalists should equally support environmentalism, and support not merely its 'shallower' but also some of its 'deeper ' versions,[1] and will do so if they are consistent. This double project will also involve comparing and relating the critiques of current evils propounded by the two camps: the developmentalist critique of underdevelopment and its economic causes, and the deep environmentalist critique of anthropocentrism. Critiques improve by taking greater ranges of factors into account, and I shall claim that each of these critiques is in danger of neglecting the factors stressed by the other.

Applied philosophy can contribute to issues such as these by close attention to concepts and principles, and by tracing their implications. But to prevent the overlooking of the intricacy and complexity of the circumstances to which the concepts and principles must be supplied, I shall begin my discussion of what development involves by reference to an example drawn from *Orbit,* the magazine of the British Organization of Voluntary Service Overseas. There a volunteer in the cause of overseas aid to the Third World, Ian Craven, who worked for three years in Indonesia as an environmental officer for the World Wide Fund for Nature, adduces his own experience in rejecting the kind of conservation which would involve 'the total exclusion of any resource utilization' or 'the segregation of land from the local population for nature's protection in certain overstressed regions'. Granted the poverty of the tribal people of the Arfak Mountains with whom he was working, and the risk that, without some financial return from the forest, they would succumb to external economic pressures (presumably from timber companies), the establishment of a nature reserve there required, and in Craven's view justifies, the preparation of the local people on its management and in particular the collection for export of butterflies. Butterfly ranching involves the collection of 'eggs, caterpillars or cocoons... from areas enriched with the butterflies' plant foods'; they are then 'shipped to butterfly zoos, collectors, taxonomists and scientists around the world'. Since the butterflies are forest reliant and the local people know this, they thus have a strong interest in preventing the destruction of the forest. Craven's short article is entitled 'Profit for the poor'.[2] The role of timber companies in Indonesia is explained on the next page of the same number in an article by Jasper Zjilstra entitled 'Rainforest Reality'.[3]

Many developmentalists would be likely to applaud Craven's plan unreservedly, on the grounds that the basic problems of Indonesia are poverty and exploitation, and that for the tribal people in question this plan appears to alleviate poverty in some degree without the further exploitation which would be involved in the destruction of the native habitat and thus their way of life. The plan also involves their active participation, another hallmark of development which is of value both in itself and because of the self-respect and the increased autonomy of previously disadvantaged people which it is likely to bring. And developmentalists who are not apologists of timber-companies would add the pertinent point that the plan would help secure the forest for future generations of Indonesians, and may well be the only way in which that can be achieved.

Others, whether environmentalists or not, would want to ask a number of questions, for example about the extent to which the plan really does save the forest ecosystem from destruction. In particular we are not told how (if at all) it is proposed to ensure that the butterfly species in question do not become extinct, at least as far as sites in the Arfak Mountains are concerned. For if they were to become extinct the forest would be impoverished and at the same time the benefits to local people would prove unsustainable; in other words they would be thrust back into the same problem as at the outset. Thus the plan could be counterproductive even from a purely developmentalist's viewpoint.

Environmentalists of a quite moderate persuasion might well add a number of points. Thus we are not told that other forest species depend on the presence of these butterflies, whether through pollination or predation, and we need to know this to discover to what extent the forest genuinely escapes destruction. This relates to a more general question: how much 'resource utilization' is consistent with conservation? And even if the answer turns out to be 'quite a lot in this case', very little follows about whether conservation should not sometimes exclude the consumption of resources, and sometimes exclude even the use of consumable resources, and thus an actual prohibition of the human use of certain habitats. Anthropocentric (i.e. human-centered) reasons could sustain all these possibilities, but they become stronger still when the interests of nonhuman species are taken into account, as advocated by environmentalists of 'deeper' persuasions.

Some readers, particularly if they are also environmentalist, may by now be aghast at any amount of consideration at all being given to the cause of development, as opposed to none at all, especially if it can adopt such manifestations as this. But this is where the concept of development and the related moral obligations need to be brought into prominence. For I shall be arguing that there are obligations here to support and foster development which in any case cannot be disowned.

In social and economic connections it is easier to define underdevelopment than development. Underdevelopment is a condition of society where several of the following factors reinforce one another: malnutrition, high infant mortality, low levels of literacy, relatively high morbidity among the young and the middle aged, poor medical facilities, poor educational facilities, low levels of income per head and low levels of productivity per head. Development may be taken as either the process or the condition resulting from the process of moving away from the cycle of underdevelopment.

But not just any departure from one of the mentioned variables amounts to development. The obvious example is productivity: for mere economic growth need not, as such, involve or indicate development of any kind. A number of other implications flow from the definition, such as the need for the active participation of the people concerned in the process of development, if that process or its outcome is to be worthy of the name. But I have written about these matters elsewhere,[4] and should here move to a centrally relevant aspect of development (as just now defined), namely its necessary connection with justice. For injustice prevails where people's basic needs are avoidably unsatisfied; and except where underdevelopment is out of people's control, many people's basic needs are precisely unsatisfied in the circumstances of underdevelopment. There is thus a strong moral obligation incumbent upon those who have the ability to help or hinder the process anywhere (whether by action or by inaction) to promote some form of development, for not to do so is to perpetuate injustice. This obligation is obviously particularly strong in the cases of the members of the society in question; but, short of stronger countervailing obligations, it is a strong one for members of other societies who (individually or in concert) have the ability (whether by action or inaction) to help or to hinder the process.

To say this is certainly to assume that there can be relations of justice and injustice not only between members of one and the same society but also between different societies and their members. But this assumption cannot seriously be denied by anyone prepared to enter into moral discussion at all.

For if the basic needs of anyone count, so do the basic needs of anyone else, insofar as an agent can make any difference to them. The fact that the one person is a member of the same society and another is not makes no difference at all in this regard. Certainly there are further moral rules requiring agents to pay special consideration to the needs e.g. of members of their family, and rules which make good moral sense; but the nature of these obligations in no way implies that all obligations depend on some special relationship or other.

Correspondingly there is a like obligation to help remove oppression wherever it is found, to the extent of one's power, and insofar as this does not conflict with stronger obligations. But where underdevelopment is avoidable, there, whether beknowns or unbeknowns, oppression exists. Accordingly, at least where other things are equal (and quite often when they are not) there is a strong obligation to combat oppression. But this is a further way of showing that it is a moral obligation to support development wherever avoidable underdevelopment is to be found. It would not be obligatory to support any and every form of development, as there are alternative forms, and some are arguably better than others. (Thus there is no general obligation to support schemes to develop tribal societies in ways which would undermine their inherited cultures). But it is morally obligatory to support some form of development in each avoidable underdeveloped society.

But if so, the needs of the poor in Indonesia must be taken seriously, whatever our beliefs as environmentalists may be. It is morally unacceptable to claim, for example, that the needs of future generations for an intact rainforest there justify us in disregarding their current needs. For if future people's needs count, so do the needs of our contemporaries. Nor is it satisfactory to maintain that what fundamentally matters in morality is the integrity and stability of the biosphere, and that as human beings sometimes subvert this integrity and stability their interests can be disregarded for the sake of the greater good. This kind of misanthropy is sometimes to be found among ecological writers,[5] but everyone should be clear that is involves disowning the intrinsic value and moral significance of the well-being of every individual, and the valuing of everyone and everything according to its relation to the biosphere instead. In other words it is an attempt to disown all the requirements of justice. But is hard to believe that even those who from time to time swallow this ethic can seriously employ it in their own interpersonal dealings, much less in their attitudes to themselves.

In any case misanthropy of this kind is no part and no implication of what Arne Naess has called 'Deep Ecology' one tenet of which concerns the equal right of all creatures to live and blossom.[6] While I should not seek to defend this 'biospherical egalitarianism', I want to draw attention to some of its less problematic implications. For the creatures which are said to have the right to live and blossom certainly include nonhuman creatures, and thus insects such as butterflies. But they also include human beings, with their more complex possibilities for self-realization. According to this approach, then, while the different interests must sometimes be weighed up against one another, there is a strong case for upholding the interests of each and every human being, (especially as in conditions of underdevelopment) where these interests are significantly unsatisfied at present. Indeed Naess explicitly maintains that the Deep Ecology Movement takes into account the needs of the Third World, alongside the interests of future generations and of nonhuman species.

Some environmentalists, however, will now maintain that all this stress on the needs of human beings exhibits species discrimination, and thus reinforces the central underlying source of oppression, namely anthropocentrism. Why, it will be asked, should the problems of people be singled out as they have been above, to the neglect of nonhuman (and in particular those sentient nonhumans whom human beings exploit for food and in experiments)? A failure to recognize anthropocentrism for what it is fundamentally vitiates any ethic and any social programme, it will be alleged. Later in this chapter I shall try to explain how much there is to be said in favour of this appraisal of anthropocentrism. Here it is more relevant to point out that drawing attention to unsatisfied human needs is quite compatible with concern for the needs of nonhuman creatures, and need not involve neglect of them. Thus the humanitarian tradition has historically made a point of protesting not only at slavery, excessive working hours and the oppression of women and children, but also at the maltreatment of animals.

But no movement should allow itself to supply too one-dimensional a critique of oppression. I shall be returning to this point in a later connection, but in the present context its bearing is that those who recognize the evils of anthropocentrism have a distorted vision if they ascribe the world's evils to anthropocentrism alone. Such a critique neglects such other sources of oppression as economic exploitation, racism and sexism. Warwick Fox has some salient remarks about one-dimensional critiques of oppression, of which mention is now in place.[7]

Such simplistic critiques, according to Fox, suffer from two minor weaknesses, in respect of which they are 'not merely descriptively poor and logically facile' but also 'morally objectionable' One of these is 'scapegoating', by which all members of a particular class are targeted for criticism to an equal degree, whereas in fact some subclasses are much more responsible for oppression than others, and some subclasses of the targeted class are actively working to challenge ecological destruction or whatever form of oppression is envisaged. By targeting all members of the class which (in the short term) stands to gain from discrimination, scapegoating is objectionably 'over-inclusive'.

At the same time, simplistic critiques suffer from what Fox calls 'inauthenticity' and at the same time 'underinclusiveness'. For such analyses can lead to a denial of responsibility in cases where some responsibility should be accepted. Fox has in mind here critiques which focus in a unidimensional manner on capitalism or again, on patriarchy; for such critiques can serve to exonerate e.g. trade unionists or women of all responsibility for oppression of any kind; but his point is not without relevance to any critique which focuses simply on anthropocentrism, and fails to ascribe responsibility for oppression to those human groups and individuals (not excluding some unionists and some women) who have the power to act oppressively and do not hesitate to do so.

Fox's points here are well taken; a critique of global problems should neither be so blunt as to bestrew blame indiscriminately nor so unsubtle as to distract attention from genuine major sources of oppression, and tacitly to exonerate them accordingly. What is needed in a critique of social or of global problems is the kind of intelligent approach which takes into account a plurality of seats of power and sources of oppression, a variety of degrees of complicity, and a range of legitimations of unjustified hierarchies, all of which need to be challenged. Such an approach has the tactical advantage that, instead of writing off all males or all beneficiaries of capitalism or even the vast majority of human beings, it facilitates alliances between diverse subgroups which either suffer from oppression or are prepared to campaign against it. But tactical considerations apart, it has the intellectual and moral advantages of being more appropriate to the actual distribution of power in society (international society included) and more just.

While Fox is primarily objecting to writers and movements which neglect anthropocentrism and environmental destruction (a theme to which I shall return), his several remarks apply similarly to those who focus on anthropocentrism and environmental destruction to the exclusion of all else besides. For the same anti-discriminatory principles which underly e.g. the Deep Ecology stance of Arne Naess apply to other instances of discrimination, of the misuse of power and of oppression also. There is, indeed, a kind of inconsistency involved in excoriating the arrogance of humankind for its chauvinist treatment of all other species besides, and lifting not so much as a finger in protest at economic oppression, sexism and racism. It is not as if these latter misuses of power involved minor discriminations within this world elite, humanity; for in many cases discrimination against humans is at least as bad as the treatment accorded to nonhuman animals. It is certainly true that nobody can campaign about everything and that different people may rightly focus their energies on one campaign rather than another. But that is no justification for asserting or giving the impression that the same principles do not apply to oppression of different kinds.

The point may be reinforced by citing the definition of chauvinism given by Richard Routley (now Sylvan) and Val Routley (now Plywood). The Routleys used this designation of 'substantially differential, discriminatory and inferior treatment by humans of nonhumans' and this is a perfectly proper extension of the use of chauvinism'.[8] But if this kind of treatment by humans of nonhumans is chauvinism, then equally so is such treatment by humans of humans, especially in connection with discrimination on a nationalist or a racist basis, the original context of application (after all) of the term. And if substantially differential, discriminatory and inferior treatment is oppressive and unjustified in the one case, so (truistically) it must also be in the other.

Thus where an environmental philosophy (or 'ecophilosophy') is partly grounded, like that of the Routleys, in opposition to unjustified discrimination, or, like that of Arne Naess, in the advocacy of egalitarianism on a global scale (at least in principle), or, like that of John Rodman, on the need for liberation,[9] the same grounds require support for opposition to injustice and oppression in interhuman relations. This remains the case even among those who maintain that the root cause of ecological problems is population growth, reluctant as the holders of this kind of theory may be to support some of the steps to development advocated by those who are not so persuaded. For even theorists of this kind would be obliged by their principles to oppose the oppression of those humans who are already alive. Their support of development programmes would, however be more uninhibited if they came to recognize that the underlying cause of population growth is poverty, and that poverty is also one of the direct causes of ecological problems;[10] indeed, once these causal connections are granted, environmentalists have additional grounds for supporting the alleviation of poverty. But even if they are not recognized, such support is in any case obligatory on grounds of justice.

There is more of a problem, however, with environmentalists of two kinds, whose positions are prone to coincide in practice. One is the kind which regards humanity as a cancerous growth, so detrimental to other life-forms that the planet would be better off without it, or with drastically curtailed numbers. The other is the kind referred to above, which locates intrinsic value in the well-being of the biosphere as a whole, and determines the value of individuals and/or species by their contribution to this well-being of which the leading criterion is diversity. Since most humans contribute little to the integrity of the whole, and since humanity has been diminishing planetary diversity, human beings would on this basis be either of neutral or of negative value and should be treated accordingly. The first kind of position is sometimes supported on a consequentialist basis, in that humans are held to do more harm than good to life-forms overall; alternatively it can be harnessed to the ethical holism of the second kind. The second kind does not attach any value to the good of individual creatures or even life-forms, but derives its entire ethic from its collectivist and holist value theory. Both kinds may fairly be described as misanthropic, and both earn the designation, coined I believe by Murray Bookchin, of 'ecofascism'.

The first kind of misanthropic environmentalism has been put forward by Dave Foreman, a supporter of Deep Ecology,[11] and has attracted from Bookchin the charge that deep ecology is essentially a misanthropic enterprise.[12] Foreman maintains that the best way to help Ethiopia is to let people starve, and that this will minimize suffering and death in the long term. Fox, however, is happy to see Bookchin taking Foreman to task for these 'personal, unhistorical and abhorrently simplistic views on population control', and is quick to dissociate deep ecology from support for them. Indeed he quotes Naess as writing that 'faced with hungry children, humanitarian action is a priority, whatever its relation to developmental plans and cultural invasion'.[13] To Fox's criticism it may be added that any kind of positive consequentialism, in which intrinsic value is attached to worthwhile life, would be inconsistent with Foreman's conclusions while if Foreman is appealing to negative consequentialism, a theory which would also, depending on circumstances, support the elimination of all sentient life in the cause of preventing suffering, the unacceptable implications require the reaction of any normative theory of this kind, and thus of whatever negative consequentialist theory he may happen to be appealing to. Ecofascism, in short, cannot be defended by the harm to people which it is supposed to prevent. It is only fair to grant to Fox here that he well shows that deep ecology does not stand for any such misanthropic position.

As for the holistic version of misanthropic environmentalism, I have already published what I believe to be fatal criticism.[14] The central problem here is that no defensible ethic can assume the form which this kind of collectivist holism assumes, for its implications conflict with almost all the central cases of agreed ethical judgements and principles. This becomes particularly clear in connection with the instrumental approach which this position requires to be taken to all individuals. Thus whatever we say about the well-being of the biosphere and the desirability of diversity, we cannot defensibly say this. (These remarks do not, of course, subvert certain other positions in which axiological holism is combined with belief in the intrinsic value of worthwhile individual life: but there is no need to argue against such positions as these in the current connection.)

The conclusion which I draw from the consideration of these two versions of environmentalism is that they are indeed misanthropic, but that there are extremely strong grounds against adherence to either of them. To put matters another way, those forms of environmentalism which are essentially opposed to development are ones which intrinsically deserve to be re-examined, while the remainder require some degree of support for development insofar as their supporters are consistent, not to mention the regard which they ought to have for justice. (No doubt the obligation to uphold justice applies also to supporters of ecofascism, but they are likely to disown it).

One footnote is needed before I move on. It should be stressed that grounds for supporting development are *pro tanto* grounds for supporting sustainable development, i.e. the kind of development which avoids harm and loss to future generations and can be sustained indefinitely. Supporters of Deep Ecology are sometimes suspicious of sustainable development; but Arne Naess himself would seem to be selectively in favour of it, to judge from his article 'Sustainable Development and the Deep, Long Range Ecological Movement.[15] Indeed this is where Naess's remark about humanitarian action sometimes being a priority is to be found.

I now turn to the issue of whether supporters of development should also support environmentalism. Now there is not much of a problem about support for environmentalism in its shallower forms. Let us presume that the developmentalists in question are moderately well versed in the findings of ecological science and also accept what is argued in *Blueprint for a Green Economy* in terms of the considerable impact of environmental factors on a country's economy as well as of the considerable impact of the latter on the former.[16] They will, if so recognize that economic development requires not only the reduction of pollution and the conservation of natural resources, but also the preservation of a good deal of wilderness (e.g. wetlands and rainforest), all in the long-term interest of humanity. Indeed the degradation of the natural environment would at some point make economic life unsupportable while the loss of a species or an area of wetlands, being irreversible, involves a cost forever to whichever humans could have benefited therefrom. Thus sustainable development calls for preservationist measures even more strongly than development does, as such.

But these are just the kind of grounds which make environmentalists of the deeper persuasion suspicious, for they are compatible with an anthropocentric approach. And this may serve as a clue to the location of possible disagreement; for developmentalists are often reluctant to support campaigns conducted in the interests of nonhuman species or their members, particularly when so much human need remains unsatisfied. To some extent this would be a matter of priorities: nonhuman interests, it might be held, matter, but can wait. Others again might hold that they do not matter at all. And both schools of thought might well maintain that to focus on anthropocentrism in one's critique of the world's problems is to divert attention from significant evils such as inter-human oppression and the excesses of capitalism, and thus from the realities of power.

In practice, concern for human interests would bring such people into many a preservationist campaign. For humans have interests in preservation for the sake of scientific research as an end in itself, for the sake of its medical and agricultural applications, for recreation, contemplation and aesthetic enjoyment. Thus campaigns for the preservation of wildlife and the necessary habitats frequently have this kind of motivation. Yet in all these connections the natural world is regarded as nothing more than a resource whether laboratory, museum, playground, temple, cathedral or art gallery. To this catalogue might be added the symbolic value of natural objects such as high mountains, cliffs (like those at Dover) and untamed rivers; nature as emblem, or perhaps as mascot. Nevertheless where human interests are paramount, other human interests will often take priority over all of these. So if preservationist campaigns are supported by some people on these grounds and by others on deeper environmentalist grounds, the alliance will be an uneasy one. Sometimes indeed, the allies may part company, such as when preservationists urge (in Craven's words) 'the segregation of land from the local population for nature's protection'.[17] But this kind of segregation would be rejected not only by developmentalists, but also by the environmentalist movements of both Germany and India, to judge from Ramachundra Guha's excellent article 'Radical American Environmentalism and Wilderness-Preservation: A Third World Critique.'[18] Indian environmentalists tend rather to support forest preservation for the sake of preventing soil erosion and flooding, and generally for the sake of human beings as well as that of forest creatures.

Nevertheless to grasp the need to support environmentalism of a deeper kind than that of an anthropocentric preservationist, a developmentalist, like anyone else, would need to see the force of the critique of anthropocentrism. This would in no way involve abandoning other forms of negative critique, concerning oppression or hierachy for instance, any more than it would involve support for the kind of segregation which debars local people from their own countryside. Rather it would supplement such a critique, and broaden appreciation of the nature of social and global problems, and of what might count as solutions to them.

There are two ways to proceed. One is to point out the inconsistency (and sometimes hypocrisy) of opposition to human suffering which stops short at opposition to comparable suffering in animals, or to argue from the intrinsic value of human health, happiness and flourishing by analogy to there being intrinsic value in the health, happiness and flourishing of nonhuman, despite the differences between the natures of the different species convened. To discriminate on the basis of species for no good ground is just as arbitrary as to discriminate on the basis of race or sex for no good ground, as Peter Singer has long been arguing;[19] and to mete out treatment which is substantially differential and inferior on no better basis amounts to what Val and Richard Routley have called 'human chauvinism'[20] These are good liberal arguments, and none the worse for that; they deserve a hearing both from supporters of possessive individualism and from its most resolute enemies, and they call for radical changes not only at the level of individual behaviour but also at the levels of public policy in matters such as agricultural methods, fisheries and land use. But there is another route by which a negative critique of anthropocentrism can be commended, at least to developmentalists, and I shall attempt to expound it now.

The critique standardly advanced by developmentalists of the causes of persistent underdevelopment concerns systems of power relations. Both within and between societies, it is held, the terms on which economic and other transactions take place are so skewed that flows of resources pass from those in economically weaker positions to those in stronger positions, in the forms of rent, debt servicing and the relative prices of raw and processed commodities. These economic relations depend on relationships of power, and are perpetuated by them; not only do governments protect business corporations, landowners and local elites, but at the international level transnational corporations and the governments which support them have enough power to dictate terms to the governments of most developing countries. This system of economic and political relations sometimes actually benefits the poor, in that they would be even worse off without the investment and employment which it offers. But for all that it is profoundly exploitative. It is also mirrored in the power relations which often hold within families and between the sexes and the generations, and is thus prone to uphold the least desirable aspects of patriarchy and of gerontocracy.

This critique depicts a hierarchy of power relations, which does a lot to explain the persistence of poverty, and suggests that lasting solutions to social and global problems depend on a radical redistribution of power. Not all developmentalists, of course, subscribe to this critique, but very many would subscribe to at least parts of it, and this accounts for an insistence on exposing capitalism, sexism and the like for what they are. As the present project is to persuade developmentalists of a further point, I will assume the essential acceptability of this critique, at least for present purposes. But if that much is accepted, is it credible that the base of the hierarchical pyramid consists of rural and urban proletariats, subsistence farmers and the unemployed?. At each of the higher levels, interest-groups and classes profit from the humbler classes. Thus, as Bahro has been pointing out,[21] the working class in developed countries has considerably profited from the much more wretched condition of the poor of the Third World. But, as Bahro would readily agree, the lives of the poor (and to some extent of the relatively rich as well) have also benefited economically from transactions between humanity and other living creatures. Domestic animals have been used for traction, transport and food; wild animals are often hunted for their hides, fur or flesh; and forests have been eradicated for timber and for farming.

Now I am certainly not suggesting that the domestication of wild species of plants and animals is reprehensible; much less, with deep ecologists like Rodman, that domesticated animals should be phased out.[22] Technology in the forms of agriculture and medicine has contributed a great deal to making civilized life possible, and thus the liberation and flourishing of humanity. Nevertheless much civilized life has depended on the toil of animals, who, to quote St. Basil, 'bear, with us, the heat and burden of the day',[23] and much has depended, and continues to depend on animal deaths, in many cases before there has been time to develop the faculties proper to their kind, and often in unspeakable conditions. In the past, certainly, the system often gave some sort of dignity at least to some domesticated animals; and the use of wild species was sufficiently restrained as to be sustainable and to avoid too drastic damage to wilderness. But now two factors have intensified the time-honoured human use of nature, on the one hand an increase in what the World Bank calls 'absolute poverty' and on the other the extension, usually driven by the profit motive of economic activity on the part of corporations and governments to the furthest corners of the globe. (Of these developments both pressures from the timber companies and the project to ranch butterflies in the Arfak mountains are but tiny manifestations.) Population growth has exacerbated the problems caused by poverty, but as it is itself plausibly a product of poverty, there is no need to supplement the inventory of underlying problems in its regard. And, as according to the usual critique of developmentalists, poverty is itself a function of the global system of power relations, all the indications are that here we have the underlying cause, at least to the extent that the critique is to be credited.

If it is now added that the actions and policies *vis-a-vis* nonhuman creatures are no more inevitable or indispensable than most inter-human relations are in their present form, it becomes extremely difficult to resist the conclusion that these actions and policies often also amount to exploitation i.e. not just use, but unjustified use. The power system which pervades inter-human relations extends also to inter-species relations, and does not become any the more excusable in the latter connection (I have hitherto avoided the use of 'exploitation' in connection with treatments of nature, as it has both a morally neutral and a morally pejorative sense; but I am in a position to use the term without the need to qualify it.) And further, the processes which issue in exploitation within human relationships are identical with those which issue in unacceptable treatments of the natural world.

But if this is correct, then the critique adhered to by most developmentalists must itself be supplemented. For oppression turns out to be manifested not only in capitalism, sexism and racism, but also in anthropocentrism and human chauvinism. The iceberg of exploitation is even larger beneath the surface than is usually imagined; and, all along, it is habituating us to legitimate oppression, and to become hardened to it. Yet oppression is often a seamless whole, at least psychologically; when a callous disregard sets in for any one class, the possibility opens up of the parallel unquestioning acceptance of oppression at any other level. And this symbolic factor is yet another reason for supplementing and developing the critique for the developmentalist.

There is, indeed, a close analogy of the case presented for environmentalists to broaden their critique of oppression beyond anthropocentrism alone; the developmentalist critique needs to be broadened similarly so as to include anthropocentrism. The reasons for this include the requirement to be consistent with one's own principles, the recognition that both underdevelopment and ecological problems have a common source and are causally interrelated, and the symbolic links between the different forms of oppression, and again, between the various campaigns which oppose it. A further reason would consist in the requirements of justice. This reason has not till now been deployed, as there is a widespread view (held, for example, by John Rawls)[24] that nonhuman creatures fall outside the scope of justice. But to the extent that the concept of exploitation has been shown to be in place, the same will apply to the concept of justice; and if so, there is yet a further similarity between the reasons why environmentalists should support development and the reasons why developmentalists should support some nonanthropocentric version of environmentalism.

As the future of the forest is apparently at stake, as well as that of numerous butterflies, it would not follow outright that butterfly farming should be rejected. But if the case which I have been making stands up, then even in that instance the grounds of environmentalists for reluctance about farming butterflies should at least be taken seriously. Those grounds turn not only on the interests of human beings, but also on those of butterflies.

Notes

1. The distinction between shallow and deep ecology movements was made by Arne Naess, in 'The Shallow and the Deep. Long-range Ecology movements: A Summary', *Inquiry*, 16, 1973, pp. 95-100.
2. Craven, 1989, p.15.
3. Zjilstra, 1989, p.16.
4. Attfield, 1986, pp.36-44.
5. See for example J. Baird Callicot, 'Animal Liberation: A Triangular Affair', *Environmental Ethics*, Vol. 2, No. 4, 1980, pp. 311-338. More recently Callicott's views have changed: See 'Animal Liberation and Environmental Ethics: Back Together Again' in J. Baird Callicott, *In Defense of the Land Ethic*, Albany: State University of New York Press, 1989, pp.49-59.
6. See Naess, 1973.
7. Fox, 1989.
8. Routley and Routley, 1980.
9. Rodman, 1977, pp.83-145.
10. See WECD 1987, Chapter 4.
11. Thus Dave Foreman, interviewed by Bill Devall, 'A Spanner in the Woods', *Simply Living* 2.12 (no date), p.43.
12. Thus Murray Bookchin, 'Thinking Ecologically: A Dialectical Approach; Our Generation, Vol. 18. No. 2, 1987, pp. 3-40.
13. Fox (p.21) reports finding similar sentiments in Bookchin, 1987.
14. Attfied, 1987, pp. 179-182; Attfield, 1983, pp. 195-208; Attfield, 1984, pp. 289-304.

15. For Naess's essay on sustainable development, see Fox, 1987, p.6 and 21.
16. Pearce, *et al.*, 1989, Chapter 1.
17. Craven, 1989.
18. Guha, 1989.
19. E.g. in *Animal Liberation, A New Ethic for Our Treatment of Animals,* London: Jonathan Cape, 1976.
20. Routley, 1980.
21. Bahro, 1984.
22. See Rodman, 1977.
23. Cited in Passmore, 1975, p.198.
24. Rawls, 1971, p.512.

14 ARE IDEOLOGIES DEAD?

Francisco Miro Quesada C.
Universidad de Lima
Lima, Peru

Methodological considerations

To approach with acceptable rigour the problem concerning the death of ideologies, we must know, first, what an ideology is all about. This is no easy task because the term 'ideology' has a heavy semantic load. Since Destutt de Tracy coined the word, its meaning has suffered several variations originated through different philosophical influences. To avoid being too long we shall limit ourselves to the way politicians and persons interested in political matters use it: as a theory or doctrine that is handled to justify political praxis.[1] When it is used this way we become aware that there are several types of ideology. So, to know if ideologies are dead or not, it is convenient to make a previous analysis of the different ideological kinds that have prevailed in the modern world. We believe that all of them can be classified into two principal types: epistemic ideologies and timetic or estimative ones. Moreover, each type can be focused according to the degree of awareness with which it is handled by the person or group that are trying to justify their political action.

Conceptual difficulties

When we want to know if an ideology is or is not epistemic we must look in which way its users are handling the concept of science. For a Hegelian or a Marxist, science is knowledge founded on the principles of dialectics. For them an ideology is scientific only if it is based on dialectics. According to this concept of science, to know if an ideology is epistemic we must know, as clearly as possible, which are the general concepts and which are the different species of dialectics. The first thing we observe when we analyze any classical dialectics is the frequent lack of rigour in the handling of words.[2] Many classical dialectical terms and sentences are vague; and many examples given to pinpoint the system of dialectical reasoning are easily invalidated through copious counter examples.

Another objection that can be made is that many of the sentences of dialectical systems are contradictory and, when this happens, the system collapses because, according to traditional and classical logic, from two contradictory propositions anything formulated in the language of the system can be derived.[3] Not long ago, the dialectical philosophers were unable to overcome this objection. But today several formal systems of dialectical logic have been created through which the difficulty can be surmounted. In one of the most rigorous and interesting of them, even classical logic results in a particular case of dialectical logic.[4]

However, the difficulty is not completely eliminated, because, today there exist many systems of incompatible formal dialectical logic. Besides, Marxist dialectics cannot be developed without serious theoretical gaps. On the other hand there is another difficulty that, on first sight, seems to be unsurmountable: Hegel maintained that the mathematical method was totally unable to formalize dialectical thought. We 'say on first sight' because, when we analyze what Hegel really meant we find that he was trying to solve one of the more profound, perhaps the most profound, problem of philosophy.

The prevailing vision in the non-Marxist philosophical communities can be called the 'deductive-hypothetical' concept of science. According to this concept, science is not necessarily dialectical, although in certain circumstances concerning the development of some theories it can present dialectical aspects.[5]

According to this conception an ideology can be scientific in two senses. First, the principles (or the principle) utilized can be evidentially true as are, for instance, the Peano arithmetic axiom, the intuition of natural numbers, the most elementary properties of sets, and including the infinite ones. In a second sense, the ideology is based on non-scientific principles (or principle) and from them important consequences for political action are deduced. So, although the supreme principles (or principle) cannot be scientifically known, the way their consequences (or its consequences) are deduced can be analyzed with a fairly logical rigour.

Critique of epistemic ideologies

As we have said an epistemic ideology is an ideology that pretends to be scientific; consequently, it is supposed to be true. For this reason it is necessary to have a clear concept about truth and about science. If we wanted to start with the analysis of truth we would never end. We begin, therefore, with the concept of science. But to make a clear analysis of this concept is, as we all know, very difficult, because there are several concepts of science which vary according to the philosophical presuppositions that support them. We shall only refer to two of them because we think they are the most important: the dialectical concept of science and the hypothetical-deductive.

The dialectical concept of science varies according to the different viewpoints adopted by important thinkers through history (Heratkleitos, Plato, Aristotle, Petrus Hispanicus, dun Scot, Abelard, Ockam, *et alia*; the German thinkers, Kant, Fichte, Schelling, Hegel, etc). Remarks here will be confined to the Marxist conception, because this ideology is the most detailed and systematic regarding the relationship between ideology and political action. According to the Marxist-Leninist doctrine an ideology is the *Weltanshauung* of the dominant class. Through it, this class reinforces and perpetuates its privileges. Not all the components of a culture are gears in the ideological machinery of domination: religion, science, economy, art, philosophy, and politics. Politics is considered by Marxists as an instrument of the domineering class to exert and preserve its power. The justification of politics, from this ideological point of view, is through a theory or doctrine whose truth is incorporated in the deepest repertoire of the people's beliefs. This is possible only when the dominant class is on the summit of its power.

The Marxist conception has several true aspects, but it has a limitation: it does not offer any criterion to distinguish a true theory or doctrine from an ideological one. If we accept that a theory or a doctrine is ideologized, we must know at least one that is not. Otherwise, how do we know that a theory or a doctrine is ideologized if we are unable to distinguish between truth and falsity? If we become aware that a theory or a doctrine is ideologized, it is because we have compared them with others that refer to the same topic and are true.

Now, the Marxist ideology pretends to be scientific. The concept on which this ideology is based is the dialectical concept of science. Dialectics, according to Engels and, afterwards, Lenin, is the law of the totality, as well as of the natural world (dialectical materialism) and of the social one (historical materialism). A political ideology, to be efficiently applicable, must be dialectical; and, this is very important, it must describe, explain, and be able to predict historical facts. This triple criterion of corroboration is the same one accepted by traditional western epistemology and, as far as we know, this coincidence has not been perceived by Marxists nor by Marxologists.[6] But then, the Marxist ideology can be empirically tested. If we find new social facts (for instance, the birth of new classes that cannot be dialectically explained), such ideology must be readjusted and, if in spite of this, it still cannot account for the new facts, the readjustment will be so great that the ideology will be hardly recognizable.

On the other hand, the exact application of the dialectical method to exact and natural sciences is very limited indeed. Although, in a pretty large sense, it can be accepted that certain aspects of these sciences could be dialectical, there are multiple examples that show that the dialectical method does not work in either of them. For instance, the famous set theoretical and semantic paradoxes (Burali-Forti, Cantor, Richard, etc.) are solved in favour of the thesis.[7]

There is still another objection, one of the strongest: the impossibility of making predictions concerning the evolution of large social processes. This failure has been observed not only in the social sciences, but also in the natural ones and even in pure mathematics. It has been shown that, in social (an natural) processes, an insignificant cause can unchain catastrophic effects. This fact that has baffled economists, sociologists and meteorologists has been baptized with the suggestive name of 'butterfly effect'.[8] It means, indeed, a very deep scientific revolution, and is especially grave *vis-a-vis* the Marxist-Leninist doctrine which is fundamentally based on economical and historical predictions.

It is possible to make many other criticisms of the dialectical conception of scientific knowledge, but we think that the ones we have made are sufficient to show that the Marxist idea of scientific knowledge does not work. However, in spite of this, we want to affirm, very emphatically, that the ultimate goal of the Marxist ideology gives sense to the process of modern history: to be able to forge a classless society.[9]

Let us have a look now at the epistemic ideologies based on the modern Western conception of science. There are not many but, as far as we are informed, there is at least one: the one proposed by the North-American philosopher Filmer Northrop. According to Northrop's conception every, political ideology (and also every ethical system) presents a double aspect. On the one hand there is a theory that can in the usual be empirically corroborated; on the other hand there is a set of normative sentences that are not verifiable. But both systems are related through the *Weltanschauung* of a determined culture. For this reason, even though the normative expressions cannot be empirically corroborated, the fact that the theoretical principles are liable to confirmation, makes it possible to consider the whole doctrine as true.[10]

Even though Northrop's theory is quite interesting, we think it cannot be maintained. In fact, a theory can be corroborated in numerous cases, but imperative sentences can never be confronted with empirical facts. The reason is simple: statements or propositions are always related to fact, but imperative expressions can never describe facts, because they do not say how facts are, but only how they ought to be.[11]

Critique of timetic ideologies

An essential trait of estimative ideologies is that they do not claim to be true and, consequently, it would be otiose trying to demonstrate that they are true or false. An estimative ideology is based on principles that need not be theoretically proved. Its principles are not propositions. For this reason they are quite different from the epistemic ones; their acceptability does not depend on any scientific theory but upon the collective acceptance of the values their principles proclaim and the decisions to realize the norms that are derived from them.

It is possible to make two objections to a timetical ideology: 1) it can be an evil one because it can lead to immoral acts (for instance, incest among the Pharaohs and the Incas); 2) its principles are so far away from human reality that it is impossible to apply them. The first objection cannot be easily dispatched because it confronts us with a deep problem: what are the criteria we apply to affirm that a determined ideology (or ethical system) is an evil one? This can only be done if we beg the question, for to judge an ethical (or ideological system) we must resort to our own. This counter objection, dear to sociologists and anthropologists, confronts us with a very difficult, perhaps impossible, problem. Which are the distinctive marks of a truly universal ethics?

The problem of finding the essential traits for a universal ethics has not been solved in spite of the great efforts made by philosophers of all times. Today the greatest part of these efforts is devoted to finding a rational foundation for ethics *more kantiano*.[12]

We see then that the first problem cannot be bluntly solved. But, the second one can be approached with a higher probability of success. Although it is certainly impossible to fulfil all the prescriptions of an ethical system and, *a fortiori* of an ideology, it is possible to approach this realization in the sense of a Kantian ideal. The approximation to difficult, realizable prescriptions can be compared to the approximation of a variable to its limit. In this sense, the problem of approximation can be considered as a mini-maximal optimization problem: to approach the ideological goals with a maximum of efficacy and with a minimum of effort by means of the best utilization of the available resources.

Eternal death and perdurable life of ideologies

If the arguments we have presented are convincing, the conclusion is clear: epistemic ideologies are dead for good, and it is highly improbable that they will reappear through some unexpected process of historical palingenesia. On the other hand, it is obvious that the timetic ideologies are far superior to the epistemic ones because they do not have the impossible task of proving truth.[13] But, as it always happens when we deal with ideological and moral matters, there are some difficulties concerning their possibility or application and their axiological ground. I think the strongest ones are the following: 1) they can be too idealistic concerning the human capacity of following their prescriptions; 2) they can be anti-humanist, that is, they try to justify the oppression of large collectivities; they can be used to perpetuate privileges, they can even be demoniac, demanding its followers to kill innocent people or commit collective suicide.

In the first case we think that if the goals of an ideology are too exacting to be truly followed, as it happens with the higher religions, the majority of persons who try to perform them will reach a certain kind of equilibrium. The ethical ends of the ideology will be followed as far as the human capacity is able to follow it. This is what happens with the principles of most religions and, of course, with the explicit or mostly implicit, ideologies with religious foundation.

The second objection is stronger. There are examples of cruel antihuman religions and ideologies. For instance the thugs of India believed that they had to make sacrifices consisting of murdering foreign people by strangling them. How can this objection be overcome? We have already seen that to judge an ideology (or an ethical system) we must presuppose its validity begging, in this way, the question. Nevertheless, it is not possible to demonstrate in a rigorous way that an estimative ideology is superior to the other ones, but it can be shown that it is either rational or irrational. We cannot follow this argument in detail because it would be too long, but we can say a few things about its general traits. To be rational we must reject arbitrariness and prepotence, and this means that we must consider our fellow beings as ends in themselves and never as instruments to fulfil our own ends. So any religion or ideology that prescribes human sacrifices is irrational. And, at least, in modern times almost nobody wants to be considered an irrational person. So, if we demonstrate that the prescriptions of a religion or of an ideology are against human reasons, because they lead to anti-human practices that must be imposed by sheer force, we have a good chance to be successful. There is, however, a point that may seem rationally objectable: to commit suicide out of religious convictions. But if we apply the Kantian maxim that a person must consider every fellow man as an end in itself, then religious suicide is irrational because it avoids the fulfilment of the personality of the suicidal one.

Of course in matters of morality there are always casuistic difficulties, for instance, the euthanatical or the heroical suicide. No doubt, concerning any theory about human affairs, it is always possible to find counter-examples. We certainly know this. But we also know that, through well founded argumentation, the number of possible counter-examples can be greatly reduced. We hope that, in the present exposition, in spite of some irreducible difficulties, we have been able to show in not too loose a way that epistemic ideologies are dead for always, whereas timetic ones will live for ever.

Notes

1. We say 'theory' or 'doctrine' because the concept of doctrine is more general than the concept of theory. Generally speaking a theory could be called a 'doctrine' without trespassing too much on the usual meaning of both words: but not every doctrine is a theory. For instance, the Christian doctrine is not a theory because most of its parts are not descriptive but prescriptive. The Marxist concept of ideology is much wider but related to ours. As we have said, according to Marx, an ideology is the *Weltanshcauung* of a definite

Francisco Miro Quesada C.

social group through which the domineering class subjects the exploited ones. An ideology, therefore, is a very complicated system of ideas, values and beliefs through which social groups and individual behaviours are conditioned. This conception is related to our own because Marx and the Marxists claim that politics is the most direct instrument of upper class domination.
2. By 'classical dialectics' we understand the Hegelian Marxist system. The systems created by Fichte, Schelling and Hegel can also be called 'classical', but they will not be used in the present text.
3. According to the usual convention of logico-mathematical circles, by 'classical logic' we mean the logic which was systematized in the monumental book *Principia Mathematica* of Whitehead and Russell. 'Traditional logic' is Greek, Medieval and non-mathematical logic before the creations of Boole, De Morgan, Schroeder Peano and Frege. As it always happens, there were anticipations, for instance, the works of Raymond Lull, Leibniz, Plouquet, Lambert and others of lesser rank.
4. The system was created by DaCosta in 1978. On the philosophical import of paraconsistent logic and, especially of DaCosta's system, see Miró Quesada, 1989.
5. These aspects need not be identical to the ones a classical dialectician would expect. On a non-classical conception of dialectics, see Miró Quesada, 1982.
6. We can find in Marx several references to the descriptive power of dialectics as well as to its explicative and predictive power. For instance in the Preface to the Second Edition of *Das Kapital;* in the *Communist Manifesto, The German Ideology,* etc. The same in Engels in a much more detailed (and wrong) exposition. In the Anti-Duhring and The Dialectics of Nature we find many references to the descriptive-explicative and predictive power of his dialectical system.
7. In any good book of mathematical philosophy. The solution of the paradoxes is clearly in favour of the thesis. Tarski, 1936; 1977; Beth, 1959; Benacerraf and Putnam, 1965.
8. About the butterfly effect, see Prigogine and Stengers, 1988; Steward, 1990; Rietman, 1989 (in this book the effect is not explicitly mentioned, but we can find functions that yield examples of its functioning).
9. On the classless society as the ultimate end of history see, Quesada, 1991.
10. Northrop, 1947.
11. We think that one of the principal problems, if not the principal problem, of ethics is to know if it is possible to deduce prescriptive expressions from categorical ones. We think that, unfortunately, it is not possible. See Flew, 1983.
12. For instance, Lorenzen, 1978; Miro Quesada, 1988, 1991.
13. To say that timetic ideologies will exist for ever, is a *facon de perler*. We are not, of course, naively thinking about ideologies of eternal duration. An ideology can be convincing only if the principles it proclaims are socially in force. In this sense an estimative ideology is born, grows, is strongly accepted, declines, and dies. If eternal, unchanging ideologies really exist, they do not concern us within the frame of this essay. What must be clearly understood when we affirm that estimative ideologies are eternal, is that we are referring to their existence in determined historical periods. We think that in an explicit or implicit way, timetic ideologies, assuming multiple aspects with respect to different historical epochs, will always exist.

15 POLITICAL MONISM AND PLURALISM IN CONTEMPORARY AFRICA

Didier Njirayamanda Kaphagawani
University of Malawi
Zomba, Malawi

Philosophy in Africa today is of varying types and has taken on different, sometimes divergent, forms. These types and forms of African philosophy are, however, generally classified into four categories. The first is *ethnophilosophy* which is basically the volume of works done by scholars on specific African ethnic groups on the assumption that in each ethnic group there exists communal thought on various issues of philosophical significance. The fundamental aim of all ethnophilosophical works is to disinter from the African myths, beliefs, customs and languages the quintessentially African world outlook. As Bodunrin has observed, ethnophilosophy conceives of African philosophy as 'communal thought' as opposed to 'a body of logically argued thoughts of individuals.'[1] Some of the founding fathers of ethnophilosophy in African philosophy are Placide Tempels, John Mbiti and Alexis Kagame.[2] Ethnophilosphy has not gone unchallenged, but I won't go into its criticisms in this chapter.

The second type of African philosophy is what Odera Oruka has ably called *sage philosophy*. This is essentially works and views of individual sages who are not only aware of the commonplace, conventional wisdoms of their particular cultures and world outlooks, what Oruka terms 'culture philosophy which is basically ethnophilosophy, but who also transcend this ethnophilosophy by being both critical of it, through ratiocination, and appreciative of it. Thus these sages recommend 'only those aspects of beliefs and wisdoms which satisfy their rational scrutiny.'[3] What these sage philosophers produce are basically metaethnophilosophies appreciative and critical of ethnophilosophy. Insofar as it is a metaethnophilosophy, sage philosophy is also saddled with a host of problems of its own which are beyond the scope of this chapter.

The third is African professional philosophy, works of trained philosophers, both African and non-African, on 'specific philosophical issues and concepts' of some significant bearing on and reflective of the African peoples and cultures.[4] Characteristic of this type of African philosophy is that it is 'engrained with argument and criticism.' What Kwasi Wiredu calls 'ethnically specific studies which 'disclose a variety of philosophies, similar in some respects, but distinct, nevertheless[5] seems to me to belong to African professional philosophy insofar as these studies are conducted by professionally trained philosophers.

Lastly, there is African political philosophy, works produced to underscore the socio-political situations in both pre-colonial (traditional) Africa and in post-colonial Africa. These works are aimed at formulating political theories of an African tinge by taking into consideration whatever lessons can be learned from the traditional African communalism and familyhood.[6]

This chapter addresses itself to some issues of current interest in the African political sphere, issues requiring immediate attention and consideration particularly now when calls are being made in various parts of Africa for the abolition of political monism and the institution of political pluralism. The vicissitudes in the political arena of the world in general and Africa in particular compels one to recall what is regarded as one of the most perennial and fundamental problems in philosophy, namely, the question whether Reality is One or Many.[7] To the surprise, and perhaps dismay, of all those who continously doubt and constantly argue about the viability of philosophy in Africa, this chapter aims at showing that this metaphysical question has significant relevance to contemporary Africa, more so now when political quibbles and debates are concentrated on whether Africa ought to have political monism or political pluralism.[8] Thus it is argued that the question of whether Africa is or ought to be politically monistic or pluralistic is logically posterior to the more fundamental question whether or not dissent, toleration of dissent and difference of opinion, is or ought to be encouraged and instituted in all African political institutions and organizations. Drawing on data from pre-colonial Africa, I argue that one of the lessons contemporary political Africa can and ought to learn from pre-colonial (traditional) Africa is respect and toleration of opposition, dissent and difference of opinion, the abdication and annihilation of which is the abdication of democratic practice in Africa.

This chapter, thus, proposes a hermeneutical solution to the problem of monism or pluralism bedeviling political Africa now, by showing that opposition, hence democracy, insofar as democratic practice presupposes respect and toleration of dissent and difference of opinion, is logically possible in both political monism and political pluralism. For, as Spinoza once wrote, 'the object of (any) government is not to change men from rational beings into beasts and puppets but to enable them to develop their minds and bodies *in security*, and to employ their reason unshackled; neither showing hatred, anger nor deceit, nor watched with the eyes of jealousy and injustice'. Spinoza continues, 'the true aim of government is liberty'.[9] And a free man, for Spinoza, is 'the man conscious of the necessities that compel him'.[10] Needless to say, such necessities abound in contemporary Africa, the awareness of which, on the part of the Africans themselves, is problematical. It is to the question of political monism or pluralism in Africa that the paper turns for consideration.

The One and the Many in Africa

At least two questions immediately present themselves: firstly, the question whether contemporary Africa *is* politically monistic or pluralistic; and secondly, whether contemporary Africa *ought to be* politically monistic or pluralistic. Admittedly, the answer to the second question is not as straightforward as that of the first; and to hazard a possible answer would require more than this paper allows. But, insofar as ought-questions are regarded as radically different in nature from is-questions, this chapter concentrates on the first question, leaving aside the ought-question for later discussion.

That almost all Africa is politically monistic cannot be gainsaid; the continent is replete with examples, too many to be mentioned. But, as Wanyande points out, political monism in contemporary Africa prevails either *de jure*, or *de facto*. In those countries where it prevails *de jure*, Wanyande believes that 'people are free to form opposition parties if they so wish'.[11]

But here I must rush to point out that this freedom Wanyande is referring to is merely theoretical; never is it practical with regard to Africa and even in those countries where political opposition has suffered a natural and untimely death, it is virtually impossible to reintroduce political pluralism. However, a sad consequence of the African political monism is the prevalence of *coups*, *coup* leaders claiming to 'save' their nations from leaders who had earlier alleged to have liberated their nations from still other allegedly corrupt leaders etc., *ad infinitum*! In fact, some African countries know more *coups* than general and free elections that the distinction between the two pales into insignificance on the part of the citizens. For reasons best known to these citizens, they seem to have resigned themselves to political monism, seeing no hope or point of political pluralism, just like the Russian, when asked whether there should be two parties is said to have answered: 'Two? Isn't one enough?' or the Yugoslav, when asked whether political pluralism, would be a good development, is said to have replied: 'If we had an opposition party, everyone would join it; and again we would have one party.'[12]

However, there are several arguments proffered to both justify political monism and refute political pluralism in contemporary Africa.[13] But this chapter only deals with what I have termed 'the traditional argument,' propounded in varying ways and forms by, for instance, Julius Nyerere, Jomo Kenyatta, Paulin Hountondji and Kwame Gyekye. This argument rests on the premise that pre-colonial (traditional) political systems were politically monistic and democratic; and this is seen as a reason for political monism extant in post-colonial Africa. In *On Socialism,* Nyerere insists that despite 'all the variations and some exceptions where the institutions of domestic slavery existed, African family life was everywhere based on certain practices and attitudes which together mean basic equality, freedom and unity.'[14] Similarly, referring to the Gikuyu of Kenya, Kenyatta also remarks that 'before the coming of the Europeans, the Gikuyu had a democratic regime'[15] because the elders, regarded as custodians of political authority and power, 'talk(ed) till they agree(d).'[16] Kwame Gyekye has made much the same observations about the Akan of Ghana.[17]

Although I am quite in agreement with the general thrust of the argument, I should point out that, insofar as human nature is regarded as continuous, ticking away without any chance or possibility of reversal, contemporary Africa should not only learn from traditional Africa alone, as I take this argument to be implying, but also from both colonial and post-colonial experiences in order for it to thrash out possible ways and options of carving out a 'future' political Africa. And since experiences in all these periods are as varied as the countries themselves, to think of one solution for all is no doubt to verge on the impossible.

But, whatever the merits or demerits of traditional Africa, some of the significant practices and attitudes to be assimilated into contemporary political Africa are, as indeed Gyekye lucidly puts, 'the pursuit of consensus' which takes into account individual views and opinions; the promotion of 'mutual tolerance and patience'; and 'an attitude of compromise' all of which are essential to democratic practice.[18]

Although Gyekye is talking about the Akan political system in particular, this also holds for quite a good number of traditional political systems in Africa. For instance, that the Chewa of Central Africa also esteemed the concept and practice of consensus is evidenced by the proverb: *Mutu umodzi susenza denga*, literally translated as 'One head never ever carries/lifts a roof'; meaning that, due to the finitude of the human mind, in any decision or action of public concern, consultation and consensus is of prime importance. Interestingly, this proverb shares similarities with the Akan proverbs: *Ti koro nko agyina* (one head does not go into council) and *Nyansa nni onipa baako ti mu* (wisdom is not the head of one person).[19] Similarly, Chewa proverbs exist which confirm both the cherishing of mutual tolerance and patience, and the valuing of the attitude of compromise.[20]

Conclusion

Traditional Africa, from the foregoing discussion, seems to be proposing a hermeneutic approach to contemporary political Africa, in its attempts to solve political problems, particularly that of whether political pluralism or monism should prevail. Why contemporary political Africa does not heed a piece of advice, as priceless as this, buried in her own cultural past, is a mystery. But, as Gadamer points out,

> hemerneutic philosophy understands itself not as an absolute position, but as a way of experience. It insists that there is no higher principle than holding oneself open in a conversation. But this means: Always recognise in advance the possible correctiveness, even the superiority of the conversation partner's position.[21]

Indeed, the caveat that hermeneutics, and traditional Africa for that matter, are issuing to all those currently quibbling about the desirability of political pluralism or monism is no doubt that whatever arguments they might think they have in their arsenal for or against monism or pluralism, they should bear in mind that their positions, or the stands they take, whatever they are, are not without flaws. For, as Gadamer rightly insists, for a conversation or discussion among them to be really genuine, it must not fall short of meeting the requirement that 'one really considers that weight of the other's opinion.'[22] Lamentably, this sort of Gadamerian conversation is glaringly absent in contemporary political Africa. And this chapter has purported to show that if toleration, dissent and genuine conversation or discussion are absent in political monism, as is the case in almost all Africa now, then the possibility of political pluralism is even more remote and reduces itself to a vanishing point. Democratic practice in Africa can be instituted in political monism even before political pluralism is made possible and implementable. Africans should genuinely take pride in belonging to their varying nations. For, as Rorty points out quite rightly, 'our identification with our community — our society, our political tradition, our cultural heritage — is heightened when we see this community as *ours* rather than *nature's, shaped* rather than *found*, one among many which men have made.'[23] Advertently or inadvertently, it is true that Africans in the first three decades of independence made and instituted political monism. But they need to move from this position with improvement. How this is to be effected, varies from one African nation to another.

NOTES
1. Bodunrin, 1981, p.161.
2. Kagame, 1971; Mbiti, 1969; Tempel, 1959.
3. Odera Oruka, 1983, p. 386.
4. *Ibid.*, p. 384.
5. Wiredu, 1987. p. 153.
6. For problems and critiques of all these four trends in African philosophy, see for instance, articles in Floistad's *Contemporary Philosophy*, Vol.V, *ibid.*
7. This text was written in 1991. Since then political pluralism has emerged like spring waters in many parts oif Africa (Editor). Russell, 1966; Ewing, 1968.
8. Ewing, 1968, p. 211, for instance, asserts the futility or irrelevance of metaphysics to politics in general.
9. Scruton, 1986, p. 96, my emphasis.
10. *Ibid.*, p. 87.
11. Oyugi and Gitonga, 1987, p. 71.
12. Schapiro, 1972, p. 26.
13. Wanyande, 1987; Simiyu, 1987; *Malawi Daily Times*, 6/5/90 and 19/6/90, p. 4.
14. Nyerere, 1968, p. 10.
15. Kenyatta, 1938, p. 131.
16. Nyerere, 1968, p. 104.
17. Gyekye, 1988.
18. *Ibid.*, p. 18.
19. *Ibid.*, p. 20.

20. For example, *Nzeru nkupangwa* (Wisdom is not inborn; it's created); *Undisokosera nkulinga utmva* (to shout 'Nonsense!' is to initially lend an ear); *Dziko ndi mafuwa achita uchirikiza* (The world is in the balance like a pot on three fire stones); and *Nzeru zayekha adaviika nsima mmadz* (The know-it-all always immerses food in water) to mention a few.
21. Gadamer, 1985, p.189.
22. Gadamer, 1975, p.330.
23. Rorty, 1982. p.166.

16 FROM SUN-WORSHIP TO TIME-WORSHIP: TOWARDS A SOLAR THEORY OF HISTORY

Ali A. Mazrui
State University of New York
University of Jos, Nigeria, and Cornell University, New York

The proposal of this chapter is to outline a solar theory of history. Considering how obviously important to human survival the sun has always been, it is the more remarkable that we have underestimated its role in the evolution of such diverse social phenomena as European racism and the miracle of industrialization in Japan after the Meiji restoration. This short discussion stands no chance of doing justice to any of those issues. We are simply putting the sun back on the agenda of social and political theory.

The solar frontiers of religion

On the evidence available so far, it would seem that Egypt was the birthplace of monotheism – where humans first focused on believing in a single elusive God. The impact of the sun on religion resulted in the evolution of monotheism along the Nile Valley. Pharaoh Akhenaton (1379-1462 BC) was the first thorough-going monotheist. His wife Naffertiti co-founded the religion of Aton (the new God). It was belief in one God, but the God was not of course the personalized King of Judaism, Christianity and Islam. Aton was represented by the sun-disk.

Over time religion evolved from Akhenaton to Moses.
- Was Moses an Egyptian in rebellion against his own pharaoh?
- Semitic versions of monotheism became more and more anthropomorphic (Judaism, Islam and Christianity).
- Man was made in the image of God, according to the Semitic vision.
- The sun-disk was no longer God, but Semitic worshippers still looked upwards towards the Heavens as the location of God.
- Christianity has a concept of ascension. Did Jesus ascend to heaven?
- Islam has the legend of Miiraj: Muhammad's ascent to Heaven from Al-Aksaa in Jerusalem. This was what made Jerusalem one of the three sacred cities of Islam.

From Sun-Worship to Time-Worship

•Seven Heavens characterized the Islamic concept of the abode of angels and Allah.

In Africa south of the Sahara the focus on godliness moved towards the universe in a different way. It is not just man who is created in the image of God. It is the entire universe. Indeed, the evolution of the universe is the autobiography of God star by star, planet by planet, tree by tree, from birth to death. The process of creation is God telling his own story. But sometimes there are residues of the centrality of the sun in our conceptions of the ultimate in Africa. The Swahili word for sun and the Swahili word for 'to know' are the same — the word is *jua*. Is the sun the fountain of all knowledge? Some of the ethnic cultures of Tanzania also link the sun to divinity, at least linguistically. Implicit in their world view is a basic solar theory of God, which has now been overtaken by alternative interpretations of divinity.

> In general the Bantu-speaking peoples in mainland Tanzania believed in the High God as creator, the ultimate origin of life. One of the most important symbols applied to him was that of the sun. For instance, the God of the Meru people in northern Tanzania, who had many different names, was sometimes referred to as the sun ... *Lyuba,* one of the names of God among the Sukuma, means God but also the Sun ... Likewise among the Nyamwezi.[1]

The solar boundaries of race

There is also the question of whether the retreat of the sun in winter in Europe was a contributory factor to the birth of European racism. Winter in the northern hemisphere helped to develop the culture of privacy, and privacy in turn helped to develop collective insularity. Winter as a cold season created the need for walls of shelter. Keeping the ecological elements out created walled enclosures. It was not just the cold weather which was kept out; it was also neighbours. Social insularity was struggling to be born. Winter as a season also created the need for elaborate clothing for warmth. But what began as clothed protection against freezing weather became protection against natural sexuality. Any form of natural nudity was equated with sexual nakedness. A concept of 'private parts' came into being accompanied by new sexual complexes and inhibitions. The culture of elaborate clothing in the Northern hemisphere helped to re-define the concept of privacy. This narrower definition of privacy was evolving alongside the walls of insularity. A combination of privacy for the body and insularity for the family helped promote acute ethnocentrism. The stage was being set for racism, including sexual possessiveness.

The advent of winter as a freezing experience in the Northern hemisphere also contributed to a culture of not only basic walls but also elaborate architecture over time. Sophistication in complex constructions gradually resulted in monumentalist criteria of what constitutes civilization. The civilized people were supposed to be those who built castles, palaces and fortresses. As the Black primitivist confessed with pride: 'My Negritude [my blackness] is no tower and no cathedral; It delves into the deep, red flesh of the soil.'[2]

Winter in Europe enriched architecture and construction. This enriched monumentalist civilization in turn became an additional basis of European arrogance. Much of Black Africa was perceived as a culture of mud-huts (since equatorial human beings did not need elaborate protection against freezing winds). It is partly to these multiple considerations of personal privacy, walled insularity and criteria of monumentalism that we must trace the origins of European racism.

From this point of view it is worth distinguishing between Germanic whites (further north with a colder winter) on one side, and Latin whites (originally Mediterranean) on the other. Germanic cultures encompass not only the Germans but also the Anglo-Saxons (British and mainstream United States) and the Dutch. Latin cultures embrace not only Italians but also the traditions of Spain, Portugal and France.

On balance, Germanic cultures have been more obsessed with the separation of the races than have Latin cultures. It may not be an accident that the most elaborate cases of segregation, and the most fanatical forms of racism in the twentieth century, have been perpetrated by Germans (Nazism), Afrikaners (apartheid), Americans (the lynching of Jim Crow culture) and the British (with a segregated empire). All these racist traditions are culturally Germanic. Of course, the Spanish, the Portuguese, the Italians and the French have had their own versions of racism. But their brand of ethnocentrism has been less segregationist, less obsessed with the social and sexual separation of the races. Latin whites have inter-married more readily with non-whites and have mixed socially with other races with greater ease than have the Germanic whites. The question which arises is whether the greater physical insularity of Germanic cultures was originally a consequence of the colder climate north of the Mediterranean. Were the walls of winter part of the genesis of social separatism and Germanic myths of keeping the blood 'pure'? Was winter the mother of racial segregation?

The evolution of racism has of course included other causes apart from climate. The basic question which is being posed here is whether walled cultures are more prone to social insularity and physical separatism than are cultures of more open habitat. Nor does winter always produce a walled civilization. It did not do so in North America before European colonization. But partly because of that the native Americans were less racist and less segregationist than were the European invaders who were soon to decimate the native populations. One of the ironies of the Americas is that the winter zone of North America produced cultures of open habitat – while pre-colonial Mexico in the tropics produced a walled civilization.

What all this means is that a walled civilization is not always produced by climate. In Europe it was; in Mexico it was not. Secondly, a cold climate does not always produce a walled civilization. In Europe it did; in pre-colonial North America it did not. But where a cold climate does produce a walled civilization, it sets the stage of social insularity – and, over time, it prepares the way for a culture of ethno-racial segregation.

Of course the Japanese still link the Sun, the Emperor and God. The implicit Japanese vision of the universe was that the Sun was king of the universe, the Emperor was the king of Japan and God was the king of kings. On earth the three did in fact fuse in the Emperor.

Did the sun have an impact on Christian conceptions of God as well? Christian conceptions of God are still royal but are no longer solar. The Christian God is still viewed as King of Kings – with a conception of a divine throne. The Semitic God expects to be worshipped, flattered with hymns, with humans prostrating themselves in tribute to their maker. According to John Milton's *Paradise Lost,* Satan rebelled against this royalist subservience. In the words of Milton's Lucifer, 'Better to reign in Hell than serve in Heaven.'

The Industrial Revolution in the West shifted Europe from indirect sun-worship to indirect time-worship. Time in Western civilization became the new king, exercising sovereign control. Time theory of value was the order of the day. Work was measured by time; wages were computed by the hour. The discipline of the clock made minutes valuable – workers 'clocked in' and 'clocked out'. Punctuality became a new moral precept. The human race was warned, 'Time and tide wait for no man.'

The Japanese after the 1868 Meiji restoration evolved the miracle of fusing Sun-worship with time-worship. Perhaps this is the explanation for the industrial success of Japan. The discipline of their solar religion has now been linked to the discipline of the temporal creed from the industrialized West. Sun-worship and time-worship have merged in modern Japan.

In Africa, on the other hand, sun-worship has declined – while time-worship has yet to be consolidated. Indeed, time-worship in Africa is still at a stage when it is culturally disruptive rather than socially disciplined. Time-worship is already having an adverse effect on the role of women.

The solar boundaries of gender
In Africa God made woman custodian of fire, water and earth. God himself took charge of the fourth element – the omnipresent air. Fire – originally the fury of the sun – is captured on earth in energy. In the rural countryside the source of fire is wood. Women are carrying heavy burdens of firewood across long distances. Fire is the symbol of light and warmth – and the African woman is the trustee. Water – originally the bounty of the sun – is represented on earth in rivers and lakes. African women traverse distances to fetch water. Water is symbol of survival and cleanliness, and the African woman is the trustee. Earth – originally offspring of the sun – is now the soil for cultivation. The woman is entrusted with *dual fertility* – the fertility of the womb (woman as mother) and the fertility of the soil (woman as cultivator). The African woman was centrally functional in matters of energy, water and cultivation.

And then the West came with time-worship. The African experience has included new mechanization from the West. Mechanization is marginalizing the African woman, while 'saving time'. Time-worship and the imperative of efficiency is 'propelling' Africa from hoe-cultivation (female-dominated) to tractor-cultivation (male-dominated). The transition from handwriting to the word processor saves a lot of time. But the woman typist has undergone marginalization.

The discipline of the clock did give new meaning to efficiency. And since technology produces more in a shorter period, economies of scale also

From Sun-Worship to Time-Worship

acquired increasing legitimacy. When the African woman works for wages and is rewarded by the hour, the discipline of the clock has helped her. But when she moves from energy, water and cultivation to the typewriter from eight to five o'clock, she has become more free but less central to society.

The solar boundaries of nation-states

What about the origins of sovereignty and national frontiers? Where does climate fit in? It is an open question as to which culture was historically the most likely to be converted to the doctrine of fixed frontiers of sovereignty. We do know which culture was the least likely to be enthusiastic about inflexible frontiers, the culture of the nomads. And nomadism has been disproportionately of the tropical and subtropical regions of the world. Today Africa has only one tenth of the total human population of the world, yet it has nearly half of the remaining nomadic population of this planet.

We may safely conclude that among the last people to be converted to the nation-state are such genuinely nomadic peoples as the Barabaig, the Maasai, the Taureg and others. The question which persists is whether it was a historical accident that the nation-state and its rigid territorial frontiers originated in the winter zones of Europe.

Snowfalls in winter played havoc with landmarks. Familiar signs of the summer and the autumn were often covered with snow in the winter. Measuring distances by the eye became difficult if the landmarks on a journey changed totally from season to season. The need to measure distances more accurately became more manifest as visual landmarks became drastically changed. Natural frontiers like rivers and lakes were notoriously liable to being frozen and covered with snow. What was a clearcut frontier in the summer could become a matter of dispute in the winter. Snowfalls and ice created visual imprecision, which in turn created a greater need for mathematical exactitude. Seasons in the temperate zones occasioned considerable visual and weather changes. These changes in turn created the need for quantifiable or measurable predictability.

By the time of the Thirty Years War in Europe in the seventeenth century, boundaries between European countries were getting to be a matter of more careful cartography. Monarchical jurisdiction was not only specific to a particular people, but also specific to a particular territory. The idea of the sovereign is older than the more abstract idea of sovereignty. The sovereign was basically a monarch, no more no less. For centuries the King had been attributed with supreme powers and authority. But now the idea had become powerfully abstract — not the sovereign, but sovereignty. Should we turn back to the notions of a people obeying the sovereign-state rather than obeying a sovereign monarch?

In some cultures the sun had helped to shape not only concepts of God but also concepts of the sovereign. We mentioned the linkage with the sun in the Japanese imperial system — sun-God and sun-Emperor. In Europe the most splendid of the sovereigns were figuratively associated with the sun from time to time. Particularly striking was Louis XIV of France as 'the Sun-King' (1638–1715) radiating his splendour.

In British imperial history the sun became the scale of how widely British sovereignty had spread — 'His Majesty's dominions, an empire over which the sun never sets' (Christopher North, 1785–1854). The sun was also the metaphor which placed England at the center of an early 'solar system' — an England which radiated 'the light of civilization' to all corners of the world.

Of all the continents of the world, Africa before the imperial Berlin Conference of 1884–85 was the least subjected to national territorial boundaries. Africa was also the most equatorial of all continents. Africa has always been, of course, the only continent which is cut almost in half by the equator. And the only continent which is traversed by both the Tropic of Cancer and the Tropic of Capricorn. Africa is the tropical region *par excellence*! And yet historically the continent is unbound by territorial frontiers, in spite of producing many grand empires and civilizations! Has there been a connection between tropicality and territorial imprecision?

Climate was only one of the factors in European history which contributed to the need for precision of boundaries between communities. But once those boundaries became part of human relations, a new arena of conflict was born. The quest of making national boundaries coincide with state frontiers was one of the central causes of the Second World War. Hitler's obsession with the larger German fatherland was one such fanatical extremity of redrawing boundaries. Reshaping Czechoslovakia and Poland were among the trigger-mechanisms of the ensuing global conflagration.

Hitler — like the philosopher Hegel before him — tried to make universal geography (global conquest) serve the cause of parochial history (the German nation). Hegel tried to make universal geography serve the cause of the Prussian state. Were Hitler and Hegel equally parochial?

In any case, in spite of a sensitivity to the parochial past, time-worship is not normally historically-oriented. This is its supreme paradox. Time after all is the dynamic of history. And the study of history is the supreme discipline of time, while the study of geography is the disciple of space. And yet the transition from sun-worship to time-worship has paradoxically been at the expense of sensitivity to the past.

Western concepts of citizenship have become very conscious of place of birth, partly in relation to territorial jurisdiction. Being born within the boundaries of the United States constitutes eligibility for American citizenship. African concepts of citizenship, on the other hand, tend to dilute the value of place of birth on its own. Under most African nationality laws, being born within the boundaries of a country is not adequate eligibility for citizenship. The accident of territorial location of birth is less important than historic membership of a local 'tribe' or clan.

The solar boundaries of generations

Western-style time-worship marginalizes ancestors. Past, Present and Future are re-organized in scale of importance. Present, Future and Past becomes the order of priorities. Indeed, fanatical time-worship finally becomes obsessed with the present — at the expense of both the future and the past.

Is the past truly dead? Cultures obsessed with the present evolve institutions which betray this bias. Western law certainly betrays insensitivity to the reputations of the dead. In the United States only the living can sue for libel damages. In 1981 a biography of Errol Flynn by Charles Higham hit the headlines. Higham alleged that Errol Flynn was a German spy. Flynn's daughter's sued for damages and invasion of privacy. The Court of Appeals in California wrote as follows: '... defamation of a deceased person does not give rise to a civil right of action at common law in favour of the surviving spouse, family relatives who are not themselves defamed.'[3]

In 1988, in the Tawana Brawley case, a dead policeman was accused of rape. He had in fact committed suicide, but his reputation suffered more because of the allegation of rape. The charge went before a grand jury who found it totally without foundation. But the grand jury was nevertheless worried that malicious and unfounded allegations could be damaging even if there was no case to follow. The grand jury recommended a law to enable relatives to sue if a dead person was 'knowingly and falsely accused of committing a felony.' In vain, the obsession with the present left the dead unprotected.

In the state legislature of New York at Albany a bill of libelling the dead did pass the Senate. Then somebody did a calculation about some of those who would benefit. They included Mafia big-shots and crooks in state prisons. This killed the Bill in the house. Again a pre-occupation with short-term issues affecting the present-day left the reputations of the dead still vulnerable.

William Safire, a columnist for the *New York Times*, opposed to censorship, admitted in April 1989 that it was easy under the law for authors in the United States to make outrageous fabrications about dead celebrities – and make a lot of money out of those sensationalist fabrications. Safire cited the case of a relatively recent book entitled *Cary Grant: The Lonely Heart*, by Charles Higham (again) and Roy Mosely. The libel was not against Cary Grant but against Gary Cooper, the famous star of *High Noon* and other film classics. A passing shot in the book said: 'Nor was Cary unaware of the political leanings of Gary Cooper, who in 1938 would go to Berlin and be entertained by Hitler.' Subsequently, on an ABC 'Good Morning America' one of the authors was reported by Safire to have gone further and accuse Cooper of having been 'a very strong Nazi sympatheizer, and in fact was received by Hitler in Berlin in great secrecy in 1938.' Was this libellous? If so, could the late Gary Cooper have legal recourse? Was there any foundation to the alleged Nazi sympathies? William Safire reached Mr. Higham, one of the authors of the book, and asked him for his source. Higham referred him to a California writer called Anthony Slide. When Slide was contacted he told Safire that the first time he heard about Gary Cooper's Nazi sympathies was from Higham. Real circular documentation was at work.

Cooper's daughter, Maria Cooper Janis, and Cooper's widow, 75-year old Veronica Cooper, were outraged but had no recourse. The Nazi rumours were based on a trip the Coopers made to Berlin in 1939. They met *a* Göring — but not *the* Göring of Nazi power. And yet the United States legal system was still obsessed with the Here - and - Now. The dead had no protection.[4]

In writing the controversial book *The Satanic Verses* was Salman Rushdie playing Charles Higham to the Muslim world's 'super-stars'? Sexual innuendos about the Prophet Muhammad's wives in *The Satanic Verses*, or more subtle innuendoes about alcohol and the Prophet of Islam himself, could be even more sensational than Nazi innuendos about Gary Cooper or Errol Flynn. Like Charles Higham was Rushdie muck-raking or outright fabricating? Is *The Satanic Verses* cheap sensationalism? However, women who died fourteen centuries ago could hardly get protection under Western liberal time–worship.

John Stuart Mill's distinction between self-regarding and other-regarding acts is another case in point. Freedom should be restricted only if it directly harms others — argued Mill. Did Mill's concept of 'other' include the dead? Could the dead be hurt? Should freedom ever be restricted to protect the dead? The Western time-scale after the industrial revolution left the dead unprotected. In any case, is the distinction between hurting the dead and hurting the living itself artificial? After all, when we accuse a man of being an illegitimate child — is that an accusation against him or against his dead mother? As Mobutu Sese Seko has affirmed: 'There are no illegitimate children. There are only illegitimate parents.'

The solar boundaries between life and death

The first humans in the history of the universe were what we would now call Africans. Were it possible, it would be worth exploring when our earliest ancestors began to let the sun influence their social and religious institutions. East Africa was the Eden or cradle of the human species. The cradle lies across the equator and the tropics. Was this close proximity of the sun a pre-condition for the evolution of the human species?

The genesis of the earliest institutions generally lie in the tropics: the invention of the family; the development of language; the taming of fire in what is today Kenya; the First Supper when eating moved from being a purely biological necessity to being a social occasion.

Was the tropical context a necessary precondition for these cultural miracles? Ancient Egypt in turn was the birthplace of the first grand civilization. That civilization was characterized by the following attributes: no great distinction between the past, the present and the future; no great distinction between the kingdom of God, the animal kingdom and the human kingdom; the crocodile could be a god; no sharp divide between the living and the

the dead. The pyramids were new residences of the pharaohs. Fineries in the tombs were to be enjoyed by the dead. To die was to change your address.

Although the Nile itself started in the Tropics (Ethiopia and Uganda) its fulfillment was further away from the Equator. Egypt under Akhenaton still recognized the majesty of the sun — and a solar approach to religion gave birth to monotheism. The sun as the source of life on earth has been recognized since the earliest days of human culture. Nor must we forget that the culture of building beautiful palaces was also the culture of building warlike fortresses. Monumentalist culture in the west produced slave forts on the West African Coast — as well as the palaces of Versailles and Hampton Court in Europe. Did the skills of brick-and-mortar encourage the skill of using explosives? Did war become more destructive as fortresses became more impregnable? Did walled cities encourage the discovery of gun-powder? Remember the Great Wall of China. Which came first? Better defence? Or worse offence? Does every new shield produce a sharper spear? Or does every sharp spear procure a better shield? Carter dreamt of the neutron-bomb which would destroy human life without destroying the surrounding walls. George Bush dreamt about smart weapons which would destroy walls without 'collateral damage'. Unfortunately Bush killed over a hundred thousand Iraqis.

This entire monumentalist culture grew out of the winter zone — the search for walls of insularity. In the English language a single letter of the alphabet could capture the whole story – from in solarity (with an 'o'), an ecological statement, to insularity, a social assertation: From the solar orbit to the insular orbit!

"Stand still, you ever moving spheres of heaven,
That time may cease,
And midnight never come!"
So prayed Faustus
But midnight came — and he left.

But now eternal time a nap has taken
And all the clocks don't know;
They think their arms with lives are laden
But all is empty show.

From Sun-Worship to Time-Worship

Tick they tick, move they move,
The minute-arm does rise
It's a cruel jest; it's a vile trick
which gives the day no size.

In her tracks, old Future brakes
A leg suspended, petrified
She dares not move, no step she takes;
By silent time nullified.

Yes, the sun is asleep —
But Faustus is dead.

Can the sun be asleep — and time still march on? Can time be asleep — while the central sphere of heaven continues to move? Is the sun the architect of human history?

Notes
1. See Westerlund, 1980, pp. 36-37.
2. Cesaire, 1939.
3. The obsession with the present was making the reputations of the dead an easy prey to unscrupulous sensationalizers.
4. Safire, 1989.

17 IDEOLOGY AND DOGMA

Mourad Wahba
Iansham University, Cairo, Egypt

It is well known that the term 'ideology' made its first appearance during the French Revolution with a philosophical school (empiricist and sensualist with a tendency to materialism) at the close of the eighteenth century and the beginning of the nineteenth century. The author of the term is Antoine Destutt de Tracy. His 'Elements d'Ideologie' (1801-1815) presents a 'Science des Idees' for which he cites the authority of Locke and Condillac. They are praised for having inaugurated the natural history of ideas, that is, the scientific description of the human mind. For Destutt, who superimposed the materialism of Cabanis upon the Lockean sensationalism of Condillac, the study of 'ideology' is part of zoology. What he means is that human psychology should be analyzed in biological terms, that is, without paying attention to religion. Thus, there is no super-sensible reality behind the individuals and their ideas (sensations and notions).

In 1795, De Tracy was entrusted with the management of the newly founded Institut de France. During the brief period of its predominance, until Napoleon in 1801 made his peace with the Church and concurrently turned against the liberal intellectuals who had helped him into the saddle, the Institut was associated in the public mind with an outlook which pre-dated the Revolution, but was now made official and was brought into relation with the practice of the new regime. The prestige of the 'Ideologues' flattered the vanity of Bonaparte, who in 1797 became an honorary member of the Institut. However, it was fear of the hold over public opinion which in January 1803 led Napoleon to cap his growing despotism by the virtual destruction of the Institut's core from which liberal and republican ideas radiated throughout the educational establishment. A pejorative connotation was quickly attached to the word 'ideologue' in the early years of the nineteenth century when Napoleon used it as a derogative. He denounced as 'ideologues' the liberal intellectuals of the Institut de France, who previously had promoted his rise to power, but whose republican and anti-religious ideas he now regarded as a threat to his church-supported absolutism. And this means that ideology, in its original meaning had been against the illusion of the possibility of appropriating the absolute.

But with time, ideologies tended to be absolute in claiming that they are not subject to compromise. Within this context, totalitarian regimes emerged and were incarnated in communism and Nazism, that is, systems proclaiming the absolute truth for their views of the world. And that is why since the 1950s ideology has been waning. In a 1950 article, Hughes identified a 'process of ideological dissolution and a wreckage of political faiths in which radical ideologies lost their force.'

The most significant impetus to the spread of the end of ideology thesis was provided by a conference on 'The Future of Freedom' in September 1955, held in Milan. There emerged a consensus along the following lines: The end of ideology thesis was due to the increasing affluence in Western countries and it was crystallized in the fact that antagonistic ideologies were moving closer together.

Since the Milan conference, a number of scholars have become involved in further elaboration of the end of ideology thesis, and the phrase, 'the end of ideology' has become a catch phrase summing up a major trend in our time. Daniel Bell chose it as the title for his published collection of essays on American politics and culture in which he hailed the end of ideology due to the exhaustion of the nineteenth century ideologies, particularly Marxism, as intellectual systems that claim the absolute truth for their views of the world and a road to action not for the sake of the present, but for a promised tomorrow. And this claim, according to Bell, is false. He says,'If the intellectual history of the past hundred years has any meaning — and lesson — it is to reassert Jefferson's wisdom (aimed at removing the dead hand of the past, but which can serve as a warning against the heavy hand of the future as well) that 'the present belongs to the living'. This is the wisdom that revolutionists, old and new, who are sensitive to the fate of their fellow men, rediscover in every generation. 'I will never believe', says a protagonist in a dialogue written by the gallant Polish philosopher Leszek Kolakowski, 'that the moral and intellectual life of mankind follows the law of economics, that is by saving today we can have more tomorrow; that we should use lives now so that truth will triumph or that we should profit by crime to pave the way for nobility. And these words echo the protest of the Russian writer

Alexander Herzen who, in dialogue a hundred years ago, reproached an earlier revolutionist who would sacrifice the present mankind for a promised tomorrow.

In this sense the end of ideology means an elimination of two concepts: the absolute truth and the future. But if these two concepts are identified with totalitarian regimes such as Stalinism and Nazism, and if totalitarianism is identified with dogmatism, then one has the right to raise the following question: Is ideology equal to dogma? Originally, the word 'dogma' signified a decree, a command and not a truth (Luk.II,1; Dan. II,13; VI, 8 Esther III,9; Maccab, X, 8). It was much, much later when it began to be used to denote the doctrinal decisions of the Fathers, the Councils and the Pope. This was afterwards called a dogma. In the 20th century the term ideology acquired an impassionate meaning. As the political struggle of the age took on the intensity of the earlier religious wars, the word came to denote in politics what the term 'faith' had meant in religion.

And in this sense as others have rightly observed, ideologies are some kind of religions, yet they differ from conventional religions in that they are based on information rather than ignorance. It is not knowledge of these events that ideology disseminates but their 'true meaning which renders.'[3] But this means that ideology is limited to the interpretation of the status quo. And consequently the end of the ideology thesis is right in stating that political theory which aims at radical social transformation has ended. This means that the end of ideology thesis embraces a value judgement based on a commitment to the *status quo* and on a refusal of radical transformation, that is, a refusal of the revolutionary ideologies.

Now the question is: Is it right to equate ideology with revolution? And is it right to equate the end of ideology with the preservation of the *status quo*?

To answer this question one has to see that ideology is related to the concept of time in the sense that the *status quo* involves the present and the concept of revolution involves surpassing the present. Thus, one has to define ideology within the concept of time. As time consists of three moments, the past, the present and the future, the priority is for the future in the sense that human history moves from the future and not from the present or the past. Thus ideology is a value system projected in the *pro quo* and when it is realized in reality it becomes culture. This culture is the objectivization of an ideology and

Ideology and Dogma

at the same time its end. Accordingly, the changing of culture necessitates the adoption of a new ideology. Thus one can conclude that human history moves from an *ism* to *de-ism*, that is, from an *ism* to the negation of the *ism*. But this negation is temporary because a new ideology, or a *re-ism* is to be constructed. Thus ideology per se is open and not closed or dogmatic.

Notes
1. Hughes, 1951, pp. 146-158.
2. Herzen, 1959, p. 469.
3. Kristol, 1955, p. 60.

18 THE ANTITHETICAL SEQUEL IN THE AFRICAN PERSONALITY

J.M. Nyasani
University of Nairobi, Kenya

Colonialism was and still is a historical fact whose implications have not been fully comprehended mainly because people choose to ignore or even suppress the concept out of embarrassment it causes in both the colonizer and the colonized. And yet long psychological treatises could be written on it even if only to rake up more and more embarrassment. Since the aim of this chapter is to analyze a tiny aspect of colonial repression, a full psychological exegesis is out of the scope and, in any case, counter-productive *vis-a-vis* the specific conclusions that I wish to draw from the negative side of colonialism as a historical phenomenon.

Any colonial adventure that aims at suppressing or subjecting other people to the will and design of the coolonizer is immoral *ipso facto* and *simpliciter*. This may sound like an extreme positiom to adopt but an objective analysis of the aims and objectives of the colonizer will reveal that there is some pervasive element in the whole colonial design: in the first place, it is invariably accompanied by the intent to suppress the will of others and secondly, to effect a cultural alienation in the people to be colonized. This in itself makes it both an injustice and an immoral act perpetrated by a powerful person against a weaker one. It is ofcourse true that in human society not everybody will be powerful and resistant of external forces of domination; otherwise Plato would never have advocated and justified the practice of keeping slaves in ancient Greece. This notwithstanding, we find great contrast and something of a contradiction in Plato's disciple, Aristotle, who argued strongly against the practice of Spartan domination without, however, condemning slavery outright. The good man of virtue is supposed to be content with what he has and does not need to go out to look for glory or greatness since, as a virtuous man, he has all the qualities inherent in him.

With or without Plato and his disciple Aristotle, domination and suppression are realities of human social existence perhaps only with one difference — the total integration of all the positive qualities of the dominated by the dominator and the recognition of his dignity in his inferior station. Again this would be more of an ideal than anything. The truth of the matter is that there has never been a brand of colonialism that was so indifferent and apathetic to the temptation to dominate and actually exploit both the natural and cultural resources of the dominated peoples since colonialism derives its true meaning and justification more or less from an abberational tendency of taking advantage in every sense of the word. Colonialism, in as far as it is double-edged in terms of its benefits and disadvantages, very heavily relies on the philosophy of despoliation materially, culturally and even spiritually. And this *modus operandi* happens to be the most harrying, the most undermining factor of the dignity and pride of any people, in this case the colonized peoples of the world. Let us now cast a critical look at each of the colonized people and see what psychological impoverishment they bring to bear upon the ego of the colonized people.

Material exploitation and the dignity of the colonized

One of the major designs of colonialism was to fully exploit and alienate every natural and mineral resource that it considered useful to the metropolitan industrial machine. The argument then was that the colonized subject had no use for it or did not how know to put it into good use. In the face of it, the argument is sound. However, looking at it from the point of view of human history and the fact of countless possibilities of diverse human evolutionary trends, the argument can only be valid in as far as it relates to and underscores a particular epoch of human evolution. And it was certainly valid and opportune at the time of the 18th and 19th centuries' Industrial Revolution in Europe. Indeed it was considered to be a sound argument for obvious reasons, namely that industrialized Europe had to endure in the end an industrial fall-out to the colonized territories in terms of their social evolution. The exploitation was further justified on the ground of occult religious motives according to which it was argued that paganism in Africa was both an evil and a retrogressive factor which, in the interests of manifest destiny, had to be wiped out completely. In this noble mission of civilizing the natives of Africa it was considered fair and just to take out whatever could be regarded as a compensation whether in economic or human terms. This total despoliation (because it also took spiritual dimensions) left the African in a perpetual bleached state of uncanny depersonalisation. And that is where the seeds of economic, social and, may I hasten to say, political woes were planted.

Colonialism and its attendant practices of maximum exploitation, humiliation, subjugation, vilification and utter contempt for human equality and dignity, has gradually and progressively brought about a sad process of mental, spiritual and social degeneration of the colonized African. It has rendered him totally naked, alienated and a shadow of his original self. Indeed, the colonialist machinations of vilification and depersonalization have rendered the colonized Africans very much a grotesque mimic, a superficial and ambivalent impostor with regard to his own values and those of alien civilization. This is to say in effect that the colonized African perpetually finds himself in a state of ambivalent psychological persuasion in that he is neither truly true to native values nor truly loyal and conversant with his adopted values. This state of hotch-potch and half-baked familiarity with things that ideally should form the basis for personal confidence, intellectual assertiveness and generally the driving force for social, cultural and political action turns into an inhibiting and enslaving force. As a consequence, instead of defending and upholding his dignity as an inalienable endowment, the colonized person succumbs to the doctrine of detraction and inferiority astutely propagated by the ingenuous exploiter.

It may be argued that material exploitation *per se* may not necessarily bring about a state of hopeless impoverishment of the ego and its attendant assertive operations. This view may be right only in as far as it may be expounded by an obsessed spiritualist who pours scorn on anything material on or about man that may enhance his well-being. The truth of the matter is that material goods were destined for man's rational use and, provided they are used rationally and in moderation, they should conduce to the enhancement of the individual, spiritually and physically. The nature of the enhancement may assume differen forms and indeed have diverse implications on the actual individual ego.

Let me now explore some of the forms and implications that material goods can have on the enhancement of man's ego and even personality. In order to do this, it is necessary to have recourse to the Aristotelian ethical doctrine on virtue and the virtuous citizen. In his ethical theory, Aristotle sees man who pursues virtue (and by implication, social happiness) as one who is capable of exploiting natural, physical and spiritual resources according to the dictates of reason and moderation. Aristotle deplores the habit or tendency to indulge in unbridled pursuit of goods without restraint. Happiness, he argued, cannot be cultivated through irrational pursuit of excessive wealth. And yet some modicum of wealth is necessary to procure happiness. For this reason, he was critical of the imperialist campaigns by Sparta which were designed to impose the will of Sparta on other subjects and to ultimately exploit them materially and spiritually. The scholastic coinage of *virtus stat in medio* would seem to summarize what Aristotelian ethical theory on happiness and the pursuit of other virtues envisaged.

It is important therefore to bear in mind that moderate wealth is pertinent in the self-unfolding of the ego in its material pursuit of happiness. Excessive exploitation of the material goods by the colonial powers deprived their subjects of this fundamental medium to the attainment of a basic virtue. This unbridled exploitation also made them (colonialists) monstrously unvirtuous at least in the eyes of Aristotle.

The colonial scheme of undertaking a systematic plunder of natural wealth in Africa has left in its wake an incurable trauma among the erstwhile colonized Africans. Its somatic symptoms are still visible in a variety of forms all of which torment the African ego and its psyche. The post-colonial African has become a classified material in the most negative sense having plunged as he was into an abyss of dismal and abject poverty. He remains perpetually emasculated, deprived and bewildered. The post-colonial African perpetually finds himself in an embarrassing economic rut of poverty and shame. The very stigma of being labelled poor, indigent and underdeveloped has continued to wreak psychological havoc on the African to the extent that he is totally flummoxed about the options he can adopt. As a matter of fact, this uncanny bewilderment has sealed a very dangerous capitulation to the forces of the apparent static economic predicament. The African finds himself perpetually hamstrung because of the dynamic nature of the global economic progress going on, whose pace he can neither arrest nor overtake. This sort of hopelessness ultimately gives way to a strange inertia which further erodes and undermines the efforts to grasp and grapple with the problem of trying to improve some of the conditions of his poverty and misery. Very astutely the so-called developed countries have created impossible conditions for the African to extricate himself from the quagmire of poverty and misery. The developed world which once exploited massively, instead of giving back some of the wealth or at least displaying good faith in the distribution of that wealth, would rather hold on to their economic advantage and maintain the harrying economic *status quo* in Africa.

Economic exploitation was compounded by an orchestrated ideology of cultural detraction and vilification. This is perhaps the saddest thing that befell the African under colonization. For his culture was not only declared *anathema* but also vandalized, manipulated and deliberately debased to create an artificial vacuum which would readily absorb the cultural recipes and value systems of the West. This was the first deliberate lie that has enthralled Africa for generations and has harried the colonized African long after political emancipation. Indeed the delusive machinations and sustained negative insinuations about the native way of life became the major stock in trade and indeed the more potent tool of emasculating African dignity and, by implication, a crucial tool of effecting an accelerated process of culture alienation and self-hate. Progressively the colonized African began to develop a syndrome of self-repression about his own self, his own dignity and his own worth. This state of affairs introduced into the life of the colonized African a germ of diffidence, subservience and incontestable timidity in the face of asserting and demanding even natural rights.

The extent to which these partly self-inflicted pangs and torments gnawed at the psyche of the colonized African is debatable. However, the important thing here is that the African was found to be easily susceptible to a treacherous brainwashing which, in the end, paved the way for a dangerous sell-out of the self and for the creation of propitious conditions for the practice of acts of self-erosion, shame and self-alienation. This tragic state became even more manifest through conduct which in essence can be epitomized as a *dolce far niente* state, mainly characterized by indolence, and lack of initiative.

Where positive and aggressive actions of self-affirmation might have predisposed to the African to undertake diverse pursuits to enhance his ego and to improve his material conditions, the leisure syndrome took the better part of him and he was therefore plunged into a state of confirming his seemingly intellectual inactivity in matters of critical appraisal of his own reality, his destiny and dignity. Gradually the leisure predisposition gained the upper hand in the day to day living of the African and completely alienated him from devoting himself wholly to productive ideational activities that change the world. Very often it may be argued and perhaps rightly so that too much indulgence in leisure is an indication of an inhibition or even a manifestation of a hidden complex. And the development of the complex itself is the result of repeated repressions which do not have an outlet. In the case of the colonized African, psychological repressions arising out of cultural deprivations such as the ones we have described above were the order of the day or were at least to be expected. In order to re-enact the suppressed culture and perpetuate its nostalgic past, it became necessary for the colonized African to resort to all kinds of indulgences and diversions which did not threaten the new exotic cultural order. And they only did so much more to the amusement and sport of the colonial masters than to their own amusement and entertainment.

It may be argued in some quarters that the colonial masters permitted their subjects to compete and achieve intellectual excellence, and only a few Africans showed the inclination and interest for that kind of striving. This may be true during the dawn of colonialism when, under the pressure of the manpower dilemma, some Africans had to be persuaded to attend school to acquire basic education and skills to man lowly colonial institutions. This notwithstanding, the majority of Africans who might have shown interest towards education for its own sake never really got the chance to pursue it. They were either interrupted by economic forces or literally plucked from it to pursue and reinforce the process of native pacification, which at that time was considered to be the top priority.

The re-affirmation process of the ego

The physical and psychological emasculation process under colonial repression in itself left a big dent in the African personality, since the devastation not only created a psychological lacuna, but also set each individual psychologically at variance with himself each in his own way and according to his colonial repressive perceptions. Thus the colonial oppressive *Weltanschauung* was experienced variously and in varying degrees of intensity so that what a colonial subject in Kenya perceived as oppressive may not necessarily have been the object of negative perception elsewhere in the British or French empire. This varying degree of perception of colonial suppression also created a novel dimension of contradiction in the Africans themselves — their general conduct, comportment, discipline and their total *Weltanshauung*. The colonial acts of indignities perpetrated against the African were themselves bewildering and astute enough to pander to the African's belief that he was indeed inferior, superior only to his own kin. Thus in almost the same degree, the colonial master pooh-poohed the African for his backwardness; the Africans themselves poured scorn on each other and in effect created haloes and auras of superiority in inferiority around themselves according to colonial experience and locale of oppression.

In the face of the above scenario, the post-independence African had real task ahead of him, namely, the task of liberating himself from the crisis for which he was partly responsible and of which he was dimly aware, but enduring the experience in the sub-conscious throughout the colonial domination period. This unpleasant exorcism was to last for a long time and to predispose, most unfortunately, the African to a further dilemma in the choice of political, social and economic alternatives. All of a sudden the African discovered that he had to contend with forces which pulled him away from his private convictions about the reality of social, political or economic phenomenon that was peculiar and unique to his tradition. Thus the era of oscillation between tradition and 'Western' was heralded by sheer colonial designs of conditioning and clever prompting. The African, as a result, never stood firmly on any tradition, either that of the West or of his own. Indeed he became, or shall I say, converted himself into a strange commodity of exchange often according to convenience and rarely according to the degree of consciousness or ignorance of the schemes and designs of the manipulator.

The larger part of our post-independence history has been devoted to the redemption of the alienated ego and convoluted personality in the hands of crude and deliberate manipulations. The battle has not been won yet, as many Africans are still basking in the sun of false colonial indoctrination or are simply lacking the requisite consciousness to rebel against the protracted brainwashing. For those who have actually joined the battle or have come face to face with this estranging phenomenon, the task is not only a difficult one, but also vexatious and trying. At one time the battle seems to be won, at another, it appears to be abandoned and still at another disparate, uncoordinated and inconsistent. This state of affairs is brought about by the dangling benefits that boost chances of personal advantage and personal glory often conjured by a smart schemer. Indeed, right in the heart of the African ego, there is a downright split or at least a potentiality for an easy split when it comes face to face with the decoys of economic advantages.

Occasions which present themselves as potentially dazzling in terms of making the right choice or at least a choice in conformity with the native tradition are many indeed and trying. Invariably, the victim succumbs to the temptation of jettisoning his native norms, beliefs and traditions in preference to a tantalizing material advantage. And there are many such material advantages that can be encountered in countries ravaged by poverty and misery where the temptation to succumb to an alleviating economic cushion need not be too high, provided it deludes one into believing that his economic status will change by taking the blind risk of succeeding in the transaction. It is sad to imagine that there may be many Africans who normally are traditionally upright and even sometimes diehards of the traditional ways of life but who are prepared to betray themselves and their culture because of the material gains they are able to procure upon repudiating and literally discarding their own priceless possession — their stoic cultural life.

Self-betrayal has become so entrenched in Africa that the alienation that it has created is difficult to assess and predict. The conscious self-betrayal is so terrifying that the victim completely loses any sense of direction and instead prefers to wallow in a quagmire of opportunism. When in the end the realization comes that a leap must be taken it takes many tortuous ways to regain himself. In essence, the process of regaining, re-asserting or re-affirming oneself becomes nightmarish and not infrequently, a frightening experience. Thus, the erstwhile colonial enticing snares give rise to a totally new dimension that requires a positive self-reassessment and subsequent decision to overcome the *status quo* of what we have termed a conscious self-betrayal. The exercise of self-exorcism is long and arduous and may at times become perverted to give rise to an ego that is intrinsically distorted and one that is pusillanimous and totally ill-prepared to take initiatives. Of course, a few succeed in discarding the psychological ambivalence, but the vast majority of people remain ensnared in their delusions emanating from the material advantages.

The above predicament becomes an important factor in determining the sanity of an individual African *vis-a-vis* his character development. In some cases, it may be the case that a sane decision is taken to break completely with the past obfuscating experience, or it may accelerate the process of psychological maladjustment which poses a big obstacle to the development of a new ego prepared to break with the past. Whatever it is, must be acknowledged that the post-colonial African is still beset with many snares which handicap him in freely undertaking duties and tasks which are exclusively in line with his native tradition.

So much time and energy is lost in the process and as a result, tasks which are intended to redress the economic, social, and political imbalance that has now become endemic in colonial Africa are invariably neglected or simply relegated to some future review, all at the expense of the accelerated pace of economic and material development. As a matter of fact the relegation never ceases because once it is about to be overcome, there is always another excuse to put it off to some other future. In this way, it would seem, no real re-adjustment is attained and the African perpetually remains fettered to the past tantalizing experience of colonial manipulations. Consequently, the progress that he makes in every sphere of development is piecemeal, retarded and out of step with his own reality and, shall I say, with even that of the metropolitan expectations. And so the spiral of contradictions continues *in saecula saeculorum*.

19 WHAT CAN THE EUROPEANS LEARN FROM AFRICAN PHILOSOPHY?

Gerd-Rüdiger Hoffman
University of Leipzig, Germany

In 1988 we published a book: *Wie und warum entstand Philosophie?* (How and Why did Philosophy Arise?) This title at least was stamped on its spine. In the bookshop at Leipzig University, I saw with my own eyes the surprised faces of those who read the full title of the book which is: *Wie und warum entstand Philosophie in verschiedenen Regionen der Erde?* (How and Why Did Philosophy Arise in Different Regions of the World?) I do not want to go into the details of the contents of this book because, since then we have been considering some of our hypotheses quite critically. In that book, we made a somewhat unusual attempt to deal with the genesis of philosophy considering the ancient India, China, Japan, Greece, the Islamic world, the sub-Saharan African region and pre-Columbian Mexico, to be of equal significance. The provocation was deliberate as the average European intellectual expects a book under the title *The history of philosophy* to mainly refer to European philosophy, as Walter Kranz expressed it in 1941: '... he who philosophizes, thinks in Greek terms anyway.' And there has hardly been any student yet who has contradicted such a point of view seriously. The European relationship to African philosophy is changing nevertheless. Although it is true that professional philosophy does to the greatest possible extent still deny its African counter-part, this does not mean that African philosophy is not mentioned at all. African philosophy is not only the subject of general research into the history of philosophy; there are also systematic treatises on different trends. Popular as well as academic studies can be found taking up the idea of the Belgian missionary Placide Tempels. He said that we (the Europeans) have to learn, more than the African (the Bantu), a more philosophical manner of reflection.[1] In my opinion, these different points of view reflect the actual trends in dealing with African philosophy in Europe. Before my short attempt to characterize these trends, I would like to make two preliminary remarks.

Firstly, strictly speaking, one can say that the term *African philosophy* is not quite exact; we indeed should speak about African philosophies or, even more precisely, *about philosophies in counties of a continent which are quite different in their cultural, political and economic situations.* However, I use the term *African philosophy* because it is easier to understand. In my opinion, the expression African philosophy is widely accepted today, and I think that all African philosophies have some common characteristics which justify a general description, in spite of all the advisable caution.

Secondly, I will not try to understand the African philosophy from inside. In other words, I am not an African insider. I do not deny my European point of view; otherwise I could be considered an arrogant charlatan or — as speakers of Kikongo could call me — a *nzonzi za luvumu* (a master of rhetoric but a liar).

I should now like to go into greater detail on the European treatment of African philosophy, especially in German-speaking countries.

Ignorance

Considering the syllabi of universities and philosophical dictionaries or books on the general history of philosophy, it seems quite normal to pay no attention to the existence of African philosophy. Even if its existence is taken note of, it seems to be quite hard to consider it being of any relevance to Europe. There is no doubt that one can find various arguments against African philosophy as a main subject of European teaching and research. Those who complain about the lack of money for this field are trying to maintain the university model of the 19th century. Only a few European universities adhered to the idea of the *universitas litterarum* in the real sense of this term, which means to study all sciences considering the totality of human knowledge. Much more often the intention was to install enclosed departments of the universities — *nihil novi sub sole* (nothing new under the sun). In my opinion it is mainly racism which prevents the unprejudiced studying of African philosophy. No one in the mainstream European academic circle would admit this matter of fact, but we should not have any illusions about it.

Exotism

As far as philosophy is concerned I would like to describe exotism as the egoistical manner of acquiring strange views of life starting from a superior or apparently superior position. Therefore it may also seem exotic to find portraits of Kant, Hegel, Fichte or Marx hanging on the wall of a department of philosophy at any African university, but this is not exotism at all. Predominant Western standards of education, publishing houses, professional journals and the mass media have already offered the desirable position to Kant, Hegel, Fichte and Marx. Therefore noone will be surprised about these portraits. Paulin J Hountondji is absolutely right when he says that the sciences in Africa are a facet of underdevelopment. Research work which also includes philosophy is as externally orientated as the economy is. Its impetuses and its theoretical results are still 'directly or indirectly given and determined by the needs of the imperialist economy'.[2] Although this view may need further qualification, it is still valid even if a so-called autochthonian African philosophy is booming at the moment again in both Africa and Europe. Despite the fact that the attempts of African colleagues to deal with the history of pre-colonial African philosophy and to reconstruct it, should be appreciated in itself, one should accept also the assumption that the European interest in their research work is often influenced by a romantic criticism of capitalism. The historical situation of African states or the concerns of the African peoples are not the main reason for African studies in Europe, but in strong terms, the reflection of the crisis of the European civilization at the end of reason and rationality. Therefore, African philosophy has to be very different from European philosophy. Such is the ignorance about modern African philosophy that terms like tradition, harmony, intuition, and real spirituality are nearly considered as its synonyms. I agree with Kwasi Wiredu who says '... there is a tendency to construe African philosophy as being identical with traditional African philosophy. This tendency has a colonial ancestry.'[3]

Tolerant missionarism

This approach is represented by those who are convinced of the higher values of their own philosophy and civilization, but who are still able to consider their own civilization, critically and are therefore ready to get to know other civilizations. The main target is to bring the real faith to the Africans and to convince them of the necessity of modernization according to the European model of the only revolutionary ideology. Deviating from the classical missionary work, the modern Christian missionaries, the apostles of capitalist concepts of modernization and the remaining teachers of the missionary variant of Marxism/Leninism, know that they can be successful only by looking for a connecting link between their own and African thinking. Examples of this new outlook are the decretal *Ad gentes* of the Vatican II,[4] the slogan of the moderate neo-colonialism "Custom-suits only fit the black man to a T,'[5] or quotations by representatives of the '3rd World' in the Marxist/Leninism compendia which did not reflect any other changes.

Inter-cultural philosophy

This notion must not be accepted today as one that takes one or only a few philosophical traditions to be valid for all regions of the world. Or as Franz Wimmer expresses it in his new book, *Interkulturelle Philosophie: Geschichte und Theorie* (Inter-cultural Philosophy: History and Theory):

> After it became possible to influence or even to determine the life of people on the planet by decisions which are taken by a small part of mankind — or even on behalf of it only — no part can claim anymore to represent the whole as the results and consequences of the thoughts and decisions also affect the other parts necessarily.[6]

Considering these conditions, it is not difficult to understand that Eurocentrism has become as obsolete as other forms of centrism. But this reason hardly ever effects consequences concerning philosophical research work and teaching. We have to solve two main problems at least.

Firstly, we must not speak on behalf of others who are able to speak in their own name. And these others have to be more resolute in speaking for themselves. As Aimé Césaire described it in his heuristic letter to Maurice Thorez in 1956, it could be considered *'une véritable révolution copernicienne.'*[7]

Secondly, we must not consider everything unknown in Europe important, without critical faculty, and we should not 'start a blind African or oriental travel.'[8] We should not try to substitute uncritical exotism for Eurocentrism which has been developed historically.

Priorities for philosophy today

In my opinion we should first accept all the following priorities. European philosophies have played — for good reason, I presume — a leading part throughout the history of world philosophy and may still be able to act an important part at the present time, but this must be only one part amongst others. Its representatives have to be careful not to lose even this part in the end which may become the real danger if firstly, they continue to embrace a concept of the progress which accepts the progress becoming true for the minority in the so-called centres of the world at the expense of the majority on the outskirts; secondly, if predominant concepts of rationality justify totalitarian forms of rulership or under the banner of 'democracy', legitimize the tendencies of militarization within international relations; and thirdly, if the Europeans have no better idea than to look for the 'totally different world' and strive to find this world in traditional Africa.

Ignorance in general prevents us from learning all that we could learn from African philosophy. To overcome this situation through enlightenment only, without labouring for changes in the present political and economic situation is unrealistic. I regard *exotism* and even *tolerant missionarism* as being capable of developing in spite of all criticism. Therefore, they could be the basis for a productive dealing with African philosophy in Europe. But this is not the essential problem. I would like to refer to another problem.

The preoccupation with the so-called traditional African philosophies leads to an enthusiasm for Africa which takes for granted that, for example, *La philosophie bantou, Yoruba philosophy of life, Hunhuism, ubuntuism or Sage-philosophy* can be adopted in their pure forms to present times and will help re-orientate an industrialized and anti-human world toward one stronger in human and spiritual values.[9] I do not want to contest the fact that it can be useful to remind people of values which have not been adjusted to technical progress and which do not accept man's domination of nature. But isn't it strange that the process of becoming aware of the civil, social and cultural crisis has led to an uncritical acceptance of non-philosophical views of life as philosophies, i.e., a picture of traditional African philosophy has been studied instead of the matter itself; even the colonial features of the Bantu philosophy have been neglected as it only suits the picture.

Referring mainly to ethnophilosophical treatises, some people believe they know what the essence of *the* African philosophy looks like. Therefore Kwasi Wiredu concludes: 'Hitherto there has been a tendency for facile generalization to be made about African traditional philosophy. It seems to be assumed that what is true of one or two African peoples is true for all Africans.'[10]

Last but not least, there is still a tendency which considers African thinking as a genuine factor. And all that was regarded to be African inferiority by the colonial ideology is at once described as especially superior in African philosophy. Then it appears as an advantage that Africans are supposed to be incapable of rational thinking and attach greater importance to intuitive thinking.

In any case, modern African philosophy has been ignored, and as the European preoccupation with traditional African philosophy reacts upon Africa to a large extent, the impression that African philosophy has not changed is strengthened. The opportunity to profit from the knowledge of African philosophy has rarely been taken. What shall we learn if we find only what we want to find? It seems to me that our chance to learn from African philosophy is the greater the more we approach the *inter-cultural philosophical basis* which has been proposed by Franz Wimmer. Inter-cultural philosophy corresponds in equal preoccupation to different philosophies which require that African philosophy be dealt with as critically as any other philosophy, and not at all like an ethnological exhibit standing about in the glass show-case of museum ethnology.

Why should we as Europeans be interested in African philosophy then? Firstly, I attach importance to the idea that we should simply think over the part which African philosophy could play in our European philosophical thoughts. This could raise questions about old structures of thinking as well as about apparently definite answers and methods of the historiography of philosophy. But we will not be efficient as long as we continue to believe that we know each answer, because this would mean that we only admit our questions.

Secondly, the preoccupation with African philosophy can be quite interesting as far as the old question of philosophy is concerned: *What is philosophy?* The old concept of philosophy is obviously not of general validity but concerns mainly European thinking. One could argue about the four trends of African philosophy as have been stated by Odera Oruka: (1) professional philosophy (2) nationalist-ideological theories, (3) ethnographical studies of traditional African beliefs labelled as philosophy — i.e. ethno-philosophy, and (4) sage-philosophy. But in my opinion his conclusions are of general interest and should not be confined to African philosophers only. As he says

> ... we should initially suspend our judgement as to what constitutes philosophy in the strict sense of the term. Yet this point of philosophy in the strict sense remains important in our research. The classification of the different trends should be seen as a means for us in Africa to identify philosophy in the strict sense from philosophy in the broad and all-embracing sense. This, if done, is one way of invalidating that some particular sense of philosophy is the authentic African philosophy while philosophy in any other sense is foreign to Africa.[11]

Thirdly, African philosophy can contribute to attempts at solving problems which have been previously ignored or neglected when European thinking and, later on, the East-West-conflict predominated philosophical thoughts throughout the world. I would like to mention especially problems such as *life in nature* as opposed to *rule over nature*, and the utopian idea about a solidarian society which has been dealt with by Nyerere in his *ujamaa* concept (that should not be reduced to the organization of *ujamaa*-villages. Perhaps there is a third way out of the crisis in Africa and throughout the world based neither on the command structure of what has been described as 'real socialism' nor on modern capitalism. Solutions as those proposed by Zera Yakob, Mbiti, Senghor, and Kaunda are hardly adequate anymore. Some of these proposals might have been useless for practical life from the very beginning. But this is not a reason to forget unsolved problems.

Fourthly, African philosophy should remind us of the fact that it is almost immoral to define philosophical work only as a dispute about other philosophies. The connecting link between philosophy and the real world must be maintained, i.e. to raise such questions as; *What is philosophy good for in a world which suffers from hunger?* or *What is the sense of such words as humanism, peace and progress?* I think that Africa does not mainly show us the limits of such ideas but the necessity of thinking in such general categories because this is the only way to draw out the global connection of local crisis. On the other hand Africa also shows that one must discuss these categories as concrete matters.

Fifthly, considering African philosophers, we as Europeans have to make up our lack of the reflection and reception of foreign philosophers. It is certainly right to say that the historical circumstances often forced the Africans to acquire European education. But in my opinion some African philosophers have done unprecedented work, for example, Frantz Fanon who has developed a liberation ideology for the oppressed peoples starting from preoccupation with Marx and other European thinkers,[12] Kwame Nkrumah who interpreted the philosophy of Kant to produce his *consciencism*[13] or Paulin J Hountondji who develops a philosophy for Africa despite his European studies of philosophy.[14]

It is still a bit difficult for me to study and teach African philosophy systematically. But it is obvious that we can profit from the preoccupation with African history of philosophy which exists up to the present time. The history of philosophy can also include 'a humanistic function while mediating and deepening the apprehension of strange views of the world and that is the way it can contribute to the friendship between peoples'.[15] I am sure that it is useless to believe in flattering speeches. But we might be able to back up the idea of solidarity, internationalism and equality in rights in spite of the scepticism which is part of our profession.

Notes
1. Tempels, 1945.
2. Hountondji, 1983, p. 14.
3. Wiredu, 1984, p. 31.
4. Abbot, 1965.
5. Ortlieb, 1979.
6. Wimmer, 1990, p. 70.
7. Césaire, 1956.
8. Wimmer, 1990, p. 114.
9. Sumner, 1986; Awolalu, 1970; Samkange, 1980; Odera Oruka, 1991.
10. Wiredu, 1984, p. 42.
11. Oruka, 1991, p. 28.
12. Fanon, 1961.
13. Nkrumah, 1964 (rev. ed. 1970).
14. Hountondji, 1983.
15. Wimmer, 1990, p. 116.

20 AFRICAN PHILOSOPHY: TWO VIEWS

Kate J. Wininger
University of South Maine, Portland, U.S.A.

In this chapter I would like to consider some of the issues being examined in academic philosophy, and in the political and social lives of the people of Africa. There are many views of what philosophy is and should be in Africa today. One of the attractions of African philosophies is their vitality. This is especially true with respect to their response to the issues of the current trends in philosophy in the West. In addition they are vital because many of the indigenous debates are ones which can have dramatic effects on social practice and on the lives of the people. Many of the philosophers are political leaders, for example, Nkrumah and Nyerere. And some of these people are called upon to adjudicate or give their opinion on legal and political issues. The connection between a philosophy in its theoretical aspects and its recommendations for practice can be seen quite vividly.

We are accustomed to looking at the etymology of the word 'philosophy' when we begin talking about the discipline or when we introduce our students to it. We say that the philosopher is one who loves wisdom or pursues it. In many contemporary cultures the word has taken on a meaning attached to its cultural contexts, and this has restricted its use to the activities of a person who is engaged in a rather technical enterprise. The activity is often sanctioned by an institution, usually a university or religious establishment. This practice has the rather, unhappy consequence of leaving out many types of wisdom, especially those which do not fit into an established discourse.

In this chapter an attempt will be made to study and consider a variety of philosophies including ones which do not have the sanction derived from being attached to an institution. To do this we have to broaden our own understanding in order to include ideas and wisdoms which are not written down. The group of philosophies which are indigenous and have grown up in pre-colonial Africa are now called ethno-philosophies. The question of their legitimacy as true philosophies is part of an important debate in the African literature.

It might not be surprising to find the legitimacy of indigenous African philosophies questioned by American and European thinkers. The Western intellectual tradition has long valued writing and a certain brand of intellectual activity as a sign of knowledge, reason and culture. There are, of course, notable exceptions. Perhaps the one which springs the most readily to mind is Plato's suspicion of the written word, and his clear preference for having conversation about philosophy with the thinkers present. He believes that this is preferable both because it is more likely to produce real understanding and because the authors of the ideas are present in order to correct what might be misapprehensions on the part of the other participants in the discussion.

In the West we have associated legitimacy with the written word. We sometimes use the test of literacy as a sign of a person's competence (as a criterion for voting, for example), rationality, and hence, humanity. Let us consider a historical example used by Henry Louis Gates Jr. in his preface to the anthology *"Race", Writing and Difference.* Gates makes this point in the context of discussing literature, but, like him, ultimately what I want to examine is how Western epistemologies allow or encourage these horrors. In 1772, the poet Phillis Wheatley went 'on trial'. She had written some poems which her 'master' attempted to publish under her name. The publisher whom they first approached thought the public would never believe that they could have been written by a young African girl. Proving that she did in fact write them meant something not only about her, but the entire Negro race. A very 'important' tribunal consisting of the Governor, Lieutenant Governor, prominent citizens and clergymen needed to be set up to determine that she was the author. Their testimony was put at the beginning of the book of her poems so that white people would believe that they were done by a black woman.

Painful ironies abound in the history of this country, where literacy is a sign of humanity. Strict prohibitions against teaching blacks to read betray the knowledge of the framers of such laws that these people had the potential to learn. If they really were incapable of reading/reasoning the prohibition would hardly seem necessary. It also betrays the association of literacy with power.

Gates hypothesizes that 'after Rene Descartes, *reason* was privileged, or valorized, above all human characteristics. Writing . . . was taken to be the *visible* sign of reason'.[1] The point I am trying to emphasize is that the relation between writing/literacy and intelligence or rational capacity is an important element in Western culture. This in turn makes us suspicious of those systems of thought which are not presented in written form. It also has peculiar effects on the ways in which the ethno-philosophies are viewed. We will return to this latter point when considering the idea of the Sage which is put forward in the writing of H Odera Oruka.[2]

The colonial presence has made the debate over the legitimacy of the ethno-philosophies an internal one, that is, within Africa. Many professional philosophers who are trained in academies have adopted Western standards of scholarship and consequently are less likely to consider the indigenous belief systems to be philosophies. In fact the philosopher Kwasi Wiredu of Ghana has associated the interest in ethno-philosophies with a colonial or neo-colonial bias. He notes:

> ...a tendency to construe African philosophy as being identical to *traditional* African philosophy, as if modern Africa is incapable of philosophy. This tendency has colonial ancestry. The underlying assumption is that if one is going to talk of African philosophy at all, then one must locate it in communal *Weltanschauung* of traditional African societies, for philosophy in the modern world is essentially a Western phenomenon.[3]

The question of the legitimacy of ethno-philosophy is not one which I personally find very interesting. It duplicates a debate within the Western tradition between those who prefer an exclusive or inclusive definition of the term 'philosophy'. It is, of course, important when a culture uses this distinction in order to exercise an intellectual domination as Wiredu has pointed out. I have felt quite comfortable using the more inclusive notion. This notion includes religious and other types of worldviews. I do not see that very much is to be gained by the more exclusive notion (except a certain type of gate-keeping). It seems especially important that the function of philosophy not be limited in a world which has many problems and where the perspective of a philosopher might help.

Accepting the existence of these ethno-philosophies as philosophies does not however make the issues much easier. In Kenya alone (where I have my experience) there are at least sixteen major, different indigenous religious and ethnic groups. These people are divided by language and custom. The people belong to Nilotic and Bantu groups. Their languages are not closely related, and even among the numerous Bantu speaking people where the languages are related, they are not related closely enough to allow for understanding of much beyond a few words. If one adds the intrusion of various cultural and religious groups one can see that the situation is indeed complex. It is worth naming a few examples. The Arabs have influenced the Swahili coast for centuries. Some people were and are being converted to Islam by traders and immigrants. There are various Christian religions which have come about largely as a result of missionary activity. There is a large population of Indians some of whom were imported to serve as workers under the colonial government, and an assortment of British ex-colonials or settlers.

The colonial presence in British East Africa/Kenya lasted only about 80 years, but it is extremely important to the political and social organization of the country. Its importance includes Kenya's existence as a nation and consequently its geographic borders. Queen Victoria apparently drew the border between Kenya and Tanzania in order that her German cousin could have a mountain too. She had Mt. Kenya and he had Mt. Kilimanjaro. The British presence is particularly important to our inquiry because the system of education, and hence, formal philosophy is modeled on the British system of the university. The courses which were taught are those which duplicate those commonly found in Western universities. Only fairly recently in the post-colonial situation (independence was achieved in 1961) has African philosophy and literature been added or made central to the curriculum. English is the language of the university, Swahili and English the languages of lower level education. For the majority of the population these are not first languages. Obviously other African countries vary a great deal. My point in speaking about Kenya is to give a sense of how varied and complex the situation is and how difficult it is to generalize about Kenya, let alone about all of Africa.

If we consider the ethno-philosophies, the presence of philosophy in Africa is obviously very ancient. The beginning of interest in these philosophies by Western thinkers is customarily traced to a Belgian philosopher who wrote the book *Bantu Philosophy* (in Baluba or Zaire). Placide Tempels published this study in French in 1945. From the Western perspective this is one of the earliest attempts to understand the Africans on 'their own' terms. As Tempels puts it we must 'understand their metaphysic. The gulf between Africans and Whites will remain and widen so long as we do not meet them in the wholesome aspirations of their own ontology'.[4] The ontological principle which Tempels finds underlying Bantu philosophy is the belief in a 'vital force'.

The view of African philosophy 'from the outside' are important in a way. They have a presence in the African literature which is partially a reaction of defense. They represent a reaction against an external definition which is often derogatory or patronizing. Their presence also seems to be the result of the beginning of a written discourse on thought in sub-Saharan Africa. This produced a certain type of self-reflection or self-consciousness in post-colonial Africa. For example, Abiola Irele's preface to Hountondji's book *African Philosophy: Myth and Reality* considers this definition of African philosophy from outside—as does H. Odera Oruka and most accounts of the state of African philosophy.

Another (aside from the revalued ethno-philosophies) significant movement in African thought is known as the theory of Negritude. The name most often associated with this is Leopold Sedar Senghor. This movement had adherents in the diaspora as well as in Africa. Basically it accepts the notion of racial or ethnic difference, but does not accept the hierarchical assumptions which many Western discourses do. Those discourses did not stop short of expressing the inferiority of the Negro or black 'Races' Thus 'difference' was not just descriptive, but also contained an evaluative element. The place of reason in the culture and discourse of the West made it devalue the cultures which were perceived to be organized around emotional attachments and superstitions.

Negritude acknowledges not only the differences between the 'races', but even the Western characterization of them. Senghor writes 'Emotion is African, Reason is Hellenic', and 'We feel, therefore we are'. He speaks of the importance of emotion to knowing. he believes that there is something in common among 'primitive' peoples (primitive meaning here before 'history' and before writing), but that something is a valuable reliance on meaning which comes from myth and community in oral traditions.

Later in his life, the American philosopher and essayist, W. E. B. Du Bois was interested in an idea of 'Race' and racial identity which had this breadth.[5] Negritude praised the irrational or non-rational aspects of African culture. It re-evaluated the values which had been used to dismiss the culture of the African peoples. The emphasis on feeling and emotion were seen as positive attributes of a different and not inferior culture, culture which could teach Europe a great deal.

There are parallel movements within feminism. Some women embraced a notion of women's culture which was different from men's, but not inferior: separate but equal. Even the content which described the differences between men and women, and Negroes and Caucasians were similar: the emphasis on emotion, and the importance of familial or group identity in the latter case was opposed to the emphasis of reason and individuality in the former.

One of the problems with Negritude, and its analogue in feminism, was that it seemed to deny too much, to give up too much. Many blacks did not want to deny their rationality and their ability to 'master' the Western discourse. They saw in Negritude a philosophy which perpetuated a Western conception of the Negro/Black as 'other'. John Mbiti's book *African Religions and Philosophy* which is quite well known in the West has been taken to share some of these characteristics. Odera Oruka writes that in it Western or European thought is considered 'logical, reflective and impersonal (African) is seen to be intuitive, personal and a lived experience'. Odera goes on to criticize the implication 'that Africans are strangers to objective, logical and reflective thought,' a claim which he believes to be already refuted.[6]

Some people have criticized Negritude because of its use of the concept 'race', that is, its acceptance of a Eurocentric view of Africa and Africans. Race is a concept which, strictly speaking, grew out of a 17th and 18th century scientific discourse. It grew up in a time when colonial expansion and 'exploration' (or conquest and domination) were important in European culture. even in early 'scientific' writings the idea of race does not have the neutrality which it claims and which is the supposed goal of scientific discourse. The works of the American philosophers Cornel West and Anthony Appiah and many others contain this kind of critique in greater detail.

In Africa there are also political and social philosophies which are extremely important. These take the form of a number of models for social organization and reorganization (following decolonization) some of which are related to the spectrum of political philosophies of the West. Many of these thinkers are political leaders who held office in their countries, for example, Nkrumah in Ghana and Nyerere in Tanzania. But we might also include the Kenyan writer in exile, Ngugi wa Thiong'o.

Ngugi is especially interesting because he rejects the romantic idea that we can go back to pre-colonial values. Yet he is anxious to fight neo-colonialism by using tradition and a wide variety of traditional cultural practices which still exist in Kenya today. Ngugi blends various beliefs in some aspects of Marxism and socialism with similar values in indigenous belief systems to arrive at strategies for a post-neo-colonial Kenya. Ngugi proliferates his ideas in novels, essays and autobiographies.[7] Before he went into exile he organized a theatre company in his home province which used the native language Gikuyu, and addressed issues of interest to the community and particularly its women. Ngugi described the project as truly collaborative with changes to its original story being made as the production progressed. The result was that the theatre was banned by the Government. This ban raises an important issue. Part of the reason Ngugi was viewed with suspicion is his avowal of principles which threaten the basic capitalism of the current neo-colonial government. But the other and equally important reason for the censure is that his decision to revalue traditional ways necessarily led him to pick *certain* traditional ways. They were the way of *his* people a particular group of Kikuyus of Limuru. Again the decision in favour of tradition is not unproblematic because it involves a choice in this disparate political entity in favour of a group and a language, and it is this 'favouring' of the Kikuyus as much as anything which was responsible for the government intervention.

I am extremely reluctant to be giving what is, because of its brevity, merely a taxonomy of various philosophical perspectives. But I believe it is extremely important to have some idea of the range of activity because of our tendency in the West to lump together such a wide range of discourses as 'other' and to deny differences, and the real and productive tensions between these views. So I pass so briefly over these philosophies with great reluctance and will welcome questions about them in the discussion.

Now let us return for a moment to the 'problem' of the oral literature of African philosophies. The literature of the Bible, of Homer and of the poetry and literature of the pre-Islamic Arab world all present a similar problem for interpretation. These works have arisen out of an oral tradition and have entered written discourse in the form in which we now have them. Of their earlier forms we know very little; only that which can be surmised by the existence of different versions, references in the text to other earlier stories or events, etc. Because of our reliance on and reverence for the written word and because of our inability to retrieve (in ways which we have come to consider legitimate) the earlier discourses, we tend to take as canonical the texts at the point when they enter into written language. We ignore their place in history partially because they are at the point of entry in what we consider to be legitimate history. I suspect that the way in which we treat ethno-philosophies is parallel to the way that we treat these texts in some respects. The colonial 'discovery' of indigenous philosophies in Africa tends to treat those views as static—as having existed in a similar form forever. There is, for the most part, only internal evidence to contradict this and much of that is considered mythic. From this attitude arises the view that these philosophers are 'primitive', having existed for centuries in basically the same state (the one which is 'documented' by its 'discoverer'). At the same time the West is seen as going through the transformations which are documented in the literary tradition it recognizes and which advance or progress producing 'true' culture. This idea needs to be looked at quite seriously and critically.

The last philosophy that I want to examine is that which considers the idea of the Sage as a helpful idea in looking at all philosophies in Europe, Africa and elsewhere. The most notable exponent of this view is H. Odera Oruka. This philosophy does not treat indigenous philosophers as if they were static. Many philosophies do consider the wise elder or 'witch doctor' to be someone who repeats and passes on the tradition as he or she got it. Odera sees the wise person or Sage in the culture as one who interprets some of the values, ideas and truths of the culture. The person is not necessarily bound by them in a conservative enterprise. by this I mean that she (or he) is not merely policing those values. This work of the Sage is a critical, reflective activity. It is rational, evaluative, and creative. Some of the valuable features of this view are that it does not deny credence to the traditional beliefs of the indigenous people. It also does not accept the exterior definition of African peoples as having certain non rational peculiarities which determine their behaviour. A critical, rational discourse is and has been part of these cultures as it has in various Western cultures. The culture has never been static; it has continually had to develop in order to respond to issues which arise in the practice of the people. Thus, it is also not a philosophy of alienation but one which has responded and still responds to the actual needs of the people as cultural living beings.

Socrates and Protagoras meet in the Platonic dialogue, the *Protagoras*. In it, Protagoras asks whether they would rather hear him tell a myth or story. There is general agreement that a myth is to be preferred. Although the text contains a disputation or argument, the story which Protagoras tells suggests that understanding is as important to his conception of philosophy as is argumentation. In the spirit of Protagoras, I present a story which is aimed to help in the understanding of the place of philosophy in African culture today. My point is not to provide a judgement in this case but rather to show how some of the issues I have been mentioning play out in an actual legal and moral dispute.

S.M. Otieno was a member of the Luo ethnic group. He became a lawyer in Nairobi and married a woman from outside his group. His wife was a Kikuyu and also a prominent citizen. When Otieno died he considered himself a thoroughly modern African. He expressed no desire to return upcountry to Luoland, the place of his birth, nor to be buried there. When his wife tried to bury his body in Nairobi, Otieno's family challenged her in the courts and a bitter court battle ensued. Khaminwa, a civil rights lawyer in Nairobi, took the case for Mrs Otieno. The philosopher, Odera Oruka, who is a Luo, was called upon to testify for the Luo family members. As a philosopher, Odera was asked about the traditional beliefs of his people. The Luo believe that if a group member is not buried in the land of his or her people, then the spirit of that person will not rest and misfortune will fall upon the members of the clan. This case caused an international uproar. It was extremely important because it was seen as a case where traditional or customary law came into conflict with the civil law. Since the civil war in Kenya is a legacy of British colonialism, this case raised issues of the legitimacy allowed to the indigenous belief systems within a neo-colonial structure. This issue is compounded in Kenya and in this case by the fact that the two ethnic groups represented rivals for power within the country.

I have only spoken about a few African philosophies. The ethno-philosophies, Negritude, some political-social philosophies, and the idea of Sagacity all represent only a few of the wide variety of theoretical frameworks by which African people understand their experience.

Notes
1. Gates, 1986, p.8.
2. Odera Oruka, 1990.
3. Wiredu, 1984, p. 31.
4. Tempels, 1959, pp. 16, 18.
5. Appiah, 1986.
6. Odera Oruka, 1984, p. 177.
7. These include *A Grain of Wheat; Barrel of a Pen: Resistance to Repression in Neo-colonial Kenya;* and *Detained.*

21 SIGN-LANGUAGE-COGNITION

Jerzy Pelc
Department of Logical Semiotics
Warsaw University, Poland

Sign

In discussing the concept of sign it may turn out useful to be aware of several distinctions: (1) sign-indication-index-symptom-syndrome-icon-signal-symbol; (2) token type; (3) qualisign-sinsign-legisign; (4) sign-sign use; (5) sign vehicle-sign functions-sign; (6) sign as individual-sign as system; (7) individual sign-system of signs. I adopt a general concept of sign recognizing indications, indices, symptoms, syndromes, icons, signals, and symbols as different kinds of signs. When I speak of the sign, I have in mind the use of it: there is no sign outside the use of something by someone in such-and-such a place and time as a sign of something else. The sign users, and in particular the sign interpreter, does not have to be a human being; however, sign users are beings capable of carrying out the so-called semiotic inference, not necessarily verbalised. An entity of any kind may be used as a sign. When something at a certain place and time is used as a sign of something else, then with regard to a circumstance C1 this use may be to such-and-such a degree indicational, and with respect to C2 it will be of signal character to such-and-such a degree, and with respect to C3 it will be symbolic to such-and-such a degree, etc,; there are no pure uses of any one kind. The above observation remains valid for the opposition natural - conventional with reference to use of signs.

Language

Some consider every system of signs to be a language, others - to be a code, still others see codes and languages as distinct among the system of signs. A general notion of language encountered e.g. in information theory, is being defined as any system of information conveyance between people, or between parts of a biological organism, or fragments of a machine. The system is an infinite set of sound or inscriptions each of which is a combination of a finite number of symbols of a fixed alphabet; a set of rules serves to distinguish well formed sentences from ungrammatical ones. Also ethnic language is being described as a system serving broadly understood communication expressing ideas, shaping emotions, performing referential, emotive, imperative, phatic, metalinguistic and/or poetic functions, involving an infinity of functionally distinct expressions, having a finite system of structure-dependent rules which determine the hierarchy of phrases and generation of new phrases, mainly by recursive embedding, allowing for modality, propositional attitude, description, presupposition, aspect, anaphora and quantification, and finally, as something acquired effortlessly. Language is characterized by double articulation: the segmentation of text into morphemes and the segmentation of morphemes into intophonemes, and by the fact that it includes two semiotic categories: words and sentences, called basic ones, and in addition, functions. The notion of language is of typological character, which means that the properties of being a language are gradable. Among its features the following ones could be added to the above list: in ethnic language we constantly keep producing new compound wholes which are meaningful and comprehensible, although their sense was not predetermined as a ready formula attached to each such compound whole. Such a whole may belong to a different semiotic category than each of its components, and the difference between the semiotic category of the components and the semiotic category of the combination they form often results in the difference between ontological categories of the extratextual counterparts of each of them. Meanings of expressions are context-dependent; both the linguistic context and pragmatic context come into paly here, and the latter is not limited to the situation of sending and receiving the expressions but includes many other factors. Consequently, a given expression may belong to different semiotic categories according to the circumstances of its use. The fact makes the distinction between language and speech necessary and explains why ethnic language is a set of languages in the logical sense, i.e., languages with one-one expression-meaning assignment.

Cognition

The term *cognition* may be seen as referring either to a certain activity, action or process, or to the products thereof; in what follows it will refer tot he activity of cognizing something. Every activity and action has its agent and its objective. The analysis of semiotic activities—the sending, receiving and processing of signs—cannot overlook the senders and receivers interpreting signs, participants of cognition and/or communication processes. Also interpretation, i.e., the activity or arriving at an understanding of signs, has its subject: the interpreter. In pronouncing ourselves in favour of the pragmatic approach to semiotics, cognition and interpretation, we are motivated by the obvious fact that for each of these activities to take place there must be an agent endowed with mind. As was stated above, there are no signs outside the use thereof; but moreover, there is no use of sign without the sign interpretation, and there is no sign interpretation without a cognizing subject. it follows that neither a plant nor a computer acts as the interpreter or understanding subject. On the other hand, the object of understanding may be an entity of any kind, on condition that the entity is used as a sign of something else: in the genetically primary sense one may understand only signs. Thus, interpreting something is a semiotic activity: it consists of making a kind of inference; namely the interpreter I, basing on the premise that in his conviction the interpreted object A occurs, and on the premise that in his conviction there exists some kind of sign relation between A and B/causal, of similarity, of similarity, conventional etc., with regard to some semiotic systems, draws the conclusion that B takes place. This inference is very often enthymematic, not verbalized fully, and unverbalized in the case of animals. The process of interpretation may include explanation, and the latter—as a passage from *explanandum* to an *explanans*, i.e., from one sentence to some other sentence—requires that we understand each of these sentences; thus we have alternating phases of interpretation and explanation within one process of semiotic. It seems that formulations of the type 'I understands A' may be reduced to formulations 'I understands A' where 'P' represents a sentence. Semiotics consists in sending, processing and receiving signs. In order to be able to use something as a sign, I must perceive it or imagine that I am perceiving it. Even if pure perception were possible, and I doubt it is, then it would not in itself suffice to use the perceived thing in the capacity of sign. One must perceive it as such-and-such an entity, applying conceptualization, single it out from the environment and recognize it as belonging to a certain system. One has to think, to believe, to conceptually apprehend in addition to perceiving, retrieving and imagining. While the semiotic process of interpreting signs consists of performing cognitive activities, the activity of cognizing some entity includes the element of interpreting the entity, except for revelation as a form of cognition, the object of which may be incomprehensible by nature and hence not subject to interpretation. Thus cognition is of indirect character and semiotic; but we should remember that the term 'indirect' is gradable here. The above approach to the concept of sign, language and cognition is expected to pave the way towards an analysis of semiotics performed from a cognitive science point of view and an analysis of mind performed in semiotic terms.

22 RE-VIEWING VERWOERD'S VISION: CRITICAL REFLECTIONS ON THE PRAXIS OF APARTHEID AND THE THOUGHT OF ITS ARCHITECT

W.J. Verwoerd
Department of Philosophy
University of Stellenbosch, South Africa

> South Africa is a country of many baffling contrasts ... Between the euphoric vision of Dr. Verwoerd and the resigned apathy of a pass-law offender ... (in) the magistrate's court stood a vast gulf of apparent incomprehension.
> *T.R.H. Davenport*

Making sense of the past, without justifying sins, one of the most difficult tasks confronting someone with an Afrikaner Nationalist upbringing who is participating in the formation of a truly democratic, future South Africa. As part of this task, this chapter reflects on the conflict between the political thought and praxis of someone who epitomizes Apartheid in its classical, most baffling form, the 'one man ... remembered as the author of our calamity ... '[1]

The question addressed here is: Why did Dr. H.F. Verwoerd (Minister of Native Affairs, 1950-1958; Prime Minister, 1958–1966) continue with his 'vision of justice'[2] despite its consequences? Why did he persist with his policy of separate development—'designed for happiness, security and the stability provided by their home language and administration for the Bantu as well as the Whites'[3]—despite the manifest injustices and unhappiness caused by his actions?

Attempts to answer these questions, to explain this baffling contrast, have emphasized, on the one hand, the ideological nature of his thoughts and actions. Some concluded that he must have been mad, that he was a Nazi/Fascist, an impractical fanatic. Others described him as a 'consummate ideologue ... who undauntedly wanted to force through his intellectual schemes, the brilliant mind with scant patience who abhorred compromise and glorified principles as the Architect of Apartheid'.[4]

On the other hand, a recent study by Lazar of the Afrikaner nationalist alliance between 1948-61, challenges the popular belief, that Hendrik Verwoerd was the omnipotent 'architect' of a consistent apartheid plan. Lazar argues that although Verwoerd was arrogant and often dogmatic, his 'legislation, speeches, reports and letters indicate that, above all else, he was a pragmatic and ambitious politician whose primary objective was to respond, on all fronts, to growing black resistance . . . '[5] This picture of Verwoerd emerges also from Adam's distinction between traditional race separation and utopian separate development, with the latter most clearly embodying the new and flexible elements in the domination of a racially separated majority by a pragmatic race oligarchy.[6] Du Toit also emphasizes that Verwoerd's shift in policy in 1959 to that of separate development was 'not so much due to ideological conviction as to an expedient and pragmatic adjustment to changed circumstances.'[7]

Thus there seems to be a conflict of interpretations between those depicting Verwoerd as an ideologue and those regarding him as a pragmatic politician. These different pictures draw attention to important distinctions with regard to the meaning and role of ideology, which can be employed to structure this chapter. Once these distinctions have been made, the rest of the chapter will be divided into three sections. Each section will be devoted to a discussion of one of these meanings of ideology in connection with the question at stake. This will be done in the order in which they have been introduced, in order to reach the conclusion that a combination of these different senses of ideology may serve as a hermeneutical key in the search for an explanation and fundamental criticism of the tension-filled relationship between Verwoerd's vision and its falsifying consequences.

Given the complexity of ideology this chapter will limit itself to two basic distinctions. A first distinction can be made between ideology as 'impractical and visionary ideas' and ideology as 'an action-oriented set of beliefs and attitudes associated with a social group'.[8] In the former particular sense of the word, ideology functions as a negative evaluation, in *contrast* with all that is supposed to be realistic.[9] Within the latter, more general conception a further distinction between two levels of ideology can be made.

On the first level, ideology functions as a consciously *constructed* political belief-system which directs and gives coherence to policy debates. On the second level, ideology denotes an *implicit* belief system, the uncritically accepted set of assumptions or prejudices ('pre-judgements') which structure the way one thinks.[10]

An ideologue's vision

The connection between Verwoerd's thought (as reflected in the policy of separate development) and ideology as impractical, visionary ideas results, from the association of this meaning of ideology with a popular distinction between ideologues and pragmatists: Ideologues are those who are committed to some general social theory or plan which they feel will solve everything and to which they will stick at any cost. They believe in the possibility of radical and systematic reform and change. By contrast, the term pragmatist is reserved for those who take a realistic, practical, common-sense approach to politics, with reforms guided as much by precedent, instinct and above all caution as by any theory or explicit ideology.[11]

This distinction reflects important differences in political culture between white South Africans. This distinction's popularity in English circles highlights the embarrassment of a utilitarian worldview with overriding moral principles or ideological blue-prints, in contrast with the Afrikaner culture which is rooted in a morality of principles (however evil their application).

Verwoerd's unique personality and political style, his intellectual vision and dogmatic advocacy of Grand Apartheid, despite its practical consequences, widened this conceptual gap between what Terreblanche called the 'ideological and religious oriented Afrikaners and the much more pragmatic and liberal minded English-speakers', making him the ideologue *par excellence*.[12]

This ideological picture, however, does not only emphasize Verwoerd's personality and different approaches to political practice—thus highlighting elements of the background to his vision. Its main use is not an illustration of a conceptual gap within white South Africa, but as a criticism of the vast gulf separating Verwoerd's policy of separate freedoms from non-white demands for freedom. It is obvious that this *contrast* between theory and practice should be condemned.

However, this important negative evaluation does not explain where this contrast came from. The complex *relationship* between ideology and practice is not dealt with. The ideologue/pragmatist distinction breaks down when it is realized that ideology can be very pragmatic.[13] Thus the obviousness of the ideological picture may become a spell which obstructs a broader explanation and more effective, more fundamental criticism. By combining two concepts which are usually contrasted in the South African context, and by making use of insights gathered from recent research, the following section will attempt to break this spell.

A pragmatic vision

By employing ideology in the broad sense of the word, the pragmatic picture introduced above makes an important contribution. It does not only *contrast* ideological preoccupations with practical caution and common sense. Instead, the *relationship* between principles and pragmatism, within *one* ideological framework, is emphasized, i.e. the practical orientation and purposes of a set of ideological principles—in 'giving one cause for doing'—are more explicitly recognized.[14] This recognition of the meaning given to collective action by ideology, implies that for an ideology to be fully understood, it must also be assessed in its own terms, apart from the necessary focus on its practical effects and on the social interests promoted via ideological rationalization.

Before looking at Verwoerd's effectiveness as a pragmatic Afrikaner Nationalist, his vision must first be reviewed from his perspective. This will help to account for the euphoria surrounding it, as well as the ineffectiveness of criticisms against the injustices accompanying his vision. Interpretations which emphasize the contrasts between ideological principles and political practice, by concentrating on the repressive aspects of the apartheid system, often under-estimate pragmatic changes in official policies, which resulted in a *theoretically* consistent policy from an Afrikaner Nationalist perspective. The shift in Verwoerd and his government's official position from racial segregation/apartheid to separate development can be seen as a move towards greater ideological clarity and theoretical consistency. As a move away from the crude apartheid, closer to the already established separationist idea.[15]

With the winds of change blowing across Africa, following the end of the era of unproblematic worldwide white domination, separate development or Verwoerdian apartheid thus became a systematic ideological package, with an

> intellectual appeal which managed to morally seduce more than the ignorant and unreflective racists in South African society... The first new and coherent post-colonial era response to the political, social and economic difficulties generated by decades of

colonial exploitation. An ideological response to a colonial situation where the whites would not and could not leave.[16]

Instead of the whites leaving, the logical alternative, on a theoretical level, was therefore that the non-white ethnic groups had to leave—in terms of the exercise of their citizenship. Of course, their labour power had to stay. The phenomenon of migrant labour in the European context, served as a precedent for the ideological justification of this illogical continues dependence.

This unique form of internal decolonization, was further differentiated by the peculiarly conservative and controlled content given to black independence in terms of the Bantu Authorities' system. A system based on a specific conception of African culture and traditional rule, which had to be protected. This was welcomed by conservative elements amongst the Africans, which strengthened the illusion that separate development was a practicable *and* acceptable solution.[17]

In comparison with the white politicians in Rhodesia, Angola, Mozambique who persisted with established colonial methods of rule, this could indeed be described as pragmatic or enlightened form of co-existence. This policy was profoundly racist in its consequences for the people who suffered from its implementation. But on an ideological, theoretical level, therefore, it cannot simply be dismissed as irrational racism, pure and simple.[18]

Emphasizing ideological coherence and the attitude underlying separate development may indeed seem like insensitivity and a luxury in the face of the suffering and poverty caused by separating development. On the other hand, as stressed by Adam: 'Only if one takes the theoretical plausibility of the Apartheid policy into consideration can the missionary zeal of civil servants committed to paternalistic aid, and the belief in the success and sincerity of their course, be understood'.[19] This may help to explain why criticisms which focused mainly on the consequences of an ideologically defined policy were so ineffective. This was partly due to the fact that the white opposition parties did not provide alternative policies with the same clarity and appeal to the imagination of an insecure white electorate. Furthermore, criticisms which did not deal with the ideological cause underlying this policy, were not only ineffective in changing this course, they actually *strengthened* the commitment to an Apartheid ideology. The more the cruelty of the means were criticized, the more important the moral principles and ideological ends became as 'the only way to attempt to validate cruelty.[20] The greater the demands for change, the more influential Verwoerd became. According to Pelzer, Verwoerd actually saw the excessive demands from an ill-informed and blindly prejudiced world as a 'challenge and opportunity to prove the honesty of our motives and the seriousness of our striving . . . '[21]

These criticisms of Apartheid practices were effective, therefore, contributing to changes in official policy, but not to changes in the principles of the Apartheid ideology. What changed was the official justification for white domination within an area described as their country, at a time of worldwide decolonization. This points to two related practical purposes of separate development. It served as a *constructed* framework within which policy discussion took place. What Verwoerd was good at—through his confidence in his own leadership and through his construction and defense of (more) coherent policies within a clear ideological framework—was to inspire many Whites with the belief in success and sincerity of the policy course. At a time of 'great doubt and uncertainty, when the people of South Africa longed for a leader who would give certainty and surety to its existence, it found such a leader in the person of Dr. Verwoerd'.[22]

Those less concerned with ideology and sincerity, especially those in the burgeoning state bureaucracies, as well as white agriculture and (low-income) white labour, were also satisfied. Separate development gave moral coherence to policies which protected their economic interests and accommodated their fears. These included fears of loss of privilege, possessions and cultural/political identity and also intense fears of a more violent nature.[23]

In retrospect, these fears appear to be exaggerated and misplaced. Whether this is true or not, these perceptions were certainly real, because their consequences were very real. This fact points to the important further practical function fulfilled by separate development. The corollary of the theoretical recognition of the eventual rights and sovereignty of Black separate(d) states was the ruling out of any idea that 'Black consent may be relevant to the legitimacy of White sovereignty and rule in South African *heartland*', while the ideological goals of total separation, also served to 'legitimize whatever coercive measures might be necessary to achieve the aims of separation itself'.[24]

The intensification of Apartheid inside the Whites' own areas thus accompanied the proposed positive developments. This reinforced and dangerously worsened most Whites' separation from the evidence against the success of their policy course, making their sincerity appear to be very baffling and very cynical indeed. Thus resistance (non-violent for many decades) continued to be interpreted—and therefore legitimately suppressed—as the work of agitators, Communists and Black Englishmen.[25] The results of this very incomprehension of pass-law offenders' non-apathy are clearly visible today. This points to section four's most explicit critical review of the consequences of Verwoerd's vision as well as the limitations of its principles.

A short-sighted vision

For someone who has not suffered from the implementation of Grand Apartheid, it is impossible to comprehend fully the nature of its consequences. However, a good summary is provided by Chief Albert Luthuli:

> To us Bantustan means the home of disease and miserable poverty... There is no hope in the Bantustan Act for and African. It is the White man's solution at ruthless cost to the African, of the White man's problems. Its only disadvantage from the White man's point of view is that it will not work.[26]

Luthuli's statement also draws attention to a further meaning of ideology which is overlooked by criticisms which focus only on the *contrast* between ideology and practice, and on ideology as a *constructed* political belief-system, that is ideology as an uncritically accepted set of beliefs or pre-judgements. This sense of ideology must be incorporated in a more fundamental criticism of the principles of Verwoerd as a white politician, of those assumptions shared by most Whites, many of whom, with good reasons, were critical of Nationalists' obsession with unrealistic policies, but whose criticisms did not extend to their own benefits from a system of White domination.[27]

Here I focus only on the fact that he took it for granted that whites had an unquestionable right to domination in what was regarded as their country. On an ideological level, in principle, this same right was granted to non-white ethnic minorities in their homelands. The heart of the conflict within white South Africa, could then be limited to (Afrikaner) Nationalism versus Imperialism.[28] As Verwoerd put it: 'This has been the basis of the conflict since 1910: A republic against the monarchical connection'.[29]

Ashforth argued convincingly that the design of the Union of South Africa (1910) structured racial differentiation into the very conditions of the existence of state power, with the direct relationship between land reservation and political citizenship forming the 'heart of the state', the fundamental basis of conflict.[30] His study has shown that Verwoerd was another white politician who overlooked this critical fact. The conflicts resulting from this were intensified and reached a decisive new phase under his ideological, pragmatic leadership. The conflicts between his adherence to the rigid political principle of separation and the dynamic, uncontrollable pressures of socio-economic development, between the siege mentality of apartheid policies and the irreversible process of de-tribalizing urbanization, highlighted the central historical root of the problem, the disunion structured into the union of white interests. Since 1912 at least, it is this foundation of a white South Africa, which has been disputed by those who had no choice when it was laid. A dispute which still has to be resolved at disputed power-sharing negotiations.

Concluding remarks

By employing different senses of ideology the preceding re-viewing and critical reviewing of Verwoerd's vision of justice for South Africa suggest both a limited answer to the baffling contrast under consideration here as well as avenues for further investigation and criticism. He persisted with his vision despite falsifying consequences: because his steadfast adherence to political principles reflected his personality and cultural background; because he believed that it was the only practicable solution; because it was politically effective; because his untested pre-judgements became totalitarian unquestionable rights; because his vision blinded him to the predictable consequences and failure of his policies.

Further investigation and criticism of this contrast between intended results and actual results may focus on the following themes: the personal and socio-economic background to an ideologue's vision; problems with the ideology of nationalism; the nature of racism; the morality of a vision which effectively justified means by ends; the importance of intentions in moral evaluations; the links between his personal power and the institutional and structural levels of power underlying Apartheid; or the relationship between individual action and the social determinism as a background to the question whether Verwoerd was a *tragic* figure or not, whether the painful absurdity, the baffling contrast of separate development can be seen as tragicomedy? (Implications for making sense, without justifying sins?)[31] With regard to the present, one may look at the implications of Verwoerd's limited pragmatism for the Conservative Party's promised return to Verwoerdian Apartheid and the remaining principles of Verwoerd's vision within a new National Party (e.g. group rights.) Without this critical reviewing, the ghost of Verwoerd will continue to haunt South Africa on the difficult road to shared freedom.

Notes
1. Luthuli, 1982, p. 176
2. De Klerk, 1976, p. 241.
3. Verwoerd in De Klerk, 1976, p. 241.
4. Suzman, 1991, p. 16; Hepple, 1967, p. 208; Oppenheimer in Harrison, 1981, p. 163; Giliomee, 1982, pp. 4–5; Kenney, 1980.
5. Lazar, 1987, p. 70.
6. Adam, 1971, pp. 52, 67–68.
7. Du Toit, 1975, p. 41.
8. Mullins, 1973; Thompson, 1984 and 1990; De Crespigny and Cronin, 1975, pp. 7 and 10.
9. This meaning corresponds to K. Mannheim's 'particular conception of ideology' and dates back to Napoleon's mocking criticism of certain French intellectuals' concern for abstract principles. See De Crespigny and Cronin, 1975, p. 7.
10. With regard to this distinction, see e.g. W.T. Bluhm's distinction between 'forensic' and 'latent' ideologies (De Crespigny and Cronin, 1975, p. 12) and Plamenatz' distinction between 'sophisticated' and 'unsophisticated' ideology (Plamenatz, 1970). With regard to 'pre-judgements' see Gadamer, 1971, on the historically transmitted 'forestructure' of understanding as an integral part of any interpretation.
11. Robertson, 1986, pp. 272–273.
12. Terreblanche, 1988. p. 371.
13. Havel, 1989, pp. 42–43.
14. Mullins, 1972, p. 508.
15. Du Toit, 1975; Cronje, 1945 and 1947.
16. Van Zyl Slabbert, 1985, p. 76. See Verwoerd's reply to H. MacMillan's 'winds of change' speech in Pelzer, 1966, pp. 336–339.
17. Scholtz, 1974, pp. 234–246.
18. Adam, 1971, p. 70; Van Zyl Slabbert, 1985, p. 76; De Villiers (1990) formulated this problematic point as follows: Apartheid was and is racism, but not all the Afrikaners, even those who supported apartheid, were or are racists. This is a crucial distinction, because unless it is understood, none of the Afrikaners' history makes any sense (and) it is impossible to understand why apartheid took the form it did. Apartheid is a complex combination of many emotions.... The complexities are not easy to see now. So much of it reads like simple racism. like mere rationalization, to justify odious acts. Which it is and it isn't. See also Kinghorn's (1990, pp. 31–41) interpretation of simple racism—discriminating attitudes of superiority and hostile actions on the basis of skin colour—as the *symptoms* of racism as an ideology, a totalitarian, pre-modern system of thought based

on biological differentiation between groups. The rejection of racism in Apartheid theory (collectivist nationalism) created a disastrous ideological illusion, he argues, which didn't recognize that a system based on 'equal, but separate nations (volkere)' couldn't function (in praxis *and* in theory) without racism as the fundamental principle of definition and administration. This illusion he believes, is central to an explanation of the tragicomedy of Apartheid, and central, I believe, also to an answer of this chapter's question.

19. Adam, 1971, p. 45.
20. Paton, 1979.
21. Pelzer, 1966. p. xx.
22. Pelzer, 1966, p. xx. See also, Ashforth, 1987.
23. Lipton, 1986, p. 361. See also, Hugo, 1988, his emphasis on the scope and emotional intensity of the (particularly Afrikaans) media coverage of the experiences of whites in a decolonizing Africa (e.g. in Kenya and the 'Congo'), pp. 567–590.
24. Du Toit, 1975, p. 40.
25. Scholtz, 1974.
26. Luthuli, 1982, p. 184.
27. Adam, 1971, p.53.
28. Pelzer, 1966, p. 180.
29. Quoted in Pelzer, 1966, p. 180.
30. Ashforth, 1987, pp. 1–5.
31. See Alford and Friedland, 1985, pp. 1–31; O'Meara, 1983; Kinghorn, 1990; De Klerk, 1976.

PART III

DISCUSSIONS ON ENVIRONMENTAL ETHICS

23 ECOLOGY AND ETHICS: EXPLOITING NATURE

Jay Drydyk
Calton University
Ottawa, Canada

In English the word 'exploit' is used often as a term of condemnation. Claiming to have been exploited is claiming to have been abused perhaps to have been treated unfairly, and both of these claims have moral import. but 'exploit' is not always used to condemn. There are contexts when it is used as a term of praise, as in the case of artisans who have 'exploited' the qualities of their materials to good advantage. So we might say that some cabinet makers are distinguished from others by the degree to which they exploit the qualities of their wood. Now, it is also true that some employers are distinguished from others by the degree to which they exploit their workers. Yet the moral force of these two statements is not the same.

Consider a third case. We humans are distinguished by the degree to which we exploit our natural environment. What is the moral force here? while we have certainly used our environment to advantage, it would be self-deceiving to think that what we have made of it bears any resemblance to a work of art. It scarcely seems appropriate, then, to praise our species for the way in which we have exploited our natural environment, in the same way that we praise some potters for the way in which they exploit the qualities of their clay, or carpenters for exploiting the burl and grain of their wood. Should anyone be condemned for exploiting the environment, in the way that some employers are condemned for exploiting their workers?

There is much to be gained by exploiting the analogy between environmental exploitation and economic exploitation. This sort of exploration has been made easier by the recent work of John Roemer, whose formal theory of economic exploitation lends itself to reinterpretation in the environmental context. Once it has been suitably interpreted, this conception of exploitation expresses certain moral intuitions about the environment which are ignored by other theories of environmental ethics.

Exploitation of humans

According to John Roemer's theory of exploitation, Group A is said to 'exploit' group B just in case A is in a position of dominance over B and the members of B would be better off (and A worse off) if B collectively withdrew from relations with A, producing and exchanging on their own with assets stipulated by the withdrawal rule. The power of this conception of exploitation is revealed in the variety of models it takes in vastly different economic formations. It is not narrowly economic; it is not tied to any economic theory of value, and it can capture various kinds of non-economic exploitation. It is applicable to any social system in which there is a division of labour and in which the participants receive discernible benefits as a result interacting with others in the system.

By considering some examples one can appreciate the power and elegance of Roemer's approach. For feudal exploitation Roemer suggests a particular withdrawal rule: assume the serfs withdraw each with the property that they had previously been allowed to work for their own benefit. If there is an alternative system, under this withdrawal rule, in which the serfs win and the manors lose, then serfs are exploited. Capitalist exploitation is captured by a different withdrawal rule, namely that wage workers bring to an alternative economic system the sum of their per capital shares of the means of production.

There is one form of exploitation that is especially significant in centrally-planned or administratively top-heavy economies, though it is also widespread in capitalism.[1] Roemer calls it 'status exploitation'. The idea here is that some people can exploit others by means of their status in state and corporate organizations. The persons who would qualify as 'exploiters' in this case are those who receive differential rewards that cannot be accounted for as remuneration for differential skills or assets. The higher salaries paid to managers in businesses and bureaucracies do not come as remuneration for capital they have contributed, nor do they entirely remunerate superior skills. In these cases, higher salary corresponds to higher status, and it secures loyalty to the company.[2] Dues to status, then, are differential payment not accountable as remuneration to capital, labour, or sill, but which remunerate status in a hierarchy and secure loyalty to the organization. Roemer puts the withdrawal rule defining status exploitation in the following way: 'A coalition will be status-exploited if it could improve the lot of its members by withdrawing with its own assets but exempting itself from the dues to status, and if the complementary coalition thereby fared worse.'[3]

Exploitation of nature

To arrive at an environmental conception of exploitation, one must interpret the groups, the withdrawal rules, and the allocation of benefits and harms in environmental contexts.

The groups. Who is exploited, environmentally? Exploitation of nature is best conceived in terms of the ways in which humans treat particular populations (global or local) of other species. Once 'exploitation' is defined in the context of species, it can be defined in regard to individuals by allowing that an individual organism is exploited in either of two cases: (a) in case its species is exploited or (b) in case its species *would* be exploited, if its members were *normally* treated in the way this organism is treated. Thus even an animal that is thriving would be said to be exploited, if it species were exploited; on the other hand, even if the species were thriving, treatment of an individual animal could still count as exploitive, in case the species would be exploited, were it to suffer this treatment in any widespread, generalized way.

Can we exploit parts of nature that are not organisms? I will not have anything to say about the exploitation of inorganic nature, except insofar as it forms part of the habitat of some living species. However, we should be able to say that nature is exploited, even by human activity that does not intentionally set about to use any particular species or organisms. If a rare species has been endangered or driven to extinction through the draining of wetlands, then one should still be able to say that this is a case in which nature has been badly exploited, even though the intent of the draining might have been to use the water or the land, not the inhabitants. Since it seems odd to say that a species has been exploited through being extinguished, it would seem equally odd to say that the habitat has been exploited, since in this example the wetlands habitat may too have been destroyed. I prefer to say in these cases that the geographic region is exploited. I propose to say that a region is exploited when use of the region affects a species within it so badly that, if we had brought about these same effects by using that species directly, we could be said to have exploited the species.

Withdrawal rules. The games-theoretic conception of exploitation allows us to say that a group is exploited only if we can show that they would do better by withdrawing from the conditions and interactions that are thought to be exploitive. The withdrawal rule must specify what sort of new patterns interactions they would enter into, and what resources they would take with them. In the environmental context two sorts of withdrawal suggest themselves. On the one hand, we might ask whether other species would do better in a world without *property* relations. Interactions would be determined, on the non-human side, by normal patterns of behaviour—of the sort that are studied by ethologists; on the human side we would have what some European philosophers called 'the state of nature', by which they meant the absence of property law. If other species would do better in such a world, where they might be subject to contact with humans but not to human ownership, let us say they are subject to 'property exploitation'. On the other hand, it would be simpler to imagine how other species might fare if they were able to withdraw from human contact altogether. If they were to do better in isolation from humans, let us refer to our exploitation of them as 'species exploitation'. Counter-intuitive results arise from relying exclusively on the property conception of exploitation. It is exploitive, under this conception, to make another species worse off by exercising proprietary control over them; however, to inflict the same harm on a species by direct use, without relying upon ownership, would not be counted as exploitive. For example, stress through overuse of fish stocks in a privately owned lake might count as property exploitation, but the same treatment of fish stocks in unowned waters would not. Species exploitation, then, is a more useful conception.

Benefits and harms. The final requirement is to interpret 'benefits' and 'harms' in the environmental context. There is much debate in environmental ethics about what should count as harm to non-humans. The three best known possibilities are (a) pain and suffering[4] (b) injury against the rights of an organism[5] and (c) vulnerability, endangerment or extinction of a species.[6] A balanced evaluation of these options is not possible in a chapter as short as this one; however, a few critical comments must be made. There is, I believe, a continuum of harms that might be done to other species, ranging from disturbing them through hurting them to making them extinct. we should be able to discuss degrees of harm throughout the entire range. But each of the three current conceptions of harm introduces a discontinuity somewhere, focussing on the harms that occur on one side, and ignoring the harms that occur on the other. Peter Singer's trans-sentient utilitarianism ignores harms that do not involve suffering or pain. On the other hand, if it is extinction or endangerment of a species that counts as harm, we are left unable to account for the degree to which we harm organisms that are not at risk. Finally, a rights conception of harm would seem not at all to allow of mistreatment by degrees.

The alternative I suggest is a *behavioural conception of harm*. I take it that species are harmed, first to the degree that local or global populations are reduced. But I also take it that benefits to a species vary with their chances to engage, with success, in certain behaviours. There are the conative behaviours in which organisms seek out certain objects, situations or interactions under normal conditions—'normal' conditions being those in which a local population can sustain its numbers. Finally a species is harmed to the extent that their chances of having to engage in aversive or defensive behaviour (flight and fight) are increased. The norms of a 'good life' for a species can be expressed by a measure of successful conative behaviour conjoined with a measure of aversive behaviour. Conceptually, then, it is meaningful to speak of a local population's chances of having a good life.

Consequently, the life quality and quantity of a population are commensurable in principle. Reducing a population's chances of a good life by any factor would be morally equivalent to preserving their quality of life while reducing their numbers by the same factor.

The behavioural conception of harm can encompass most of the harms to organisms that are emphasized by animal-utility, animal-rights and species preservation theories. Animal-utility theories give priority to pain, suffering and death as forms of harm. Since pain mechanisms are among those which cause organisms to avoid or flee certain objects, interactions or situations, anything which causes pain will also cause aversive or defensive behaviour and will therefore also count as harm under the behavioural criterion. The behavioural criterion is broader than the pain criterion, since it also allows us to take as indicative of harm the aversive reactions or organisms which cannot be said to experience pain. This view also takes seriously the notion that organisms are subjects of lives, on the assumptions (1) that this subjectivity is mythical if it is not revealed in behaviour, and (2) that if the non-humans have anything like what we call 'preferences', then these are best detected ethologically, by observing the organism's behaviour. Finally, the behaviour view takes extinction seriously, since either local population loss can be employed as criteria of harm to the species.

Some consequences

Special consequences emerge from employing the behavioural conception of harm within the conceptual framework of exploitation.

First, no obligation to avoid exploitation would require that humans treat other species better than they would fare on their own-better than they would treat each other, in effect. There may, in addition, be some degree of exploitation which is morally permissible. If a moral community could not be sustained and developed, if certain exploitive practices were discontinued, then those practices are morally permissible. I assume (since I have insufficient space to argue the point here) that a moral community must equalize its members' opportunities for development, and since development requires good health, a moral community must enable its members to stay healthy. If this requires reduction in populations of infectious and parasitic organisms, then, though this is exploitive, it is a morally permissible form of exploitation.

It will be said that if we commit ourselves *only* to avoid exploiting other beings, and if some exploitation is morally permissible, then the door may be left open for us to cause sentient beings to suffer and die for our own benefit. Do sentience and suffering not matter? Various characteristics, including sentience having a good of one's own, goal-seeking and self-regulation,[17] are claimed to confer moral standing on a creature. The arguments as to why these characteristics should count rest on analogies between other species who possess them and humans, who are known and assumed to have moral standing. While these arguments are not entirely without strength, the most compelling reasons why a moral community should accord moral status and consideration to beings with a given characteristic are that otherwise (1) the community would die out, (2) the community could not function—e.g. through lack of trust, lack of allegiance, lack of understanding, etc., and (3) the community could not employ moral language without inconsistency or hypocrisy. All three are reasons for giving standing and consideration to all potential *moral agents*. Until we encounter other species capable of guiding their behaviour by conceptions of right and wrong, humans will remain the only known species capable of moral agency. Neither the survival nor the functioning of a moral community requires the extension of moral standing to sentient creatures who cannot become moral agents.[8] Nor does consistency require this, unless one is already a trans-sentient utilitarian—which is to assume what is to be proven. On the other hand, consistency within a moral community does require equalization of development opportunities for moral agents. If it happens that the interests of equality within a moral community conflict with interests of other creatures—even sentient creatures—which are incapable of moral agency, then it is equality among the moral agents that should prevail.

It may also be said that it is unjustified and unfair, if not brutal as well, to allow the quality of life to be traded against quantity of lives among non-humans, which we would not tolerate in relation to our own lives. But the alternative is to treat each non-human life as having equal value. But we cannot act as though every organism's life has equal value to our own, without sacrificing ourselves as a moral community; nor can non-humans treat each other's lives as having equal values. Consequently, a requirement of moral equality and incommensurability among all individual organisms is both naturally and morally unenforceable.

In spite of this, good life for one species is not commensurable with good life for another species. Within a species there is, at least conceptually, a common behavioural standard for a good life. To arrive at such a standard among species one would have to compare the value of one species' behaviour to the value of another species' bahaviour. Aside from the capacity of a species to support and develop a community of moral agents, there are no standards by which to say that a good life for one species is better than another's. Consequently, every non-human species has equal value; the value of preserving a species is not commensurable with either the life quality or quantities of organisms in other species.

The framework of exploitation suggests an agenda for reforming our treatment of non-humans. Worst of all, and most urgently requiring change, are practices which endanger other species. Since the value of species is incommensurable, extinction if the most serious form of exploitation. Other forms of exploitation deserve attention and redress to the degree that they make other species worse off (in life quality and population size) than they would be in our C absence. Some exploitation may be morally tolerable, if it is required for the survival, functioning, consistency or equality of a community of moral agents.

Notes
1. Roemer, 1982, p. 247: 'Status exploitation is a problem not only for socialism but also for capitalism. Indeed, the status exploitation of capitalist society may be even more severe than in existing socialism. In large corporations, salary is set on an internal hierarchy and includes a large element of remuneration to status, to secure loyalty to the company, and so on. Perhaps the status exploitation is not so noticeable under capitalism as under socialism ... it is small in comparison to the capitalist exploitation which exists as well. Capitalism has no pretensions to egalitarianism and annihilating privilege, as does socialism, and hence capitalist status exploitation is less remarked upon.'
2. Roemer, 1982.
3. Roemer, 1982, p. 243; Wright, 1986.
4. Singer, 1975.
5. Regan, 1982 and 1983.
6. Gunn, 1984.
7. Singer, 1979; Regan, 1982; Taylor, 1981; Goodpaster, 1978.
8. This objection also holds against Van DeVeer's 'Weighting Principle', that 'the interests of beings with more complex psychological capacities deserve greater weight than those with lesser capacities—up to a point.' Donald Van DeVeer, 'Interspecific Justice,' *Inquiry* 22: 55–79.

24 TECHNOLOGY, ETHICS AND THE 'END' OF NATURE

Frederick Ferré
University of Georgia, Athens, Georgia, U.S.A

The 'end' of nature

In a widely read book, *The End of Nature*, Bill McKibben affirms, in some detail, his reasons for considering us to be living in 'postnatural' history.[1] It is an eloquent lament and a disturbing indictment of the heedless ways in which we human beings — especially we of the industrial modern civilization — have pushed the world to an utterly unprecedented condition. That is the condition of nature's both *seeming* to us and *being* largely a product of technological activities.

Those activities have not been witty or wise. We have frequently thrashed about without environmental forethought or even awareness. McKibben goes into much detail on inadvertent climate changes we have set in motion, the destruction of the protective ozone layer, acid rain, and so on. But worse is the loss of sense of nature being separate and independent, ruled by its own awesome forces. 'We have changed the atmosphere,' he observes, 'and that will change the weather. The temperature and rainfall are no longer to be entirely the work of some separate, uncivilizable force, but instead in part a product of our habits, our economies, our ways of life.'[2] Even consulting such seemingly objective measurements as temperature highs and lows will be misleading from now on.

> Those "record highs" and "record lows" that the weathermen are always talking about – they are meaningless now. It's like comparing pole vaults between athletes using bamboo and those using fibre glass poles, or dash times between athletes who have been chewing steroids and those who stuck to Wheaties. They imply a connection between the past and the present which does not exist...; we live in a postnatural world.[3]

This postnatural world, according to McKibben, is in many ways dangerous to our health as well as to our spirits. From now on we had better get used to hotter summers and to more cancers from postnatural sunburns. Good croplands will burn and wither in postnatural droughts. Forests and lakes will die from the artificial acidity in postnatural rain. And behind it all will be human tools. We will have no one else to blame, since culture has now intruded on nature.

> The storm that might have snapped the hot spell may never form, or may veer off in some direction, not by the laws of nature as they have been rewritten, blindly, crudely, but effectively, by man. If the sun is beating down on you, you will not have the comfort of saying, "Well, that's nature." Or if the sun feels sweet on the back of your neck, that's fine, but it is not nature. A child born now will never know a natural summer, a natural autumn, winter or spring. Summer is going extinct, replaced by something else that will be called "summer". The new summer will retain some of its relative characteristics – it will be hotter than the rest of the year, for instance, and the time of year when crops grow — but it will not be summer, just as even the best prosthesis is not a leg.[4]

As McKibben shows, this recent change is not only profoundly *practical*, threatening our entire civilization in its food supply, the location of its cities, the health of its citizens; it is not intensely *aesthetic*, undermining human perceptions of nature as 'eternal and separate' and replacing them with images where the world outdoors is not essentially different from the world indoors;[5] it is – beyond both of these – an essentially *religious* problem. He cites the important warning in the book of Job 'that we may not judge everything from our point of view – that all nature is not ours to subdue.'[6] He compares the prideful Western industrial way of life with the gentle attitudes of St. Francis of Assisi. For better or worse, we are now in charge. 'As a species we are as gods – our reach global.'[7] This realization brings with it a crisis of faith. Just as the occurrence of the Nazi Holocaust led to extreme spiritual pain for many who could not understand how a good and powerful God could allow such horror; similarly others today are (soon will be) suffering from the undermining by profane human technology, of the eternal integrity of nature. 'Why did he not stop us? Why did he allow it?'[8]

Agriculture and environment

'Human technology', in general is too broad a topic to handle in making a response to McKibben. I propose to give a little more focus to what follows by taking agricultural technology as the key example. Nothing is more intimately entwined with the natural environment and with the long story of humanly designed responses to human need.

Agriculture, after all, began it all. As hunters and gatherers, our ancestors pretty much left nature alone, to provide (or not) according to the operations of conditions far beyond our control or understanding. Our stone axes made up for our lack of effective claws or fangs, but did little to control nature. Our camp-fires may have added a tiny bit of pollution to the atmosphere, but they were negligible compared to the forest fires set by lightning or to boiling lava flows. The first significant attempts by *Homo sapiens* to change and master nature came with the age of agriculture, usually dated to the Late Stone Age, or Neolithic, about 10 000 years ago.[9] We must remember that the whole idea behind agriculture was (and is) the effort to tease and stroke and bully nature into giving us a crop. Only in that way can we settle down and have villages, towns, cities, nations and empires. Only in that way can we have chiefs and priests, books and trade, accountants and even philosophers – i.e., civilization.

Thus 'nature', in McKibben's sense of being separate from and other than the products of human purposes, started to 'end' about 10 000 years ago. It was at that crucial point that the intelligence of *Homo sapiens* became an important causal element in the natural environment surrounding us. The grains and tubers that we selected for planting and re-planting, the animals that we decided to gather around us for food, hides, labour and companionship, all quickly became artifacts of purpose, skill and luck. It sounds odd at first to speak of man's best friend, the dog, for example, as an artifact; but in a very important sense that is exactly the case. Sheep dogs, bird dogs, tracking dogs – these did not evolve by accident. Neither, as we all know, did modern strains of corn, or wheat, or rice. These are all artifacts, in that they were fashioned in important part by 'art'; they owe their existence to intelligent and consistent purpose applied over time.

But if they are *artifacts*, they are to that extent *artificial*! They are alive, they breathe and breed; they have their own natures; but at the same time they are artifacts and artificial. Is this a paradox? If our minds are filled with McKibben, this sounds paradoxical, indeed. The 'natural', for him, is exactly what is *not* mixed with human purpose, what is *not* the outcome of human control. 'Nature', then means what is 'separate', what operates 'of its own accord'. For McKibben the terms 'natural' and 'artificial' are mutually exclusive. 'Nature' is the opposite of 'culture'.

Must it be that way? No. Every dog, every cow, horse and ear of corn are counter-examples to any dualist, either/or, view of nature *versus* culture, environment *versus* man. There is of course, one popular sense — let us call it 'wild nature' — in which, like McKibben, one may define nature as 'all that exists apart from the artificial'[10]; but there is another sense, equally legitimate and widespread, in which 'nature' — let's call it 'universal nature' — simply means 'all there is (apart from the supernatural, if such there be) in the universe'. In the second, more inclusive sense, houses and boats and bombs are just as much within universal nature as rocks and hills and trees. In this wider sense it is perfectly understandable that a tree, perhaps a highly selected peach tree in a Georgia orchard, could be *in significant extent* 'artificial' (and to that extent less purely part of wild nature) though at the same time fully part of universal nature. The logical moral: 'artificial' often comes in a variety of degrees. Our world of nature, since the establishment of agriculture ten millennia ago, has had an opportunity to become profoundly mixed with the artificial.

Sometimes, however, matters of degree can suddenly turn into differences of kind. We all know just how minor drops in degrees of temperature can suddenly turn liquid water into solid ice. Likewise, normal expectations can reverse when 'matters of degree' have gone far enough. All of a sudden, water no longer contracts when further cooled, but expands. Perhaps the degree to which nature has been made part of culture has reached such a crisis point. Then McKibben's warnings would be well taken, even if his all-or-nothing approach should be rejected.

I think that engineers and environmental ethicists should take this possibility seriously and ponder its application in their practice. Have we in recent years passed such a threshold point in engineering nature? Are our assertions of domination and control at a level where we are putting not only the long-term future of nature at risk, but also our own psychological — aesthetic and spiritual — health? In looking for such a threshold-passing event, McKibben himself cites the advent of nuclear weapons. As he puts it: 'The invention of nuclear weapons may actually have marked the beginning of the end of nature: we possessed, finally, the capacity to overmaster nature, to leave an indelible imprint everywhere all at once.'[11]

Is the nuclear threat to nature a lonely exception, or is the situation found elsewhere, as well? In recent agricultural technology, for example, is there anything that has a similar universal, overmastering and indelible effect on nature?

Some might answer that the heavy 'chemicalization' of agriculture in our century has gone beyond the point of no return. The radical dependence of American agriculture on chemicals such as fertilizers, herbicides and pesticides has been well recognized. In many ecologically aware quarters, it has been criticised. Problems include pollution of land, surface water and ground water; problems of monocultural vulnerability; problems of deficit energy accounting; and problems of long-term sustainability. These criticisms have begun to be heard, however, even within the orthodox agricultural establishment. At a recent meeting of national agricultural society, for example, the theme was 'Risk/Benefit: A Way of Life'. The organizers even invited a philosopher to address a plenary session on agricultural ethics.[12] It seems to me, therefore, that high-intensity chemical agriculture may not be the threshold phenomenon that one could identify as 'universal' and 'indelible' in its transformation of nature. This is a matter of speculation, but it seems still possible, and even likely, that the big, mainstream agriculture will pull back from the brink and that even more biologically effective methods of interacting with nature will be researched and will replace our over-reliance on chemicals in the coming decades. This will not be without costs, pains and struggles; but it seems not to be scientifically or technically beyond hope. And travelling down our worn out chemical highway will almost certainly lead us to still worse costs and pains in the long run. My tentative verdict, at any rate, is that our chemical binge of the last few decades has not triggered what we could reasonably call the 'end' of nature.

On the other hand, the human race has already stepped gingerly over the brink of another technological intervention that may, in fact, be much more analogous to the release of the nuclear genie out of the bottle than we like to think: namely, the engineering and release of life-forms into the natural environment. Here is a paradigm case of artificial life. Our domestic species may still be dominantly natural despite being in significant part what they are because of the intervention of intelligent human purpose into their causal history. But in the case of purely invented life-forms, the proportions have changed. By the time organisms are sufficiently artificial to be patentable, it is clear that the relative weights of nature and culture have reversed themselves.

Culture is in the driver's seat and nature is hanging on for dear life (literally!) as we hurtle down unexplored roads, with poor visibility, and with uninspected and untried brakes.

We may not have passed that 'point of no return' yet in agriculture. The release of genetically engineered, artificial micro-organic life into the environment qualifies as 'indelible', since it is an irreversible process. No one can be sure that mistakes, when they happen, can be cleaned up and put back into the bottle. But it is not necessarily the case that genetic agricultural engineering is yet 'universal'. The overwhelming tendency in American barnyards and fields is still toward nature, at least in the modified, mixed mode that we have learned to live within during the past 10 000 years. Should we try our best to keep it that way? Or should we redouble our efforts to engineer improvements that will boggle the mind and enrich the bank account? When we seriously ask ourselves that sort of 'should' question on environmental issues, we are trekking into environmental ethics. We need, therefore, to take a square look at that subject.

Environmental ethics

One thing is unavoidable for normal, adult humans: moral responsibility. To be exempted, one must be an infant or an idiot or be otherwise incapacitated. For the rest of us, responsibility must be taken for what we do and — just as much — for what we fail to do. Therein lies one significant rub: we are just as responsible for *not* doing something as we are for doing something. The old adage 'Damned if you do, and damned if you don't', is true to the human condition. Jean-Paul Sartre told us that we are 'condemned to be free', like it or not; in the same spirit I want to begin these final reflections with the recognition that we are 'condemned to be morally responsible towards the environment.' That is, as far as we can tell, not true for any other species. If a beaver builds a dam and floods a forest, there is no moral issue and no moral praise or blame; but if a person builds a similar dam,it is appropriate to ask the 'should' question. Sometimes we may answer, 'Yes, he should have', sometimes, 'No, he shouldn't have'. That will depend upon the assessment of the facts of the situation and our standards of judgement. But the question itself, whether asked out loud or not, is unavoidably laid upon us. That is what makes us what philosophers call 'moral agents'.

What, then are the standards we moral agents should use? In addition to this being itself an ethically challenging question, illustrating the literally inescapable character of the quest, it is the most difficult one to settle. Engineers are likely to use the standards of efficiency or economic least-cost in assessing their recommendations. But what if economic standards clash with ethical ones? In personal life it may not be hard to choose: e.g. if it could be proved that it would be more economically beneficial to kill (in an undiscoverable way) one's old and useless parents than to support them in a nursing home, one would doubtless unhesitantly override the economic standard for the ethical. In professional life, however, it might be different. What if additional economic profit in an already profitable concern called for the ruin of hundreds of families through unemployment? A carefully studied example from agricultural engineering is the development of the mechanical tomato harvester, which has displaced many thousand of workers.[13] Even if compensation had been given to those who bore the costs for this technological change, the technological innovation would have remained tremendously profitable; but compensation was not provided for retraining, relocation or retirement of the people who were harmed while others were profiting. Was it right to work on this as an engineering project without at the same time working on the fairness of the social and economic results? Or, to take a non-human example, what if efficiencies called for significant increases in frustration and pain for countless numbers of barnyard animals? Would the ethical standards be the controlling ones? This is what I meant earlier by pointing out that the choice of the ruling standards is itself an ethical question. And if ethical standards are chosen as the controlling ones, which ethical standards are to be chosen?

At the moment, the greatest debate on these matters, as they pertain to the human relationship to nature, is over the choice of standards that focus exclusively on the good for human *versus* the choice of standards that broaden the focus to include the good for other species or, indeed, the whole natural order as relevant for ethical consideration. This choice is sometimes put as the choice between 'anthropocentric' standards and 'non-anthropocentric' or 'biocentric' standards.

My suggestion is to look for a balance. Ethical standards, exercised by human beings, that would put the good of other species ahead of — or even on exactly the same level as — the good for humans would not only require a level of altruism beyond that urged even in the great religions[14] but would also run counter to the quite normal species-preference that virtually all animals exhibit. Dogs are quite normally interested in other dogs; why, as Mary Midgley asks, should human beings not take a special interest in our own species?[15] These observations are not ethically decisive, of course. Just because human beings may share this trait with other animals does not prove that we *ought* to tolerate it in ourselves. Just because the major religions of the world pay special heed to human persons does not preclude us from trying to go further. Still, there is one logically inescapable fact we must face about our ethical decisions: however mean or however generous, they will and must continue to be made *by human beings* This is implied by the fact that human beings alone, so far as we know, are moral agents.

If this seems to make my starting point anthropocentric, so be it; but I do not think it must. I will admit to what might be called 'logical anthropocentrism', but that does not require substantive 'ethical anthropocentrism'. The distinction means that, unlike dogs, human beings are capable of taking thought beyond their initial interests and preferences. We are not able to stop being members of our species, true; but we are able to care for more than our species alone. Likewise, we are not able to avoid being located physically somewhere in space and time, true; but we are capable of extending moral concern from beyond our own immediate family or neighbourhood or region. We can be expected to be concerned with fairness to unemployed tomato workers we have never met. We can be expected to give moral consideration to poor, sick or starving strangers around the world. We can even be expected to give ethical attention to non-existing, merely *possible* persons like our great-great-grandchildren. Such *possible* people are incapable of returning the favour ('What has posterity done for me, lately?'); therefore they are not in any way moral *agents*. Instead, they are to us moral *patients*, the non-reciprocating recipients of our ethical concern.

In a closely similar way, we human moral agents are capable, if we will, of troubling ourselves over the good of *non-human* moral patients. The pain or frustration of other species, the vandalizing of natural beauty, the pillaging of species, the destruction of oceans,or the destabilization of atmosphere — these can be taken as legitimate ethical concerns *along* with our concerns for hungry distant strangers, the anonymous sick, and even those in our immediate circle of friends and enemies. We may, in sum, come to recognize the ethical duty to behave with due respect toward value, actual or potential, wherever found. Among the wider ethical concerns flowing from this principle might well be an ethical concern for nature, 'proud and free', worthy of respect on its own terms, but not wholly domesticated or subservient to human whim. At this juncture Bill McKibben's ethics and mine flow together.

Ethical standards and world views, however, go hand in hand. If a world view has no place in it for beings other than human beings who are worthy of respect and concern, then an ethic of extended responsibility like the one I am sketching would have no footing. But worldviews seem to be changing these days. One of the prophets of change is Wes Jackson, Director of the Land Institute at Salina, Kansas. Jackson sharply criticises what he call the 'knowledge-based worldview' on which, for example, genetically engineered organisms would be introduced into nature on the proud assumption that we know exactly what we are doing. He advocates, instead, what he calls an 'ignorance-based worldview', in which we would take proper account of how we are a 'billion times more ignorant' than we are knowledgeable about nature's complexities.[16] On such an 'ignorance-based worldview', clearly, engineers would be obliged to be far more tentative and careful with their recommendations affecting the environment. And we should be obliged to give up entirely on such projects as genetic engineering.

Wes Jackson and Bill McKibben would agree on this, and their case, in view of our undoubted ignorance, had better be taken seriously. It is not, however, quite where I come out. To summarize my agreements, I would strongly urge that we remember our frailties. For one thing, we really do not know a great deal about the long-run consequences of the irreversible train of events we are today setting loose. For another thing, we are not very good at sorting out our motives, either. It is easy to think of ourselves as serving the noble abstract causes; it is hard to face how much we may be lured by financial incentives and pushed by competitive pressures in the profession both inside and outside our academic settings. And for still another thing, it is easy to be attracted to the bright new possibilities of a new technique we have been developing and to overlook the many ways in which 'doing good' can go wrong. Our culture itself tends to praise the well-intentioned intervener and to overlook those who also serve by simply refraining from doing harm. But the principle of not doing harm is at least as fundamental to sound ethics as the principle of increasing good. For all these reasons I prefer neither a 'knowledge-based' nor an 'ignorance-based' worldview, but a 'modesty-based' worldview that is capable of intervening, with great caution, but one that holds back — out of proper concern for avoiding harm — until all circumstances and all motives have been examined with great care. This 'modesty-based worldview', linked to an ethic of extended responsibility, will in my view guide us away from the road that leads to the 'end' of nature.

We have not, after all, ended nature. Even McKibben, for all his rhetoric, toward the conclusion of his book realizes that it is counter-productive to talk as though the battle for harmony between nature and culture had finally been lost. As he says, 'If nature were about to end, we might muster endless energy to stave it off; but if nature has already ended, what are we fighting for?'[17] Indeed it is hard to imagine what could be morally allowed to count as a sign of such a decisive failure. As long as we are moral agents, we cannot in principle be exempted from responsibility to work for better outcomes and against worse. Wild nature is wounded, threatened, diminished because of unwise human intelligence and dangerous human values, embodied in ruthless technologies that must be stopped and reversed. We therefore need to look to engineers for new, wiser, more sensitive technologies, designed to heal what has been damaged and to distribute good effects more justly, not only among humans but also between humans and other moral patients.

Nature will never again exist as though the human race had not evolved in it and changed it by increasingly powerful technologies. But nature, though irretrievably changed in many ways by technology, has not ended and cannot end. This is why we cannot afford to settle for the rhetoric defeat. Quite the contrary, the damage our technology has already inflicted on nature makes the spread, to engineers as well as to the public, of an environmental ethics — a moral conscience of widened responsibility — all the more urgent for our future and the future of nature.

Notes
1. McKibben, 1989.
2. *Ibid*, p. 47.
3. *Ibid*, p. 60.
4. *Ibid*, p. 59.
5. *Ibid*, p.48
6. *Ibid*, p. 76.
7. *Ibid*, pp. 78-9.
8. *Ibid*, p. 79.
9. Breasted, 1944.
10. Ferré, 1988, p. 28.
11. McKibben, 1989, p. 66.
12. Ferré, 1990.
13. Schmitz and Seckler, 1970.
14. Regan, 1986.
15. Midley, 1986.
16. These views were expressed by Dr. Jackson at a public lecture at Athens, Georgia, held on February 26, 1991, and sponsored by the Department of Agronomy, the Environmental Ethics Certificate Program, and the Institute of Ecology of the University of Georgia.
17. McKibben, 1989, p. 210.

25 ECOLOGY AND ETHICS: A RELATIONSHIP

A.T. Dalfovo
Makerere University, Kampala, Uganda

The present way of life appears to be threatened by global, vital, and urgent challenges, such as the south-north divide, the economic order, demographic growth, and the environmental situation. They demand common terms of reference for an answer that must be universal to be adequate. Growing opinion suggests that this reference be found in a 'return to ethics', and in this connection one hears of environmental ethics, a specification that some consider rather naive for its lack of clarity.[1]

For a long time, environmentalism nourished the theory that the environment determined the human being. About 30 years ago, this theory began to be inverted by a fast growing awareness that the human being was determining the environment through science and technology. This 'Copernican' awareness had been prepared for by a century of ecological study initiated by E.H. Haeckel.[2] But it was only from about 1960 that its results came to the attention of a public beyond scientific circles. Since then, ecology has become a central theme in literature, in politics, in education, in the mass media, and in other aspects of life. It has also been suggested that ecology be considered an all embracing synthetic science.[3]

Although the term *environment* is broader than *ecology,* the present understanding of ecology specifies to a great extent the manner in which the environment is currently perceived and experienced. And although there remains an 'ecology-narrow' within the field of natural science, the prevailing interest today seems to be in an 'ecology-wide' involving the social sciences, philosophy, and other disciplines, and extending to almost every aspect of the environment.

Environmental information, fostered by its problematic urgency, has reached a vast public. This information appears vested in scientific language, thus imposing itself in an unquestionable manner, and prompting a demand for a quick and concrete answer. The outcome is a series of 'oughts' that are not always consistently connected among themselves, thus giving rise to an ethics considered by some to be naive. While environmental issues need to be kept before the eyes of the public and the attempt to have them solved ethically is to be encouraged, philosophy should provide some clarification's concerning the 'oughts' arising from environmental issues and ethics. Such clarifications can also demonstrate the contribution that the environmental challenge offers to ethics.

The fundamental issue to be clarified concerns the position of the person in this environmental context. One of the most significant discoveries of ecological research is the interdependence of ecosystems and the holistic nature of the ecosphere namely, the fact that the ecosphere constitutes a global whole, structured and organized in a network of relations and essential interdependence among living organisms. But the integrity of the ecosphere is not only a datum of cognitive interest. It is also, and above all, a condition for the existence and survival of humanity; a condition that is seriously jeopardized by the increasing environmental degeneration of the last twenty years. This degeneration is the result of an interface by the human being on the equilibrium of the ecosphere, and an interference resulting mainly from technology. The human being is therefore at the centre of the ecological issue, threatened by it because of threatening it; the human being is here again the source of his own problem. Hence, the way to the solution of the ecological problem leads to human behaviour as an affect to its to its cause.

When technological action is considered and assessed, opposite conclusions arise; some reject technology as an enslavement, others accept it as a fulfilment. According to H. Marcuse, for instance, human beings in a technological society have reached an unprecedented level of alienation. For G. Marcel, technological civilisation embodies that is worst in a modern society, an evil grip from which the modern person cannot free himself. On the other hand, B.F. Skinner argues fir a deliberate adoption of a 'technology of behaviour' in view of social and political engineering; the person is totally conditioned by his environment and he must make the best of it, giving up the illusions of freedom and dignity. F. Dessaur sees technology as the transforming force in a new philosophy of culture appropriate to the contemporary world; technology is the new foundation of a comprehensive metaphysics; philosophy of technology is the foundational discipline of an adequate contemporary philosophy.[4] These contrasting philosophical positions are further complicated by the alleged split between humanistic and scientific cultures.[5] In this case, the humanistic language of philosophers would not be scientifically understandable enough to provide a philosophical synthesis.

One writer states that 'the present models of production and development inevitably lead to a blind alley, namely to an ecological deadlock.'[6] A way out of this deadlock would seem to be by a negative attitude toward technology, which appears to be fostered particularly in some humanistic circles and in some technologically advanced societies.[7]

At the same time, one should realistically ask whether it is at all possible for a human being to set aside his 'faber' vocation and deny himself his typical use of instruments ad techniques. This question appears to be particularly crucial within the context of developing countries. In developing countries, the development model has been that of growth along the path that all societies seem to have been traveling, marked by agriculture, industry, and technology. This understanding of development had been subsequently improved to include a guarantee of justice and the full involvement of the people concerned with the constant stress of passing from exogenous to endogenous development.[8]

In this elaboration of the development model, technology has constantly remained a necessary tool, and sometimes also a target, of development. It may be a simple technology at first, but at the ultimate aim is to master its most advanced type. The thought of A.A. Mazrui in this connection is significant. He sees the gap between the north and the south as being not in riches (the south has more than the north) but in technology. A technological redemption is needed, brought about by a south-south organic solidarity and a south-south strategic solidarity.[9]

Hence, the arguments of taming technology and curtailing progress to save the environment become dubious. If development postulates technology, then there is no deadlock over a choice between the two. Both are needed. Thus the issue is not 'what', but 'how'. And the 'how' is solved in a human behaviour. The central issue in technology and development, and in the environment is the responsible behaviour of human beings, which is the subject matter of ethics. Ethics ought to provide the way out of the apparent deadlock of ecology and development, to resolve the dualism of science and humanity, and to elaborate the 'how' in the contrasting challenges of environmental issues.

The focus on the person as central to the environment contributes a fundamental clarification to the environmental ethics. In fact the environmental equilibrium seems to have become a rule for human behaviour, changing ethics from an anthropocentric to cosmocentric, or from egocentric to ecocentric. However, what the cosmos and ecology do *vis-à-vis* ethics is not to change the source of ethical rule, but to emphasize a new ethical concern. Human awareness of the balanced interdependence of living things becomes ethical awareness of service to life; it becomes a deontological awareness, a categorical imperative to respect the life equilibrium of the ecosphere in order to safeguard life; and this life is ultimately human. The imperative is thus from and for human life, though mediated through the environment.

The first contribution from a clarification of environmental ethics is thus re proposing a categorical imperative that has its roots in the person. The point emphasizes also the deontological dimension of ethics *vis-à-vis* its technological dimension that has led to unwarranted stress utilitaristic speculations.

A second contribution bears on the presupposition of freedom and responsibility. Technological interventions in the environment have become drastic, but they do not represent the inevitable or inexplicable result of determinism. These interventions can be checked by the person checking his behaviour. Human power over nature can be tamed; the person can act responsibly.

The third contribution relates to ecological equilibrium and recalls an ethics of balance and harmony. Here one is reminded of the harmony in Greek philosophy that touches on justice and of the harmony in African philosophy that points to human wisdom.[10] Justice and wisdom support a human equilibrium that attains the philosophy of respect for nature suggested by P. Rossi, by which the human being renounces both a wild dominion of nature and a utopian submission to it, thus avoiding being either a sadistic exploiter or a masochistic release of it.[11] In this way, human equilibrium renders environmental equilibrium possible.

The fourth contribution refers to the social dimension of ethics. The environmental challenge involving global society cannot be met by simply transferring individual ethics to it. The environment with its problems created by human beings, conditions ethical behaviour and the ensuing challenge needs to be met by a social effort, implying that ethical individualism and relativism need to be contained. An encouraging example of this social ethics comes from the Igbo celebration *Mbari* that brings together all aspects of significant human experience, including the threatening ones.[12] It may also come from Lugbara dances that gather in a communal dimension every aspect of the life experience, including death.[13] Like these dances and Mbari, ethics needs to celebrate the whole of existence together.

The fifth contribution is in the demand that the solution to the environmental problem is practical. The problematic basis of ecology has become an integral part of it outweighing other theoretical considerations and pressing for concrete solutions, like the 'green' movement appears to be. If ethics want to heed this message, it needs to go beyond its descriptive and analytical contribution, and to provide a normative pattern that singles out principles and elaborated norms able to change the behaviour that had led to the present environmental crisis.

The sixth contribution ensues from the need for an agreement on the meaning of basic terms and issues related to the environment in order to be able to formulate a common and effective answer to the environmental challenge. As said, this agreement could be found in ethics. But an ethical agreement postulates in turn a foundation in the form of a common perspective or orientation or worldview or metaphysics. Hence, it is ultimately a unitary vision of reality that can solve the environmental problem through a shared ethics.

Notes

1. Angelini, 1990.
2. In 1873, the German biologist Ernst Heinrich Haeckel (1834-1919) first derived the term *ecology* from the Greek words *oikos* 'house, place in which one lives', and *logos* 'discourse, science'.
3. Strassoldo, 1987.
4. Marcuse, *et al.*, 1974.
5. Snow, 1960.
6. E. Brovedani, 'La Crisi Ecologica e' Problema Morale'. *Jesus*, XII June 1990, p.14.
7. E.g., N.O. Schedler, 'Our destruction of tomorrow: A philosophical reflection on the ecological crisis'. W.R. Durland and W.H.Bruening, eds., *Ethical Issues*, Palo Alto, Ca., 1975, pp. 247-269.
8. Harrison, 1983 pp. 23-42.
9. Mazrui, 1986, pp. 170-177.
10. D. Nothomb, *Un Humanisme Africain,* Bruxelles, 1965, pp. 14, 118-119. A.P. da Postioma, *Filosofia Africana,* Milano, 1967, pp. 49-52.
11. P. Rossi, 'L'eta' del rispetto'. *Airone,* Year VIII, No.88, August, 1988, p.158.
12. Achebe, 1990.
13. From the author's experience among the Lugbara and his research on their dances.

26 DEEP ECOLOGY'S APPROACH TO THE ENVIRONMENTAL CRISIS

Michael E. Zimmerman
Tulane University
New Orleans, Louisiana

Despite some advances in curbing air and water pollution, and in protecting wilderness areas from development, governmental decrees and legislation have not been particularly effective in preventing environmental destruction. Increasingly, some critics argue that such reformism cannot deal with the problems created by the twin problems of industrialization and unchecked human population growth. Reform environmentalism, so these critics charge, are far too willing to arrive at compromise positions with big industry and the government—positions which jeopardize the well-being of the ecosphere. One group of critics, belonging to a branch of radical environmentalists called 'deep ecology', claim that only a transformation of Western society can save the living Earth—and humanity itself—from potentially dire consequences. Environmental reformism will fail, because it does not question the technological system which, apparently craving power for its own sake, is destroying the conditions needed for life on Earth. Deep ecology examines critically the metaphysical presuppositions of this self-destructive system.

A noted Norwegian philosopher and mountaineer named Arne Naess coined the term 'deep ecology'.[1] Later, two California academics, George Sessions and Bill Devall, expanded upon his idea.[2] Deep ecologists maintain that the environmental crisis results from Western humanity's anthropocentric, atomistic, dualistic, and exclusively utilitarian attitudes toward the natural world. Insofar as it remains human-centered, reform environmentalism merely tries to curb some of the worst problems created by the industrial system, but does not challenge the system itself. Deep ecologists maintain, however, that the good of the whole biosphere—not just of humans—should be taken into account when we assess the consequences of our action.

Deep ecologists may sometimes exaggerate the difference between their own position and that of reform environmentalists. Many alleged 'reformers' believe they are moving beyond a narrow anthropocentrism, which regards nature merely as raw material for human ends.[3] Deep ecologists, then join with many other environmentalists in maintaining that preserving a richly variegated, complex ecosystem is a noble, vital endeavour and that only a basic shift away from Western anthropocentrism and toward 'ecocentrism' will make such preservation possible.

Deep ecologists trace the roots of Western anthropocentrism back to the Greco-Roman tradition, especially Stoicism, to certain tendencies in the Jewish and Christian traditions, and to the Enlightenment humanist ideologies of maximum and capitalism, which may be regarded in part as secularized versions of the Jewish and Christian traditions.[4] Enlightenment anthropocentrism, combined with a doctrine of universal progress, led Westerners—whether capitalist or communist—to regard nature solely in instrumental terms. Capitalists exploit nature privately; communists do so collectively.

Not all radical environmentalists agree with deep ecology's emphasis on anthropocentrism as a major factor in the environmental crisis. Eco-feminists, for example, criticize deep ecologists for overlooking what are supposedly the real roots of the environmental crisis: the patriarchal attitudes governing all modern societies.[5] The same fear of and anger at women which leads men to subjugate them also leads men to dominate 'Mother Nature'. While agreeing that sexism is an important ingredient in our destructive attitude toward nature, many deep ecologists maintain that anthropocentric humanism is a more important ingredient. Warwick Fox has argued, for example, that one can imagine a society in which sexism, racism, and authoritarianism, and hierarchy are overcome, but which still regards nature as raw material for human purpose.[6]

Some deep ecologists argue that even more important sources for environmental abuse than anthropocentric humanism are metaphysical atomism and dualism. Atomism, first developed in ancient times by thinkers such as Democritus, was revitalized by Newton and others during the scientific revolution. According to atomism, everything is made up of externally related, separate parts. Dualism, especially as developed by Descartes, emphasizes that mind and body are radically distinct: humans are non-extended *res cogitans* or intellect: bodies (Nature) are composed of an inert, value-free totality of matter in motion. Stripped of all intrinsic value and depicted as radically separate from humans, natural things stand revealed merely as resources for human ends. According to Warwick Fox, however, the 'central intuition' of deep ecology is

> the idea that there is no firm ontological divide in the field of existence. In other words simply is not divided up into independently existing subjects and objects, nor is there any bifurcation in reality between human and non-human realism. Rather all entities are constituted by their relationships. To the extent that we perceive boundaries, we fall short of a deep ecological consciousness.[7]

Subject-object dualism is accompanied by profound feelings of isolation, alienation, separation, and death anxiety. Such dualism, a basic factor in all anthropocentrism, leads people to view nature and their own bodies both as alien and as threatening to the stability of the subject or ego. Death anxiety leads people to engage in the 'God project', the attempt to deny death by making the ego and its products (works of civilization) immortal.[8] Arguably, then the environmental crisis becomes acute when people have developed scientific and technological powers sufficient to give the illusion of control over nature.

While many deep ecologists appeal to trends in contemporary science as evidence that the dualistic way of thinking is being overcome, they are also critical of early modern science, which enthroned the atomistic way of seeing things. Yet if the modern scientific worldview was atomistic, it was not necessarily anthropocentric; indeed, by describing humans as clever animals living on an insignificant planet in the middle of an incomprehensibly vast universe, modern science punctured the anthropocentric myths of the Middle Ages. When the modern scientific view was combined with anthropocentric humanism during the Enlightenment, however, there occurred a synergistic effect which greatly enhanced the human domination of the natural world. According to naturalistic humanism, humans are both: (1) clever animals competing in an ultimately meaningless struggle for survival and dominance with all other forms of life, and (2) the source of all meaning, purpose, and value. At first glance, of course, naturalism and humanism would seem to be incompatible, if not contradictory; in fact, however, modern people have successfully reconciled them in the following, often unspoken, principle: humans are justified in their domination of nature not only because this is simply natural law, but also because humans are the source of all value. Hence, humans have the 'right' to do what they want with non-human beings. The ratification of human 'rights' over nature is a central dimension to both communism and capitalism, each of which is a representative of naturalistic humanism. Both of these leading political systems have an exclusively economic-utilitarian view of nature. Nature is simply assumed to be human property.

Deep ecologists argue that we must replace anthropocentrism with ecocentrism, atomism with relationalism, dualism with non-dualism, and utilitarianism with an attitude of respect and love for all human and non-human beings alike. Deep ecologists do not believe that these new attitudes can be developed by tinkering with existing Western ethical systems, for example, assigning rights to non-human beings.[9] For one thing, the notion of rights for animals, plants, and rivers seems incomprehensible, since rights are generally correlated with responsibilities. Moreover, the doctrine of rights seems inextricably involved with the metaphysical atomism, which deep ecology seeks to overcome.[10] Further, anthropocentric attitudes are often discernible in the ways in which we assign value to non-human beings; for example, animals are said to be more valuable than plants because animals are more conscious or more sentient. But consciousness or sentience is what humans prize most about themselves.

Deep ecologists argue that in establishing a new humanity-nature relationship, ontology must precede ethics. Only a new mode of understanding what things are can bring forth ethical norms consistent with that understanding. For example, since Western humans think nature is merely raw material, we have few ethical norms limiting our treatment of the natural world. Because I identify myself with other humans, I treat them with respect. If I were to expand my sense of identity to include beings other than myself, however, I would spontaneously begin treating them with a measure of respect as well. Deep ecologists, then, call for an expanded identification with all beings, in a way consistent with the teachings of Buddhism and other non-dualistic traditions.[12] Non-dualistic awareness discloses the self in all things; such awareness spontaneously generates an attitude of care toward all things.[13]

While non-dual experience is often associated with mysticism, deep ecology also appeals to the findings of contemporary science to support its search for an alternative to atomistic-dualistic categories. In physics and biology, for example, researchers now maintain that the atomistic and mechanistic worldview is no longer tenable. Instead of the universe being a machine composed of separate parts, it is much more like an organism which is internally related and still in the process of evolving. Current findings suggest that Leibniz may have been on the right track in saying that every aspect of the universe mirrors or reflects every other aspect. Deep ecologists maintain that one way in which the universe becomes aware of itself is through humanity. The universe contains the capacity for generating carbon-based forms of life capable of thinking about the universe.

Arne Naess uses the term 'self-realization' to describe the expanded sense of self required for the deep ecological attitude. By this term Naess does not mean the achievement of the atomized ego's goals of infinite expansion and acquisition. Following Buddhism and Spinoza, Naess defines self-realization as a revelation that a person's authentic destiny involves identifying not just with one's body and desires, or even with one's own species, but with the living cosmos, the larger self of which we are all manifestations.[14] Naess, then, calls for a higher humanism to replace the anthropocentric humanism which is largely responsible for the technological domination of nature.

Some critics, including social ecologists, fear that deep ecology is promoting a kind of eco-fascism.[15] There is some reason for such fear. Deep ecologists sometimes regard the Enlightenment in wholly negative terms, as a drive to control nature. Deep ecology fails to see that there was an authentic emancipatory dimension to the Enlightenment, despite the limited character of the Enlightenment's scientific and political vision. Deep ecologists must be sure that their critique of anthropocentric humanism and metaphysical atomism does not undermine one of the major achievements of Enlightenment modernity, namely, the notion that individuals have the right both to form democratic institutions and social relations, on the one hand, and to protect themselves from authoritarian, irrational, and racist regimes which would sacrifice individuals and their freedom for the sake of 'higher good,' on the other.

Only as respect for human persons grows can we expect to see the demand grow for respectful treatment of the living Earth itself, for we will see ever more clearly that destroying the Earth undermines the conditions necessary for healthy human life. It may be that we increasingly perceive the relationship between healthy, flourishing people and a healthy, flourishing planet, anthropocentrism will gradually give way to ecocentrism. In the light of our growing comprehension of the interrelationship and interdependence of all people and all things, we may learn to extend respect and care to the whole living Earth. While important, such extension would not yet overcome the dualism which currently characterizes humanity's relationship to the natural order. But overcoming such dualism will require centuries of continuing human evolution. In the meantime, it is important to sustain the political, social, and cultural conditions necessary for this step in human evolution. Above all, we must be clear that attempts to overcome humanity-nature dualism by a regression to earlier collectivist stages of human awareness have proved and will continue to prove catastrophic.

In conclusion, let me reiterate that deep ecology provides a very different 'risk assessment' of modern technology than do people uncritically committed to the project of 'mastery of nature'. For deep ecologists, the risk posed by modern technology is planetary in scope; hence, nothing less than a profound critical reflection on our world-view is required if we are to avert global disaster. In calling for an end to anthropocentric humanism, metaphysical atomism, dualism, and resource utilitarianism, deep ecologists are reminiscent of Heidegger's critique of modernity. Deep ecologists use Heidegger's phrase that we must learn to 'let things be', but Heidegger's relation to National Socialism rightly gives us pause when we think of his conceptual proximity to deep ecology.

Deep ecologists differentiate themselves from Heidegger, however, in two ways. First, they adopt the liberatory language of the Enlightenment, despite their critique of its anthropocentrism. The Enlightenment postulated the notion of human progress; without a commitment to the possibility that humans can evolve and progress beyond anthropocentric humanism, deep ecologists would have no reason to hope for a better future. Second, deep ecologists also take more seriously than did Heidegger the possibility that post modern science might reveal something true about human existence.[16] Hence, while deep ecologists criticize modernity, they are far less likely than Heidegger to reject out of hand its political achievements and to adopt a reactionary social attitude which would be disastrous if it were resurrected in today's world. Deep ecologists have the advantage of being able to learn from the mistake made in the first part of this century. Hence, they recognize that while they may continue to harbour utopian hope for a radical transformation of the humanity-nature relationship, they must nevertheless face up to the dangers posed by the politics of redemption.

Michael E. Zimmerman

Notes

1. Naess, 1973; for a fuller exposition see also Naess 1989.
2. Devall and Sessions, 1985; Drengson, 1983, as well as his journal of 'ecosophy', *The Trumpeter*: Evernden, 1985; Fox, W., 1990; LaChapelle, 1978, 1988; Roszak, 1978; Snyder, 1974, 1980; Zimmerman, 1983, 1986; for an outstanding bibliographical review of deep ecology see Sessions, 1981.
3. In reviewing Bill Devall's *Simple in Means, Rich in Ends: Practicing Deep Ecology*, for example, the Executive Director of Sierra Club, Michael McCloskey, strongly disagreed with Devall's criticism of so-called reform environmentalism: 'Basically, (Devall) believes that deep ecologists are biocentric and that reform environmentalists are anthropocentric. Here Devall is just plain wrong. It is the developers who champion the Dominant Social paradigm, and environmentalists of almost all stripes who champion the New Ecological Paradigm. There are differences among environmentalists in interpreting and applying this new paradigm, but it is grossly misleading to suggest that reform groups have the same views as developers, or that they are basically anthropocentric.' *Sierra* (January/February, 1989), pp. 162-164.
4. Passmore, 1974; White, 1967; Mitcham and Grote, 1984; Fox, M., 1988.
5. Warren, 1990, see especially the first footnote for a good bibliography of essays on ecofeminism; Diamond and Orenstein, 1990; Zimmerman, 1987.
6. Fox, W., 1989.
7. Fox, W., 1984, p.196.
8. Wilber, 1981.
9. Fow, W., 1990 for the best critique of the axiological approach to the humanity-nature relation.
10. Zimmerman, 1985.
11. Rodman, 1977, p.94.
12. Naess, 1979, 1984a, 1985; Fox, W., 1990.
13. Fox, W., 1990.
14. Naess, 1984b.
15. Brookchin, 1987, 1982.
16. Griffin, 1988. This outstanding collection of essays shows the extent to which contemporary scientific research calls into question the dualistic, mechanistic, and often anthropocentric attitudes of classical modern science. They show that these have profound implications for our own self-understanding and for our conception of humanity's place in the natural order.

27 ETHICAL PRINCIPLES FOR ECODEVELOPMENT

Alejandro Herrera Ibáñez

Universidad Nacional Autónoma de México
Instituto de Investigaciones Filosóficas

The principles proposed in this chapter are based on a holistic non-anthropocentric ethics. Environmental ethicists usually claim that environmental concerns require the adoption of a holistic ethics. This is warranted insofar as it means that ethics must take into account beings other than human and the global consequence of human actions, i.e. the consequences of human actions upon the entire planet in regard to the welfare of human and other living beings. In other words, a holistic ethics claims that the range of applicability of ethical principles should be extended or expanded to beings other than human.

A non-anthropocentric ethics is a necessity if by this it is meant that human beings are no longer considered the exclusive centre of attention of moral considerations. In other words, non-anthropocentrism claims that the centre of such considerations are not only human beings, but all beings with inherent value. This claim implies that—contrary to the assumption—not only human beings have inherent value; all sentient beings have inherent value.

The position of philosophers who claim that all living beings have inherent value (not to speak of those who claim that all members either of our planet or of the Universe have such value) has been described as 'radical biotic egalitarianism'. One of the consequences of this position is that to take the life of a carrot away is as wrong as to kill a human being. Our non-anthropocentric ethics accepts, however, the establishment of a hierarchy among sentient beings for situations of irreconcilable conflicts.

The principles proposed here are aimed at providing some specific guidelines for action within the context of ecodevelopment. The notion of ecodevelopment was popularized by Ignacy Sachs, who characterized it as 'development without destruction,' meaning by this phrase, economic technological development without destruction of ecosystems in general and human environments in particular. Therefore, ecodevelopment is any kind of development (economic, scientific, technical etc.) that takes into account not only the welfare of human beings but of all sentient beings affected by its actions. In other words, ecodevelopment is development guided by environmental ethics.

The need to have scientific ethical guidelines for specific situations is urgent. The aim of this chapter is to provide a set of such guidelines that, on the one side, does not pretend to be exhaustive and, on the other side, does not pretend to be casuistic. These principles fall between the most general ethical maxims (such as the principles of benevolence, of justice or of equity) and concrete answers to very concrete problems (such as whether I should plant a tree or build a studio in my backyard). Ignacy Sachs says that we should see the concept of development as an ethical concept guided by the principles of solidarity (synchronic and diachronic), social justice and ecological prudence. These and other principles are elaborated below.

Usually, when economic development and environmental quality clash, the latter gets the worse part. This gives rise to the first principle: When there is a conflict between the economic development of a human population and the quality of its environment, the latter must be preferred to the former if the harm that would be caused by the former cannot be repaired. If the harm caused by the former can be repaired, it must be kept to a minimum, and the results of economic development should provide the means to repair the harm caused. Transnational corporations, in particular, have usually had a negative impact of ecosystems at home and abroad. Therefore, it is necessary to state a second principle which serves as a criterion of guilt: Any activity of transnational corporations that does unnecessary harm to any ecosystem of our planet is guilty of directly assaulting the well-being of the human and non-human populations of that ecosystem. In such a case, transnationals must either remedy or pay for the harm caused. Unnecessary harm is done to an ecosystem when there are ecologically healthy ways of achieving the same goals and the ecologically harmful ones are preferred. Often transnationals allege in their defense that they contribute to the economic development of the human population of the ecosystem in question. In this case, the first principle must be applied.

Another source of human conflict is the relation between environment and urban development. Such development has usually been realized to the expense of natural environments: Any action aimed at urban development must avoid destroying or altering ecosystems unnecessarily. When destruction or alteration of natural ecosystems is necessary, the result sought must be the balance between building and green areas. Urban landscape does not have to be synonymous with masses of concrete, glass and iron without trees. A more delicate problem is that of the relationship between our species and other animal species. A non-anthropocentric ethics allow us to state the following principle: Any human intervention in ecosystems must take into account the survival and well-being of the various animal species that live in them. The concern for animal well-being must not be merely conservationist. Efforts must be made to obtain better conditions for our fellow animals: As long as others are not necessarily harmed, efforts must be made to increase or to improve the conditions that make the well-being of the population of the ecosystems within their respective trophic levels possible. This principle is in accordance with the more general maxim of not only avoiding doing harm, but also trying to do good for other beings.

Responsibility is a virtue that has been neglected for a long time, especially in regard to our use of science and technology. Misuse of science and technology has led to the verge of ecological catastrophe. The worship of an unqualified idea of progress inherited from the last century must end, and a goal the idea of responsible progress should be adopted. We propose the following principle: Any scientific or technical innovation that contribute or can in principle contribute to the global well-being of human and non-human populations without directly or indirectly causing unnecessary harm to any species of the biosphere is a contribution to responsible progress. Failure to follow this principle leads to the victory of irresponsible progress, which is destroying life on our planet: Any scientific or technical innovation that directly or indirectly causes unnecessary harm to any species of the biosphere must be considered irresponsible progress. A non-anthropocentric ethics is concerned not only with the survival and conservation of species—endangered or not—but also with the well-being of their members. It is of utmost importance that technical progress take into account animal suffering: We must not produce or use techniques that contribute to the unnecessary suffering or death—in the short, medium or long range—of sentient beings. It is also important to define when a species is unnecessarily harmed: Harm is done upon a species when an action contributes to the reduction of its population to critical levels, thus making it an endangered species. A species is unnecessarily harmed when it is put in danger of extinction, despite the fact that it has not seriously threatened the health or life of human and non-human populations.

All sentient beings deserve equal consideration in similar circumstances. There are, however, limited situations in which the survival of a group makes it necessary not to give equal consideration to all its members. These abnormal situations are fortunately infrequent. The typical 'life-boat' situation in an extended ethics establishes priorities even when the members of the group are all human. Decisions are rooted more in the survival instinct of the species than in considerations of equal treatment: Not only the members of the human species have inherent value. There is, however, a descending order of priorities among beings, ranging from those with inherent value to those with instrumental value. In cases of irreconcilable conflict, the interests of beings with inherent value must prevail. If there is an irreconcilable conflict among the latter, the interests of the members of the human species must prevail. However, before determining that a conflict of interests is irreconcilable, all possible efforts to reconcile such interests must be made.

In more normal situations, there is the problem of the relation between the search for social justice and the search for environmental quality: Creative formulae must be sought in order to achieve social justice without worsening the environmental conditions or harming ecosystems. In the case of an irreconcilable conflict between these goals, social justice must be preferred and somehow the remedy to the harm caused to the ecosystems or to the environmental conditions must be sought. All possible efforts of conciliation must be made before deciding that the conflict is irreconcilable.

If national and international communities cooperated together for a better world, the problem of social justice would not arise. We must practise solidarity first: At the ecological and environmental levels, there must be national and international solidarity among human populations. This means that first, no population must base its economic development on the ecological and environmental deterioration of any other population; second, every population must treat responsibly the natural resources on its territory, avoiding a management that could have negative effects on the whole planet or parts of it; and third, mechanisms of international cooperation must be established in order to help less economically developed populations to fight the deterioration of their environmental conditions and their ecosystems.

Synchronic solidarity is advocated above, but duties to future generations must be met by the practice of diachronic solidarity. This cannot be done sacrifice: Present generations must sacrifice part of their comfort in favour of the well-being of future generations. Particularly, certain types of ecologically destructive comforts must be abandoned in favour of a better environmental quality for future generations. However, the life of the present generation must never be sacrificed for the improvement of future environmental conditions.

The ethical dimension of the practical decisions we take daily is critical to environmental and ecological consequences. The set of principles briefly sketched above, can serve as a starting point for discussion of the urgent measures we have to take on the ethical level.

28 THE BUSINESS OF ETHICS: DEVELOPMENT AND THE ENVIRONMENT

Daniel W. Skubik
Florida Atlantic University
U.S.A.

A plethora of stories recounted over the past few years in internationally-respected news media and academic writings around the globe can leave one confused, frustrated, concerned and saddened. Consider the following examples:

- In a special item to the *New York Times* in July 1988, James Brooke observed that 'From Morocco to the Congo, virtually every country on West Africa's coast reports receiving offers... from American and European companies seeking cheap sites to dispose of hazardous waste. Fees offered African recipients have gone as low as $3 a ton'.[1] He goes on to cite the example of Guinea-Bissau's contract with European tanneries and pharmaceutical companies to receive and bury some 15 million tons of wastes over five years; in return, the government would receive US$120 million each year, nearly doubling the country's GNP of $147 million.

- When industrial wastes cannot be dumped on land, they are often disposed of at sea. Responding to this practice, representatives from 65 countries 'adopted a resolution to place an international ban on the incineration of toxic wastes at sea as of 1994' at the 1988 annual meeting of the London Dumping Convention.[2] Meantime, burning at sea continues.

- The military government in Burma—feeling an urgent need of funds for refurbishing its weapons stockpiles as well as meeting some of the more urgent needs of its people, is selling off its large natural reserves of teak to Thai logging companies who come to work from across the border now that Thailand is virtually denuded of its own teak reserves.[3]

- Brazil and Indonesia, countries containing respectively the two largest rain-forests in the world, continue to find it appropriate to burn off or cut down large stands of its ancient trees to satisfy needs for generating foreign exchange to service their international debts and to attempt to raise the standard of living of their peoples. Indeed, during a recent visit to Japan an Indonesian government minister, confronted by a fledgling environmentalist group, defended the pulping of its forests in cooperation with Japanese paper companies by charging the nay-sayers with interfering in the internal affairs of a sovereign nation as well as hypocrisy in that the protesters apparently wanted to maintain their standard of living while keeping Indonesians poor.

I cite these examples not to incite any vision of global environmental disasters or to point the finger of blame and abjuration, but rather to note that in each of these cases we see otherwise rational political and business leaders taking decisions that are neither fully economically rational nor morally justifiable. From the perspective of a philosopher concerned with rational deliberation and moral justification, I would suggest that these cases throw up issues which are too often overlooked in the current environmental ethics debate: issues which I would like briefly to address here.

In a recent paper delivered at an ethics conference in New Zealand, I argued that theoretical ethics, particularly in the Anglo-American analytic tradition, had created or evolved little ground suited to applied ethical decision-making. That is, we theoretical ethicists have surprisingly, and intolerably, little to say to ordinary political and business people who must confront the day-to-day clashes and conflicts which arise in situations such as the cases noted above about how they *should* go about the business of taking fully economically rational and morally justifiable decisions.

One philosopher who has taken this applied ethics task seriously is Thomas Donaldson of Georgetown University. He has developed a provocative *ethical algorithm* for corporate decision-making in a recent book, *The Ethics of International Business*, in an attempt to address practical ethical problems in international business operations. There, he defends a typology of conflicts grounded on the sorts of economic and non-economic justifications offered by moral agents for a variety of business practices, and proffers corresponding formulae for resolving them. Now, his typology assumes that conflict arises from a practice which is permitted in one state, specifically the host country of a transnational corporation (TNC), but is not permitted in the TNC's home state, i.e. the country of the company's incorporation. Where there exists such a clash in permitted business practices (e.g. in permissible pollution levels), Donaldson tells us we can discern and divide the moral judgments offered to support these disparate practices or standards into two broad types according to their categories of reference and then apply his devised appropriate formulae for reaching morally justified resolution. In the same paper alluded to above, I criticised Donaldson's scheme on a number of grounds, and proffered a formulaic scheme of my own for resolving TNC-versus-host country conflicts which I thought better suited for use by corporate managers in their decision-making.

Yet, what neither of us, nor others in my reading, have clearly offered is some means for resolving cases where there are no such conflicts, but where there are still a variety of economic and moral problems present, again such as the cases with which we began. While authors such as Donaldson and Henry Shue have addressed issues of exporting hazards, or more generally exporting risks, the context is always that of industrialized-versus-developing countries and the justificatory role moral concepts such as autonomy play in resolving any conflict. I wish here to begin to address two different but related problems. First, what is to be done when industrialized and developing countries and companies alike agree about what business practices to sanction, but disagree about what it means for the states and businesses involved to get on with managing their affairs? Second, how are we to think about environmental duties that extend not only across borders but across generations?

As noted in the fourth example above, Brazil continues to 'harvest' substantial rain-forest acreage. It does so to generate direct income from the felled wood (paper product exports are substantial), and indirect income both from the use of the wood for curing its tobacco crop, and from beef cattle grazed on this freshly cleared land. The government has come under intense domestic and international pressure to cease all clearings, especially in the Amazon basin. Even the International Monetary Fund, not usually reputed for social and humanitarian conditionality, is playing a role by urging Brazil's finance minister to develop an economic restructuring programme which provides for rain-forest preservation before the Fund will sanction debt rescheduling. Meanwhile, in efforts to head-off a potentially costly consumer boycott, McDonalds has been taking out expansive advertisements in newspapers and magazines declaring that it never will use beef for its hamburgers from cattle grazed on land 'reclaimed' from Brazilian rain-forests, and will not utilize rain-forest paper products for its packaging.

Most commentators applaud these moves, economists, politicians, consumer activists and philosophers alike. Still, such exercises ought to give us pause. For however pragmatically laudatory these restraints, they are after all heteronomous: i.e. they are not autonomously given through the moral actors' reason; they are externally imposed constraints on state and business behaviour. So how might they be justified?

One common class of argument which could be advanced is utilitarian. Of course, in simple classical utilitarian terms, both Brazil and McDonalds are morally required to take these measures so as to globally produce the greatest good for the greatest number. In brief, even though Brazil (and its citizenry) and McDonalds (and its shareholders) could realize substantial benefit from continued rain-forest logging, greater benefit quite arguably accrues to the global majority from their restraint, QED. This sort of calculation is problematic, supposing as it does that the calculator is classically a disinterested, omniscient, benevolent spectator, but if 'ought implies can' we may accept probabilistic good faith judgments based on available scientific and social information.

In broader consequential terms, the actors themselves might also attempt to calculate the direct and indirect harms which are the probable outcomes of their unrestrained activities, and conclude that future generation will incur considerable costs without enjoying offsetting benefits. Since (as Rawls reminds us in his *A Theory of Justice*) there is no greater utilitarian moral ground for discounting future costs today than for discounting present benefits tomorrow, a straightforward weighing of costs and benefits should result in the recognition that the economic benefits of currently expending Brazilian natural resources (relieving to some degree Brazil's balance of payment deficit and reducing McDonalds' sourcing and operating costs) is substantially less than the costs which will accrue to future generations (leaving Brazilian and other citizens susceptible to risks associated with environmental degradation and costing McDonalds' shareholders profit losses associated with a world-wide boycott along with a significant dent in the company's reputation).

This latter calculation and conclusion correlate well with contemporary interpretations of a Millian harm-to-others principle that other-regarding action which results in significant harm can justly be proscribed by appropriate authorities. Certainly, as J.S. Mill himself recognized, the calculation that coercive proscription is morally appropriate requires the additional calculation that the benefits of coercion outweigh the relative costs of proscription. But given our context of developmental harm to environmental stability, it is far more likely than not a presumption favouring proscription is in order. The onus is thus on those who would argue for freedom of action to demonstrate greater benefit to overcome this presumption.

For all that, one of the issues in question which is usually eyed when such consequential principles are applied is how to determine who or what constitute 'appropriate' authorities for enforcing these proscriptions. The current international political and (arguably) moral order is comprised of some moral agents such as nation-states which are sovereign entities, being by definition agents who are free *vis-à-vis* other actors. Since there is no formal higher, i.e. supernational, political or moral institutional authority or enforcement body such as a global cosmopolitan parliament, each nation must act according to its own best construal of the duties it owes its citizens. As a corollary, no other body is properly situated to critique the decisions taken by another actor. Actors can only proceed as they judge best in the context of the global situation created by the actions of surrounding agents. Thus, firms or nations might decide to refrain from doing business with some other state (e.g. trade sanctions applied against South Africa for its apartheid policies), but moral criticisms, approbation, or condemnation all will miss the mark as each agent simply talks past the other, much as two ethical subjectivists merely swap noncognitivist preferences.

This anarchical state is a permanent feature of the international landscape, unless and until it can first be shown that each actor shares relevantly similar politico-moral judgments. In that case, dialogue can practically proceed in conjunction with the give-and-take which comprises persuasive discourse in community. But if relevant judgments are not shared, there exists no such common ground for dialogue; there is only place for submissive tolerance or coercive use of might. In the Brazilian case, we might conceive the role of international political and consumer coercion to be a moral prick or hint to the actors that they seemingly have miscalculated the relevant levels of benefits and harms, and so should redo their sums until they get it right. This is plausible, possible and legitimate just because broader judgments concerning the desirability of promoting only environmentally sustainable development are in fact shared by the relevant moral agents. Thus, Brazil and McDonalds may be said to have been heteronomously moved to assent to recalculations, but it can also be shown that restraint is fully warranted and so can be autonomously adopted.

What of our other examples? Are they subject to similar analysis and resolution? Or do they throw up some other issues as well? In the first example of Guinea-Bissau's toxic waste contract, we might reach what some would think to be disturbing conclusions. For while the contract was in fact repudiated after it was made public, the outcry that embarrassed the government and subsequently led to the contract's cancellation was not clearly justified. Considering that some industrial wastes can safely and securely be transported and buried, it makes quite clear consequential sense to dispose of those wastes in low density population territories. Such space offers the best placement at least cost. Now most of Europe is quite densely populated, ranging on average 300–3000 persons per square mile, and the interested companies represented here were located in states where densities average 1000–3000/sq mi. On the other hand, the West African coast averages 30–300/sq mi, with some states like Mauritania averaging just 5 inhabitants per square mile. Guinea-Bissau itself has an average density of 70/sq mi. Thus, it is not at all clear that industrialized nations' companies were engaging in 'toxic terrorism' as was alleged by some. Rather, their calculations on economic and utilitarian moral grounds were sound.

Too, the direct benefits of US$600 million income over the 5-year term of the contract (= $40/ton for 15 million tons of waste) offered quite significant development prospects for business and social projects in the country. Recall this new income would have virtually doubled the nation's GNP at a time when life expectancies average only 42 years, infant mortality rates were and remain amongst the highest in the world, illiteracy rates hover around 70 per cent and clean water is available to less than 10 per cent of the population. Repudiation of realisable potential benefits and projects which could dramatically alter these statistics and improve people's lives would be warranted only if one could demonstrate future probabilistic harms significant enough to counterbalance the clear benefits available here. That demonstration might be accomplished if one could show there exists certain transactional externalities which would unfairly be borne by future generations, but that had not been, and I think cannot be, shown. No, if there is sound moral reason to reject such contracts it won't be consequentially grounded. What other grounds might there be? Let's turn to the third example for some insight.

As noted above, the Burmese *junta* is selling off its teakwood forests to Thai loggers. Both governments and their companies involved substantially benefit from these contracts. The loggers and associated teak furniture and *objets d'art* crafts(wo)men and exporters are kept employed, the world market is supplied with good teak at reasonable prices, and the governments receive revenue for spending as they deem appropriate for their respective countries. The arrangement is a straightforward commercial deal entered into at an arms length between two equally situated parties. This is not after all a matter of an industrialized country or its company overreaching a developing country to exploit its natural resources. Who could possibly object?

Well, how about the people of Burma? They might well object, if they could, to this wholesaling of their country's reserves by an administration which seized power contrary to the democratic expression of the peoples' wishes at the polling booths, by an administration which, as poor as the country is, budgets over $1 billion for defense and internal security. In short, objection to this arrangement is based not simply on utility, but on the deontological value of any development decision being—and being seen to be—representatively taken, i.e. that the autonomous wishes of the people are respected and acted upon. We morally bristle at the Burmese *junta*'s decisions, whatever they might be and whatever the sums of the utility calculations, just because they do not, indeed cannot, reflect the desires and aspirations of the Burmese people.

So, too, we might query the Guinea-Bissau government's decision. Not because I mean to liken the *junta* in Burma with Guinea-Bissau's republican government. Rather, that the waste contract decision was not seen, by an important number of its own people and the peoples of neighbouring countries, to be representatively sensitive. Albeit the utility factors all point in favour of the decision first taken, this felt lack of representation in the decision-making process provides independent grounds for that decision's reassessment and ultimate repudiation by the government officials responsible. It might too be noted that government representatives of industrialized countries responded to this and some other toxic waste episodes with proposed legislation to curb the movement of wastes from their countries to areas such as West Africa: the Parliament of the European Community has called for a total ban where safe disposal cannot be guaranteed, and perhaps more to the point the U.S. Bush Administration has implemented the Basel Convention's restrictions on vast exports by stipulating that no hazardous materials can be transshipped unless any proposed shipment conforms to an international agreement between the U.S. and the receiving country. In this way, the U.S. can determine that there is fully informed consent on the part of the receiving country's administration. The U.S. Congress is now considering widening the scope of the provisions to cover all solid wastes and to extend (perhaps paternalistically) U.S. inspection/regulation of foreign waste treatment facilities.

This deontological concern for and recognized the value of representativeness in decisions having environmental impact also help explain the dubious nature of incinerating wastes at sea (note the second example). Those actions directly implicate no contemporaries; nor do they clearly implicate future generations. So while there may be some consequential concerns about harms flowing from abuse of a global commons, those calculations are for now scientifically quite inconclusive. What must not be dismissed however, is the largely shared and still evolving judgment concerning some resources—for example conservation of seabed resources under the high seas—being the common heritage of mankind (as the phrase is often put in international legal documents such as the UNCLOS treaty of 1981). As such, decisions here must bear the stamp of global representativeness. Unilateral state or business decisions to burn wastes at sea cannot then represent the developing consensus of the world's peoples. How much less so when a significant number of state representatives at an international conference adopt a contrary policy?

Returning then in conclusion to our original query, how might we justify constraint on state and business behaviour? We can always begin by asking for straightforward utilitarian accounts of benefits and harms, and broader consequential accounts which rightfully consider the internalisation of externalities over time for future generations. Should these all return a positive assessment for a particular development project, we must still ask one further query: is that decision deontologically representatively based? If the answer is 'yes', the development project can go forward as being morally well grounded as well as being economically rational; if the answer returned is either 'no' or 'we do not know whether representation is itself well grounded', the project remains without moral justification, however desirable it might otherwise be. At that point, constraints *are* morally justified unless or until an affirmative answer can be given.

Notes
1. Brooke, 1988, p. 1.
2. *Keesing's Record of World Events*, 1988, p. 36252.
3. Australian Broadcasting Corporation, 'Indian Pacific' (radio programme), May 1991.

29 WHETHER THE WESTERN WORLD WILL WEATHER THE WEATHER: A NEO-MARXIST DISCUSSION ABOUT AVERTING 'ECOLOCAUST'

Paul Allen III
East Stroudsburg University
U.S.A.

The likelihood of ecolocaust

People worry about exploitation of the environment because of concerns about endangered animals and the balance of nature; about a lowering of the quality of life for this and future generations; about people in this and future generations lacking adequate food, clean air, clean water; and so on. However, some argue that much *more* is at stake, namely, the very survival of civilization. Jose Antonio Lutzenberger, Brazil's Special Secretary for the Environment, said, 'We are acting as if we were the last generation on the planet.' He added that without a radical change in course, the earth will end up 'like Venus—a dead planet.' (*New York Times*, 30 April, 1991, p. C4).

Destruction of the environment is due to various factors such as the growth of population and the rapid expansion of technology and industrial society. If we use the word 'capitalism' loosely to refer to the market economy and the modern Western lifestyle associated with it, we can say that capitalism also is a major cause of destruction of the environment. For example, to keep the world economy thriving, there is great pressure to build and sell more and more automobiles. This leads to more driving and more carbon dioxide accumulating high up in the atmosphere. At the same time poor nations, because of their need to grow economically (and to go along with business interests from elsewhere), are cutting down rain forests which are needed to convert the carbon dioxide into oxygen. All this extra carbon dioxide, along with certain other gases, results in the so-called greenhouse effect. That is to say, these gases are enveloping the earth, trapping the sun's heat, and causing global warming.

Some predict that in future decades the global warming will turn major farm lands into deserts and lead to massive famines even in the richer countries. Also the warming is expected to melt polar ice, raise the sea level, and cause flooding of coasts and destruction of major coastal cities. Then millions of people living along coasts will be forced to migrate to regions of higher elevation.

Global warming from the greenhouse effect is just *one example* of *many kinds* of traumas we are inflicting on the environment. It seems that the cumulative effect of all of these over the next 100 years or so, together with a tripling of the world's population to 15 billion people, will be more than civilization can sustain. The global famines, epidemics, migrations of populations, and other forms of economic and social disruption will lead to wars, crime, and a breakdown of social fabric on a scale that is hard for us to imagine. In short, if the present trends of population growth and industrial and capitalist exploitation of nature continue, we seem headed for a situation so dire that it could be called ecological holocaust; so I will call it 'ecolocaust'.

Averting ecolocaust

Some would say we can avert ecolocaust by persuading corporations, business leaders, and other people that recycling, conservation, and strict pollution controls are *good business*. Others hope that *governments* will become sufficiently enlightened to impose guidelines and laws that will force everyone to conserve, recycle, and stop polluting.

But I am afraid that these measures cannot work because the whole capitalist system depends on the vast and complex dynamic of environmental exploitation: exploitation of the environment is essential and integral to civilization's present capitalist system. Therefore, governments and other institutions cannot afford to impose guidelines and laws strong enough to really stop the exploitation of the environment; for if they did, the world economy would crash. Thus, continuation of our present lifestyle and economic system seems destined to lead to ecolocaust.

For Marx, the source of all the troubles with capitalism was the material, economic processes which inexorably determined the bourgeoisie to dominate and exploit the proletariat. He thought that capitalism's ills would be cured only after the workers revolted and ushered in a new social and economic order in which there was no domination or exploitation of one group over another. Now I would like to offer a rather different explanation for the problem we face today (the threat of ecolocaust). It seems that the root of this problem is the way our worldview makes all of us dominate and exploit nature. Accordingly, we will avert ecolocaust only by somehow acquiring a new worldview whereby we relate to nature in a non-dominating and non-exploitative way.

Compare our Western attitude of domination and exploitation of nature with the worldview of indigenous cultures such as the Native Americans. At least some indigenous people had a worldview whereby they saw themselves as an integral part of nature. Nature was not something they dominated, controlled, owned, and exploited at will but was a realm of conscious beings who deserved respect. That is to say, many native Americans and other so-called 'primitive' people viewed the animals, trees, mountains, and other things in nature more like family members with whom they had an I-thou relationship. So, dominating and exploiting them was inconceivable.

Of course, it would be naive to assume that we could or should regain the worldview of indigenous people. But perhaps we can acquire a worldview with features that are somewhat like those of some indigenous worldviews. If we could somehow acquire a worldview whereby we no longer view nature as something for us to dominate and exploit, perhaps then we would be intellectually, psychologically, and socially ready to invent and build an economic and social system by which we would happily respect and take care of nature—and thereby avert an ecolocaust.

How we acquire our present worldview

Plato. To get insight about acquiring a new environmentally friendly worldview, let's discuss how we got our present worldview. In an earlier paper I outlined how, thanks largely to Plato, during the Middle Ages a worldview evolved which depicted nature as a temporary realm of secondary value. Nature was viewed as inferior to us superior spiritual beings and as a system that could be fully conceptualized, scientifically mastered, managed, and used for our own higher purposes.

But that worldview encouraged by Plato did favour the environment in at least one respect. That is to say, Plato did leave us with the view that things on earth have meaning and purpose namely, the purpose of becoming more and more like the ideal forms which they imitate. So we should not wantonly cut down a tree, because the tree has its own inner purpose: to grow and become a bigger, healthier tree. Augustine and other Christians later on helped popularize Plato's view of nature as being less permanent and less valuable than Heaven above, etc. And of course, Aristotle and Thomas Aquinas especially developed Plato's ideas about earthly things having meaning and purpose.

Hobbes. The Renaissance brought great changes in worldview and, of course, many individuals and cultural forces contributed to the changes. As I did with Plato, I will take the liberty of being simplistic and single out only a few representative thinkers to concentrate on.

In the 1600s, Thomas Hobbes viewed things in nature with even less respect than Plato did. Hobbes even robbed them of their meaning and purpose. Hobbes taught that all of nature is just one huge machine consisting of mechanical matter which is meaningless. Hobbes' mechanical materialism was so extreme and total that he argued even human beings were nothing more than mechanical matter—that we have no spiritual mind or soul. Thus, for Hobbes, rocks, trees, and people are all made of the same stuff—mechanical matter. One might argue that Hobbes, in a backhanded way, was implying that the rocks, rivers, and trees deserve at least a little respect and consideration because they are made of the same stuff that we humans are made of.

Descartes. But our next representative thinker, Descartes, robbed nature even of that last vestige of respectability. Descartes left us with the view that trees and rocks are not composed of the same stuff as a human self is. Nature is composed purely of matter while our true selves are spiritual substance—and never the twain shall meet. (We don't need to discuss Descartes' futile attempt to explain how body and mind interact by means of the pineal gland.) Thus, thanks to Descartes' dualism, we now tend to construe our personal identity as our minds. What I really am is my mind, not my physical body. Consequently, thanks to Descartes, we now tend to view ourselves as totally different from and cut off from all matter—from all things in Nature. We see ourselves as absolutely different from and fundamentally alienated from all the animals, trees, rivers, and other things in the environment. Accordingly, while Hobbes had implied that we have something in common with things in nature, namely, we are both made of matter, Descartes says that we have nothing at all in common with anything in nature. Plato and company had encouraged us to feel alienated from nature by viewing ourselves as superior spirits who can intellectually master nature; but Descartes now deepens the alienation by clearly construing us as composed of entirely different stuff from everything in nature.

Just as Christianity with its powerful influence on people's thinking had helped popularize Plato's ideas, another powerful and practical movement starting around 1400, namely, the new science and technology, helped to popularize Hobbes' and Descartes' ideas. That is, science and technology presented the masses with a vivid display of the effectiveness of machinery and of the way trees, hills, rivers, etc., can be fixed up, operated on, and used as if they are machinery. Science and technology, by demonstrating their feats, deeply ingrained in the minds of the masses the view that nature indeed *is* inferior to us, is separate from us, and is purposeless, mechanical matter to be manipulated.

Capitalism. Of course, capitalism soon began adding fuel to fire the 'progress' of civilization. John Locke, eased the way for capitalism by finally putting into words a revolutionary new concept that had been emerging since the end of the Middle Ages, the idea that fields, woods, and other areas of nature are real estate to be bought, sold, and owned. Then ownership of property, of other material possessions, and of money became a widespread passion. And this passion for wealth stimulated factory owners to seek more efficient machinery so that they could manufacture and sell more products and could get richer by selling the products to the consumers who likewise were hungry for possessions. The lure of money motivated scientists and technicians to figure out more powerful and economical ways to manipulate and manage nature. And these successes demonstrated to people ever more dramatically that all of nature is machinery to be manipulated. No wonder that after the industrial revolution people felt justified and free to use and abuse the environment as much as they desired.

But we felt not only free and justified in exploiting the environment; capitalism also indoctrinated us to do so aggressively. Capitalism's value system made us feel that our own worth as individuals depended on how much we owned insofar as we were consumers, and on how extensively we could dominate and exploit nature insofar as we were scientists, engineers, industrialists, business executives, or craftsmen. Thus capitalism gave us a powerful impetus to exploit nature aggressively.

To recapitulate briefly, thanks to Plato, Hobbes, Descartes, Locke, and other individuals, plus other forces such as capitalism, we now have a worldview, whereby we see nature as mechanical matter to be mastered, manipulated, and merchandized.

How our own worldview precludes any other
Now that we have a better idea of where we are coming from, we must discuss where we want to go and how to get there. So here are a few observations about the dynamics of worldviews.

Our worldview has largely programmed our consciousness, and now determine how we think and feel about everything. It also determines how we perceive things. In some sense a worldview can be called unconscious or *a priori* because a person is seldom aware of how much control it has over his thinking and perceiving. Therefore, we tend to downplay and deny even to ourselves how our thoughts, feelings, and perceptions are subjectively patterned by our worldview.

Therefore, all of us, even experienced and cautious philosophers, tend to assume that Reality has an objective character close to the way we conceive of it. When we hear any descriptions of what the world might look like under a new worldview, the descriptions tend to sound absurd. And if someone suggests to us that we try to acquire a new worldview, we normally will consider the suggestions to be unrealistic and will reject it out of hand. But we are poor judges of any other worldview precisely because our judgment is so thoroughly programmed by our present worldview.

Describing the new worldview
Despite our poor judgment in these matters, let me offer a few guesses about what sort of worldview we would need in order to avert an ecolocaust.

Sublation. I speculated above that the new worldview might share some features of an indigenous one. To most, this surely would seem an absurd proposal—tantamount to a recommendation that we turn back the clock and settle for a savage primitive-communal stage of history. But if my thesis is to be viable, we must be somewhat like Marx here and think in terms of sublation. We must think in terms of a worldview that would take the best in the indigenous cultures plus the good features of modern civilization, and result in a synthesis that is qualitatively new and better than either.

Beyond alienation. In order to overcome our alienation from nature, it seems that the new worldview would have to have a feature somewhat like the indigenous one which construes trees, mountains, etc., as conscious beings who deserve respect. Thus, with the new worldview we might have an I-Thou relationship with things in nature, or an attitude somehow similar or analogous to that. According to this scenario we would no longer have any desires or other inclinations to exploit the environment. Then it would no longer be necessary to lure business leaders into conserving, recycling, etc., by telling then that it is 'good business'; nor would laws be needed to force people to take care of the environment; nor would we need to frighten or shame people into doing so. Working with nature and taking care of the environment would 'come naturally' to us; and mastering, manipulating, and merchandising nature would seem distasteful, abnormal, absurd, and out of the question.

Beyond capitalism and Marxism. Of course, if we could reach this stage, we would have gone beyond capitalism, or at least would have radically transformed it. So as a bonus, we would have gotten rid not only of alienation between ourselves and nature but also the rampant alienation among individuals and groups which is causing great misery and violence throughout today's world.

The new orientation could also be interpreted as taking us beyond Marxism in that it would not be humanism. If we still viewed human beings as more important than animals, plants, rivers, etc., *à la* humanism, that would foster alienation and the very exploitation of nature that must be avoided. So, presumably, under the new worldview, we would view the animals, plants, rivers, etc., as being as important as ourselves.

How might a new worldview develop?

Of course, many people believe that our environment, capitalist system, and present worldview will remain intact for centuries to come and that a new worldview will evolve only very gradually over many centuries of interaction of economic, spiritual, and other kinds of forces. Marx, on the contrary thought that the capitalists' exploitation of workers would relatively quickly precipitate a violent revolution leading to a new world order and new worldview. But it will be the impending ecolocaust.

A neo-Marxist agreeing with this might add that we will have to let the material forces do their work, that is, that the ecolocaust will actually occur, that it will wipe out civilization, and that only then, after the ecolocaust, will our miserable descendants finally start rebuilding a new non-capitalist society. But I am afraid that after the ecolocaust too little would be left of either the environment or society for much rebuilding to be possible.

I myself, as only a quasi-neo-Marxist, am idealistic enough to hope that we will not have to wait for the material factors to force us to change. I suggested a more idealistic explanation earlier: that at the root of our exploitative capitalistic lifestyle is our worldview and that the cure must be a new worldview. Thus, I think that we human beings may be free and creative enough to find a way to generate the sort of new worldview that is required. And we may be able to create the new worldview before the ecolocaust itself materially forces us to do so, i.e., soon enough to take advantage of an environment that is still intact enough to build on.

Conclusion

Ecolocaust is threatening to wipe us out. We are so locked into or addicted to our present environmentally exploitative capitalistic economic system and lifestyle that only a new worldview will enable us to invent and build the radically different philosophical, theological, cultural and economic systems that are needed to avert ecolocaust. One may judge the prospect of developing the new worldview and subsequent non-capitalistic world as being too unrealistic, impossible, and utopian to waste time discussing. But this judgment might well be due to the way our present worldview is shaping our thinking and keeping us from entertaining new patterns of thinking. Because from our present vantage point we cannot be sure that developing the new worldview is possible, and because getting the new worldview might be the only way to avert ecolocaust, it would be unreasonable not to at least examine the possibility of acquiring the new worldview that is needed.

So I would like to make a concrete proposal—that we initiate an investigation of the possibility of developing a new worldview. It might seem that what I am recommending will turn out to be just more discussion of alternative metaphysical, theological, or ethical systems, in other words, what philosophers have always done. On the contrary, I am talking about something very different, namely, zeroing in on the question of worldview per se. Our work would be more epistemological than metaphysical or ethical, and would have to do with questions such as the following:

- Exactly what do we mean by worldview? How is a worldview different from a set of metaphysical, religious, and ethical beliefs?
- What metaphysical, religious (etc.) beliefs and concepts would we need in order to avert ecolocaust, and how can we describe the worldview we would need in order to produce those metaphysical and religious beliefs?
- How is a worldview formed and changed? How might we go about acquiring the worldview we would need and what would the chances of success be?

I do not know what form this investigation should take—a meeting, a conference, a newsletter, an organization, or what. But I would very much like to discuss with you the possibility of taking some such action.

30 MATHEMATICAL-SCIENTIFIC-TECHNICAL COMPREHENSION OF NATURE VERSUS ORGANIC IMAGE OF NATURE

Karen Gloy
Lucerne, Switzerland

The ecology debate with its increasing intensity and vehemence, as we have witnessed it for about twenty years in all industrial nations and the reverse of which is the technology and industry criticism, is not new. It represents a variant of the older civilization criticism, which is as old as life in highly developed urban cultures and in the alterations to nature on the whole that go with it. Whether the opponents appear under names such as country and city, sound, healthy and decadent world, vitalism and degeneration, asceticism and luxury, or under notions such as nature and intellect, nature and art, nature and technology, is of secondary significance and does not modify the archetype. This criticism is neither restricted to single epochs nor to single countries or continents, but occurs at all times and globally.

Civilization criticism already occurs in ancient China, where in the 4th century, B.C. Chuang-Tzu contrasted the hermit's life close to nature with the courtly intrigues. In Europe, we find on the same level the bucolic poetry of the anacreontics in ancient Greece with the glorification of the Arcadian scenery or the praise of the golden age. During the Roman era the ideal of rural solidarity with nature gained increasing importance over the striving after power and wealth. The simple, rural, rustic life was praised. Statesmen such as Cincinnatus exchanged the sword for the plough and returned to the soil after the battle. In Horace and Vergil country life is the basis of simple, austere existence, a view which returns in Tasso and Petrarca during the Renaissance, and which remains valid until the 18th century. The more the luxury of city and court life grew in the era of absolutism, the more extensive became the flight into an often fake idyll of shepherds' romanticism. Since the initiation of the industrial age in the 19th century with its technical and technological revolutions, the flood of counter and reform movements has never ended and is manifested in the *Wandervogel* and pathfinder movement, the gymnasts' federation, and in garden city and allotment gardeners' associations. Today their places have been taken by large national and international ecological mass movements with a new, altered environmental consciousness. Their purpose is to stand up for the protection and preservation of remaining natural living spaces and their animals, plants, and natural resources. Environmental associations, landscape and species protection associations, institutions for the establishment of national parks, etc., have been established. The object of criticism is everything which interferes with nature in a destructive way such as atomic power plants, nuclear and chemical armament, pollution of air and rivers and seas by industrial emissions and exhaust fumes, and gene manipulation as interference with human idioplasm.

At the bottom of the basic controversy are different conceptions of nature, the theoretical dispositions of which are connected with normative, ethical implications. On the one hand the organological, perhaps ever zoomorphistical or anthropomorphistical image of nature is predominant, which considers nature as a living organism and the human being as an integrated partner within it. On the other hand the mathematical, scientific, technical, respectively, comprehension of nature is predominant. It is based on the subject-object difference, understands nature as the other, strange reality, which is often opposed to the human being, and over which a claim of dominion is to be enforced. In this case nature becomes the object of experiments and manipulations.

The periodical occurrence of this conflict model (which appears throughout) seems to confirm the supposition that conflict is a matter of fateful coincidence, an irreversible process. The mathematical-scientific view of life, a product of the European, ancient Greek mental attitude, has since its origin developed with unalterable consequence and stringency. Opposed to it and just as unalterable is the human being's dream of paradise lost, which leads to the future utopian restoration of this world.

The development process of the mathematical-scientific-technical comprehension of nature has its origin in a certain constellation of occidental philosophy, i.e. in the conception of science in ancient Greece, and it has since that time developed with irresistible consistency enhanced by the influence of Christianity. In the course of this process three stages can be distinguished:

(1) the antique stage, which for the first time in history introduces the conception of construction and availability by orienting knowledge on ποιεtν on making, on producing, but stopping at an intellectual construction; (2) the medieval-Christian stage, for which nature is the real product and construction of a divine creation and structural act, which the human being is able to reconstruct intellectually because he is God's image; (3) the modern stage, in which, after secularization and after the suspension of God nature becomes the artificial and technical product of the human being. An artificial nature has taken the place of natural nature, the world of robots, computers, automatons, and artificial intelligence. Alternatives can only be found when the immanent necessity of this process is understood.

The wide-spread thesis, pleaded above all in this century by Bergson and Heidegger, that upon the weighing of theory and practice, knowledge and action, practice is the more original principle and knowledge derivative of it, which arises upon man's decreasing interest and lesser involvement with nature, and which represents as it were the quiet, solidified product of an original procedure. *Mutatis mutandis,* this thesis is also valid for the antique conception oriented on the process of acting. To know is to make, and that is an intellectual construction; it is not just mere reception. As the artisan or the artist, according to a preceding plan, in a real production process forms the matter, the thinking subject in an intellectual process comprehends the forms of nature.

The paradigm for this conception is given in Plato's 'Timaios', wherein he records his cosmology, and his knowledge of the universe. Confronted with the question of how man can comprehend the pre-existent world into which he is born, Plato answers with a creation myth: just as a human artist viewing a pre-existent idea, e.g. the conception of the chair, forms the material he finds, so the divine artisan and architect viewing the pre-existent cosmos of ideas created the world. The re-execution of this original creation and construction by reconstructing thinking enables man's insight into the building-up, the laws and structures of the cosmos. Behind this is the insight that we can really understand only what we can produce and reproduce ourselves.

That the foregoing is a myth emerges from the fact that the antique ontology only knows an eternal, non-originated and everlasting cosmos. It is therefore the task of the myth to elucidate the non-temporal laws of the cosmos in temporal, successive form, i.e. in their genetic origin. With this technical conception of nature according to which the φύσεψöν is a *TÉχöν*, and a constructivistic theory of cognition, Plato became the founder of a tradition reaching to modern times. Lactantius (*De opificio dei* 14, 9, in: *Opera omnia* I-II, ed. according to S. Brandt, Prague-Vienna-Leipzig 1890–93) says: 'Only the author knows his work'; in Cusanus' *Idiota de mente*, it is said that the human being can precisely understand only by proving to be God's equal and by reconstructing the divine creation process. And in Kant we find the conception that we make the experience ourselves, Kant's *Opus postumum* constantly repeats this stereotypical phrase: 'We make the experience ourselves, which we believe to have learned by observation and experiment.' Kant's entire epistemology is based on the idea that we can perceive in objects and objective connections only what we ourselves constitute *a priori* according to our subjective perception conditions. We ourselves are the creators of the laws of nature, which we believe are abstracted from nature. This is nevertheless only valid in formal, not in material, respect.

Whereas antique constructivism was merely intellectual, this changes with the Christian influence. The world, all along pre-existent according to antique ontology, now becomes a real product of God, which the human being because of his equality with God is able to reconstruct and comprehend by intellectual re-execution of divine ideas. Christian thinking may be distinguished from antique thinking in three ways:

(1) According to the Genesis report, God created heaven and earth and everything on it: plants, animals, and man as the coronation of creation. Even though other religions and myths know a creation of the world, lies the Indian myth from the man Purusha, the Germanic myth from the world ash-tree or from the giant Ymir, they are, however, only shapings of a pre-existent material, and not a *creatio ex nihilo*, a creation from nothingness according to Christian dogmatics. Bound up with the absolute creation of the world is an enhancement of God's power to unlimited omnipotence, which deepens the gap between creator and creature.

(2) Bound up with the creation is a division of existence into a creating and a created existence (*ens creans* and *ens creatum*), which is at the same time the basis of a dialectic. On the one hand the creation is God's *product*, not he himself, released, dismissed, or delivered from him. On the other hand the

creation is not the *entirely* different, strange, and anti-divine. Upon this dialectic of divinity and non-divinity the Christian attitude towards nature and the Christian ethics are based. These radicalize man's relation to nature in two different directions. On one hand, nature is positively valued, estimated as a divine product, respected, adored. Representatives of this optimism are Augustinus and Leibniz, the latter with his conception of our world as the best of all possible worlds. On the other hand, nature is depreciatorily, devaluatingly, negatively judged, and degraded to a merely non-divine product.

(3) Christian anthropology based on the statement in Genesis 1:27 about man's God-likeness, as well as on the statement in the New Testament about the filiation (Galatians 4: 1–10), also follows this ambivalence. These statements establish the excellent position of man within the hierarchy of existence, and guaranteed him a position between God and creature. On the one hand man is God's creature like all other creatures. On the other hand, however, he is placed above nature; he is the master of nature. This pre-eminent and powerful position is entirely missing in the Greek way of thinking and has been of greatest efficiency in intellectual and cultural history.

Biblical statements such as Genesis 1:28: 'Subdue it (the earth) and rule over the fish of the sea and over the birds of the sky, and over every living thing that moves on earth', have often been considered as the Magna Carta of technology. It legitimizes man's claim of dominion over nature and entitles him to interventions of any kind, from mere working and utilization for his subsistence, to exploitation. It becomes therefrom intelligible that the realization and rapid expansion of the mechanistic, technical view of life would have been impossible without Christian influence. In his book, *Philosophie der Technik. Das Problem der Realisierung* (Bonn, 1927), Friedrich Dessauer already saw the innateness of the human being in the predominance of technology, not only in post-industrial, modern, but already in pre-industrial technology, and even more fundamentally in all forms of man's condition as *homo* investigator, *homo* inventor, and *homo faber*. In view of the ecological crisis, not only the positive, but above all the negative, fatal consequences of scientification, mechanization and industrialization, are criticized today.

During the secularization process of modern times, God as creator of the world and guarantor of human cognition of objects and nature faded more and more within the hierarchy of existence. Man took his place as the *alter deus* not only in epistemological, but also in practical respects, with the consequence that nature not only became the intellectual construction, but more the real construction and product of man. We are not only in a position to imitate inorganic, inanimate nature—let's think of plastic materials, artificial energies, artificial scenarios consisting of concrete, foam rubber and neon light; we are also about to imitate living organic nature.

31 F.E. ABBOT AND THE ENVIRONMENTAL CRISIS

Creighton Peden
Augusta College
University System of Georgia
Augusta, Georgia, U.S.A.

The environmental crisis facing humanity is due in part to the philosophy of possessive individualism, in the tradition of Hobbes and Locke, which has strongly influenced the development of Western industrial societies. Today we are witnessing the spread of possessive individualism in such diverse cultural forms, as pluralistic democracy and the free market economy become the dominant political and economic norms as humanity approaches the twenty first century. If humanity is to survive very complex environmental crises, a shift in philosophy from individualism to universalism as the foundation principle of ethical theory is required. Francis Ellingwood Abbot (1836–1903), a noted 19th century American philosopher, provided an insight into what such a philosophical shift might entail.

While Abbot was a graduate student at Harvard Divinity School, his philosophy began a radical transformation under the influence of Charles Darwin. The immediate results of this transformation were two articles by Abbot in the *North American Review* in 1864, establishing him as the first American philosopher to support Darwin. Due to the radical nature of his philosophical and theological views, Abbot, like Chauncey Wright, C.S. Peirce and other philosophers of his day, was excluded from academic appointments at Harvard, Johns Hopkins and Cornell universities.

Abbot was a member of Peirce's Metaphysical Club. Within this company Abbot participated in the movement of philosophical thought from idealism to pragmatism, but he never identified his position with pragmatism. Sharing with Idealism a strong concern for the rational and moral side of human nature, he developed a philosophy that rejected Idealism in light of the Darwinian revolution and emphasized experience and reason as the foundation of knowledge. Abbot presented a vitalistic, relational, organic philosophy which began with experience, and was then rationally tested by employing the scientific method until a consensus of the competent was reached. Yet there was always a conflict within Abbot due to the inherent conflict between his Puritan up-bringing and empiricism. Because of this conflict, Abbot was unable to compromise politically and philosophically, always remaining a radical even as empiricism was gaining as the new philosophical direction for American thought.

In his most noted work, *Scientific Theism*, Abbot argued that real relations are the ultimate ground of intelligibility; things do not exist apart from relations nor do relations exist apart from things related. By 1893, in his unpublished 'Grand Logic' Charles Peirce had shifted his focus in considering the problem of universals from genera to relations and directly attributed to Abbot.[1] In his 'Pragmatic Lectures' at Harvard in 1903, Peirce abandoned phenomenalism 'under the impact of Abbot's critique of phenomenalism', and thereafter dropped the 'inferentialist position in favour of a certain kind of immediacy,'[2] In an obituary note in *The Nation* Peirce spoke of the benefits of an acquaintance with Abbot:

> The unsophisticated purity of his love of and apprehension of truth, oblivious of the tide of opinion, was a quality without which the Introduction to his 'Scientific Theism', wherein he put his finger unerringly (as the present writer thinks) upon the one great blunder of all modern philosophy, could not have been written. The perfect clearness and simplicity of his argument will blind many a mind to it that could thread its way through the most abstruse turtuosities of law ... In each writing of a philosophical nature that he produced, he brought put some undeniable and important point that had almost entirely overlooked by philosophers ...[3]

As Abbot considered the situation facing humanity in his day, he became convinced that a shift from individualism to universalism was required as the foundation principle of ethical theory. A position is essentially individualistic which seeks the ideal end of individual life in the primary ethical welfare of humanity, with individuals being a part of humanity.

Historically, ethics has focused on the ideal of the individual while excluding the insights provided by the physical and cosial sciences. In the Orient the ideal of the individual is seen in the 'superior man' of Confucius and Mencius and in the 'awakened man' of Buddhism. For Greece and Rome ethical speculation focused on determining the essential qualities of the 'philosopher' or ideal person, qualities which were inapplicable to society except as a sum of individuals as such. A student of the history of Western philosophy will recognize a consistent application of ethics of this central conception of Greek philosophy, which germinating in Socrates and Plato, found its full expression in Aristotle's theory of universals: 'Namely, that the pure universal, or Form, inheres in the individual, or union of Form with Matter, as at once efficient cause, final cause, and formal cause or constitutive essence ...'[4]

Following in the tradition of Aristotle, Kant contended that universal humanity is immanent in the individual. Thus, the individual is conceived as a universally self-legislating individual or as the sole absolute source of universal moral law. In the tradition of Kant, Hegel made the individual the centre of ethics and supported the 'autonomy' of the individual will as Conscience. Hegel, like Kant, made the individual a universally self-legislating will, denying any ethical authority over the subjective conscience of the individual as such. It is true that Hegel proclaimed the individual's highest duty to be a fellow-member of the State, but this duty was dependent upon the individual's self-recognition. The root of the ethical individualism of Kant and Hegel is to be found in the Aristotelian theory of universal in metaphysics.

What the individualistic theories overlooked was the notion that every organism, and every organ in it, functions partly for self and partly for others. This means that it is both means and ends for itself and for others. There is a reciprocity between these two functions. If either function is impeded, then the organisms perish together. A proper scientific ethical theory will rest on an understanding of the organic constitution of all life, with its characteristic principle of reciprocal finality as both immanent and exigent. The organic constitution is to be found in each person and ripens in the course of evolution into ethical self-consciousness. As the individual ideals coalesce into a universal social ideal, the social organism emerges into self-conscious knowledge. Thus, the proper aim of philosophy as ethical theory is to effect this coalescence. Philosophy should engage in this task because Nature's idea of the 'good' is the organic constitution based on this reciprocal process. Health is the clear proof of Nature's good, and disease is unmistakable proof of its partial defeat. Abbot indicates that nature establishes a pragmatic criteria of health and disease for determining whether conduct conforms to the organic constitution.

The reason why I should do it is that, by willing it, I will the health of the social organism, while, by willing the opposite, I will the disease, and so far the death, of the social organism. For in vain shall I seek (and Herein lies the failure of all individualism in ethics) to separate my own healthy or my own disease from that of the organic body of which I am merely an organ or member.[5]

To will reciprocity, largely understood, means to do the right. That is the law of nature and ignorance of the law is no excuse. What is required by humans as rational beings is that they understand and obey the principle of the all-pervading reciprocity of ends and means as the total constitution of all living things.

When the individual and society function according to the law of the organic constitution, there will be a harmony of organ and function according to the law of the organic constitution, there will be a harmony of organ and function between the person and society—a healthful ethical equilibrium which is described as justice, equity, and equality. Reciprocity between the individual and society is well formulated in the old saying 'each for all and all for each ...'[6] Reciprocal justice is the social ideal. It seeks to cultivate in each organism individual differences while subordinating these differences to the universal social ideal of reciprocal justice. A person is of 'moral worth' to the degree that he develops individual differences while subordinating the self to the social organism. Being right involves more than the intentions or 'good will,' for good will is mere subjective justice. Abbot contends that the only scientific criterion and only truly ethical criterion for 'right' is human conduct, which is the basis of objective justice. While the personal ideal may focus on subjective justice, the social ideal demands objective justice. What is required for individual and social health is a reciprocity between subjective and objective justice.[7]

As a social philosopher and social reformer, Abbot was not content only to explain theoretically the difference between individualism and universalism in ethics. He was equally concerned about this ethical position being applied individually and socially. What one must do is acquire conviction regarding one's own ideal and worth. One needs to come to grips with the question, 'What is life for?' In determining the nature of worth, one becomes convinced as to what constitutes the highest good. If one determines one's worth in terms of acquiring outward advantage—i.e. money, power, or social position—'if we really believe at bottom that our own selfish pleasure or happiness is the thing to live for—then we shall live for that, and our life will not be worth living.'[8] Yet, if one becomes convinced that life contains, for each living thing, an ideal and, then the primary question becomes 'What is my ideal end?' However, an understanding of the ideal requires an understanding of the real. Abbot explained that the soul of ethics is to be found in the contract of antithesis of Real and Ideal: 'The real is that which is. The Ideal is that which ought to be. Science is accurate knowledge of their Real. Ethics, or ethical science, is accurate knowledge of the Ideal.'[9]

As we face the potentially catastrophic environmental crisis, Abbot reminds us that our ethical decisions must be based on the substitution of universalism for individualism which requires that we understand and obey the principle of the all-pervading reciprocity of ends and means as the total constitution of all living things. Due to our intense possessive individualism, we have failed to realize the ideal immanent in the Real. When we understand the immanence of the Ideal in the Real. When we understand 'the identity of Nature and Spirit in God.'[10] Yet, we need to understand, if we are to participate with Nature in dealing with the environmental crisis, that the universal Ethical Ideal, which is immanent in Nature and humans, is also immanent in the organic constitution of all living things—plants and animals. As the ethical ideal of any living thing is realized in the whole, the Good of Nature flowers. F.E. Abbot reminds us that for our health, our ethical actions must be committed to helping Nature flower.

Notes
1. Burks, 1958.
2. O'Connor, 1985, p. 561; Raposa, 1989.
3. Peirce, 1903, p. 77.
4. Abbot, 1874, p. 195.
5. *Ibid.*, p. 214.
6. *Ibid.*, p. 216.
7. For a discussion of the difference between action being subjectively right or wrong and being objectively right or wrong see F.E. Abbot, *The Syllogistic Philosophy*, Vol. II, pp. 263–268.
8. Abbot, 1897, p. 5.
9. Abbot, 1897, p. 8.
10. Abbot, 1897, p. 12.

32 THE PRINCIPAL ATTITUDES OF HUMANITY TOWARDS NATURE

Juhani Pietarinen
University of Turku
Finland

European culture has at times been compelled to revise its conception of nature. What is nature? What is the place of man in it? How are we entitled to treat nature? These questions have once again become of current interest.[1] I shall approach the questions by considering four attitudes of man towards nature which have played an especially important role in the history of our civilization. I call them utilism, humanism, mysticism and naturism.

By 'utilism' I mean an attitude or way of thinking that nature exists only for the welfare of humankind. Its substantial characteristics might be stated as follows:

(i) End: A high level of welfare for people. (ii) Conception of nature: Nature is a system regulated by causal laws; it provides a huge and valuable source of energy and raw materials. (iii) Legitimization: Humanity has an unlimited right to use nature for the welfare of people. (iv) Relation to technology: Science and technology are all-important, especially technology which helps us improve the effectiveness of production and thereby improves human welfare. (v) Optimism: All problems related to the welfare of humankind can be solved by promoting science and technology.

From the historical point of view, utilism together with the idea of possessive individualism is a product of the breakthrough of a new mode of scientific thinking in the 17th century. We are now familiar with the serious damage that life founded on utilism caused in natural ecosystems. The growth of human population, intensive building and pollution have caused great changes in natural ecosystems. The main problem of utilism is that it probably turns out to be contrafinal. Of course it is difficult to state with certainty what kind of development turns out to be fatal for the welfare of humankind, but if we do not find tenable solutions to the problems caused by pollution and the growth of human population, the contrafinal nature of utilism will soon prove true. Continuing a utilistic way of life presupposes that we believe in the power of science and technology, along with rational economy and politics, to solve all problems. If this belief turns out to be groundless, as might be expected, alternatives to utilism must be found.

One alternative is what I call 'humanism'. Like utilism, it is a purely human-centered attitude, but its ends are different. Humanism postulates the intellectual and moral perfectibility of mankind and promote such Socratic virtues as intellectual activity, moral strength, the sense of beauty, friendship and mental harmony. The main features of humanism are as follows: (i) End: Intellectual and moral development of man, i.e. promotion of Socratic virtues. (ii) Conception of nature: Nature, as such, is raw and primitive, but it contains possibilities for the development of human culture. (iii) Legitimization: Humanity has the right to use nature for promoting the intellectual and moral development of people through education. (iv) Relation to technology: Science and technology are necessary, but they should be developed and used in accordance with the ends of humanism. (v) Optimism: The development of culture is believed to be progressive, even though from time to time humankind has to suffer trials and tribulations.

Humanism is a rational attitude. It rates knowledge and science highly, as well as technology that is needed for human education. But the rationality of humanism encompasses more than mere technical and economical rationality. Such ideals as justice, mental peace and friendship must be counted among rational human aims. We might speak here of ethical rationality in contrast to technical rationality.

Of course humanism must accept the use of natural resources for human welfare. But, moreover, it requires that nature should provide aesthetic satisfaction for people and advance their moral character. Nature should also promote mental health and positive relations (feelings of friendship, etc.) between persons. Therefore, in our treatment of nature we must consider aesthetic values and remember our responsibility for nature. Pure utilism does not concern itself with these values.

But is it possible to fulfill all the various demands of humanism? Is it possible to advance the human culture with Socratic virtues without causing damages similar to those of the utilistic way of life does? Is it possible to invent technology and production that would serve humanistic ends but would avoid the problems of utilism? This is the main challenge for humanism.

Unlike humanism, 'mysticism' does not trust rational knowledge and human intellect. It seeks something beyond reason. Mystical movements become especially popular during cultural crises, when old habits, values and norms lose their significance and new ones have not yet become established. Mysticism aims at the experience of unity, a feeling that one is united with something infinitely great and powerful. When this feeling of unity occupies one's mind, the limits of time and space are removed and one feels everywhere the presence of something infinite, eternal and sacred.

European mysticism has often been a minor branch of the humanistic tradition. Plato's philosophy contained a large measure of mysticism. It was also easy to move towards mysticism from German romanticism and Hegelian philosophy, as in fact happened during the first half of the 19th century when American transcendentalism developed. The writings of Ralph Emerson and Henry Thoreau contain clear elements of mysticism. Of the present mystically oriented attitudes towards nature, Rudolf Steiner's anthroposophical 'science of spirit' and Henrik Skolimowski's 'ecophilosophy' might be mentioned. Both of these trends of ideas have gained some popularity for instance in Finland. The main characteristics of mysticism are as follows: (i) End: Experience of the unity of humankind and nature through intuition or some other method of immediate access to the spirit of nature. (ii) Conception of nature: Nature is essentially a spiritual and divine totality. (iii) Legitimization: Nature represents sanctity, the achievement of which is the highest end for human life. (iv) Relation to technology: Science and technology should be rejected, because they violate the spirituality of nature and undermine the human potential to achieve the experience of mystical unity. (v) Optimism: Although humanity can cause serious damage to nature, its divine force can never be destroyed.

Respect for the natural world is inherent in mysticism. However, mysticism faces the same problem as humanism: how can the welfare of people and respect for nature be reconciled? This problem is especially serious because a true mystic must keep nature as intact and as untouched as possible. Should we go back to a primitive natural economy? This is hardly what the mystics want. On the other hand, if we want even a reasonable standard of welfare for mankind, we need science and technology—but a mystic cannot accept them! Although mysticism may be a valuable solution to the personal problems of life, as a world-wide programme it would lead to an intolerable situation for humankind.

The development of biological research in the modern age is associated in an interesting way with the principle of plenitude or the idea that all possibilities will be realized in nature, and with the closely related principle of continuity the idea that no gaps can exist between species.[2] These principles paved the way for the idea of equality between species: each species should be regarded as equally important in the sense of making the world as plentiful and perfect as possible, and as having therefore the same right to exist. The special position of humanity began to be questioned. Charles Darwin's *The Origin of the Species* (1859) showed decisively that humankind is descended from other species according to the principles of natural selection. Humanity thus belongs inseparably to nature. This forms part of the background of 'biocentrism' which as a general attitude towards nature can be characterized by the following principles: (i) End: The conservation of nature in as original and as primordial condition as possible. (ii) Conception of nature: Nature is a uniform system acting according to the laws of ecology, and man is part of the system. (iii) Legitimization: All parts of nature are of equal intrinsic value, and people should respect the intrinsic value of nature. (iv) Relation to technology: All technology that endangers the life of other species and causes excessive ecological disturbance must be rejected. (v) Optimism: If humanity abandons the privileges with respect to nature and accepts *Homo sapiens* as a species among others, nature can be conserved. Otherwise it will be destroyed.

The inherent value of nature has been justified in various ways. David Ehrenfeld suggests what he calls the Noah principle: 'Species and communities should be conserved because they exist and because this existence is itself but the present expression of a continuing historical process of immense antiquity and majesty.'[3] Other authors have argued that animals, at least sentient ones, have the same basic moral right to life and freedom as humanity has.[4] It seems also meaningful to talk in an Aristotelian manner about the good of any living being, because living beings can be said to be well or ill, to thrive, or to flourish. Not only higher animals, but also plants and even simple organisms such as one-celled protozoa have a good of their own in this sense. Paul W. Taylor has recently developed a system of environmental ethics which is based on the principle that we should equally respect the good of all living beings.[5]

The main practical difficulty of biocentrism is obvious: men do not easily reject the privileges they have gained—their welfare, technology, science, civilization and comfort. Taylor suggests certain principles for solving the difficult problem of adjusting the good of man to the welfare of other living beings, but it is doubtful whether they will achieve the goal intended. Biocentrism requires that men reduce their influence on nature to a minimum, and live under primitive conditions. These ideas will probably not attract very many people.

Which one of the four basic attitudes is best justified? Utilism will most probably turn out to be contrafinal. The moral legitimization of humanism seems to be firmer. However, it is an extremely difficult task to find a reconciliation between the intellectual and moral progress of human beings and the vitality of nature. Until this problem is solved, the legitimate basis of humanism remains unsatisfactory. Mysticism, if embraced generally, could save nature from disaster. But because it does not give a satisfactory answer to the problem of human welfare, it will only provide an escape from rather than a solution to the serious difficulties humankind is encountering. Biocentrism is without doubt morally appealing, but it requires that people renounce their interests for the well-being of nature to such an extent that it cannot be expected to receive very much support.

Perhaps we have to conclude that it would be best to have proponents of all of the four attitudes, altering, however, their relative strength from utilism towards the other three attitudes. But would it help? Nobody knows. It is quite possible that no proper balance between our interests and the tolerance of nature can be found.

Notes
1. Passmore, 1974, p. 33.
2. Lovejoy, 1960, chapter 8.
3. Ehrenfeld, 1978.
4. Regan, 1983; Singer, 1980.
5. Taylor, 1986.

33 HUMANS, ANIMALS AND ENVIRONMENT: INDIAN PERSPECTIVES

S.S. Rama Pappu

Miami University, Oxford, Ohio
U.S.A.

In the past two decades philosophy, especially Western philosophy, took an applied turn. Philosophers at present are venturing into the value dimensions of science and technology, engineering and business. The ethics of environment, in particular, is widely discussed by philosophers and humanists, scientists and statesmen. In this paper I shall give a prolegomena to an environmental ethics from an Indian perspective. Indian environmental ethics is both descriptive and prescriptive. It is descriptive because the positions I shall be enunciating are found in Indian literature and they constitute the dominant belief system of the Indians. It is also prescriptive because they are also the norms which govern Indian lives.

Discussions on environmental ethics in recent Western philosophy generally centre around the following issues: (a) whether ethics is purely human-centred and anthropocentric; (b) whether the scope of ethics includes all sentient-creatures, not just humans alone; and (c) whether ethics is ecocentric, i.e. whether non-human objects such as plants, rocks and rivers also have a moral standing.

The position Indian philosophy takes on these three issues is: (a) Ethics is not just human-centred, but *dharma*-centred; (b) all life is sacred and the ethical relationship between humans and animals is one of equality, and (c) natural objects like rivers and hills, trees and rocks are sacred and therefore deserve respect. Indian philosophy maintains that 'humans are in nature' and rejects other positions like 'humans against nature', 'humans and nature', 'humans guide nature', etc.

Indian philosophy does not accept ethics as 'man-given' or 'God-given'; nor is ethics 'human-centred' or 'God-centred'. Ethics in India is '*dharma*-centred.' As early as the *Rg Veda* morality was conceived of as an aspect of *Rta*. *Rta* is the Eternal law of the Universe which, when applied to Nature, becomes

Natural Law and when applied to living beings, becomes Moral Law. From the time of the Upanishads, the Vedic concept of *Rta* becomes the concept of *Dharma*. The nature of *Dharma* is said to be subtle, says the *Mahabharata*. *Dharma* has the same connotation as *Rta* but the implications and applications of *Dharma* are widely discussed in later Indian literature. *Dharma* means 'that which holds together'. It is the eternal law which governs every aspect of the universe; it is the very foundation of the universe itself. It is all-encompassing, manifesting itself in every aspect of nature and life. Even God does not give us the *dharma*; He is the 'immutable protector of the eternal *dharma*.' (*Bhagavadgita* XI 18). Indian ethics which is *dharma*-centred is therefore not anthropocentric but universal in nature including in its fold not only humans but also all living beings and the physical environment. Starting with the assumption that human beings are the paradigm for having goods and interests, recent discussions in the West raise the following question: 'What (other) kind of beings can have 'good', interests, preferences, etc.?' Because Indian ethics starts with the paradigm that existence itself has value, the question whether non-humans have intrinsic value or are conferred value by humans is never raised. The *Yajur Veda*, for example says: 'The person who sees all animate and inanimate creation in God, and God pervading all material objects, falls not a prey to doubt.' *(Yastu sarvani bhutanyatmannevanupasyati; Sarvabhutgesu catmanam tao na vicikitsati (Yajur Veda*, 40.6).

In Indian thought, the fundamental moral belief which governs the relations not only between humans but also between humans and non-human species is the principle of *ahimsa* (non-violence). The first principles of Indian ethics are: *ahimsa paramodharmah*—'Ahimsa is the Supreme Religion'; and *na himsyat sarvabhutanam*—'Do not kill any living being.' The expression *sarvabhutanam* is important here as it refers to all living beings and not to human beings alone. The reason for this ethical commandment lies in the Indian doctrine of 'Unity of Life', a doctrine which recognizes not only the 'brotherhood of humans', but also the 'brotherhood of all living creatures'. Indian thought recognizes that it is the same life principle which exists in all life forms from amoeba to man. The life forms do not differ in kind but only in the degree of evolution.

What is the nature of this life principle which connects all living creatures, including humans? It is consciousness. Even the essence of Brahman (Absolute, God) is also consciousness. Thus, God, humans and all living creatures have the same essence which is consciousness. Indian thought, therefore, does not maintain: 'Man is made in the image of God'; it maintains : 'God, Man and all living creatures have the same essence, *viz.* consciousness.' In their *essential* nature, therefore, God = Humans = All Living Creatures. This essential unity of God and all living creatures is manifested, for example, in the Hindu conception of *avataras* or 'incarnations of God'. These are: *matsya* or fish; *kurma* or tortoise; *varaha* or wild boar; *narasimha* or man-lion; *vamana* or dwarf; *parasurama* or Rama with axe; Rama, Krishna, Buddha and Kalki. We may note here that God in Hinduism did not keep Himself aloof in Heaven, totally distancing Himself from living creatures. He incarnated Himself not only as human beings but also as sub-human beings like fish, turtle, boar, etc.

Because of the 'Unity of Life' doctrine, God does not show, in Indian religion, any favouritism to humans. Humans alone are not God's chosen creatures. *Moksa* or salvation (attainment of Heaven) is possible not only for humans but also for sub-human creatures. In the famous Indian epic *Ramayana* Rama's monkey-servant, Hanuman helps in the release of Rama's wife, Sita, and attains Heaven. Likewise, the giant vulture, Jadayu, sacrifices his own life preventing Sita's abduction by the demon King Ravana, and Rama performs the *sraddha* or funeral ceremonies for this bird on a par with his own father, King Dasaratha. The Inhabitants of Heaven in Indian religion are not humans and human-like gods alone, there are animals as well. Most of the Hindu gods are very closely associated with animals: the mouse with Lord Ganesa, who himself is half-man and half-elephant; the eagle with Lord Vishnu; the snake and the bull with Lord Siva; the tiger with goddess Durga; the swan with the goddess, Sarasvati; etc. Of all the non-human creatures, the cow symbolizes the sacredness of all non-human life. The cow is not just the first among animal equals. Killing a cow is one of the 'five deadly sins,' and thus the cow sometimes occupies a more superior position than some humans! In addition, Indian thought which argues for a rebirth doctrine states that animals can be (re)born as humans and humans may be reborn as animals depending on their moral merit and demerit. An animal, therefore, is on its way to being human in successive rebirths and ultimately reaching a state of 'birthlessness' and attaining Heaven (*Brahmaloka*). And humans too, by a 'fall' in their moral lives may be reborn as animals. In other words, in the rebirth doctrine, human and animal lives are interchangeable.

Just as 'unity of life' and 'equality' characterize the relationship between humans and animals, 'unity of existence' and 'reverence for Nature' describe the relationship between humans and the environment in Indian philosophy. Unlike Western theories which conceive of the human-environment relationship as one of domination, superiority, stewardship, separation, etc., Indian thought conceives of the relationship in terms of 'unity' and 'togetherness'.

'All that dwelleth therein and the dwelling itself is Brahman (Absolute)' summarizes the Hindu conception of Reality. The *Upanisads* which form the warp and woof of Indian religion, culture and society put forth this idea of unity of existence in several ways. Just as a 'lump of salt cast in water would dissolve right into the water' and 'wherever one may take, it is salty', (*Brhadaranyaka Upanisad, 2.14.12*), the essence of everything that exists is Brahman itself. 'All this is verily Brahman', says the *Brhadaranyaka Upanisad* 'produced from it, absorbed into it and living by it' (III.14). Not only everything that exists is Brahman, in the sense that there is no separation between Brahman and the world, the creation of the world and all that dwell therein is conceived as an *emanation* of Brahman itself. Creation, in Hindu thought, is not creation *ex nihilo*. Rather, the One becomes the Many, without the One ceasing to be the One. The seers say in the *Chandogya Upanisad* 'My dear! In the Beginning there was only this Being, one and without a second ... Let me be many and be born. into these three divinities (Light, Water and Food) with this life, namely my own Self.' (VI.2; also 1–4; III.2). 'This true being, this subtle source of the world, that is the soul of everything; that is Truth. (*Chandogya Upanisads*, VI 8.4; 6.7). In other Upanisads, the creation of the world by Brahman is compared to 'a spider emitting and drawing in (its thread)' (*Mundaka, Upanisad*, 1.1.6).

The Upanisads not only state that the world has emanated from Brahman, they also give details of such emanation. Thus the *Taittiriya_Upanisad* states: 'From this Atman (Absolute), has the space arisen, from the space the air, from the air the fire, from the fire the water, and from the water the earth' (2.1); in the *Aitereya Upanisad* (3.3) the 'five great elements' (*panca mahabhutani*) are identified with Brahman. 'He is Brahman, he is Indra, he is Prajapati, he is all gods; He is the five elements, earth, air, space, water and light or fire.' And Sir Krishna says in the *Bhagavad Gita* (7.4) 'Earth, water, fire, air, space, mind, reason, and egoism—thus is my nature divided eightfold.'

The philosophical position that everything that exists is an emanation from and is, in essence, Brahman (Absolute) leads the Indian philosophers to use the language of 'Man *is* Nature', 'Man in Nature' and not 'Man against Nature'. Since it is the same Divine that is manifested in Man and Nature, the Indians also avoid all issues of domination and subordination in ecological ethics. When it is the same Brahman that is manifested in humans and in Nature, the religious attitude of the Indians towards Nature is one of respect, reverence and worship. The Vedic hymns are replete with prayers and worship of Nature. For example, the Vedic hymn called *Bhumi Suktam* or 'Hymn to the Earth' addresses 'Mother Earth' in an inspiring way:

Your hills, O earth
your Snow-clad mountain peaks,
your forests, may they show us kindliness!
Brown, black, red, multifarious in hue
and solid is this vast Earth, guarded by Indra
I have on her established my abode
Invincible, unconquered and unharmed.

Another Rg Vedic hymn addressed to 'water' says: 'Waters! Friends of men! Give your unfailing protection and blessings to our sons and grandsons; for you are the most motherly physicians, the mothers of all that stands still and that moves.' (*Rg Veda* 6.50.7). Again, in the *Vamana Purana* (14.26) it is said: 'Earth with the quality of smell, water with the quality of viscosity, fire with the quality of energy, sky with the quality of sound, air with the quality of touch and all the *Mahatatvas* let all these elements bless our mornings.'

By adopting the 'Unity of Existence' doctrine, Indian religion develops the attitude that Nature is 'sacred' and an object of worship. An assortment of natural objects which the Indians worship consist of the sun (*surya*), the moon (*chandra*), fire (*agni*), air (*vayu*), the rivers Ganges, Yamuna, Sarasvati, Godavari, Krishna, Kaveri, etc.; the Himalay and Vindhya mountains, and mountain-peaks such as Kailasa, trees such as the pipal, banyan, neem, tulasi, and so on. The Indian worship of objects of nature should not be interpreted as fetishism or animism but as an expression of the religious attitudes which follow from the philosophical doctrine of 'Unity of Existence' and the immanence of Brahman (Absolute).

Indian philosophy also has a theistic tradition according to which the world is created by God. Unlike Western traditions which adopt an archetectonic theory of creation where God creates the world with a purpose, viz. for human beings to live in it, Indian theories of creation adopt an organic model of creation, i.e. humans and environment are organically related to each other. An organism is a unity and no one part can dominate the other. Sometimes, however, the Indians conceive of God's creation of the world as *lila* i.e. a spontaneous, joyful, playful activity. Here too, for there is no 'purpose' in play. Play becomes a sport or a game, when we give a purpose, for example, winning. The last verse in the Rg. Veda, which is a prayer, best summarizes the Indian conception of the unity of existence:

United be our resolve, united our hearts
May our spirits be at one,
that we may long together
dwell in unity and concord.

34 THE EARTH AS FAMILY: A TRADITIONAL HAWAIIAN VIEW WITH CURRENT APPLICATIONS

D.M. Dusty Gruver
Hawaii University
Honolulu, Hawaii, U.S.A.

The elements and dimensions that constitute the definition of family in any given culture directly translate to the way such a group impacts its immediate natural environment. It is within the context of relationships that the individual infers personal position in reference to the surrounding biosphere. Depending on perceived familial bonds, the idea of kinship posits a human being in a social matrix that implies varying degrees of exclusivity or inclusivity. The implications of different modes of maintaining positive environmental standards are profound, as the following explication will show.

The traditional worldview of Polynesia offers an interesting contrast to the mainstream Western notion of limited family kinship. Certain key constructs that define the position of the human individual in the overall scheme of creation lead to a radically different concept of human responsibility in and with the biological community. The Hawaiian tradition serves as a representative example for the purposes of this investigation.

In the Hawaiian Islands, the traditional concept of family adumbrated a system of social relationship that was essentially pan-Polynesian. 'Family', or *ohana*, in this sense comprised a matrix of genealogical kinship that extended to include all elements of creation. Human beings occupied a position of parity within a familial structure that originated with the dual macro-elements of the environment: the earth and the sky. These were personified, respectively, by Papa (the Earth Mother) and Wakea (the sky Father). Other aspects of creation, such as plants, animals and geographic features, were also family members, with each deriving its specific position in the scheme of things from its order of birth. The ordering of these relationships was preserved and communicated in the great cosmogonic creation *oli*, or chants. A purpose of these bodies of oral literature was to keep straight specific genealogies in the context of

Hawaiian cosmology. One of the more prominent *oli*, the *Kumulipo*, stands today as a paradigm of the indigenous Hawaiian philosophy.

The *Kumulipo*, or 'fertile beginnings,' traces in detail the ancestry of a particular eighteenth-century royal baby to the primary female-male analogues of Papa and Wakea.[1] The child's genealogy stretches back through time to the origin of all things in the primal darkness. In this listing of direct ancestral relationship all life forms and aspects of the universe are represented. This genealogy rivals the book of Genesis in its scope and complexity: it contains within its structure the multiple layers of meaning that comprise the working structure of the Hawaiian worldview. Independently composed long before the time of Darwin, the *Kumulipo* enumerates in deductive detail the evolutionary biological relationship among all things.[2] The limits of the present discussion allow for a general explication of only single theme of the many that compose the *Kumulipo'* namely, the specific inclusive genealogy that defines the boundaries of family. The following gloss of this story-line is adequate for the immediate purposes but is not intended to represent the entire *oli*.

The results of Papa and Wakea's first unions were two of the islands themselves: Hawaai'i and Maui. Next was born a daughter, Ho'ohokukalani. Through an involved series of circumstances, Wakea mates with his own daughter and fathers more children: Haloa the taro, Haloa the chief, the island of Lana'i and the island of Moloka'i. Eventually Papa and Wakea reunite and parent the rest of the Hawaiian islands: O'ahu, Kaua'i, Ni'ihau and Kaho'olawe. Haloa the chief went on to become the progenitor of the Hawaiian people who were, in a direct genealogical line, next of kin to the islands they lived on. They were also related, as immediate family, to the taro, their major food source.

The Hawaiian creation story mirrors the biological myth of the Hawaiian people. Papa and Wakea are more than metamophoric parents: the earth Mother and the Sky Father are the actual progenitors of every object in the universe. In this sense, the process of creation is procreative and is meant to be taken literally: that is, it takes place in terms of human sexuality and reproduction. For instance, in the birth chant for Kaukeaouli, the son of the great Hawaiian king Kamehameha I, the travail of Papa is mentioned repeatedly. She gives birth to the islands in a manner that is unmistakably human.

The fact that Papa, Ho'ohokukalani, and Wakea mate and reproduce in an anthropomorphic sense sets the stage for a fundamentally non-Western sense-of-place for members of the human community. The Polynesian outlook allows that the earth is the ancestral mother of each person in precisely the same way that specific individuals occupy particular niches in the matriarchal lineage. Such a direct biogenetic kinship engenders a moral standard that is founded on reciprocal duty within the family structure. This sense of responsibility resonates closely with certain indigenous familial value systems found in many of the world's seminal cultures. However the concept is expressed, the recognition of a common kinship bond among all elements of the biosphere is a powerful agent for self-regulation within the environment. This obligation to strive for balance within the all-inclusive extended family is grounded in general intellectual and psychological realities.

The biological reality of parental nurturing and the reciprocal service by the offspring to the parents and other siblings are not only utilitarian in terms of survival, but are also deeply satisfying emotionally. This kind of relationship is especially significant because it is an involvement between blood relations. This is prominent even in the relatively restricted pattern of American kinship. The example of a mother's love for her children occupies a solid place in the construction of the national cultural mythos.

The recognition of blood kinship is universal and usually generates specific codes of mutual support between members of a family. There is a responsibility to sustain patterns of reciprocal caring for the welfare of all. We see this in the Hawaiian culture as a fundamental idea: the good of the individual is inextricably bound to the good of the entire world. The basis for this is the inclusion of all elements in the web of relationship that constitutes family.

The bilateral duty to care for one's kin in Hawai'i was expressed by the word *malama*. *Malama* means 'to take care of '. Other shades of meaning include 'to tend', 'to preserve', and 'to maintain'. To *malama* another person or thing was to engage in a symbiotic act of caring or maintenance in full recognition of the reciprocal dynamism inherent in such action.

By way of comparison, consider that the Western tradition also applies the same kind of definitions when describing an individual's relationships in the world. But in America there is a significant difference in the implied limits of duty when speaking of 'taking care of ', or 'tending to', one's aged mother and when referring to, say, one's automobile or parcel of rented real estate. The cleavage occurs when different modes of action are dependent upon the class to which the particular object or group of objects belongs: is it 'family' or is it something else? This boils down to a values dualism in praxis, with specific biogenetic kinships on one side and the rest of the world on the other.

Among the Polynesians the moral imperative to care for and respect each member of one's family was continuous with concern for the well-being of the earth. Philosophically, once it is accepted that the relationship and bond between an individual human being and the earth is either literally or figuratively one of mother-child, it follows that by no standard can one in good conscience act in a manner that brings harm to the land, to one's closest kin. The Hawaiians felt that it is obvious that we all one family: rocks, trees, sharks, clouds, wind, humans. There is no choice; we have to care for each other. Each individual is fundamentally bound to all that there is. To mistreat any aspect of the biosphere, of the extended family, is to mistreat ourselves.

Modern civilization appears to be arriving at the same conclusion. Increasingly, the realization that the viability of the biosphere *in toto* is necessary for the physical well-being of the human species, and every human individual is an influence for both individual and collective action. The web of interrelationship, of inter-dependency, that intimately connects the individual with all aspects of the biotic community hardly needs to be illustrated to everyone today. The point is not that traditional biological myths such as that of Polynesia are coming to the fore. Instead, it seems that there is an increased understanding of the natural laws of this planet by a considerable segment of the world population. One by-product of this emerging understanding is the ability to appreciate elements of philosophical systems once considered archaic or irrational.

Behind the biological myth and metaphor modern environmental philosophers and the ancient Hawaiians hold one concept in common: the human being is not the be-all and end-all of creation. There is a place on the planet for the human species. However, this specific niche can sustain our species only to the degree that a reciprocally caring relationship is maintained with all other components of the biotic matrix. In order to sustain this kind of balance, an attitude of *malama* grounded in a knowledge of inherent relationship is suggested. In a very elemental way the traditional Polynesian model can contribute to a code of environmental conduct appropriate to our times.

Notes
1. For an excellent scholarly explication of this *oli* see Johnson, 1981.
2. Johnson, 1981, i.

35 WITHIN THE SCOPE OF ENVIRONMENTAL ETHICS

Jan Wawrzyniak
Adam Mickiewicz University
Warsaw, Poland

The subject matter of environmental ethics is the moral aspect of the co-existence of *Homo sapiens* with the natural surrounding. Environmental Ethics, or the ethics of inter-specific relations, belongs to the realm of bio-ethics which includes moral dimension of all actions and intentions referring to vital values, or the attributes and necessary conditions of being a living creature. Bio-ethics also contains the natural history of moral sensitivity, or evolutionary ethics. Environmental ethics formulates norms basing itself on the establishments of evolutionary ethics concerning the natural functions of a moral sense, the range of morally relevant situations and the moral status of culture.

The eco-crisis is primarily caused by the moral underdevelopment of culture. The ecological malfunctioning of culture follows from the peculiar value-aberration called *speciesism* and only in terms of social sciences can we explain why culture, a way of existence typical for the human species, has become a 'cancer' of evolution. Hence the task of environmental ethics is to work out a new definition of *Homo sapiens* in the real world and a new model of value-preferences in the relations between humans and the natural environment. In that model, moral values would be fundamental for the regulation of these relations. The main aim of environmental ethics is the defense of nonhumans against human hyper-aggressiveness, or cultural pressure. Environmental ethics, in addition, proposes basic normative categories of a new *pronatural* paradigm of the development of human civilization.

The eco-shock is a value-shock, for it proves that humankind, just like all other living beings, must be subordinate to the biological order of being and that a person is not 'the measure of all things.' The most dangerous cultural phenomenon is a feed-back relation between a poor quality of food and immuno-deficiency, spiritual degeneration and the pathology of the aggressive behaviour in humankind, for it has proven inefficient in the ritualization of aggression and has developed human sub-limitations of aggression: economico-political and mechanico-chemical.

The *neo-naturalistic* environmental ethics is directed against economic priorities in the present philosophy of environmental policy. Bentham's principle of utility introduced the impersonal statistics of the right and wrong, convenient for corrupt practices. At present, his philosophy is the universal way of thinking for politicians, producers and consumers. John S. Mill introduced into utilitarianism the value-hierarchy of species. The utility for *Homo sapiens*, subordinated to the cultural spiral of seemingly necessary needs and to economic profits, became the criterion of moral evaluation. In the utilitarian model of environmental protection, the environment has the status of a commodity and is always offered for sale. Each part, not yet destroyed, of the natural environment presents a potential source of financial profits if the advertising media arouses human needs. The environment cannot survive when its devastation can be sold profitably.

The utilitarian-pragmatic attitude towards nonhumans is biologically destructive, for it is morally wrong. The efficacy of environmental protection depends on the intentions of protective actions. The actions must be undertaken for the purpose of environmental protection and not with the aim of economic profits achieved through protection. Environmental ethics shows that techno-economic growth cannot be reconciled with the preservation of the balanced genotypic wealth of life, that is with actions undertaken for the sake of ecology. Environmental ethics unequivocally determines the following value preference: it subordinates financial interest, and artistic satisfaction as well, to superior *vital values* (such as health or eco-equilibrium), or the most important states-of-existence of all living beings. The neo-naturalistic ethic is based on autotelic valuation of the variety of the forms of life. The level of diversity at which the biospherical equilibrium is set decides life is survival. Life exists only in the form of various living beings, belonging to various species.

The basic value-related problem is the criterion of the norms of environmental quality standards. Until now, this criterion has not been the capacity of an ecosystem for self-renewal, but the measurable influence of pollution. Pollution, which does not seem to be dangerous for human animals, becomes a permissible norm. The present level of environmental 'protection' is reduced to mean the accumulation of human garbage in the environment in such a way that it cannot be recorded by common consciousness. Through eco-colonialism, people selectively exploit Earth in order to protect human consumerism. People want to protect themselves against the wastes of culture without protecting the biological environment. The right to share in the environment is treated as one belonging exclusively to *Homo sapiens* as the only breathing creature on Earth.

The environment of life, or biosphere, is the structure of living beings and conditions of life, which has created and nurtured *Homo sapiens*. But there is the natural value-based right of nonhumans to a pure environment. Nonhumans also have their role in biosphere homeostasis. They are treated as raw materials or objects for the release of human aggression. They pay with their lives for politico-propagandistic and legal satisfaction of human beings in the field of so-called environmental protection. The height of cynicism is designing forests to be buffers absorbing pollution and noise.

Evolutionary ethics operates with concepts of 'humanity' and 'animality' in their descriptive modes. 'Humanity' does not denote any special merits but is a quasi-taxonomic qualification referring to the features peculiar to *Homo sapiens*. 'Animality' comprises properties common to *Homo sapiens* and other animals. Therefore, 'humanity' also covers the specific faults of *Homo sapiens* (like the loss of functional animality) and the sublimations of animal (historical) traits.

In current usage, 'humanity' is a dream of humankind as a perfectly noble and spiritually efficient entity. At the same time, such an understanding of *Homo sapiens* is the devaluation of the animality identified with an invasive aggressiveness, spiritual primitiveness and evil. Environmental ethics unmasks that axio-normative model of humanity which justifies any actions by the fact that they are human ones. The properties that humans ascribe (idealistically or truthfully) to themselves such as the control of aggression exist also (or only) in the nonhuman world. On the other hand, 'animality', as it is interpreted by *Homo sapiens*, is an exact specific and human quality. Discovering real humanity, humans ascribe animality to nonhuman animals. Not being able to stand the truth, human beings secondarily create evolution by interpretive manipulations such as the evaluative usage of the words 'man' and 'animal'.

Environmental ethics includes an analysis of the failures of human cognition which influence human valuation and conduct towards nonhumans. *Homo sapiens* project this teleological manner of thinking into natural processes, and therefore evolution appears as a process tending to a definite end, and presents humankind as its perfect fruit. These projections make the nonhuman animal the enemy, and the natural environment appears to be the monster waiting to destroy humankind. Few comprehend the Darwinian metaphor: 'the struggle for life.' People usually take it to be a literal physical inter-specific aggression with an intent to kill.

Evolutionary ethics distinguishes the relevant meaning of the term 'nature': (1) the structure of biotic and abiotic (not created by human work) components making biosphere, or the natural environment of life; (2) the pre-cultural stages of evolution, or the primitive environment; (3) the nonhuman forms of life organization; (4) the laws of biology and evolution, or the impassable limits of safe cultural behaviour or *Homo sapiens*; in this meaning it is stressed that *Homo sapiens* does not create laws of life, and ignoring these laws must end in the annihilation of the environment of life; (5) what is normal and typical in a given environmental context; (6) the essential traits, or the unique traits of a species as well as the ones common to other species within the greater taxonomic units; and (7) the unique traits of a species, its differential, or the Aristotelian form.

The distinctive mark of culture is the category of 'work', that is the element of the form of *Homo sapiens*. Restoring humans to full ontological bio-cultural dimension, evolutionary ethics opposes both the reductionism of positivistic naturalism and an antinaturalistic (humanistic) reductionism that explains *Homo sapiens* only by (mostly alleged) specificities. Culture is not conducive to the survival of *Homo sapiens*, for it destroys the teleonomic animality (biological normality) of the species in the name of the morally wrong and ecologically absurd ideal of absolute freedom (biological independence) of humankind in the natural environment. The domination of humankind proves the malfunctioning of the species in relation to biosphere homeostasis. According to eco-succession laws, *Homo sapiens* transforms the environment into disadvantageous states, and the future climax of biosphere needs another niche for the entire species.

If the contents of moral judgments are created socially and directed to people, then we must ask to what faculty of understanding they refer. Just as the contents of thoughts are not inborn but only the faculty of thinking, so too are the contents of moral norms not inborn but only the moral sense itself. The situations of danger to vital values are stimuli releasing moral instinct (sense) that is the structure of three genetically conditioned elements: (1) 'conscience', or a *sui generis* emotional imperative to defend vital values; (2) provital behaviour (including unconditioned reflexes) not connected with procreation and nutrition; (3) the ability to ritualize aggression. The moral sense teleonomy is determined by the structure of abilities of the organism and its references to the environment. Moral sensitivity is evolutionarily selected and serves, in the living being's spirituality, as a counter-balance for aggressiveness, free will and intellectual efficiency. Cultural imprinting abuses elementary moral reactions by the promotion of transient politico-economic states-of-affairs to vital-values status. In the instance of *Homo sapiens*, the moral sense is a neglected instrument of the struggle for survival.

The emergence of a human degree of freedom, understood as adaptive plasticity of the species, means complementary reduction of natural mechanisms of inter-specific balance control and the complication of intra-specific relations as well. Human freedom is ecologically dangerous, therefore simultaneously the moral control of human development is naturally possible as necessary. The non-specialized *Homo sapiens* can prey on all existing nature, and this comfortable hyper-consumer position is an ecological trap. The standards of evolution, including the states of eco-equilibrium, constitute the limit of human freedom.

Natural selection has favoured freedom, or spiritual adaptive inventiveness, for each successive species found a more complicated environmental situation where possible niches had been occupied by specialized species. What must have emerged then, were beings capable of non-instinctive and counter-instinctive actions. This self-controllability makes the human niche morally and intellectually the most difficult among species. Culture does not change the laws of organic evolution, and its duration depends on whether *Homo sapiens* respects these laws. Such an adjustment of human behaviour to the standards of ecological normality, which are innate to other animals, is a task adequate for the creative ambitions of human beings. The novelty that human beings can initiate within the evolutionary process is an ecologically correct adaptation of his freedom and power to the natural environment by means of moral solutions. *Homo sapiens* is such a mighty species that other animals never had a chance to compete. Morally *ergo* ecologically correct, is the attitude of respect and care towards the nonhuman environment. The environmental life quality, as a structure of vital values, is the premises of moral responsibility of human species for biocommunity survival. This responsibility is the proper functional niche of *Homo sapiens* in the biosphere. The evolutionally, or spiritually, mature *Homo sapiens* is expected to understand the subtle principles of survival including the observance of the ecologically functional value hierarchy.

As there is no level of natural *Homo sapiens* consumers, intra-specific aggression has not been dangerous for the existence of the species. Human life has been cheap and easy to reproduce. Overpopulation causes an aggressive economic competition which is ritualized in ideologies and hyper-consumption, and is released in eco-colonialism and direct pressure on nonhuman animals. The entire human educational system prefers the aggressive type of personality. Aggression is, for the sake of social safety, directed out of the species.

Culture has selected a type of man unable to react properly to environmental changes and extracultural information and has caused spiritual *ergo* evolutionary inertia of *Homo sapiens*. The moral greatness of humankind consists in 'self-consumption': procreation limitation, a change of value-criteria of procreation, the value-revisal of cultural needs, and their subordination to biosphere preservation. At present, the role of a selector towards *Homo sapiens* is executed by the environmental conditions that people have created (e.g. HIV epidemic).

The late Renaissance gave a double answer to the supernaturalism of the Middle Ages. First, it was the humanistic answer that became the basis of modern speciesism. Humanism is aggressively inclined towards the natural environment. Science has the purely utilitarian task of studying the laws of nature in order to utilize and subjugate the natural environment for human needs. Nonhumans are regarded as dead objects. This is the Bacon-Descartes line.

The post-Cartesian ideal of value-free science makes crimes of scientific practices and causes their conclusions to be untrue. Experiments on living, or sentient organisms, just because of their matter, are not morally neutral. Positivism, as a methodological instrument of utilitarianism, is a moral abuse within science.

Humanism actually devalues human freedom, or the possibility of self-creation carrying responsibility at the same time, because this worldview operates with the static picture of humankind as creatures complete in perfection. Humanism is an ecologically catastrophic ideology of isolation and contempt towards Nature. Normative neonaturalism also stands against all teleological and axio-anthropocentric visions of history like Christianity or Hegelianism-Marxism.

On the other hand there exists a naturalistic answer in the renaissance legacy. This option, according to the spirit of inter-specific egalitarianism, regards *Homo sapiens* as such a member of the biocommunity which is obliged, in view of his power and participation in common (inter-specific-transcendental) values, to protect the community. This is the Montaigne-Gassendi option, based on Epicurean tradition and continued by Schweitzer. The neo-naturalistic environmental ethics is placed within this tradition.

36 HUMAN NATURE AND THE ENVIRONMENT

Vincent Luizzi
Southwest Texas State University
U.S.A.

As I write this paper during the fall of 1990 in San Marcos, Texas I am to understand that both nature and we are gravely endangered by an ever-diminishing ozone layer of the atmosphere; and I am to understand that such is now the case in Nairobi and that such will be the case both in San Marcos and in Nairobi in July 1991 when we gather in Nairobi to share our insights on 'Philosophy, Man, and the Environment' at the World Conference of Philosophy.

Although, to many of us, this way of always thinking and talking about ourselves, our activities, and nature on a planetary basis depicts the true and now even the obvious, it still requires a rethinking on our part. For I do not think that in the face of the immediacy of quotidian demands, we easily bring to the fore an understanding of ourselves as beings on a vulnerable planet both of which are suffering from our destructive acts. Again, recognizing the truth of this is one thing, but internalizing it is an ever-present and significant feature of our self-concept is quite another. As difficult as the latter may be, it is still, given the current climate of opinion, the politically, socially, and intellectually correct and responsible thing to do.

What troubles me about this approach is its crisis management orientation in that it narrowly identifies a specific and urgent problem that has arisen, and identifies a narrow solution in which each of us can participate. In what follows, I would like to make these charges a little clearer and, more importantly, present a theory of human nature that can, on an on-going basis, guide our thinking about ourselves and the environment. Ultimately I argue that we should construct, in an on-going fashion, conception of ourselves and our environments which carry with them advice for our conduct. The current claim on us to think about nature in a reactive fashion and about ourselves as citizens of an endangered planet then becomes but an instance of how my more general view can be employed.

Let us first clarify the invitation to think of ourselves as beings on an endangered planet. Carl Sagan does a good job depicting for the layman the problem that chlorofluorocarbons (CFCs) have caused the planet. Our use of such things as hair-sprays and deodorants in aerosol containers and our use of air conditioning and refrigeration systems release CFCs. These diminish the ozone layer which has served as a shield from the sun's harmful ultraviolet rays (UV). This means, for one thing, the loss of millions of lives from the cancers caused by these rays. But this is not the main problem, Sagan explains. The UV is killing unicellular life forms on the ocean's surface. They are at the beginning of the food chain, so, if destroyed, so is life. Sagan's advice amounts to our having to realize and take to heart some things about ourselves and nature. Seemingly insignificant actions we perform have grave consequences for the planet, and we must think of ourselves in this fashion. Further, nature as we have known it is far from indestructible; nature is vulnerable. Sagan says that we should begin to think and act not merely in terms of our nation and generation, but in terms of the entire planet.

This approach is too much tied to some obvious measures we can take to deal with the problem at hand, and is too little part of any theory that would assist us in thinking about problems that arise. Sagan, the scientist, has us applaud the ingenuity of university scientists who discovered the effects of CFCs on the ozone layer; and we can well suspect that he appreciates, and would want us to appreciate, both the complexity of the topic and the investigation and the rigor and care with which the results were presented to the scientific community. Yet, outside the arena of science, it seems that issues of a social nature have such simple solutions if we could but get ourselves to conform our conduct to what reason so clearly prescribes: think of nature as vulnerable and act accordingly. I have a hard time seeing social issues as being so easy to define or solve, and I think we need a theory that allows us to perceive and solve them in a more sophisticated fashion.

My view, simply put, is this. Our nature allows us to construct, in an on-going process, conceptions of ourselves ranging from specific roles we occupy to our humanity itself, with these conceptions suggesting guidelines for our conduct. Suppose, for example, that our thinking about ourselves as humans leads us to conceive of ourselves as rational beings, as competitive but social and striving to progress. Going hand in hand with this construction are such evident guidelines and admonitions for conduct as: act not on impulse, act rationally; compete, and progress. The constructed concept is in effect a normative one and, as such, brings with it rules to govern our experience. Highlighting as the distinctive feature of this view the idea that humans can develop an understanding of themselves together with the idea that tied to this conception are rules for conduct, I refer to humans summarily as the constructors of rule-referring conception of themselves.

I cannot here go into the full scope of my argument for this position, but I will offer a few considerations that might incline you to see the truth of this thesis. My experience, along with that of my students, is that almost every one of the many theories of human nature that we study has one ring of truth; all of us view ourselves quite differently at different times. Further, we find over and over that ethical theorists have in some way grounded their ethical advice in their estimation of human nature. Kant, for example, sees us as rational beings in effect, and commands us to act rationally; Bentham sees us as pleasure seekers, and commands us to produce the greatest pleasure for the community. And each of these commands seems plausible given the view of human nature that the theorist has offered. From such data, I gather something quite general about our nature: that we can and do see our nature in a variety of plausible ways, each of which provides a basis for constructing guidelines for conduct. We are thus free to construct a fruitful view of our nature from which we can reasonably determine guidelines for conduct. For example, the pragmatist's insight about reality and various aspects of it are a function of a pragmatic conceptual framework. This can be rethought in terms of how we have talked about human nature and our roles, and a consistent theory governing all of this can be formulated. The main insight is that these external environment are extensions of how we are choosing to see ourselves—in these cases, how we choose to see ourselves in the world. Once this move is made, these constructions too can be seen as carrying with them normative advice for conduct.

Relating this to our discussion of the environment and to Sagan's analysis, we might rethink our notion of our planet and recognize its vulnerability, in which case the normative advice would be to act more responsibly toward it. And we might rethink our notion of ourselves so that we recognize that we are inhabitants of a planet. In this case, we would have to assess the consequences of our acts for not just our more restricted environments like state and nation but for the entire planet. But this is portraying Sagan's analysis in the very best of lights. It is apparent that these new conceptions that he offers us are not the result of a critical analysis of competing alternatives, or an endeavour to construct an optimal view.

In what follows I wish to identify some significant variables that seem to weigh in any intelligent assessment of how we should conceive of nature and of ourselves, especially with regard to our relation to nature. First is the debate regarding nature's vulnerability. At one extreme, nature is portrayed as passive, inert and separate from people who can and do treat it as an entity that can be manipulated or exploited for human purposes. At the other extreme, nature is portrayed as an active, living entity of which we are a part, that responds to our interacting with it as any organism would and that commands our respect and appreciation. My theory would have us disentangle the various threads of each of these views, look for further competing alternatives, and then have us decide on each variable, seriatim. Thus, as an example, we would separate from this description the activity-passivity issue, ask how else we might think of nature, and finally select the optimal descriptor. We would begin to construct an adequate conception with the understanding that we may modify it as we see how it fits with other descriptions we select, or as we are advised by experience. One obvious move is to recognize that this either-or dilemma posed for us by the debate is too rigid, with an obvious alternative being that nature is both. This alternative probably accords better with some of our experiences and it sets up the inquiry of just which aspects of nature are active and which are passive. While I am not prepared on this limited ground to argue that this is the best way of thinking about nature, I do want to underscore the point that our theory fostered the identification of this alternative.

With regard just to the few matters at issue in this polarized debate, we would proceed similarly with another question. Is nature living or dead, and what are the alternatives? If we choose to see nature as living, what kind of a living entity are we likening it to? A lower animal, a mammal, an elm? We would then break beyond the matters at issue in this narrow debate and raise others, some of which surround Sagan's suggestion. For example, should we think of nature as the planet, as he suggests, or as the solar system, or as the universe? And, if the universe is selected, for example, we would ask how this fits with our initial decision to regard nature as living. Further, pursuing Sagan's recommendation that we think of nature as vulnerable, we find that his suggestion opens a host of matters. Is nature vulnerable in a destructive and irreparable way or in a destructive but reparable way? Are we altering it temporarily for an acceptable purpose, altering permanently for an acceptable purpose, altering temporarily for an unacceptable purpose, or altering permanently for an unacceptable purpose?

This theory of human nature has been introduced because it gives us the latitude to construct cogent conceptions about ourselves and our environments that at once are responsive to the ways in which on-going experience demands assessment and re-assessment. It also recognizes the deep complexity of the variables available to us, from which we can forge these conceptions. The adoption of this approach makes our dealing with such matters a more difficult task, but it does so with the promise of providing solutions that we can endorse as optimal within the context of our continual search for better ones.

37 ENVIRONMENTAL PHILOSOPHY WITHIN THE RELATIONSHIPS OF HUMANITY, ENVIRONMENT, CULTURE AND ECONOMY

U. Ozer
Uludag University
Bursa, Turkey

Humanity, environment, culture and economics are four variables that reciprocally influence each other.[1] In this equation, which has four unknowns, it is possible to reach a judgment about the fourth without keeping the other three constant by analyzing the philosophy of the subject. The problems we face within the environment are due to the negative outcomes of industry-man, industry-culture and industry-economy relationships. They may be overcome firstly by determining environmental philosophy, and secondly by the determination of environmental policies. In order to reach concrete results from the relationship between humanity, environment, culture and economics, it is necessary to study the philosophy of the subjects that these concepts cover. In this way we may explain other concepts and disciplines that are related inseparably to the above-mentioned.

The relationship of humanity to nature has always existed in 'nature', and since the time of Aristotle, scientists and scholars have been busy with improving living standards. Humankind has been involved in a long struggle for survival, the only assistant being 'nature' or the environment. The term 'environment' may be considered in its strict sense as the whole of the conditions of the natural surroundings, or in its broad sense as the whole of the conditions of the surroundings including social conditions.[2] Therefore it should be stated that the concept of 'environment' can be concrete as well as abstract; it should be studied within the scope of being developed and undeveloped. With such an approach, 'environment' is defined as 'the conditions that affect development'. Environment is thought of differently by people belonging to different social and culture strata. The sun, soil, rocks, rain, creeks, trees, people: these objects can be considered as environment. Therefore, the concept of the environment is shaped depending on the living standards and the educational levels of the people.

As the cultural environment also affects the behaviour of people and other living things, besides the biological, physical and psychological environment, we should first have a glance at the relationship between culture and environment. Culture is a multi-dimensional event. Malinowski defines 'culture' as 'things and tools that are used directly or indirectly, customs physical and intellectual, habits to satisfy human needs'.[3] This means that culture is the whole of things that are produced by man which are different from things created by nature itself. Therefore things with which a person is in frequent contact in the environment form the environment culture. Here the question whether culture is a part of the individual, of society, or environment may arise. The answer to this question changes, depending on the individual or the environment under study. For instance, for people who live in cities, culture is acquired from the environment. Since the mind develops influenced by environment, the environment will determine culture.

Humanity should be educated about environment, since people are a part of it and are its creator and user. On the other hand, as education is an economic problem, the relationship of man, environment and culture should be handled together with economics. Economics is a branch of science which investigates the ways to satisfy human needs in the most effective way despite sometimes scarce resources. Humanity obtains and uses air, water and natural resources from the environment to produce goods and services to satisfy needs. The end of this production often results in 'polluted' water and residues in the environment. Environmental pollution and other environmental problems are caused by production which is necessary to satisfy human needs. Population increases and economic development necessitates further increases in production. Often inappropriate technologies are applied, leading to further environmental pollution.

The general level of education and knowledge of a society reflects that society's production capacity. The average level of knowledge of each society is proportional to that society's level of production and is limited by it. Because the economics of education is determined by educational costs and profit calculations, it is only industrialization that can bring education to more people. In addition, technological advance depends on financial conditions. Only industrial activities form real wealth. The scientific and technological facilities that industry provides may bring more or less adequate solutions to every kind of environmental problem. However, the environmental destruction that industrialization causes is far greater than that caused by agricultural societies. Additionally, it is known that industrialization inevitably causes social changes. As was stated in the Brundtland Report,[4] sustainable development and environmental problems are closely related to humanity and educational problems. This means that understanding the environment is critical to establishing a harmonious balance.

When the statistics of population increase are studied along with the extension of technology to more countries, it becomes obvious that no one place in the world will remain in its natural form. As it is true that industrialization causes urbanization and urbanization causes industrialization, population increase can only contribute to the continuance of this vicious circle. Therefore, we have to work for an idea of development which is balanced and in accordance with the environment, instead of an idea of development that destroys the environment in a world which does not grow bigger but in which the number of people who want to share its blessing increases with every day that passes. It is obvious that at the end of the synthesis of culture, environment, man, and economics, industry is the main factor that determines these four variables. Because of this, environmental education is expected to treat the environment as a whole and thereby establish a balance between the natural environment and the environment that people have built. Such a balance can be established only if the social, economic, political, technical, cultural, ethical and educational aspects of humanity and the environment are taken into consideration.[5]

Notes
1. Oguz, 1986.
2. Dura, 1985.
3. Malinowski, 1984.
4. Brundtland Report, *Our Common Future*, WCED, 1987.
5. Ozoglu, 1988.

38 THE ENVIRONMENT AND THE EPISTEMOLOGICAL LESSON OF COMPLEMENTARITY

Henry J. Folse
Loyola University
New Orleans, Louisiana, U.S.A.

As soon as the ethical questions raised by the environmental crises pass beyond a concern with merely anthropocentric prudential considerations, philosophy quickly becomes engaged in *metaphysical* reflection on the relationship between human existence and the natural world around us. The so-called 'deep ecologists' have frequently argued that the foreboding threat of future ecological catastrophe is—at least partially—the consequence of a western scientific worldview which robs nature of its inherent value and awesomeness, thereby alienating human consciousness from the natural world which forms its object and out of which it arises.[1] Thus the philosophical dialectic moves from metaphysical questions to an inquiry into the *epistemological* status of scientific knowledge. Here I analyze the implications of what Niels Bohr called the 'epistemological lesson' of the quantum revolution for understanding environmental issues.

The quantum revolution and environmental issues
The 'dehumanization' of nature is often associated with a subject/object dualism which irrevocably dichotomizes value and fact by assigning them to the separate and incommunicable ontological categories of mind and matter.[2] As mind recedes to the vanishing point of the subjective ego—carrying with it all value—nature is reduced to the purely factual configuration of mere valueless matter. The *spectator epistemology* inherent in this metaphysical dualism reaches its apex in the positivistic enthronement of scientific knowledge as objective fact, excluding any other avenue of epistemic access to the natural world. Thus links are drawn between positivistic scientism, metaphysical dualism, the estrangement of human consciousness from nature, and the catastrophic devaluing of nature for its domination by an anthropocentric

humanism. Evaluating these conceptual stepping stones surely requires a careful look at the presuppositions of the scientific description of the natural world.

In freeing itself from those positivistic assumptions to which it has been moored for the greater part of this century, recent philosophy of science has become preoccupied with the *axiological* question of the aims of science and their evolution as exhibited in the concrete history of science.[3] Even the positivists had to concede that the real theories which comprise mature scientific knowledge are not the logically consistent algorithms they imagined, but historically evolving constellations of belief exhibiting few of the fine points of mathematical calculi. But now nearly everyone recognizes that not only the empirical evidence adduced to support theories, but also the conceptual schemes by which they try to map the essential cartography of nature evolve together with theories and human theorizers in a complex interrelated dialectic. Hence out of the chaos of recent philosophy of science has emerged a dawning recognition that we must learn to understand the changes in the very aims which characterize the values which science aspires to achieve.

Of the changes in science's conception of its aims, none has affected the physical sciences more than the explosive development of atomic physics which we call the *quantum revolution*. The major consolidator of the quantum revolution, Niels Bohr, tried to express the essential consequence of the new physics by saying that it called for a more general 'viewpoint' or 'framework', called 'complementarity' which in effect provides a new goal for the 'scientific description of nature.'[4] He was fond of summarizing the epistemological lesson of this new framework by saying that 'it has forcibly reminded us of the old truth that we are both onlookers and actors in the great drama of existence.'[5] Surely this has a nice sound to any environmentalist's ears, but the consequences of Bohr's framework for environmental concerns have never been explicitly formulated.[6]

Objectivity and the aim of science

We must begin by asking what the aim was which motivated the description of nature on the old mechanical causal ideal that preceded the quantum revolution. This goal can be expressed in terms of the value placed on the 'objectivity' of its description of nature. But what were the criteria for determining that it had been attained? In a framework dominated by subject-object dualism, 'objectivity' by definition excludes 'subjectivity.' With respect to the phenomena of physics, 'subjectivity' can be eliminated by excluding all reference to what appears to the subjective perceiving consciousness. The observer must withdraw from the world observed, leaving behind a description of how that world is in itself. Thus science must aim for knowledge expressed solely in terms of properties allegedly possessed by the physical object, the primary properties inherent in the thing described.

On the classical spectator epistemology science describes these properties by 'representing' the object as it would 'appear' detached from any interaction with a subjective observer. This was possible because classical mechanics gave the physicist the ability to determine a spatio-temporal moving picture which represented the mechanical processes of the cosmic machine as it would look from a 'God's eye' point of view. Theoretically this cinema of the universe as it looks to no one was expressed by means of the mechanical state of the interacting components of a closed system. Thus the stories unfolded in this cinema could be interpreted realistically as true descriptions of the structure of reality because they pictured a mechanically and dynamically isolated ensemble of entities; the universe as it is 'undisturbed' by interaction with the observer who records such a picture. Since only the universe as a whole is a truly closed system, ultimately the 'Observer' who provides the empirical basis for such a picture must be pushed out of the cosmos entirely into some netherworld of the non-natural; but for metaphysical dualism, as an ideal this goal was logically consistent. Furthermore, practically speaking in the world of ordinary physical objects, the actual interaction between observer and observed could be made negligibly small.

Bohr's comment that we must remember we are actors as well as spectators may be taken as intending to eradicate the dualist distinction between the consciousness which knows and the objective nature which it seeks to comprehend, on which the classical mechanical ideal of description depended. Some physicists have indeed argued that precisely this is the crucial move of the quantum revolution.[7] But it was not Bohr's point nor the intention of complementarity to reject the classical goal of objectivity in favour of embracing a new kind of subjectivity as the goal of science. Indeed Bohr frequently cautioned against this move which he clearly took to be mistaken.[8]

That Bohr maintains his point about the interaction of the observer with the object is a consequence of the surprising discovery of the quantization of 'action'. The concept of 'action' involved in this discovery is definable only with respect to what can be characterized as physical objects, not subjective knowers. So the interactors on the stage whom the physicist seeks to describe are both physical interactors, whether they be the bodily sense organs of human scientists or complex 'detectors' interacting with the physical systems described by quantum physics. Bohr's point is not that the subjective consciousness as the seat of values invades the arena of the formerly purely physical, thereby eliminating the subject/object distinction, but that the goal of description in science cannot be what it was classically thought to be, namely the picture or 'representing' of the properties possessed by a substance apart from all interaction with anything separated from it.[9] After the quantum revolution we must recognize that the goal of description is to characterize the observational interaction between systems in terms of the properties exhibited in those interactions. Furthermore Bohr took this to be the case not only in atomic physics, but also at least in biology, psychology, and anthropology as well.[10]

Separability and interaction

Although as far as Bohr's framework is concerned, it is a mistake to say that the quantum revolution brings subjective values into the objective domain of fact, what we do learn is that the classical mechanical goal of describing nature by representing the cosmos in terms of a moving picture of the careers of self-subsistent essentially spatio-temporal individual entities, simply located in, and ontologically separated from all other individual entities by, space and time cannot be read as a literally true description of an independent natural world. Why has the quantum revolution brought such a change? Today the best answer we can give to that question is to say that the quantum revolution has forced physics to discard the 'principle of separability' presupposed by the image of nature which was distilled from a realistic reading of classical physics.[11] According to such a principle, entities existing at distinct loci in space and time possess separate independent 'mechanical state' which the classical picture aims to define. This principle was necessary in order to interpret the classical cinema of the cosmic machine as a true description of the natural world in terms of the interactive behaviour of its spatio-temporally distinct parts.[12] Bohr wrote before talk of violation of separability became commonplace, but he expressed this point by claiming that in an observational interaction observer and observed systems exist in a single indivisible state.

Bohr regarded the indivisibility of interaction as a new kind of 'wholeness inherent in atomic processes, going far beyond the ancient idea of the limited divisibility of matter.'[13] From this physical consequence of the empirically discovered quantization of action he drew profound epistemological consequences for the scientific description of nature. When interacting, physical systems share a single indivisible quantum of action, thereby uniting them into a single quantum mechanical state. To observe an object, that object must interact with an observing system, uniting them into an indivisible whole state, but to interpret the observation as providing information about the state of the observed object, the states of observing and observed systems must be unambiguously distinguished. This apparent tension can be overcome by recognizing that the descriptive concepts are limited to the description of observed phenomena.

Bohr regarded the ability to provide unambiguous description of the object as the essential criterion of objective description, and hence the aim of physics. He thereby offered a new ideal of objectivity replacing the classical ideal of the mechanically detached observer of a physically isolated, closed system. But such unambiguous descriptions require that the properties used to characterize the observed object are attributed to it not as possessed by it apart from observation, but as arising only in the observational interaction. Thus in different observational interactions the same observed object can be described as exhibiting different observational phenomena, descriptions which Bohr called *complementary descriptions of complementary phenomena*. But because of the unity of nature, and the consistency demanded of science, Bohr held that no contradiction will arise as long as each description is careful to specify the state of both the observed object and the observing system and to recognize that the properties attributed to the object can be said to belong to it only in the context of the observational interaction. Thus what it is that is described in quantum physics—and Bohr took this to be true of all empirical science—cannot be understood to be properties possessed by the object independently of its interaction with observers, but rather the observational interaction itself.

Interaction and the environment

For Bohr it is observational interaction as an indivisible whole phenomenon which becomes the object that science aims to describe unambiguously, and his comment that 'we are actors as well as spectators in the drama of existence' should be understood in this light. The framework of complementarity seeks to replace the classical ideal of representing nature detached from interaction with the goal of being able to describe in different complementary ways the phenomena which emerge in different physical interactions. The need to describe such interactions unambiguously, i.e. objectively, requires a careful distinction between the interactors in the description which is belied by the holistic character of the phenomena of interaction. This fact, in turn, forces science to accept the necessary recourse to embodying the knowledge of nature it seeks in the form of complementary descriptions of complementary phenomena arising in different interactions among the same objects.

This framework presents a viewpoint attractive to environmentalism for viewing the ecological description of the biosphere. *Prima facie* what ecology seeks to describe objectively are the relations among the interactors—both human and non-human, organic and inorganic—that populate the biosphere. But the lesson of complementarity contains more than the commonplace reminder of environmental literature to think holistically. At least two consequences of Bohr's outlook tell us that the attempt to associate the physicists' worldview with the dehumanization of nature is simply outdated.[14]

First, because we must divide the whole ecosystem into its interacting components, for the sake of an objective description of the phenomena exhibited, we tend to think that the properties attributed to the components are possessed by them independently of the interactions in which they are exhibited. This was precisely the mistake of the classical picture of nature as an isolated closed system, detached from any interaction with the observer. To speak of the properties of any living organism—much less a social organization of such organisms—in isolation from its environment is to use terms which cannot be well-defined, precisely because no organism can exist in isolation from some environment and yet continue to live. Thus the properties by which we characterize living organisms, including especially humans and their societies, can provide an objective description only in the context of a full specification of the environment with which they interact.

Second, the fact that the properties by which we characterize the natural world arise only in indivisible observational interactions can be extended to valuational properties. In this respect there is no reason to limit the antecedent of 'we' to humans, for all sentient organisms can be seen as 'observing' their environment in some way. This outlook provides a natural, non-anthropocentric basis for objective value judgments.[15]

Third, since the need to characterize separately the interacting components of a complex whole is one which arises from the demands of objective description, from a natural point of view these distinctions are imposed arbitrarily, and may be drawn differently, resulting in different complementary descriptions of the same interactive unity. For the sake of describing the world as experienced by us it is natural enough to draw the distinction between observer and observed at the line separating human and non-human. But spectator epistemology and metaphysical dualism elevated this arbitrary distinction for providing one possible description out of many possible complementary descriptions into an essential ontological distinction making possible the one and only possible true description. The resulting dehumanization of nature and denaturalization of humanity, whatever its role in causing current environmental crises, has certainly been no friend to resolving them.

It is of course absurd to think that the quantum revolution could provide a viewpoint from which the solution to environmental crises will become clearly discerned. But I hope what Bohr's framework could provide is a perspective from which to overcome our environmental blindness which not only is founded on the objectivity of scientific knowledge, rejecting a relativistic subjectivism, but also stays true to the finest achievements of human reason without resorting to a super-rational mysticism.

Notes

1. *Cf.* Zimmerman, forthcoming, for a compact characterization of this outlook and its sources.
2. *Cf.* Zimmerman, 1988, for a discussion of this association, which in turn discusses Callicott, 1985. I am much indebted to Prof. Zimmerman for calling my attention to this discussion.
3. *Cf.* Laudan, 1984.
4. *Cf.* Folse, 1985.
5. Bohr, 1934, p. 119; similar statements appear in Bohr, 1958, p. 20, and Bohr, 1948, p. 348.

6. Callicott (1985) provides the closest approach to such an effort, but he defends a subjectivist reading of the quantum revolution contrary to Bohr's intention.
7. *E.g.* Of the 'Copenhageners,' W. Pauli appeared to have the view of Laurikainen, 1988, but though advocates of this view have often attracted philosophic attention, Callicott is misled into thinking this is the majority view.
8. Bohr, 1963, p. 7; *cf.* Folse, 1985, pp. 198–206 for further discussion of this confusion.
9. *Cf.* Callicott, 1985, pp. 269–271. Bohr's view is compatible with Callicott's interpretation that quantum physics eliminates primary properties, but not with his contention that it eliminates subject/object dualism; Bohr does not address the question of mind–body interaction. Zimmerman, 1958, pp. 11–12 calls attention to this error.
10. Had Bohr written in times of current environmental concerns, I have no doubt he would have added ecology to this list. Indeed he would have said this discovery is surprising only in the case of physics; in other sciences this epistemological lesson has been learned more or less intuitively. Concerning Bohr's views on biology, *cf.* Folse, 1990, pp. 211–224.
11. *Cf.* the essays by Howard, Wessels, Teller, and Folse in J. Cushing and E. McMullin, eds., 1989.
12 Today there is increasing agreement among physicists that we have produced phenomena (so-called 'Bell phenomena' which provide experimental tests of Bell's inequality) which exhibit correlation between spatio-temporally separated entities revealing that though separated, such entities exist in a single indivisible quantum state.
13. Bohr, 1963, p. 2.
14. I do not want this comment to suggest that the clockwork of classical physics was guilty, as commonly charged, for our environmental crises. I doubt any intellectual construction—science, philosophy, or religion—could have such widespread efficacy (witness the ecological havoc wrought in many non-modern, non-western societies), and I suspect it is far more plausible to lay blame on the selfishness and drive to dominate which lurk in the human heart, a fact which can easily and naturally be explained by evolutionary selection.
15. Though Bohr disagrees with the subjectivist reading of quantum physics on which Callicott bases his argument, this agrees with his view that values would be 'inherent' though not 'intrinsic' *cf.* Callicott, 1985, p. 262.

39 SOCIAL ECOLOGY AND THE FUTURE OF THE EARTH

J.P. Clark
*Loyola University, New Orleans
Louisiana, U.S.A.*

Social Ecology is a comprehensive holistic conception of the self, society and nature. It is, indeed, the first ecological philosophy to present a developed approach to all the central issues of theory and practice. It sets out from the basic ecological principal of organic unity-in-diversity, affirming that the good of the whole can only be realized through the rich individuality and complex interrelationship of the parts. And it applies this fundamental insight to all realms of experience.

In affirming such a holistic approach, Social Ecology rejects the dualism that has plagued Western civilization since its beginnings. A dualism that sets spirit upon matter, soul against body, humanity against nature, subjectivity upon objectivity, and reason against feelings. A dualism that is intimately related to the social division that are so central to the history of civilization: ruler versus ruled, rich versus poor, urban versus rural, 'civilized' versus 'savage,' male versus female, in short, the dominant versus the dominated.

In opposition to this dualism, Social Ecology proposes a principle of ecological wholeness, which Bookchin defines as 'a dynamic unity of diversity' in which 'balance and harmony are achieved by ever-changing differentiation.' As a result, 'stability is a function not of simplicity and homogeneity but of complex and variety.'[1] The entire course of evolution is seen as a process aiming at increasing this diversification. Thus, there is an ever-increasing richness of diversity, not only in the sense of biological variety and interrelatedness, but also in the sense of richness of value.

Accordingly evolution should be looked upon as a process of planetary development having directiveness and involving the progressive unfolding of potentiality. Social Ecology thus forms part of a long teleological tradition extending from the ancient Greeks to the most advanced 20th century process philosophies. Yet Bookchin rejects the term 'teleology' because of its deterministic connotations, and its association with a hierarchical worldview that looks to some transcendent source of order and movement. There is no pre-determined, necessary path of evolution and world history. The unfolding of potentiality is best described as 'tendency or nisus,' rather than the inevitable outcome of much classical teleology. This directionality of nature is much like the kind of immanent teleology discovered by the early Taoist philosophers. They explained that each being has got its own Tao, 'way', of striving toward its own particular good. Yet, reality as a whole (or that part of it that was most vividly experienced, living Nature, the biosphere) has a more universal 'way' that can only unfold through the harmonious realization of all individual goods.[2]

It is in this sense that the entire process of development of life and mind is a movement toward the attainment of value. For Bookchin, 'the universe bears witness to an ever-striving, developing, not merely moving-substance, whose most dynamic and creative attribute is its increasing capacity for self-organization into increasingly complex forms.'[3] Life and mind are not random, chance occurrences in a dead and unconscious universe. Rather there is a tendency within substance to produce life, consciousness, and self-consciousness. A tendency to differentiate itself, to issue in diversity and complexity in all realms of being. In nature, all stages of such development are incorporated in the subsequent stages. As a result, there is an important sense in which a being consists of its own history. Social Ecology comprehends, in a way that the tradition never has, that mind, like all phenomena, must be understood as rooted in nature and in history.

If natural history is the history of the emergence of life, consciousness, and self-conscious mind, it is correspondingly the history of the development of freedom. Social Ecology sees freedom as essentially meaning self-determination. In this sense, it is found to some degree to all levels of being: from the self organizing and self-stabilizing tendencies of the atom, through the growth and metabolic activities of living organisms, to the complex self-realization processes of persons, societies, ecosystems and the biosphere itself. For Bookchin, 'freedom in its most nascent form is already present in the directiveness of life as such, specifically in an organism's active effort to be itself and resist any external forces that vitiate its identity.' It is this 'germinal freedom' that develops along the path of evolution, and finally becomes the 'uninhibited volition and self-consciousness' that is the goal of a fully-developed human community.

It is important to see this planetary evolution as a historic process, rather than merely as a mechanism of adaptation by individual organisms or species. Progressive unfolding of freedom depends on the existence of symbiotic cooperation at all levels—as Kropotkin pointed out almost a century ago. According to Bookchin, recent research shows that this 'mutualistic naturalism not only applies to relationship between species, but also morphologically—within and among complex cellular forms.'[4] We can therefore see a striking degree of continuity in nature, so that the free, mutualistic society at which we aim (the ecology society) is rooted in the most basic level of being.

According to Social Ecology, this holistic, developmental understanding of organic systems and their evolution has enormous importance for ethics and politics. Indeed only if the place of humanity in nature and natural processes is understood can we adequately judge questions of value. We can see our own experience of valuing and seeking the good as part of the vast process of the emergence and development of value in nature. Value is achieved in course of each being, according to its particular nature, attaining its good to the greatest degree possible.

Yet, from an ecological point of view, the realization of the planetary good is not merely the sum of all the particular good attained by all beings. For the biosphere is a whole of which these beings are parts, and a community of which they are members. The common planetary good can therefore only be conceptualized in a non-reductionist, holistic manner. The essential place of humanity in the attainment of this good cannot be underestimated. This has become even more obvious today as we confront our unprecedented dilemma: continued participation in this evolutionary development through judicious and restrained cooperation with nature—or reversal of the process through nuclear annihilation or degradation of the biosphere. But in a more fundamental sense, humanity's role in nature results from its inextricable interrelationship to the biospheric whole, and from its character as the most richly-developed realm of being to emerge thus far in the earth's evolutionary self-realization.

To say this is not to adopt an anthropocentrism that makes humanity the final or even the only end of nature. Neither is it narrow biocentrism that would ignore evolutionary developments for the sake of a biological egalitarianism.

Rather, it is ecocentrism, in the sense that it requires humanity to situate its good within the larger context of the planetary good, and to transform our often narrow rationality into truly planetary reason. As Bookchin states, 'the greatest single role' of an ecological ethics is 'to help us distinguish which of our actions serve the thrust of natural evolution and which of them impede it.'[5]

Human society must therefore transform itself, and renew itself, using ecological wisdom, so that it becomes a social ecological whole within a larger natural ecological whole. It must be seen as 'an ecosystem based on unity-in-diversity, spontaneity, and non -hierarchical relationships.'[6] This demands that a new ecological sensibility pervade all aspects of our social existence. Such a sensibility perceives 'the balance and integrity of the biosphere as an end in itself.'[7] It also recognizes the intrinsic goodness of the self realization process (the Tao or 'way') of all the diverse beings that shares our planetary eco-community. As the mentality of non-domination replaces the prevailing hierarchical outlook, there will emerge 'a new animism that respects the others for its own sake and responds actively in the form of a creative, loving and supportive symbiosis.'[8] The mutualism found throughout nature thereby attains its highest development in a mutualistic system of values and perceptions. This new sensibility will give direction to the process of regeneration that must take place at all levels, for nature, to the community, to the individual person.

The renewal of nature is perhaps the most self-evident task today for an ecological movement. According to social ecology, it is necessary to create eco communities and eco-technologies that can restore the balance between humanity and nature, and reverse the process of degradation of the biosphere. An ecological community will not attempt to dominate the surrounding environment, but rather will be a carefully integrated part of its ecosystem. Rather than continuing the system of obsessive, uncontrolled production and consumption, the community will practice true economy, the careful attending to and application of 'the rules of the household.' The extent to which humans can have a desirable impact on the ecosystem can only be decided through careful analysis of our abilities to act on behalf of nature and of the detrimental effects of our disturbances of natural balances.

A precondition for achievement of harmony with nature is the attainment of harmony and balance within society itself. Mechanistic organization based on political and economical power must be replaced by an organic community regulated through common ecological values and a commitment to a common life. The post-scarcity society advocated by Bookchin does not transcend the 'realm of necessity' through vastly increased production and consumption of commodities, nor by more 'equitable' distribution of existing material goods to 'the masses.' A society does not fight addiction to harmful substances by evenhandedly administering increased doses to each citizen. Rather, the eco-community will achieve abundance through a critical analysis and reshaping of its system of needs. The development of an ecological sensibility will create an awareness of the importance of cultural and spiritual richness: that which come from close human relationships, from aesthetic enjoyment, from the unfolding of diverse human potentialities, from spontaneity, play, and all activities liberated from the deadening hand of productive and consumptive rationality. The eco-community will seek greater simplicity and reject the mystifying and dehumanizing economic, technical, and political systems that prevail in mass society. It will highly value the complexity of developed personality, of subtle skills, of disciplined intelligence, of liberated imagination. In short, the greatest wealth of an eco-community will consist in the flowering of a richly-elaborated libertarian and communitarian culture. The social forms that will emerge from such a culture will themselves embody the ecological ideal of unity-in-diversity. A fundamental unit will be the affinity group, a closely-knit, small community based on love, friendship, shared values, and commitment to a common life. It is founded on the most intimate 'kinship,' whether or not this kinship is also biological. In addition, co-operative institutions in all areas of social life will be formed: mutualistic associations for child care and education, for production and distribution, for cultural creation, for play and enjoyment, for reflection and spiritual renewal. Organization will be based not on the demand of power, but rather on the self-realization as free social beings.

Such a transformation requires vast changes in our conception of 'the political.' Bookchin states that a society conceived of as a diversified and self-developing ecosystem poses a very distinct notion of politics that stresses decentralization, communitarianism and face to face interaction. The ideal method of decision-making is consensus, which requires an outcome based on a full recognition of the worth and competence of all involved in the process. But to the extent that this is impossible, the most participatory forms of democracy are necessary, if the values of the freedom and the community are to be synthesized in practice. Ultimate authority must be retained at the level of the local community—the level of lived experience. For this reason, a political form that is of a crucial importance is the town or neighbourhood assembly. This assembly gives the citizenry arena in which to publicly formulate its needs and aspirations. It creates a sphere in which true citizenship can be developed and exercised in practice. While it is conceivable that ecological sensibility and ecological culture can flourish through a diversity of affinity groups, co-operatives, collectives, and associations, the community assembly creates a forum through which this multiplicity can be unified and co-ordinated, and allows each citizen to conceive vividly of the good of the whole community.

Martin Buber wrote that 'the whole fate of the human race' depends on the question of whether there will be a 'rebirth of the commune.'[9] He perceived clearly that if the world is ever to emerge from its self-destructive path, it must become a universal community. And such a community, he says, can only consist of a 'community of communities.' If human beings cannot develop a deep sense of community—that is, become communal beings—through the actual practice of living in an authentic community of friends and neighbours, then the vast gulfs that separate us from one another (whether others persons or other life-forms in the biospheric community) can never be bridged. Such a possibility depends on a renewal at the most personal level: that of the self. As Bookchin has formulated it, social ecology sees the self as a harmonious synthesis of reason, passion, and imagination. Hierarchical power has always demanded the repression of many dimensions of the self. As early as *The Odyssey*, we find Odysseus, the paradigmatic model of civilized man, vanquishing, in the forms of Circe, the Sirens, the Lotus-Eaters, Scylla, Charybdis, and so on, the forces of nature, desire, the feminine, the primitive, the unconscious. And in Plato, the first great ideologist of domination, civilized rationality is exalted as the only true human part of the psyche, while desire calumniated as the 'many-headed monster' that destroys and devours all.

Social Ecology affirms an ideal of a many-sided self, in which diverse aspects attain a mutually-compatible development. The self is seen as an organic whole, yet as a whole in constant process of self-transformation and self transcendence. The myth of the self as a completed totality, as a hierarchical system with a 'ruling part', is a fiction designed to facilitate adaptation to a system of domination. The self contains on the one hand, its own individuality:

its own internal telos, its striving toward a good that flows in large part from its own nature. Yet the nature of that good and the development toward it is incomprehensible apart from one's dialectical interaction with other persons, with the community, and with the whole of nature. The goal is thus the maximum realization of both individual uniqueness and social being.

This conception of self and society does not accept the myth that all tension and conflict can ever miraculously disappear. Indeed, this delusion is more typical of reactionary psychologies of adaptation. Instead, it must be recognized that personal growth takes place only through dialectical interaction within the self, and between the self and others. The interrelationship between reason, passion, and imagination will always be dynamic and tending toward discord. In recognizing the inevitable multiplicity of the self, Social Ecology is in the tradition of the great utopian philosopher Fourier, who exhorted us to never deny or repress the vast diversity of human passions and interests. Instead, all should be recognized, affirmed, and harmonized to the greatest degree possible, so that the self can be as much a complex unity-in-diversity as are the community and nature.

Bookchin has aptly said that the creation of a true ecological community is, above all, a 'work of art.' In the same spirit, we might say that the certain creation of the organic self, this complex unity of multiplicity, is the most exquisite work of art ever undertaken by humanity and nature.

Notes
1. Bookchin, 1982, p. 24.
2. Clark, 1984, Chapter 7.
3. Bookchin, 1984.
4. Bookchin, 1984.
5. Bookchin, 1982, p. 342.
6. Bookchin, 1980, p. 69.
7. *Ibid.*, p. 59.
8. *Ibid.*, p. 268.
9. Buber, 1955, p. 136.

40 OF SUFFERING AND SENTIENCE: THE CASE OF ANIMALS

Purushottama Bilimoria
Deakin University
Geelong, Australia

The first of the Four Noble Truths of Buddhism states that there is suffering *(duhkha)*. This universal recognition of a state that afflicts all sentient beings led the Buddha to found a new philosophy of life whose sole objective was to liberate the sentient being from the ravages of this affliction. His fully worked-out program for enlightenment, however, appears to have applied to the human sentient being alone and did not encompass other forms of sentience which Buddhism (and the older Indian tradition from which Buddhism emerged) recognized, namely, animals and gods. In some respects human birth was considered to be privileged simply because it was believed that the human is endowed with certain faculties (especially insight) that animals are thought not to possess, and a body which gods do not appear to have. Nevertheless, the moral principle of *ahimsa* (or nonviolence) to which the Buddha gave exceeding prominence in Buddhist praxis, was to prevail irrespective of the status of the sentient being. Its emphasis though was weighed more in the interest of the spiritual progress of the human than a blanket concern for the welfare of the creature or being at issue.

But of course, in certain human contexts and circumstances decisions have to be made which may require qualifications and exceptions to this and such noble principles. For instance, on the question of consuming flesh of animals, the Buddha appeared to have held a rather ambivalent position; some say he took the middle path, meaning that practical considerations went towards moderating the extremes of idleness on the one hand and impractical or idealistic tendencies on the other.

The details of the disputes the Buddha and later his followers had with other hard-nosed protagonists of *ahimsa* and non-flesh-eating are too extensive to go into here.[1] All that needs to be said is that the view favoured by the Buddhists was, very generally, that if an individual is not directly responsible for the killing of an animal, then he is justified in eating its flesh. The argument turns on the motive or intentionality of the partaker, in consonance with the Buddhist theory of *karma*. Namely, if you were not aware of the animal when it was alive and it was not your intention to kill the animal, moreover, you did not possess the means of killing it, nor did you carry out the act that led to its death, then you are not responsible for its death and you invoke no bad *karma* (demerit). This means that you could turn up at the butchershop and without asking any questions buy whatever meat you might fancy and take it home for the sizzling oven. This also means that since the butcher was not expecting you, neither he nor you can say that the animal was killed for you in particular, for someone else could just as well have come by the butchershop before you (or after you) and bought the same meat; it follows therefore that you cannot be held responsible by guilt of association.

The Buddhists were challenged, particularly by a parallel sect of Jainism, on the faulty logic used in this argument, and they were charged with merely passing the moral buck, as it were, onto someone else. Does it mean that your desire to eat meat in no way contributes to the killing of the animal? After all, it is the collective wish on the part of the meat-eating community that makes it possible for there to be a butcher and his cronies who provide him with the regular supply of meat that ends up on one's plate. The market forces work only because there is an actual or projected demand for such and such an item. In the long chain of cause and effect that leads to the supply of an item X, it would seem naive to rule out any accessory contribution that its procurer makes. A consumer society such as ours indeed thrives on the desires we each have for material possessions of all kinds; far from thinking that it is our privilege to, say, use as much paper as we like, we have had to stop and think how each of us might be responsible for the demise of two trees each year! Similarly, how could my or your desire to consume meat be completely severed from the 'motive' of whoever it is that actually kills the animal, whose intention as it were is fed in large part by our desire and unacknowledged wish that there be meat in the butchershop? One could call this a 'deferred motive' syndrome.

In any event, to give due credit to the Buddhist claim of impunity, there are still two things that are intriguing about the Buddhist account. First, the Buddha's programmatic emerges from the recognition of the fact of suffering rather than the sacrosanct state of being human. So the question of 'rights', i.e. natural or human rights, does not arise here. Second, suffering is endemic to all sentient life. But on the question of priority the Buddhist wants to give to human life over animal life, there appears, to me at least, to be a few issues here. I shall address these and then ponder whether Peter Singer's scheme casts a better light.

As I mentioned a little earlier, the Buddhists were persuaded by soteriological motives for alleviating the plight of human suffering. After all the Buddha was a human and the Brahmanical ritualistic worldview had not delivered the promised goods. The human condition was desperately in need of saving. Gods and animals will need to take care of themselves. This, however, is not exactly correct. For on the brink of attaining *nirvana* the adept pledges to postpone entering the penultimate state until all sentient beings have been liberated, and he assumes instead the role of a Bodhisattva, similar to a saint or a mini-saviour, to work towards this end.

Still, it is considered that birth in a human body, somewhere in the vast cycle of birth and death, is incumbent on all sentient beings who desire to reach the state of *nirvana*. Why? Because the particular kind of insight into the nature of reality and the fulfillment of certain requisite precepts may not be possible in other forms of sentient existence. This claim, of course, cannot be decided one way or the other without accepting or rejecting other presuppositions of ontological and religious kinds which themselves do not necessarily rest on arguments (what after all is the state of *nirvana*?), and so they need not concern us here.

But the reference to 'insight' (Sanskrit, *prajna*), gives a clue to the possibility of a claim that appeals to rationality. There is a long and drawn-out debate as to whether *prajna* stands for some sort of reflective and meditative intuition or whether it has to do with systematic reasoning or ratiocination. Either way, it appears to be a conscious and self-conscious process through which some understanding of the state of nature and human nature is achieved. Now it goes without saying that in the Buddhist worldview this capacity, let us say in short, for self-reflection is absent in the animal world or is not there to the same degree. Hence, despite the universality of suffering, a hierarchical ordering is assented to here, wherein the human world is positioned above that of the animal world on the grounds that animals lack a certain intellectual faculty that human beings possess. But assuming or imposing this kind of hierarchy is problematic, in the same way that the subtle hierarching involved in the discourse of (human) rights is. The latter comes about partly as a result of valorising the individual above the social or communal whole, and partly by elevating the human world above other sentient worlds, nature and indeed above the whole cosmos. (The Copernican Revolution notwithstanding, the human moral world was never quite decentred. With God gone or dead who else could claim the centre of the court?).

I suppose what I am struggling to come to terms with is the claim that the possession by the human being of a self-consciously rational or quasi-rational (in the case of Buddhist psychology) disposition is itself a justification for prioritising different forms of sentience.

A very similar kind of argument appears in Peter Singer's thinking as well. Though certainly not one for speciesism (his case for the defence of animal interests being based on the rejection of placing human species over and above other species),[2] in a curious way his argument appears to appeal at some point to a species-specific consideration where the question of saving an endangered human life over an animal life is concerned. Some would submit that there is no philosophical way of resolving this impasse once the fact of sentience, conscious living and so on, is admitted in respect of both the species. But Singer's argument, if I am right, turns on the claim that human beings possess awareness of themselves as a distinct entity with their own life-narratives. (Of course, he doesn't deny this to all non-human animals, but the range is too large such as to include all animals under this category.)

There are any number of epistemological problems in such claims, not the least of which is, how do we know that all non-human animals do not have the same mental capacities, at least in the same respect as a fully-recognized human baby, without obvious defects, has? Well, perhaps because they don't have language, poetry, history books, universities and so on. But nor do human children have these to the same degree that the adult human community has. On parity, dolphins, for example, seem to show greater intelligence than a human infant does; yet we would not attribute the same respect and moral interests to the dolphin as we would to the human infant. Of course, the human infant has the potential of growing into a developed human adult in the way that the dolphin does not. But the argument from 'potential person' reeks with the same defects as its use in anti-abortion and 'right to life' rejection of embryo experimentation and so forth. At the baseline, we seem to be returned to the old Cartesian divide between animal and man, if not the Chomskian-Bennett divide between animal behaviour and human language. This might be too general and I don't here want to get trapped in the thorny issues.

I am basically puzzled by the move that first of all detaches the human from the natural cosmic world, and then claims for it an entitlement on grounds of its being rational and self-conscious, and presumably not simply because of its being human *qua* species. But this is tautological, for if only human beings are rational and self-conscious, then all beings that are self-conscious and rational would have to be humans. This strikes me to be another form of speciesism that makes coveted recourse to the fact of rationality, which by definition only human beings possess! What has to be shown, I believe, is that in the whole wide world there is something particularly significant and special about being rational and self-conscious, and that being rational and self-conscious is not merely a characteristic human beings historically evolved as a matter of survival, just as bears developed thick furs to protect themselves against the chill of the Arctic wind, or giraffes' necks grew longer in the face of increasing competition for the short seasonal supply of fruits on tall trees.

Of course, an evolutionary argument can be made for the pre-eminence of reasoning as a capacity that has aided and guided human beings in their quest for survival and self-fulfillment, with its culmination in the European Enlightenment. Such arguments are not uncommon. Without this commitment to reason and the power of reasoning, the human race might be worse off than it presently is; or conversely, with a better use of reason, the human race could have done much better than it has. But notice that we seem not to be able to speak of reason without speaking of human beings: it is this that makes it species-specific. But reason also makes us attentive to the interests of non-rational animals.

Still, however, if our yardstick or bench-mark is to be rationality then we might *vis-à-vis* other species be as much part of the circle as, say, Christians were when they felt concerned about the spiritual plight of the non-Christians. Internal and external critiques of Christian beliefs showed that at least this aspect of its concern is incoherent and fundamentally flawed. A self-critique of reason, Kant showed, revealed a number of antinomies in the concept of reason, which could leave some of our rational solutions ambiguous. Perhaps the overly cognitive emphasis betrayed in the concept of rational self-consciousness overlooks the connotative, affective and subjective dispositions of human beings which bring them rather closer to the animal being than it has otherwise appeared. After all, suffering or the capacity for suffering might not itself be sufficient grounds to warrant a concern for animals; hence Mill, who acknowledged that animals feel pain, did not see any obligation on the part of the human to redress the pain of the animal species. Alternatively, in our narrow individualistic cosmology, where we are more prone to assert human rights than to consider our obligations, hence rites, toward other beings, our ethics does not force us to give equal weight to the conditions of humans and other sentient beings.

Since we have mentioned (moral) rights, in respect to humans, let us pause for a moment and consider the question of whether it is ever appropriate to speak of 'animal rights'. This is familiar territory in many ways, particularly from the work of Tom Regan[3] who bases his popular defence of animal well-being on precisely these grounds, *viz.*, the rights of the animal and the recognition of this principle by (human) moral agents. Some have argued on the other hand that it is logically absurd to assume that animals can have rights, not least since animals do not claim for themselves such moral rights (and it is doubtful whether animals recognize rights of humans and of other members of the sentient world). Besides, can we assume that animals are capable of being moral agents in the same terms as human beings are (such that, for example, they would acknowledge their corresponding obligation or responsibility and agree to resolve disputes in a rational communicative manner)? In the absence of a (shared) language who is to specify moral rights in respect of animals, and how are the requirements of reciprocal duties to be determined?

There are, then, a host of difficulties that would seem to militate against the attempt to extend the concept of rights to animals. While admitting such difficulties, it must nevertheless be acknowledged that the concept of moral rights even in respect of human beings is not without its own difficulties. We do not wish to divert to this larger problem here, except to draw attention to two issues that are relevant to this present discussion. These are, namely: Firstly, should rights be restricted to human beings, and persons at that? Put another way, ought a human-centred viewpoint (or human ethics) occlude the virtue of certain intuitively persuasive moral principles from having a legitimate place in the quest for an ethics of the environment, and second, even in the context of human rights there are situations where rights are extended to those members who are not capable of determining their own rights, or who have no consciousness of (or voice in) any of the deliberations that might proceed on their behalf (e.g. in the case of the intellectually challenged, mentally retarded, the patient in severe coma, the unborn and the dead). Again, put another way, there are ways of negotiating the extent of the moral rights an agent might legitimately be required to recognize regardless of the capability or otherwise of the claimant to assert such a right.

In short, there is principle at stake here, namely, of the universality of a 'rights' ethics if its place within the sentient spectrum is not heeded. We may in the end settle for a sliding scale system which allows humans (and persons among them) to have, on balance, more rights than say a species of the far end of the spectrum, however that status is to be determined. The argument is that the conception of rights risks slippage into an anthropocentric discourse unless it is extended and integrated into a wider framework of environmental ethics. Of course, there are other ways of addressing the issue of animal well-being and protection, such as through the recognition of the interests and intrinsic value of animal species. I should like to think that human beings are intelligent enough to be able to come to terms with the fact that they have certain basic duties to other species in the common eco-sphere (such as not to harm, not to disturb, not to forego trust, be willing to make restitution, be compassionate); these duties may ensue either in recognition of the rights of others *or* in respect for the interests and values of others. While a stronger moral case can be made by basing the argument on interests and values than on the moral rights of animals, there is no reason why animal ethics need to favour one over the other. It would seem to me that a case for the *respect* of animals (of the kind that Paul Taylor has made as part of his case for respecting nature[4]), can only be strengthened by finding a mean between rights and interests. But since our present inquiry concerns critiquing the Buddhist position, we must now return to this.

Now one can appreciate without accepting the Buddhist position that since it is human life that presents the gateway to *nirvana* it is more important to preserve human life against animal life where hard choices have to be made.

But if our present day concerns do not coincide with Buddhist soteriology and when faced with the choice between saving a healthy human and a healthy animal, how are we to decide, on theoretical grounds, which way to go? We cannot fall back on the fact of sentience qualified by rational, etc., properties, for reasons we have already considered. Consider also, on purely consequentialist grounds, that the saved human might occasion more damage, say, to the environment than the rival animal were it saved, what great good would follow from our action? From a broader perspective, the question does arise as to what rights the human kingdom has over the animal and the natural kingdom? Once we admit the fact of sentience and the capacity for suffering, this, it would seem, must guide all our decisions.

Of course, it might be retorted that human beings, because of their self-consciousness and reason, are capable of greater suffering than are animals. But in what way does being able to reason make the burden of suffering more onerous? One could also turn the argument around and say that since humans can reason and establish the source of their suffering, they cope with it better than animals can and might even be sage enough to suffer on behalf of the animals! Gandhi, for example, preferred and utilized the human capacity for greater suffering against the traditional belief that suffering at all costs has to be rid of. So perhaps after all it is better that animals more than human beings be spared the burden of suffering. But apart from the difficulty of making quantitative measures of suffering, the argument creates problems in other areas: where an unhealthy and suffering human life (infant or adult) is concerned, it would be reasonable to argue for the perpetuation of that life; but where the terminal suffering of an animal life is concerned it might seem more reasonable to put the animal to rest. Under the 'capacity for greater suffering' argument, human euthanasia would appear to be an incoherent position.

Thus, either there is equal regard for the suffering of all sentient beings or there is not. And finally, should the greatest good for all leave out or bracket the interests of animals where it conflicts with human interests? Most utilitarians, such as J.S. Mill, who were sensitive to the animal's capacity to feel pain, invariably came around to arguing that human interests ought to prevail over animal interests. Again, I cannot see how utilitarian considerations can be sufficient, necessary though they might be, to clinch the argument without sliding back into humanism[5] (by which I mean preference for the human species).

One implication of the line of thinking I have presented above is that just as we have grown wary of talking in terms of rights ('right to life', 'right to abortion', 'animal rights' and so on), we might be more cautious in conflating the discourse of dignity (a concept that has its roots in Aquinas' division of human and nature), and deserving or not-deserving of life with arguments based on self-consciousness and rationality, not because there is anything substantially wrong with the argument, but because it is not self-evident that these and these alone can constitute the criteria for the implicit hierarching of sentience, which in traditional philosophy was achieved by reference to sacredness, the Will of God, the capacity to attain *nirvana*, Brahmanical liberation and so on.

Notes
1. Rahula, 1988.
2. Singer, 1979.
3. Regan, 1983.
4. Taylor, 1986.
5. Bilimoria, 1992.

REFERENCES

Abbot, F.E. 1874. The advancement of ethics. *Monist.* vol. 5, pp. 195–216.
Abbot, F.E. 1897. 'The Scientific Basis of Ethics.' Free Church Tracts, No. 7, Tacoma, Washington: First Free Church.
Abbot, W.M. (ed.) 1965. The Documents of Vatican II. New York.
Achebe, C. 1990. African literature as restoration of celebration. *New African,* no. 270, pp. 40–41.
Adam, H. 1971. *Modernizing Racial Domination: South Africa's Political Dynamics.* Berkeley: University of California Press.
Aldo, L. 1949. *A Sand County Almanac.* New York: Oxford University Press.
Alford, R. R. and R. Friedland. 1985. *Powers of Theory: Capitalism, the State and Democracy.* Cambridge, U.K.: Cambridge Univ. Press.
Angelini, G. 1990. Ritorno all 'etica'? *Il Regno,* vol. 35, no. 643, pp. 438–499.
Anyanwu, K.C. 1991. 'The concept of man-nature in Dogan philosophy.' A paper presented at the Nairobi World Conference of Philosophy, Nairobi, 1991.
Anzenbacher, A. 1971. *Einfurung in die Philosophie,* Vienna.
Ashforth, A. 1987. On the 'Native Question': a reading of the grand tradition of commissions of inquiry into the 'Native Question' in the 20th century South Africa. University of Oxford, PhD. thesis.
Attfield, R. 1983. *The Ethics of Environmental Concern.* New York: Columbia University Press.
Ausubel, J.H. 1991. Does climate still matter? *Nature,* vol. 350, pp. 649–652.
Awolalu, J.O. 1970. The Yoruba philosophy of life. *Presence Africaine,* no. 73, pp. 20–38.
Ayres, R.E. 1989. Chapter in *Taking Sides: Clashing Views on Controversial Environmental Issues,* edited by T.D. Goldfarb, p. 114. Guilford, Ct: Dushkin Publishing Group.
Benacerraf, P. and H. Putnam. 1965. *Philosophy of Mathematics.* Oxford: Blackwell.
Bernal, M. 1987. *Black Athena: The Afroasiatic Roots of Classical Civilization, Volume I. The Fabrication of Ancient Greece, 1785–1985.* New Jersey: Rutgers University Press.
Beth, E.W. 1959. *The Foundation of Mathematics.* Amsterdam: North-Holland Publishing Co.
Bilimoria, P. 1992. 'Moral Enfranchisement of Nature.' In *Environmental Ethics,* edited by P. Bilimoria and J. McCollogh. Australia: Deakin University Press.
Blackstone, W.T. 1974. 'Ethics and Ecology.' In *Philosophy and Environmental Crisis,* edited by W.T. Blackstone. Athens: University Georgia Press. (Wiredu)
Bodunrin, P.O. 1981. The question of African philosophy. *Philosophy,* vol. 56, no. 216, p. 161.
Bohr, N. 1934. *Atomic Theory and the Description of Nature.* Cambridge, UK: Cambridge University Press.
Bohr, N. 1948. On the notions of causality and complementarity. *Dialectica,* vol. 2.
Bohr, N. 1958. *Atomic Physics and Human Knowledge.* New York: Wiley.
Bohr, N. 1963. *Essays 1958–1962 on Atomic Physics and Human Knowledge.* New York: Wiley.
Bookchin, M. 1980. *Toward an Ecological Society.* Montreal: Black Rose Books.
Bookchin, M. 1982. *The Ecology of Freedom.* Palo Alto: Cheshire Books.
Bookchin, M. 1984. 'Toward a Philosophy of Nature.' In *Deep Ecology,* edited by Michael Tobias. Montreal: Avant Books.
Bookchin, M. 1987. Social ecology vs. 'deep ecology'. *Green Perspectives,* nos. 4 and 5, Summer.
Borlaug, N.E. 1989. 'Overview of the Global 2000 Agricultural Projects in Africa.' In *Feeding the Future: Agricultural Development Strategies for Africa,* Proceedings of a workshop in Accra, Ghana, August 1–3, 1989.

Breasted, J.H. 1944. 'The Earliest Food-Producers.' In *Ancient Times: A History of the Early World*, pp. 26–48. Boston: Ginn.
Brooke, J. 1988. *New York Times*. 17 July, p. 1.
Brown, L. and C. Wolf. 1985. *Reversing Africa's Decline*. Washington, DC: Worldwatch Institute.
Buber, M. 1955. *Paths in Utopia*. Boston: Beacon Press.
Burks, A.W. (ed.) 1958. *The Collected Papers of Charles Sanders Peirce*. Cambridge, MA: Harvard University Press.
Callahan, D. 1981. 'Ethics and Population Limitation.' In *Environmental Ethics*, edited by K.S. Shrader-Frechette. Pacific Grove, Ca: Boxwood.
Callicott, J. 1985. Intrinsic value, quantum theory, and environmental ethics. *Environmental Ethics*, vol. 7, pp. 257–275.
Callicott, J.B. 1989. Chapter in *Defense of the Land Ethic: Essays in Environmental Philosophy*. Albany: State University of New York Press.
Campbell, R.R. and J.L. Wade. 1972. *Society and Environment: The Coming Collision*. Boston: Allyn and Bacon.
Carmody, D.L. and T.J. Carmody. 1988. *How to Live Well: Ethics in the World Religions*. Belmont, Ca: Wadsworth.
Cartwright, R. 1987. 'A Neglected Theory of Truth.' In *Philosophical Essays*, edited by R. Cartwright, pp. 71–95. Cambridge, Ma: MIT Press.
Césaire, A. 1939. *Return to My Native Land*. Paris: Presence Africaine.
Césaire, A. 1956. *Lettre à Maurice Thorez*. Paris.
Clark, J. 1984. *The Anarchist Moment: Reflections on Culture, Nature and Power*. Montreal: Black Rose Books.
Cronje, G. 1945. *'n Tuiste vir ons nageslag*. (A home for posterity). Cape Town.
Cronje, G. 1947. *Regverdige rasseapartheid*. (A just racial separation). Stellenbosch.
Cushing, J. and E. McMullin (eds). 1989. *Philosophical Consequences of Quantum Theory*. Notre Dame: University of Notre Dame Press.
Davenport, T. R. H. 1986. *South Africa: A modern history*. Johannesburg: Macmillan.
De Crespigny, A. and J. Cronin. (eds.). 1975. *Ideologies of Politics*. Cape Town: Oxford University Press S.A.
De Klerk, W. A. 1976. *The Puritans in Africa*. London: Penguin.
De Villiers, M. 1990. *White Tribe Dreaming*. London. Penguin.
Devall, B. and G. Sessions. 1985. *Deep Ecology: Living as if Nature Mattered*. Layton, Utah: Gibbs M. Smith, Inc.
Diamond, I. and G.F. Orenstein. 1990. *Reweaving the World: The Emergence of Ecofeminism*. San Francisco: Sierra Books.
Drengson, A. 1983. *Shifting Paradigms: From Technocratic to Planetary Person*. Victoria, BC: LightStar Press.
Dubow, S. H. 1986. *Segregation and 'Native Administration' in South Africa, 1920–1936*. University of Oxford, PhD. thesis.
Dumos, R. 1971. 'A Theology of the Earth.' In *The Dying Generations*, edited by T.R. Harney and R. Disch. New York: Dell.
Dura, C. 1985. *Çevre Sorunlari ve Ekonomi*. Ankara.
Ehrenfeld, D. 1978. *The Arrogance of Humanism*. Oxford: Oxford University Press. *Ethics*, vol. 12, Summer, pp. 125–146.
Evernden, N. 1985. *The Natural Alien*. Toronto: University of Toronto Press.
Ewing, A.C. 1968. *The Fundamental Questions of Philosophy*. London: RKP.
Fanon, F. 1961. *Les Damnes de la Terre*. Paris: Presence Africaine.
Ferré, F. 1988. *Philosophy of Technology*. Englewood Cliffs, NJ: Prentice Hall.
Ferré, F. 1990. Risks and benefits in the context of a comprehensive agricultural ethic. *Proceedings of the Southern Weed Society*. 43rd Annual Meeting, 15–17 January, 1990, pp.

18–20.
Flew, A. (ed.) 1983. *The Is Ought Question.* London: Macmillan.
Folse, H.J. 1985. *The Philosophy of Niels Bohr: The Framework of Complementarity.* Amsterdam: North Holland Physics Publishing.
Folse, H.J. 1990. Complementarity and the description of nature in biology. *Biology and Philosophy,* vol. 5, pp. 211–224.
Fox, M. 1988. *The Coming of the Cosmic Christ.* New York: Harper and Row.
Fox, W. 1984. Deep ecology: A new philosophy of our time? *The Ecologist,* vol. 14, no. 5/6, pp. 194–200.
Fox, W. 1989. The deep ecology—ecofeminism debate and its parallels. *Environmental Ethics,* vol. 11, Spring, pp. 5–26.
Fox, W. 1990. *Toward a Transpersonal Ecology: Developing New Foundations for Environmentalism.* Boulder, CO: Shambhala.
Frankena, W.K. 1979. 'Ethics and the Environment.' In *Ethics and Problems of the 21st Century,* pp. 3–20, edited by K.E. Goodpaster and K.M. Sayre. Notre Dame: University of Notre Dame Press.
French, A.P. (ed.) 1979. *Einstein: A Centenary Volume.* London: Heinemann Educational Books, Ltd.
Gadamer, H . 1985 . *Philosophical Apprenticeships* R. Sullivan (trans), Cambridge, Ma: MIT Press.
Gadamer, H. 1975. *Truth and Method.* London: Sheed and Ward.
Giliomee, H. 1982. *The Parting of the Ways: South African Politics 1976–82.* Cape Town: David Philip.
Goldfarb, T. 1989. *Taking Sides: Clashing Views on Controversial Environmental Issues.* Guilford, Conn.: Duskin.
Goodpaster, K. 1978. On being morally considerable. *Journal of Philosophy,* vol. 75, pp. 308–325.
Griffin, D.R. 1988. *The Re-enchantment of Science.* Albany: State University of New York Press.
Gunn, A.S. 1984. 'Preserving Rare Species.' In *Earthbound: New Introductory Essays in Environmental Ethics,* edited by Tom Regan, pp. 289–335. Philadelphia: Temple University Press.
Gyekye, K. 1987. *An Essay on African Philosophical Thought.* New York: Cambridge University Press.
Gyekye, K. 1988. 'The Idea of Democracy in the Traditional Setting and its Relevance to Political Development in Contemporary Africa.' Paper 30 of the International Conference of Philosophy on Focus on Culture and Traditional Thought Systems in Development, Mombasa, Kenya, 23–27 May 1988.
Hardin, G. 1972. 'Parenthood: Right or Privilege?' In *Society and Environment: The Coming Collision* edited by R. Campbell and J. Wade. Boston: Allyn and Bacon, Inc.
Hardin, G. 1974. Life-boat ethics. *Bioscience,* vol. 24, October.
Hardin, G. 1981. 'The Tragedy of the Commons.' In *Environmental Ethics,* edited by K.S. Shrader-Frechette. Pacific Grove, Ca: Boxwood Press.
Harney, T.R. and R. Disch. (eds.) 1971. *The Dying Generations.* New York: Dell.
Harrison, D. 1981. *The White Tribe of Africa.* Johannesburg: Macmillan.
Harrison, P. 1983. *The Third World Tomorrow.* Harmondsworth: Penguin.
Havel, V. 1989. *Living in Truth.* London: Faber & Faber.
Heisenberg, W. 1971. *Schritte Uber Grenzen.* Munich: Piper.
Hepple, A. 1967. *Verwoerd.* London: Penguin.
Heyer, P. 1982. *Nature, Human Nature, and Society: Marx, Darwin, Biology and the Human Sciences.* Westport, Ct.: Greenwood Press.
Hountondji, P. 1983. *Wissenschaft in Afrika—eine Facette der Unterrentwicklung.* Wis-

senschaftliche Welt. London/Berlin, no. 1 S. 14–17.
Hugo, P. 1988. Towards darkness and death: racial demonology in South Africa. *Journal of Modern African Studies*. Vol. 26, No. 4.
Johnson, L.E. 1991. *A Morally Deep World: An Essay on Moral Significance and Environmental Ethics*. Cambridge, UK: Cambridge University Press.
Johnson, R. 1981. *The Kumulipo*. Vol. 1. Honolulu: Topgallant Publishing Co.
Juma, C. 1989. *The Gene Hunters: Biotechnology and the Scramble for Seeds*. Princeton: Princeton University Press.
Kagame, A. 1971. 'L'ethnophilosophic de Bantu.' In *Contemporary Philosophy*, edited by R. Klibansky, vol. IV. Florence.
Keesings Record of World Events. 1988, vol. 34.
Kenney, H. 1980. *Architect of Apartheid. H. F. Verwoerd—An Appraisal*. Johannesburg: Jonathan Ball Publishers.
Kenyatta, J. 1938. *Facing Mount Kenya*. London: Secker and Warburg.
Kinghorn, J. (ed.) 1986. *N. G. Kerk en Apartheid*. Johannesburg: Macmillan.
Kinghorn, J. 1990. *'n Tuiste vir almal*. (A home for all). Stellenbosch: Centre for Contextual Hermeneutics.
Kinghorn, J., B.C. Lategan, L.M. du Plessis and D.E. de Villiers. 1987. *The Option for an Inclusive Democracy*. Stellenbosch: Centre for Contextual Hermeneutics.
Kuide, C. 1989. 'Man vs. Nature and Natural Man: One Aspect of the Concept of Nature in China and the West.' In *Man and Culture: The Chinese Tradition and the Future*, edited by T. Yi-Jie, L. Zhen, and G. McLean, pp. 131–141. New York: University Press of America.
Kupilik, M. 1982. 'The Environment and Socialism.' In *International Dimensions of the Environmental Crisis: The Soviet Model*, edited by R.N. Barett. Boulder, Co: Westview Press.
LaChapelle, D. 1978. *Earth Wisdom*. Los Angeles: Guild of Tutors Press.
LaChapelle, D. 1988. *Sacred Land, Sacred Sex, Rapture of the Deep*. Silverton, CO: Finn Hill Arts Press.
Langenberg, D.N. 1991. Science, slogans and civic duty. *Science*, vol. 252, pp. 361–363.
Laudan, L. 1984. *Science and Values*. Berkeley: University of California Press.
Laurikainen, K.V. 1988. *Beyond the Atom*. Heidelberg: Springer-Verlag.
Lazar, J. 1987. *Conformity and conflict: Afrikaner Nationalist politics in South Africa, 1948–61*. University of Oxford, PhD. thesis.
Levine, D. (In press) 'The Sorcerer's Apprentice: The Revolution in the Family and the World We Have Made.' In *Proceedings of the First DeLange Conference on Human Impact on the Environment*. Rice University, Houston, Texas, 5–7 April 1991.
Lipton, M. 1986. *Capitalism and Apartheid, South Africa, 1910–1986*. Great Britain: Wildwood House.
Lorenzen, P. 1978. *Theorie der Technischen und Politischen Vernunft*. Stuttgart: Philip Reclam.
Lovejoy, A.O. 1960. *The Great Chain of Being*. New York: Harper.
Luthuli, A. 1982. *Let My People Go*. Glasgow: Collins.
Marcuse, H., G. Marcel, B.F. Skinner and F. Dessauer. 1974. 'Philosophy of Technology.' In *New Catholic Encyclopaedia*, Vol. XVI. Washington, DC: Catholic Press of America.
Mazrui, A.A. 1986. *The Africans: A Triple Heritage*. London: BBC.
Mbiti, J. 1969. *African Religions and Philosophy*. London: Heinemann.
McCloskey, M. 1989. Book review of Bill Devall's *Simple in Means, Rich in Ends: Practicing Deep Ecology*. *Sierra*, January/February, pp. 162–164.
McKibben, B. 1989. *The End of Nature*. New York: Random House.
Meadows, G.H. *et al.* 1974. *The Limits to Growth*. New York: New American Library.
Midgley, M. 1986. *Animals and Why They Matter*. Athens, GA: The Georgia University Press.
Miro Quesada, F. 1982. *Latinoamericana de Investigaciones Juridicas Y Sociales*. Venezuela:

References

Valencia.
Miro Quesada, F. 1988. *Hombre, Naturalza, Historia, Actas del Congreso International Extraordinario de Filosofia.* Argentina: Universidad de Cordoba.
Miro Quesada, F. 1989. 'Paraconsistent Logic: Some Philosophical Issues.' In *Paraconsistent Logic, and Essays on the Inconsistent.* Munich: Philosophia Verlag.
Miro Quesada, F. 1991. 'Ensayo de una Fundamentacion Racional de la Etica.' VI Congreso Internacional de Filosophia Lationoamericana, Universidad de Santo Tomas, Bogota, 1991.
Mitcham, C. and J. Grote. 1984. *Theology and Technology: Essays in Christian Analysis and Exegesis.* Lanham, MD: University Press of America.
Moffat, A.S. 1991. Research on biological pest control moves ahead. *Science,* vol. 252, pp. 211–212.
Moodie. T.D. 1975. *The rise of Afrikanerdom: power, apartheid and the Afrikaner civil religion.* Los Angeles: University of California Press.
Moore, G. 1903. *Principia Ethica.* Cambridge, UK: Cambridge University Press.
Moore, G. 1953. *Some Main Problems of Philosophy.* (Lectures from 1910–11) London: Allen and Unwin.
Moscovici, J. 1982. *Versuch Uber die menschliche Geschichte der Natur.* Frankfurt: Suhrkampf.
Mullins, W. A. 1972. On the concept of ideology in political science. *American Political Science Review.* Vol. 66.
Naess, A. 1973. The shallow and the deep, long-range ecology movement: a summary. *Inquiry,* vol. 16, pp. 95–100.
Naess, A. 1979. Self-realization in mixed communities of humans, bears, sheep, and wolves. *Inquiry,* vol. 22, pp. 231–241.
Naess, A. 1984a. A defence of the deep ecology movement. *Environmental Ethics,* vol. 6, pp. 265–270.
Naess, A. 1984b. The arrogance of anti-humanism? *Ecophilosophy,* vol. 6, p. 9.
Naess, A. 1989. *Ecology, Community, and Lifestyle: Outline of an Ecosophy* (trans. and revised by David Rothenberg), New York: Cambridge University Press.
Naess. A. 1985. 'Identification as a Source of Deep Ecological Attitudes.' In *Deep Ecology,* edited by Michael Tobias. San Diego: Avant Books.
Nietzsche, F. 1967. *The Will to Power,* edited by W. Kaufmann. New York: Vintage.
Nkrumah, K. 1970. *Consciencism.* London: Panaf Books.
Norse, D. 1991. Feed the world: save the environment. *Shell Agriculture,* vol. 9, pp. 7–10.
Northrop, F.S.C. 1947. *The Logic of the Sciences and of the Humanities.* New York: Macmillan.
Nyerere, J. 1968. *Ujamaa: Essays on Socialism.* Dar-es-Salaam: OUP.
O'Connor, D.D. 1986. Peirce's Debt to F.E. Abbot. *Journal of the History of Ideas,* vol . 25, pp. 561–575.
O'Meara, D. 1983. *Volkskapitalisme: Class, capital and ideology in the development of Afrikaner Nationalism.* Johannesburg: Ravan Press.
Odera Oruka, H. (ed.) 1990. Sage *Philosophy, Indigenous Thinkers and Modern Debate on African Philosophy.* E.J. Brill, Leiden, Netherlands, 1990 and ACTS Press, Nairobi, 1991.
Odera Oruka, H. 1983. Sagacity in African philosophy. *International Philosophical Quarterly.* vol. 22, no. 4, pp. 383–393.
Odhiambo, T.R. 1991. Designing a new science-led environment-conscious development in tropical Africa. *Discovery and Innovation,* vol. 3, pp. 9–15.
Oguz, B. 1986. *Çevre üzerine düsünceler.* Ankara: Nisan.
Ortlieb, H.D. 1979. 'Dem schwarzen Mann pabt nur ein Mabanzug. Technik, Zivilisation und die Seele Afrikas.' In Die Welt 17./18. Februar no.41, Beilage *Geistige Welt S I.*
Oyugi, W.O. and A. Gitonga (eds.) 1987. *Democratic Theory and Practice in Africa.* Nairobi: Heinemann.

Özoglu, S.C. 1988. *Çevre ve Kalkinma Illskileri*. Ankara.
Parsons, T. 1963. 'Christianity and Modern Industrial Society.' In *Sociological Theory, Values and Sociocultural Change,* edited by E. Tiryakian.
Passmore, J. 1974 . Man's *Responsibility for Nature* . New York: Charles Scribner's Sons.
Paton, A. 1979. 'The Afrikaners' in E. S. Munger (ed.) *The Afrikaners*. Cape Town: Tafelberg.
Peirce, C. 1903. Francis E. Abbot. *The Nation*, 5 November, p. 77.
Pelzer, A. N. (ed.) 1966. *Verwoerd speaks: speeches 1948–66*. Johannesburg: APB Publishers.
Plamenatz, J. 1970. *Ideology*. London: Pall Mall Press Ltd.
Posel, D. 1987. *Influx control and the construction of apartheid, 1948–1961*. University of Oxford, PhD. thesis.
Prigogine, I. and I. Stengers. 1988. *Entre le temps et L'eternite*. Paris: Fayard.
Rahula, T. 1988. 'Buddhist Attitude Toward Meat-eating and Non-violence.' In *Religious and Comparative Thought, Essays in Honour of the Late Dr. Ian Kesarcodi Watson,* edited by P. Bilimoria and P. Fenner, pp. 101–112. Delhi: Satguru Publications.
Raposa, M.L. 1989. *Peirce's Philosophy of Religion*. Bloomington: Indiana University Press.
Reed, F.W. 1982. 'Human Ecology, Desertification, Nationalism, and Population Growth.' In *International Dimensions of the Environmental Crisis: The Soviet Model,* edited by R.N. Barrett. Boulder, Co: Westview.
Regan, T. (ed.) 1986. *Animal Sacrifices: Religious Perspectives on the Use of Animals in Science*. Philadelphia: Temple University Press.
Regan, T. 1982. *All That Dwell Therein: Animal Rights and Environmental Ethics*. Berkeley: University of California Press.
Regan, T. 1983. *The Case for Animal Rights*. Berkeley: University of California Press.
Robertson, D. 1986. *Dictionary of Politics*. England: Penguin.
Rodman, J. 1977. The liberation of nature? *Inquiry,* vol. 20, pp. 83–131.
Roemer, J. 1982. *A General Theory of Exploitation and Class*. Cambridge, MA: Harvard University Press.
Rolston III, H. 1988. *Environmental Ethics: Duties to and Values in the Natural World*. Temple University Press.
Rorty, R. 1979. *Philosophy and the Mirror Nature*. Princeton, New Jersey: Princeton University Press.
Rorty, R. 1982. 'Pragmatism, Relativism, and Irrationalism.' In *Consequences of Pragmatism.* Brighton: Harvester.
Rosenberg, N. and J.R. Birdzell. Science, technology and the Western miracle. *Scientific American,* vol. 263, no. 5, pp. 18–25.
Roszak, T. 1978. Person/Planet: *The Creative Disintegration of Industrial Society*. Garden City, NY: Anchor Doubleday.
Ruse, M. 1986. *Taking Darwin Seriously: A Naturalist Approach to Philosophy*. Oxford: Blackwell.
Russell, B. 1966. *Philosophy Essays*. London: Allen and Unwin.
Safire, W. 1989. Libeling the dead. *The New York Times,* April 13.
Samkange, S. and T. Samkange. 1980. *Hunhuism or Ubuntuism. A Zimbabwe Indigenous Political Philosophy*. Salisbury.
Schapiro, L. (ed.) *Political Opposition in the One-Party State*. London: Macmillan.
Schmitz, A. and D. Seckler. 1970. Mechanized Agriculture and social welfare: the case of the tomato harvester. *American Journal of Agricultural Economics,* vol. 54, no. 4, pp. 569–577.
Scholtz, G. D. 1974. *Dr. Hendrik Frensch Verwoerd: 1901–1966*. Johannesburg: Perskor.
Scruton, R. 1986. *Spinoza*. Oxford: Oxford University Press.
Seligman, R.A. (ed.) 1984. 'Culture.' In *Encyclopaedia of Social Science*. New York: Oxford University Press.
Sessions, G. 1981. 'Shallow and Deep Ecology: A Review of the Philosophical Literature.' In

References

Ecological Consciousness: Essays from the Earth Day X Colloquium, edited by R.G. Schultz and J.D. Hughes. Washington DC: University Press of America.
Shrader-Frechette, K.S. 1981. 'Voluntary Simplicity and the Duty to Limit Consumption.' In *Environmental Ethics,* edited by K.S. Shrader-Frechette. Pacific Grove, Ca: Boxwood Press.
Singer, P. 1975. *Animal Liberation.* New York: Random House.
Singer, P. 1979. *Practical Ethics.* Cambridge, UK: Cambridge University Press.
Singh, R.J. 1991. 'Gandhi and Environmental Ethics.' A paper presented at the Nairobi World Conference of Philosophy, Nairobi, 1991.
Snow, C.P. 1960. *The Two Cultures.* London: Macmillan.
Snyder, G. 1974. *Turtle Island.* New York: New Directions.
Snyder, G. 1980. *The Real Work.* New York: New Directions.
Sparks, A. 1990. *The Mind of South Africa.* New York: A.A. Knopf.
Stone, C.D. 1974. *Should Trees Have Standing?* Los Angeles: William Kaufman.
Strassoldo, R. 1987. 'Ecologia.' In *Nuovo Dizionario di Sociologia,* in F. Demarchi, A. Ellena and B. Cattarinussi, pp. 726–735. Milan.
Sumner, C. 1986. *The Source of African Philosophy: The Ethiopian Philosophy of Man.* Stuttgart.
Suzman, H. 1991. *Vrye Weekblad,* 22 February.
Tarski, A. 1936. *Semantics, Metamathematics.* Oxford: Clarendon Press.
Tarski, A. 1977. 'Truth and Logic.' A paper sent by the author to the Second Latin American Symposium of Mathematical Logic.
Taylor, P. 1981. The ethics of respect for nature. *Environmental Ethics,* vol. 3, pp. 197–218.
Taylor, P. 1986. *Respect for Nature: A Theory of Environmental Ethics.* Princeton: Princeton University Press.
Tempels, P. 1945. *La Philosophie Bantou.* Paris: Presence Africaine.
Terreblanche, S. 1988. 'Interactions between Afrikaans- and English-speaking whites in South Africa: an historical perspective'. *International Relations.* vol. 9, No. 4.
Thompson, L. and J. Butler. 1975. *Change in Contemporary South Africa.* Berkeley: University of California Press.
U.S. Agency for International Development. 1990a. *Reports to the United States Congress, I.* Integrated Pest Management: AID Policy and Implementation. Washington, DC: U.S. Congress.
U.S. Agency for International Development. 1990b. *Reports to the United States Congress, II.* Pesticide Use and Poisoning: a Global View. Washington, DC: U.S. Congress.
Van DeVeer, D. 1979. Interspecific justice. *Inquiry,* vol. 22, pp. 55–79.
Van Zyl Slabbert, F. 1985. *The Last White Parliament.* Johannesburg: J. Ball Publishers.
Warren, K. 1990. The power and the promise of ecological feminism. *Environmental*
WCED. 1987. *Our Common Future.* Oxford: Oxford University Press for the World Commission on Environment and Development.
Westerlund, D. 1980. *Ujamaa na Dini: A Study of Some Aspects of Society and Religion in Tanzania, 1961–1977.* Stockholm: Almqvist and Wiksell.
White, L. 1967. The religious roots of our ecological crisis. *Science,* vol. 155, pp. 1201–1207.
White, L. 1967. The religious roots of our ecological crisis. *Science,* vol. 155.
Wilber, K. 1981. Up *From Eden: A Transpersonal View of Human Evolution:* Boulder, CO: Shambhala.
Wimmer, F.M. 1990. *Interkulturelle Philosophie:* Geschichte und theorie, Band 1. Wien.
Wiredu, K. 1980. *Philosophy and African Culture.* New York: Cambridge University Press.
Wiredu, K. 1984. 'Philosophical Research and Teaching in Africa: Some Suggestions.' In *Teaching and Research in Philosophy: Africa.* (Studies on Teaching and Research in Philosophy Throughout the World - 1) Paris: UNESCO.
Wiredu, K. 1987. 'The Concept of Mind with Particular Reference to the Language and

Thought of the Akans.' In *Contemporary Philosophy, A New Survey, Vol. V African Philosophy*, edited by G. Floistad, p. 153–179. Dordretcht: Jihoff.

Worster, D. 1985. *Nature's Economy: A History of Ecological Ideas*. Cambridge, UK: Cambridge University Press.

Wright, E.O. 1986. 'What is Middle about the Middle Class?' In *Analytical Marxism*, edited by J. Roemer, pp. 114–140. Cambridge, UK: Cambridge University Press.

Young, R. 1985. *Darwin's Metaphor: Nature's Place in Victorian Culture*. Cambridge, UK: Cambridge University Press.

Zimmerman, M. (in press) 'Applying Heidegger to Radical Environmentalism.' In *Applied Heidegger*, edited by H. Dreyfus and M. Zimmerman. Evanston, IL: Northwestern University Press.

Zimmerman, M. 1983. Towards a Heideggerean ethos for radical environmentalism. *Environmental Ethics*. vol. 5, Summer, pp. 99–131.

Zimmerman, M. 1985. The crisis of natural rights and the search for a non-anthropocentric basis for moral behaviour. *The Journal of Value Inquiry*, vol. 14, pp. 43–53.

Zimmerman, M. 1986. Implications of Heidegger's thought for deep ecology. *The Modern Schoolman*, vol. 64, November, pp. 19–43.

Zimmerman, M. 1987. Feminism, deep ecology and environmental ethics. *Environmental Ethics*, vol. 9, Spring, pp. 21–44.

Zimmerman, M. 1988. Quantum theory, intrinsic value, and panentheism. *Environmental Ethics*, vol. 10, pp. 3–30.

NOTES ON THE CONTRIBUTORS

Evandro Agazzi
Evandro Agazzi studied philosophy and physics in Milan, Oxford, Marburg and Münster. He taught mathematics and logic at the universities of Milan and Genoa and at the Higher Normal School of Pisa before and after he became Professor of Philosophy of Science at the University of Genoa in 1970. He has also lectured at the universities of Düsseldorf, Berne, Pittsburgh and Geneva. At present, he is Professor of Philosophical Anthropology, Philosophy of Nature and Philosophy of Science at the University of Fribourg, Switzerland. He was president of FISP 1988-1993 and has been president of the Académie Internationale des Sciences and director of the Centre for Contemporary Philosophy of the Italian National Research Council. His publications include *Science et foi/Scienza e fede; Weisheit im Technischen;* and *Philosophie, Science, Métaphysique* as well as various articles on the philosophy of science, logic, ethics, bioethics, language and philosophical anthropology. He is now president of the International Academy for Philosophy of Sciences and the International Institute of Philosophy.

Paul Allen III
Paul Allen III (Philosophy Department, East Stroudsburg University, Pennsylvania, USA) has degrees from Harvard University, Columbia University, and the New School for Social Research. His published works include *Exploring the Computer* and *Proof of Moral Obligation in Twentieth Century Philosophy,* as well as articles on meta-ethics, the nuclear arms race, environmental epistemology and human beings as super-human computer beings.

Robin Attfield
Robin Attfield is a professor of Philosophy in the University of Wales, Cardiff. He is the author of over a hundred articles and reviews, and of books *God and the Secular, The Ethics of Environmental Concern* and *A Theory of Value and Obligation;* and the joint author of *Values, Conflict and the Environment* and *International Justice and the Third World.* He has taught in Nigeria, Kenya, England and Wales.

John P. Clark
John P. Clark is a professor of Philosophy at Loyola University in New Orleans, and teaches in the Environmental Studies Program. He has written a number of books, including *The Anarchist Movement: Reflections on Culture, Nature and Power,* and has edited *Renewing the Earth: The Promise of Social Ecology* and co-edited *Environmental Philosophy: From Animal Rights to Radical Ecology.* He is an editor of *Mesechabe: The Journal of Surre(gion)alism* and is a long-time activist in the Green Movement.

A.T. Dalfovo
A.T. Dalfovo is Head of the Department of Philosophy at Makerere University, which he joined twenty years ago. He holds a PhD in Sociology (Brunel, London). He has been visiting professor at the universities of Bergen, Bologna, Padua and Brescia and External Examiner in the universities of Kenya, Malawi and Zambia. Among his publications are *The Foundations of Social Life: Ugandan Philosophical Studies* and *Lugbara Proverbs.*

Richard T. DeGeorge
Richard DeGeorge is University Distinguished Professor of Philosophy and Director of the International Centre for Ethics in Business at the University of Kansas. Past president of the American Philosophical Association and past vice-president of FISP, he has authored 16 books, including *Competing with Integrity in International Business* and *The Nature and Limits of Authority.*

David Evans
David Evans is a professor of Logic and Metaphysics at Queen's University of Belfast, Northern Ireland. He took his undergraduate and graduate degrees from Cambridge University. He is the author of *Aristotle's Concept of Dialectic, Truth and Proof, Aristotle and Moral Philosophy* and *Contemporary Problems*, as well as numerous articles. He has been a member of the FISP Steering Committee since 1988.

Frederick Ferré
Frederick Ferré is a research professor of Philosophy at the University of Georgia and editor of *Research in Philosophy and Technology*. He was the organizer and chairman of the Environmental Ethics section at the Nairobi World Conference of Philosophy in 1991.

Karen Gloy
Karen Gloy studied philosophy, literature, physics and psychology at the universities of Hamburg and Heidelberg. She obtained her Doctorate from Heidelberg. She has been a professor and the Director the Institute of Philosophy at Lucerne, Switzerland. She has been a visiting professor at the universities of Beijing, Taiwan, Basel and Fribourg. Her main publications are *Kant's Theory of Natural Science* and *Unity and Manifold*.

Gerd-Rudiger Hoffmann
Gerd-Rudiger Hoffmann studied philosophy at Leipzig Karl Marx University and in 1984 completed his doctoral thesis on African Philosophy. He has taught at Leipzig University and Berlin Humbold University. His publications include *Wie un warum entstand Philosophie in verschiedenen Regionen der Erde, Texte zur afrikanischen Philosophie* and *African Philosophy—Myth and Reality*. His articles have appeared in *Quest, Asien, Afrika, Lateinamerika, Deutsche Zeitschrift fur Philosophie* and *ZAST*.

Calestous Juma
Calestous Juma is the founder-director of the African Centre for Technology Studies (ACTS) which specializes in research on biodiversity, biotechnology, environmental governance, capacity-building and information science. Dr. Juma has won the Pew Scholars Award and is a Global 500 laureate. His publications include *The Gene Hunters, Innovation and Sovereignty* (ed. with J.B. Ojwang) and *Biodiplomacy* (ed. with V. Sánchez).

D.N. Kaphagawani
D.N. Kaphagawani is a graduate of the University of Malawi, Sussex University, and Leeds University. He is a former Head of Department of Philosophy at the University of Malawi and is currently Dean of the Faculty of Humanities at the same university.

Yersu Kim
Yersu Kim is a professor of Philosophy at Seoul National University. He is Chairman of the International Exchange Committee of the Korean Philosophical Association, Secretary General of the Afro-Asian Philosophy Association, President of the Korean Society for Analytic Philosophy and was President of the Harvard Club of Korea and Fellow of Woodrow Wilson International Centre for Scholars. His main publications include *Die bedeutungs theoretische Problematik in der Philosophie Husserls und Wittgenstein; Modernization: Problems and Prospects; Cultural Policy in the Republic of Korea; World and Language; Understanding Wittgenstein*. He is the author of more than twenty articles in English and Korean.

Notes on Contributors

Wolfgang Kluxen
Wolfgang Kluxen studied at the universities of Koln, Bonn and Louvain. He has been a professor of Philosophy at the University of Bonn since 1969. His publications include *Philosophische Ethik bei Thomas von Aquin, Duns Scotus De Primo Principo, Ethik des Ethos, Thomas von Aquin im Philosophischen Gespräch, Sprache und Erkennthis im Mittelalter, Beiträge zur Geschichte der Philosophie und thaologie des Mittelalters*. He has been the president of the 'Societe internationale pour l'etude de la philosophie medievale', president of the 'Allegemeine Gesellschaft fur Philosophie in Deutschland' and a member of the Steering Committee of FISP.

Ioanna Kuçuradi
Ioanna Kuçuradi studied philosophy at Istanbul University. Since 1969 she has been Head of the Department of Philosophy, Hacettepe University, Ankara and a founding member of the Philosophical Society of Turkey (and President since 1980). She is a member of the Steering Committee and is the Secretary General of FISP. Her publications include *The Tragic in Max Scheler and Nietzsche, Nietzsche's Conception of Man, Schopenhauer's Conception of Man, Man and Values, Problems of Art from a Philosophical Perspective* and *Among the Events of the Time*. She has published various articles on social and political philosophy, human rights and problems of culture in Turkish, English, German and French.

Mihailo Markovic
M. Markovic studied in Belgrade and London. He is a professor of Philosophy of Science at the University of Belgrade and Director of the Institute of Philosophy. He has lectured at the Academy of Sciences, Poland and the Academy of Sciences, Moscow, as well as at various universities in the Netherlands, Finland, Sweden, Denmark and the USA (universities of Michigan and Pennsylvania). Publications include *Dialectical Theory of Meaning, Reexamination* and *From Affluence to Praxis, Philosophy and Social Criticism*.

Ali A. Mazrui
Ali A. Mazrui is the Albert Schweitzer in the Humanities and Director of the Institute of Global Cultural Studies, State University of New York at Binghamton, USA and Albert Luthuli Professor-at-large at the University of Jos, Nigeria. He is also a senior scholar at Cornell University, USA. He has published more than twenty books, the most ambitious being *A World Federation of Cultures: An African Perspective* and *Cultural Forces in World Politics*. Ali Mazrui is a Kenyan with a PhD in political studies from Oxford.

J.M. Nyasani
J.M. Nyasani is a former chairman of the Department of Philosophy and former dean of the Faculty of Arts in Nairobi University. He is currently the Principal, College of Humanities and Social Sciences in the same university. He holds degrees from the University of Cologne, New York University, Oxford and Urbanian University. He is currently a professor of Philosophy specializing in metaphysics. Among his publications are A *Treatise on General Metaphysics*, and *An Introduction to Traditional Logic*.

H. Odera Oruka
Odera Oruka has degrees from Uppsala (Sweden) and Wayne University (Michigan). He is founder chairman of the Department of Philosophy, University of Nairobi and the Philosophical Association of Kenya. He has written and published almost fifty articles and reviews. His books include *Punishment and Terrorism in Africa, Sage Philosophy, Trends in Contemporary African Philosophy, Ethics, The Philosophy of Liberty* and *Oginga Odinga: His Philosophy and*

Beliefs. He is a member of the Executive Committee of FISP and former Secretary-General of the Afro-Asian Philosophical Association. He has received an honorary cultural doctorate from the World University Round Table and the Fil Dr. *Honoris causa* from Uppsala.

Thomas R. Odhiambo
Thomas R. Odhiambo is a graduate biologist of the University of Cambridge (UK). He is the founder-director of the International Centre for Insect Physiology and Ecology (ICIPE) and is currently President of the African Academy of Sciences (AAS). He has received honorary doctorates from the universities of Oslo, Nigeria (Nsukka), Johns Hopkins and Notre Dame. He is also a co-sharer (with President Abdou Diouf of Senegal) of the First Hunger Prize for the Sustainable End of Hunger in Africa (June 1987).

Jerzy Pelc
Jerzy Pelc is a professor at Warsaw University and is the Head of the Department of Logical Semiotics. He was the President of IIP, President of the International Association for Semiotic Studies and a member of the Comite Directeur, FISP.

Juhani Pietarinen
Juhani Pietarinen is a professor of Practical Philosophy, Department of Philosophy, University of Turku, Finland. His publications are on logic, philosophy of social sciences and ethics.

Francisco Miro Quesada C.
Francisco Miro Quesada is the Head of the Institute of Philosophical Investigation at the University of Lima. He founded the Peruvian Philosophical Society and is a former president of it. He has been Minister of Public Education. He is also President of FISP and President of the Co-optation Committee of IIP.

Daniel W. Skubik
Daniel W. Skubik is currently visiting professor at Florida Atlantic University. He has taught at various universities throughout Australia and the United States. He holds degrees from the Australian National University and the University of California.

Ernest Sosa
Ernest Sosa is Romeo Elton in the Philosophy Department of Brown University (USA). He is the author of many journal articles, some of which have been collected in *Knowledge in Perspective*. He has long edited the journal *Philosophy and Phenomenological Research*. He was a vice-president of FISP and a member of its Executive Committee. He has published mainly on issues of epistemology and metaphysics (including issues of moral objectivity).

Anna-Teresa Tymieniecka
Anna-Teresa Tymieniecka (Zaremba) is a Polish-American philosopher. Her numerous books and treatises are about the phenomenology of life and the human condition. Her metaphysics offer the groundwork for ecology and interdisciplinary challenges. She is editor of *Analecta Husserliana, The Yearbook of Phenomenological Research* and *Of Phenomenological Inquiry* and President of the World Institute for Advanced Phenomenological Research and Learning.

Wilhelm J. Verwoerd
W.J. Verwoerd is a lecturer in Philosophy at the University of Stellenbosch, South Africa. His areas of specialization include political philosophy and development ethics. He holds degrees from Stellenbosch and Oxford.

Notes on Contributors

Mourad Wahba
Mourad Wahba is the founder president of the Afro-Asian Philosophical Association (AAPA). He has organized numerous international philosophical conferences in Cairo. Wahba has edited and published over a dozen books among which are *Philosophy and Civilization, Roots of Dogmtism, Unity of Knowledge* and *Philosophy of Mass Man.*

K.J. Wininger
K.J. Wininger is a professor of Philosophy at the University of Southern Maine. Her works include articles on ethical theory, Friedrich Nietzsche moral and aesthetic theories, decolonization and the ethical implications of European cinematic portrayal of colonized people. She has taught at Temple University, Earlham College and Villanova University, USA. She taught philosophy and women's studies in Kenya in 1987.

Kwasi Wiredu
Kwasi Wiredu is currently a professor of Philosophy at the University of South Florida, but formerly professor and Head of Department of Philosophy, University of Ghana. He is a vice-president of the Inter-African Council for Philosophy. Wiredu is the author of more than ninety articles and papers on epistemology, philosophy of logic, philosophy of language, human rights and African philosophy and editor or co-editor of seven philosophical journals in Africa. Main book publications include *Philosophy and an African Culture, Person and Community: Ghanaian Philosophical Studies* and *God, Mind and Destiny.*

Michael E. Zimmerman
Michael E Zimmerman is a professor of Philosophy at Tulane University, USA. He is the author of two books on Heidegger, *Eclipse of the Self* and *Heidegger's Confrontation with Modernity.* He has just completed *Contesting Earth's Future: Radical Ecology and Postmodernity.*

INDEX

Abbot, F.E. 116, 120, 121, 285–289
Abelard 152
absolutism 178
abstentionist 72
Academy Science Publishers 57
acquisition 39
actualization 112, 113
Adam Mickiewicz University 306
Adam, H. 213, 216
Africa ix, xii, xiii, xv, 18, 30, 31, 41, 42, 43, 44, 45, 47, 49, 51, 52, 53, 55–58, 158–164, 167ff, 171, 181–189, 190–197, 198–207
African Academy of Sciences 57
African Centre for Technology Studies 115
African folklore 35, 202, 204
African personality 181–189
African philosophy 158–164, 190–197, 198–207, 247
African worldview 46
Afrikaner 212ff
Agazzi, E. ix, x, xv, 3–14
aggression 306ff, 311
agriculture 52, 54, 234–238, 320
air 169, 298
Akan 38, 39, 45, 48, 161, 162
Akiiki, A. xv
alienation 80, 81, 103, 104, 181, 188, 276
Allen, P. 270–278
America 126, 303
American 168
animality 308, 309
animals xv, 5, 16, 22, 23, 24, 29, 99, 117, 121, 138, 146, 227, 229, 239, 240, 252, 258, 270, 272, 282, 289, 293, 295–300, 301, 308, 310, 311, 316, 336–344
animism 15, 18, 28, 116, 299, 332
anthromorphization 77, 78, 80
anthropocentric predicament 23
anthropocentrism xii, 4, 5, 8, 12, 15–29, 78, 116, 117, 118, 134, 135, 138, 139, 140, 143, 144, 145, 147, 239, 240, 247, 249, 250, 253, 255, 295, 321, 331, 342
anthropology 324
anthropomorphic 165, 303
anti-Duhring 157
Anyanwu, J. 122
apartheid 167, 212–221, 265
Appiah, A. 203
Aquinas, T. 117, 344
Arabs 201, 204
Arafak Mountains 134, 135, 147
Archimedean 107
Aristotelian logic xiv, 73, 95, 121, 287, 293, 309
Aristotle 7, 32, 67–69, 74, 98, 99, 101, 102, 117, 121, 152, 181, 183, 184, 273, 287, 318
art 97, 98, 99
artificial environment x, xiv, xv, 98–106
artificial intelligence 60
Ashforth, A. 219
Asia ix
astronomy 29
atomism 250, 252, 254
Aton 165
atrophization 11
Attfield, R. 37, 133–149

Augusta College 285
Augustine 273
Augustinus 283
Australia 133, 336
Ayer, J. 61, 68

Bacon, F. 32, 61, 104, 118, 311
Bahro, J. 146
Bantu 194, 200, 201, 202, 212, 216
Bantustan 218
Barabaig 170
Basel 268
belief 86, 88, 89, 90, 278, 295, 296, 340, 343
Bell phenomena 328
Bell, D. 178
Bentham, J. 307, 315
Bergson, J. 281
Berlin 173
Berlin Conference 171
Bernal, M. 57
Bilimoria, P. 336–344
bio-ethics 306
biocentrism 293, 294, 331
biodiversity 128
bioinsecticide 54
biology 67, 73, 252, 309, 324
bios 108, 109, 111, 113, 114
biosphere 12, 137, 142, 249, 258, 304, 308, 309, 311, 326, 330, 331
biospherical egalitarianism 138
Birdzell, J.R. 55
Bodunrin, P. 158
Bohr, N. 321, 322, 323, 324, 325, 326, 327, 328
Bonaparte, N. 177, 220
Bookchin, M. 141, 329–335
Booke, P. 157
Borlaug, N. 52, 53
Bourdien, P. 63
Brahman 295, 298, 299,

359

300, 338, 344
Brawley, T. 172
Brazil 127, 261, 263, 264, 265, 266, 270
Britain 133
British 201, 206
British East Africa 201
Brooke, J. 261
brotherhood xiv
Brown University 86
Brundtland Report 320
Buber, M. 334
Buddhism 252, 253, 286, 336–344
Buddhist 15, 31
Burali-Forti 153
Burma 261, 267
Bursa 318
Bush, G. 175
butterfly 1324, 135, 138, 147, 148
butterfly effect 153, 157

Cabanis, J. 177
Cairo 177
Calton University 225
Canada 225
Canarp, J. 77
Cantor,R. 153
capitalism 274–275, 276
Cardiff 133
Carter, J. 175
Cartesian 311, 340
Central Africa 162
cereal 52, 53
Césaire, A. 193
chauvinism 140, 145, 147
Chewa 162
China 15, 18, 35, 36, 124, 175, 279
Chinese philosophy 15, 17, 28
Chomskian-Bennett 340
Christian 32, 34, 47, 119, 156, 168, 192, 201, 250, 273, 281, 282, 283, 340
Christianity 31, 46, 116, 118, 165, 274, 280, 312
Chuang-Tzu 279

Cicero 117
Cincinnatus 279
citizenship 172, 334
civilization 102, 167, 168, 174, 192, 233, 234, 251, 274, 276, 277, 279, 290, 304, 329
Clark, J.P. 329–335
climate 49, 233
Club of Rome 80
cognition xv, 107, 108, 109–111, 12, 208–211
coherence theory 88
coherence-compromise 25–29
collectivist nationalism 221
colonialism 81, 126, 168, 181, 182, 183, 186, 206, 308, 311
colonization 184ff, *see* colonialism
Columbus, C. 126
communalism x, xi, 47, 159, 334
complementarity 310, 321–328
compromise 249
Compte, A. 61
computers xii, 60
conception 290–294
Condillac, D. 177
Confucianism 15, 18, 31, 84, 95, 268
Congo 221, 261
conscience xiii, 62, 121, 287, 310
consciencism 197
consciousness xii, 64, 94, 96, 110, 114, 252, 275, 297, 321, 323, 330, 338, 341, 342
consequentialism 142, 264, 265, 343
conservatism 61
conservative 28
constructivism 282
consumerism xi, 308, 337
consumption 39, 40, 45, 48, 311
contrivance 67–69
Cooper, G. 173, 174
Cooper, V. 173
Copernican 29, 78, 244, 339
correspondence theory 88
cosmic 108, 109, 113, 324
cosmology 78, 122, 123, 341
counter-culture 22, 121
Craig, G. 62
Craven, I. 134, 144
creationist 8
cultural evolution xi, 5
cultural transformation 84, 85
culture 10, 61, 62, 63, 65, 68, 74, 75, 82, 84, 88, 97, 9, 102, 152, 159, 167, 168, 170, 172, 180, 199, 200, 203, 214, 234, 235, 236, 238, 245, 290, 291, 298, 301, 306, 309, 310, 318–320, 334
Cusanus 282
custom 62, 67–75, 102, 200
Czechoslovakia 171

Da Costa, J. 157
Dalfovo, A.T. 244–248
Darwin, C. 69, 119–120, 126, 285, 293, 302, 309
Davenport, T. 212
Davidson, D. 87, 88
Davran, Z. xv
de Morgan, J. 157
de Tracy, D. 150, 177
Deakin University 336
death 174–176, 251, 338
decolonization 216ff, 221
Deep Ecology 138, 140, 141, 143, 148, 249–255, 321
deflationism 88, 90

DeGeorge, R.T. ix, xi, 15–29
demiurgos 78
Democritus 250
Descartes, R. 32, 61, 78, 104, 199, 250, 273–274, 311
desertification 44, 45
despoliation 182
Dessaur, F. 245, 283
determinism 247, 330
Devall, B. 249
development xviii, xix, xx, 3, 59,133–149, 246, 257ff, 262–269, 290, 320
developmentalists 133, 134, 135, 143, 144, 145, 146, 147, 148
dharma 121, 295ff
dialectics 150, 151, 152, 153, 157
Digby, K. 117
dogma 177–180
Dogon 122
Donaldson, T. 262, 263
Dower, N. xv
doxa 107
Drydyk, J. 225–232
Du Bois, W.E.B. 202
Du Toit, J. 213
dualism 28, 250,251, 252, 254, 273, 304, 321, 323, 327, 328, 329
Dumos, R. 32
dun Scot 152
Dusty Gruver, D.M. 301–305

Earth Summit 127
Earth x, 5, 6, 17, 102, 105, 122, 123–126, 169, 249, 253, 254, 270, 298, 299, 301–305, 308, 329–335
East Stroudsburg University 270
Eastern Europe 47, 124
eco-crisis 306
eco-equilibrium 307, 310

eco-ethica 94–97
eco-ethics xiv
ecocentrism 250ff, 332
ecodevelopment 256–260
ecofascism 141, 142, 143
ecofeminism 250, 255
ecological degradation 59, 139
'ecolocaust' 270–278
economy xii, 51, 56, 79ff, 115, 118, 125, 143, 145, 261ff, 270ff, 285, 307, 318–320
ecophilosophy 115–129, 140, 292
ecosophy 255
ecosphere 245, 247, 342
ecosystem 21, 22, 135, 257, 258, 307, 326, 332, 333
Eden 174
egalitarianism 140, 232, 312, 331
ego 186–189, 251, 299, 321
Egypt 165, 174, 177
Ehrenfeld, D. 293
Einstein, A. 58, 66
eliminativist 91
Ellingwood, F. 116
Emerson, R.W. 292
emigration 55
empiricism 286, 325
empiricist 177
energy 80
Engels, F. 152
England 55, 56, 171
Enlightenment 250, 251, 253, 254, 336, 340
enthnocentrism 167
environmental conservation 59
environmental crisis 30, 33, 36, 40, 115–117, 249–255, 285–289, 321, 327, 328
environmental degeneration 245

environmental ethics xvi, 15–29, 73, 119, 121, 223–344
environmental problems xvii, xviii, xx, 3, 319, 320
environmentalism 133–149, 244, 249, 326
environmentalists 29, 66, 133, 135, 137, 138, 141, 143, 147, 148, 249, 250, 255, 322
Epictetus 64, 65
Epicurean 312
episteme 107
epistemic 87, 151–154, 321
epistemic ideology 151–154
epistemological xix,xx, 67, 69–70, 73, 74, 75, 86, 88, 90, 93, 99, 109–114, 115, 153, 282, 283, 321–328, 339
ethics xv, 17, 29, 67, 71, 94–97, 115–129, 154ff, 157, 223–344
Ethiopia 141, 175
ethnophilosophy 158, 194, 198, 200, 201, 202, 205, 206
Euclid 90
Eurocentrism 193, 203
Europe ix, 161, 167, 168, 170, 175, 182, 266, 279
European 31, 57, 78, 80, 190–197, 203, 216, 262, 280, 292, 340
European Community 268
Evans, J.D.G. 67–75
evolution 5, 6, 9, 100, 119, 182, 254, 306, 308, 309, 322, 329, 330, 331, 332
existence 101, 103, 293, 299, 300, 321, 326, 338
exotism 191–192, 194

361

exploitation 225–232, 271, 272
extinction 229

familism 84, 85
family 123ff, 301–305
Fanon, F. 197
FAO 52
Fascist 212
Faust 79, 175, 176
feminism 203
Fermi, E. 66
Ferré, F. 233–243
Fichte, B. 152, 157, 192
Finland 290, 292
fire 169, 298
FISP xx, 3
Florida Atlantic University 261
Flynn, E. 172, 174
Folse, H.J. 321–328
food security 51
Foreman, D. 141, 142
forests 22, 28, 44, 134, 135, 146, 233, 261ff, 308
Fox, W. 139, 140, 141, 142, 250, 251
France 55, 167, 171
freedom 65, 104, 106, 111, 174, 220, 247, 265, 293, 309, 310, 312, 330, 331
Frege, J. 90, 157
French Revolution 177
fundamentalism 59
fundamentality 92

Gadamer,H. 162,163
Galileo 61, 78, 90
Gandhi 121, 343
Gassendi, E. 312
Gates, H. 199
Geelong 336
gender 169–170
generations 172–174
Genesis 32, 33, 116, 282, 283, 302
Georgetown University 262
Georgia 285
Germany 55, 98, 133, 144, 197
Ghana ix, 38, 44, 45, 161, 200, 203
Gikuyu 161, 204
global warming 270, 271
Gloy, K. 279–284
goals xvii–xx
God xiv, 7, 8, 17, 33, 100,116, 119, 165, 166, 168, 171, 234, 251, 281, 282, 283, 295ff, 339, 344
Göring, H. 173
Gotthelt, J. 62
Grant, C. 173
Great Wall of China 175
Greece 21, 57, 181, 279, 280, 286
Greek 57, 74, 94, 98, 107, 190, 247, 280, 283, 287, 329
Green Parties 133
Gruver see Dusty Gruver
Guha, R. 144
Guinea-Bissau 261, 266, 267
Gyekye, K. 161, 162

Haeckel, E.H. 244, 248
Hampton Court 175
Hansfer, F. 63
harm 229, 242, 259, 264
Harvard 285, 286
Hawaii 301
Hawaiian 122, 301–305
Hegel, F. 121, 150, 151, 152, 157, 171, 192, 287, 292, 312
Heidegger, M. 254, 281
Heisenberg, W. 78
Heliocentric 78
Heraclitus 35, 152
Herzen, A. 179
Higham, C. 172, 173, 174
Hindu 297, 298
Hinduism 31
history xiii, xiv, 7, 13, 81, 124, 152, 153, 157, 165–176, 180, 187, 191, 194, 197, 199, 220, 233, 276, 281, 290, 322, 329, 330
Hitler, A. 66, 127, 171, 172, 173
Hobbes, T. 68, 273, 274, 285
Hoffman, G. 190–197
Homer 204
homo economicus 79
Horace 279
Hountondji, P. 161, 197, 202
hubris 82
Hughes, R. 178
human condition 108, 111, 338
human environment ix, x
human nature 313–317
human rights x, 23, 40, 65, 66, 338, 342
human survival 59–66, 82, 310
humanism 250, 251, 252, 253, 276, 290–294, 311, 312, 322, 343
Hume, D. 17, 61, 68
Husserl, E. 110, 112
hypothermia 16

Iansham University 177
Ibánez, A.H. 256–260
ICIPE 49, 53
ideology 32, 61, 118, 150–157, 177–180, 192, 213, 214, 215, 216, 217, 218, 220, 250, 311, 312
Igbo 248
image of humanity 76–85
image of nature 76–85
Imamichi, T. ix, xiv, 94–97
imperialism 218
Incas 154
India ix, 144, 156, 295
Indian philosophy 121, 295–300, 336

Indian xiii, 121, 144, 295–300, 336
individualism 286, 287, 288, 289
Indonesia 134, 135, 137, 261, 262
Industrial Revolution 55, 56, 168, 174, 182
industrial civilization 79, 80, 81, 82, 84
industrialization xviii, 19, 42, 47, 80, 83, 165, 249, 319, 320
insects 53
Institut de France 177
insularity 166, 167, 168
integrating vision 111–112
inter-cultural philosophy 193–197
interaction 324–325, 326–327
International Centre for Environmental Philosophy xv
Irele, A. 202
irrigation 49
Islam 46, 47, 165, 174
Italy 124

Jackson, W. 241, 243
Jainism 337
Janis, M.C. 173
Japan ix, 55, 94, 165, 168, 169, 262
Japanese xiv
Jefferson, T. 178
Jerusalem 165
Jesus Christ 31, 165
Jewish 250
Johnson, L. 37
Judaism 165
Judeo-Christian x, 7, 115, 120
Juma, C. 115–129
justice 84, 121, 136, 137, 141, 148, 246, 257, 288, 291
justification 86, 87, 88, 93, 117

Kagame, A. 158

Kampala 244
Kant, E. 17, 32, 33, 68, 78, 107, 121, 152, 155, 156, 192, 197, 282, 287, 315, 340
Kantian challenge 76–77, 83
Kaphagawani, D.N. 158–164
karma 337
Kaunda, K. 196
Kenya Freedom from Hunger Council 66
Kenya ix, xvi, 49, 53, 115, 161, 174, 181, 186, 200, 201, 204, 206, 221
Kenyatta, J. 161
Khaminwa, J. 206
Kikuyu 206, *see also* Gikuyu
Kim, Y. 76–85
kinship 123ff, 301, 303, 333
Kluxen, W. ix, xiv, xv, 98–106
knowledge 35, 38, 48, 51, 52, 56, 58, 61, 76, 82, 86, 88, 104, 150, 153, 199, 241, 285, 287, 319, 321, 322
knowledge industry xiii, 51, 54, 55–58
Kolakowski, L. 178
Kranz, W. 190
Kropotkin, V. 331
Kucuradi, I. xv, xvii–xx

Lactantius 282
Lambert, J. 157
Langenberg, D. 50
language xv, 69, 76, 77, 83, 131–221, 244, 246, 340
laws of nature 16, 18
laws of physics 16, 17
Lazar, J. 212, 213
legitimization 290, 291, 292, 293, 294
Leibniz, R. 157, 253, 283
Lenin, N. 152, 153, 193

Leopold, A. 22, 23
Levine, D. 56
liberation 140, 146, 148, *see also* freedom
life 174–176, 295ff, 308
life-functions 110–111
Lima 158
linguistics 76, 77
literature 202, 204, 295ff, 301
Locke, J. 177, 274, 285
logic 37, 90, 151, 157, 286, 337
Logos 107, 108, 109, 111, 112, 113, 114
London 42, 261
Louisiana 249, 321, 329
Loyola University 321, 329
Lucerne 279
Lugbara 248
Luizzi, V. 313–317
Lull, R. 157
Luo 206
Luthuli, A. 218
Lutzenberger, J. 270

Maasai 170
machines 8, 61, 62
Makerere University 244
Makokha, J. xv
malaria 43
Malawi 158
Malinowski, B. 319
Manhattan Project 63, 66
manifestation 107–109, 109–114
Marcel, G. 245
Marcuse, H. 245
Markovic, M. xi, xii, 59–66
Marx, K. (Marxism) 150, 151, 152, 153, 156, 157, 178, 192, 193, 197, 204, 271ff, 312
material exploitation 182–186
materialism 152, 177, 273, 337

363

mathematics 78, 151, 153, 157, 279–284
Mauritania 266
Mazrui, A.A. ix, xiii, xiv, 165–176, 246
Mbiti, J. 158, 196, 203
McCloskey, M. 255
McKibben, B. 233, 234, 235, 236, 241, 242
mechanization 169
Mediterranean 167, 168
Mencius 286
Meru 166
Mesopotamia 49
metaphysics 23, 29, 109, 121, 163, 245, 248, 250, 252, 287, 321, 327
Mexico 109, 256
Miami University 295
Middle Ages 78, 251, 272, 274, 311
Midgley, M. 240
Milan 178
Mill, J.S. 174, 264, 265, 307, 341, 343
Milton, J. 168
Miro Quesada, F. 150–157
mirror of nature 76–77
misanthropy 138,141, 142
misplaced expertise xii, 18–21
Mobutu 174
monism 17, 28, 158–164
monotheism 165
Montaigne, J. 312
monumentalism 167, 175
Moore, G. 61, 89, 90. 92
moral agents 231, 238, 240, 265, 341
morality 36, 61, 96, 97, 121, 122
Morocco 261
Moscovici, J. 78
Mosely, R. 173
Moss 165
Mount St. Helen 16, 23
Mozambique 216
Mt. Kenya 201

Mt. Kilimanjaro 201
Muhammad 165, 174
Murty, K.S. ix, xiii
Muttes, W. 63
mutualism 332, 333
mysticism 61, 290–294, 327
mythology 78, 304

Naess, A. 138, 140, 142, 143, 148, 249, 253
Naffertiti 165
Nairobi Conference ix
Nairobi xv, 49, 206, 313
nation-states 170–172, 265
national boundaries ix, xiii, 170
nationalism xiii, 59, 73, 309
Native American 272
natural history 330
natural science 8, 67, 79
natural selection 310
naturalism 86–93, 290–294, 312, 331
naturalistic epistemology 69–70
nature x, xii, xiii, xv, 3–129, 225–232, 233–243, 250, 270ff, 279–284, 287, 288, 289, 290–294, 313ff, 322ff, 330ff
Nazi 16, 167, 173, 174, 178, 179, 212, 234
negotiation 27, 28
Negritude 202, 203, 206
neo-colonialism 193, 200, 204, 206
neo-Marxist 270–278
neopragmatism 88
New Orleans 249, 321, 329
New York 165, 173
New Zealand 262
Newton, I. 61, 90, 250
Ngugi wa Thiong'o 203, 204
Nietzsche, F. 17, 81–82
Nigeria 165
nihilism 81

Nile Valley 165, 175
Nilotic 200
nirvana 338, 342, 344
Nkrumah, K. 197, 198, 203
noncognitivism 88, 89, 90, 91
North America ix, 133 168
Northrup, F. 153, 154
Nyamwezi 166
Nyasani, J.M. 181–189
Nyerere, J. 161, 196, 198, 203

objectivity xii, 322–324, 327
observation 325
Ockam 152
Odera-Oruka, H. ix–xvi, 115–129, 158, 195, 200, 202, 203, 205, 206
Odhiambo, T.R. ix, xi, xii, 49–58
Odysseus 334
Ogut, G. xv
Ohio 295
omniscience 35, 41
oppression 137, 138, 139, 140, 144, 145, 147, 148
optimal synthesis 82–83
optimism 290, 291, 292, 293
Orient 31
Otieno, S.M. 206
Ottawa 225
Ottoman 124
overpopulation 311
Oxford 42
Ozer, U. 318–320
Ozone Agreement 30, 40
ozone 313, 314

pan-Polynesian 122
pantheism 17
Pappu, *see* Rama Pappu
parental earth ethics 115–129
Parsons, T. 79

364

Pascal, J. 111
Passmore, J. 32, 33, 36, 37
Pax Americana 80
peace ix, xii, xiii, xiv, 51, 196, 291
Peano, S. 151
Peden, C. 116, 121, 285–289
Peirce, C. 87, 285, 286
Pelc, J. ix, xiv, xv, 208–211
Pelzer, A. 217
Peru 150
pesticides 53
Petrarca 279
Petrus Hispanicus 152
Pharaohs 154, 165, 175
phenomenalism 286
Philosophical Society of Turkey xx
physics 322, 323, 324, 325, 328
Pietarinen, J. 290–294
Plato 7, 152, 181, 199, 272–273, 274, 281, 282, 287, 292, 334
Platonic 78
plenary sessions ix, x–xv, xvi
Plessner, H. 101
Plouquet, R. 157
pluralism 28, 158–164
pluralistic democracy 115, 285
Poland 171, 208, 306
politics 131–222, 291, 331
pollution 19, 20, 27, 28, 30, 31, 40, 42, 47, 143, 235, 249, 263, 280, 290, 307, 308, 319
Polynesia 301, 303, 304, 305
population xviii, 31, 40, 44, 141, 142, 147, 170, 229, 230, 232, 290, 320
positionality 101
positivism 61, 311, 321, 322

possessive individualism 115, 116, 145, 285, 289, 290
poverty 31, 133, 134, 135, 141, 146, 147
pragmatist 88, 307
preservation 26, 27
preservationist 143, 144
primitive truth 86–93
primitivism 88, 89, 90, 91
property 228
propositional knowledge 86
Protagoras 206
psychology 76, 87, 177, 324, 339
Ptolemy 78
Puritan 286
Putnam, H. 87, 88

quality of life 10, 11
quantum revolution 321–322, 323, 324, 327, 328
Queen Victoria 201
Quine, W. 91

R&D xiii, 51, 52, 57
race 166–169, 199, 202, 203, 220
Rama Pappu, S.S. 121, 295–300
ratiocination 40, 338
rationality 107, 109, 110, 111, 112, 113, 114, 199, 291, 338, 344
Rawls, J. 148, 264
reality 67–75, 87, 92, 103, 159, 248, 298, 338
reason 107–109, 112, 199, 340
reciprocity 27, 121, 288, 289, 304
reconciliation 103
reductionism 309
redundancy 88
reformism 249, 255
Regan, T. 22, 341
relativism 28, 327

relativist 88, 247
religion 61, 97, 122, 156, 165–166, 175, 177, 201, 240, 298, 299, 328
Renaissance 8, 279, 311
research 64, 65, 107, 192, 252, 293
resolutions xv, xvi
revisionist 28
Rhodesia 216
Richard, T. 153
Rodman, J. 140, 146
Roemer, J. 225, 226ff
Roman 124, 127
romanticism 292
Rome 49, 80, 286
Rorty, R. 88, 163
Rosenberg, N. 55
Rossi, P. 247
Routley, R.&V. 140, 145
Rta 121, 295ff
Rushdie, S. 173, 174
Russell, B. 66, 89, 157
Russia 124

Sachs, I. 256, 257
Safire, W. 173
sagacity 206
Sagan, C. 313, 315, 316, 317
sage philosophy 158, 195, 200, 205
Sahara 43, 44, 166
Saint Benedict 32
Saint Francis of Assisi 32, 234
Sardinia 49
Sartre, J 238
scapegoating 139
scepticism 70, 197
Schelling, K. 152, 157
scholarly press xiii, 57
scholars xii, xiii, 59–66, 116, 118, 318
Schweitzer, A. 312
science ix, xi, xii, xv, 12, 13, 15–29, 41, 47, 49–58, 60, 61, 62, 63, 66, 73, 76, 93, 104, 143, 150, 151, 152,

365

244, 246, 251, 252, 254, 255, 258, 274, 279–284, 290, 291, 292, 311, 322–324, 325, 328
scientific theism 286
scientism 41, 321
Second World War xvii, xviii, 124
security 51, 125, 160
self-consciousness 101, 287, 330, 331, 338, 341, 342, 344
self-realization 138, 253, 331
self-reflection xii, 64, 338
semiotic 208ff
Semitic 165, 168
Senghor, L. 196, 202
sensationalism 177
sensualist 177
sentience 336–344
Seoul National University 76
separability 324–325
separate development 212–221
separatism 168
Serbian Academy 59
Sessions, G. 249
Shintoism 31
Shue, H. 263
Sicily 49
sign 208–211
Singer, P. 145, 229, 338, 339
Singh, R. 121
Skinner, B.F. 245
Skolimowski, H. 292
Skubik, D.W. 261–269
Slide, A. 173
social ecology 329–335
social organization 102
social technology xiv
Socrates 7, 206, 287, 291
Sodipo, J.O. xv
Sophists 7
Sophocles 99, 100
Sosa, E. 86–93
South Africa 212–221,
265
South Korea 76
Southwest Texas State University 313
sovereignty 170, 171, 217, 265
Soviet Union 47, 124
Spartan 181, 184
speciesism 306, 311, 339
Spencer, H. 120
spheres of influence 49, 74
Spinoza, R. 17, 160, 253
spirit 15, 16
spiritual freedom xiii
St. Aquinas 273
St. Basil 146
Stalin, J. 179
Steiner, R. 292
Stevenson, G. 61
Stich, S. 87, 88
stoicism 250
Stone, C. 22
subjectivism 321, 327,328
sublation 275–276
suffering 336–344
Sukuma 166
sun-worship xiv, 165–176
sustainable development xii, xiii, 51–54, 133, 143, 149, 320
Switzerland 279

Tanzania 166, 201, 203
Tao 330, 332
Taoism 31
Tasso 279
Taureg 170
Taylor, P. 37, 293, 294, 342
teak 261, 267
technology ix, xi, xii, xiv, xv, 4, 6, 8, 11, 13, 15, 17, 18, 20, 25, 34, 41, 47, 49–58, 60, 72, 94, 95,103, 104, 105, 146,169, 233–243, 245, 246, 258, 274, 290, 291, 292,
293, 320
teleology 329, 330
teleonomy 310
Tempels, P. 158, 190, 201, 202
Terreblanche 214
Thailand 261, 267
themes ix–x
theocentric 8
theology 33
Thoreau, H.D. 292
Thorez, M. 193
Three Mile Island 48
timber 134, 135
time-consciousness xiv
time-worship xiv, 165–176
timetic ideology 154–155, 157
Tokyo 94
Tokyo University xiv
tolerant missionarism 192–193, 194
trees 22, 272, 273, 276, 282, 295
truth 76, 86, 87, 88, 89, 92, 93, 151, 152, 286, 298, 308, 336
Tulane University 249
Turkey 318
Tymieniecka, A. 107–114

Uganda 175, 244
ujamaa 196
UK 133
Uludag University 318
UNCLOS 268
underdevelopment 134, 136, 138, 148, 306
Unesco xix, xx, 52
unity 107–114, 122
universalism 116, 120, 285, 286, 288, 289
University of Belfast 67
University of Bonn ix, 98
University of Fribourg ix, 3
University of Georgia 233, 243
University of Jos 165

University of Kansas ix
University of Leipzig 197
University of Lima 150
University of Malawi 158
University of Nairobi 115, 181
University of South Florida 30
University of South Maine 198
University of Stellenbosch 212
University of Turkey 290
University of Wales 133
university system xiii, 57
Upanishads 296ff
Uruk 49
USA 30, 34, 48, 54, 55, 80, 86, 107, 172, 198, 233, 261, 268, 270, 285, 295, 301, 313, 321, 329
utilism 290–294
utilitarian 214, 229, 231, 252, 264, 266, 268, 307, 311, 343

values xi, xiii, 16, 62, 64, 76, 79, 81, 82, 141, 304, 306, 307, 308, 310
VanDeVeer, D. 232
Vergil 279
Versailles 175
Verwoerd, H.F. 212–221
Verwoerd, W.J. 212–221
virtuality 112, 113
virtue 38
von Linné, C. 118–119, 120

Wahba, M. xv, 177–180
wandervogel 279
Wanyande, A. 160
Warsaw 306
Warsaw University ix, 208
water 169, 170, 298
Wawrzyniak, J. 306–312
Weber, M. 79
weighting principle 232
Weltanshauung 152, 154, 156, 186, 187, 200
West Africa 43, 175, 261, 266, 268
West, C. 203
Western Europe 124
Western philosophy xiii, 7, 17, 37, 46, 115, 118, 121, 287, 295, 300
Western view xi, 32ff, 117, 203, 252, 321
Western world 30, 59, 115, 116, 270–278

Wheatley, P. 199
White, G. 117–118, 119, 120
White, L. 32
Whitehead, J. 157
Williams, B. 68
Wimmer, F. 193, 194
Wininger, K. 198–207
Wiredu, K. ix, x, xv, 30–48, 122, 159, 192, 194, 206
wisdom 35, 38, 164, 178, 332
withdrawal 226ff
Wittenstein, H. 77
World Bank 146
World Conference of Philosophy xv, 313
World Congress of Philosophy ix, 94
World Institute 107
worldview 272–277
Worster, D. 117
Wright, C. 285
WWF 134

Yakob, Z. 196
Yugoslavia 59

Zaire 201
Zimmerman, M.E. 249–255, 327
Zjilstra, J. 134
Zomba 158